Design History: An Anthology

Design History: An Anthology

edited by

Dennis P. Doordan

The MIT Press

Cambridge, Massachusetts

London, England

The contents of this book were first published in Design Issues (ISSN 0747-9360), a publication of The MIT Press. Except as otherwise noted, copyright in each article is owned by the Massachusetts Institute of Technology.

David Brett, "Drawing and the Ideology of Industrialization," vol. 3, no. 2 (Fall 1986); 59–72; Bradford R. Collins, "The Poster as Art: Jules Chéret and the Struggle for Equality of the Arts in Late Nineteenth-Century France," vol. 2, no. 1 (Spring 1985): 41–50; Paul Shaw, "Tradition and Innovation: The Design Work of William Addison Dwiggins," vol. 1, no. 2 (Fall 1984): 26–41; Enrich Satué, "Super Veloz: A Typographic System for the Small Printer," vol. 2, no. 2 (Fall 1985): 9–17; Gyorgy Haiman, "Imre Kner and the Revival of Hungarian Printing," vol. 8, no. 2 (Spring 1991): 43–53; Ellen Mazur Thompson, "Alms for Oblivion: The History of Women in Early American Graphic Design," vol. 10, no. 2 (Summer 1994): 27–48; Roland Marchand, "Part One: The Designers go to the Fair: Walter Dorwin Teague and the Professionalization of Corporate Industrial Exhibits, 1933–1940," vol. 8, no. 1 (Fall 1991): 4–17; Roland Marchand, "Part Two: The Designers go to the Fair: Norman Bel Geddes, The General, Motors 'Futurama,' and the Visit-to-the-Factory Transformed," vol. 8, no. 2 (Spring 1992): 23–40; David Gartman, "Harley Earl and the Arts and Color Section: The Birth of Styling at General Motors," vol. 10, no. 2 (Summer 1994): 3–26; Dennis P. Doordan, "Design at CBS," vol. 6, no. 2 (Spring 1990): 4–17; Dennis P. Doordan, "Promoting Aluminum: Designers and the American Aluminum Industry," vol. 9, no. 2 (Fall 1993): 44–50; James A. Schmeichen, "Reconsidering the Factory, Art-Labor, and the Schools of Design in Nineteenth-Century Britain," vol. 6, no. 2 (Spring 1990): 58–69; Larry D. Lutchmansingh, "Evolutionary Affinity in Arthur Mackmurdo's Botanical Design," vol. 6, no. 2 (Spring 1990): 51–57; Mitchell Schwartzer, "The Design Prototype as Artistic Boundary: The Debate on History and Industry in Central European Applied Arts Museums, 1860–1900," vol. 9, no. 1 (Fall 1992): 30–44; Matthew Turner, "Early Modern Design in Hong Kong," vol. 6, no. 1 (Fall 1989): 49–78; Shou Zhi Wang, "Chinese Modern Design: A Retrospective," vol. 6, no. 1 (Fall 1989): 49–78; Svetlana Sylvestrova, "That Was the Beginning," vol. 3, no. 1 (Spring 1986): 54–63; John Turpin, "The Irish Design Reform Movement of the 1960s," vol. 3, no. 1 (Spring 1986): 4–22.

Library of Congress Cataloging-in-Publication Data
Design history: an anthology/edited by Dennis P. Doordan.
p.cm.—(A Design issues reader)
Includes bibliographical references.
ISBN 0-262-54076-2 (alk. paper)
1. Design—History. I. Doordan, Dennis P. II. Series
NK1525.D43 1995
745.4'4—dc20 95-24677
CIP

Contents

Acknowledgments

We are indebted to the following individuals who have contributed their editorial skills, insights, time, and passion to *Design Issues* during the period of publication from which the essays in this anthology were drawn: Leon Bellin, Stephen Bloom, Richard Buchanan, Marco Diani, John Heskett, Martin Hurtig, Victor Margolin, Lawrence Salomon, and Simon Steiner. We also acknowledge others for their efforts on behalf of the journal during the same period: John Cullars, Bonnie Osborne, Faith Van Alten, and Diane Stadelmeier. In addition we would like to thank Karen Moyer for her design assistance. The School of Art and Design at the University of Illinois at Chicago (under the directorship of Martin Hurtig, then Susan Sensemann, and finally Judith Kirshner) served as the original home for *Design Issues* and sustained the journal for its first nine volumes (1984–1993). *Design Issues* is now edited at the Department of Design at Carnegie Mellon University and published by The MIT Press.

Introduction

Design Issues was founded in 1983 by a small group of designers and design educators at the University of Illinois, at Chicago, who were interested in creating a forum for design discourse. In the first editorial, the founders described their vision of the journal as "a place for ongoing deliberation" concerning design.[1] The scope of the proposed deliberations included design history, theory, and criticism, and from its inception, *Design Issues* has regularly published articles dealing with the history of design. The first volume of the journal contained a long two-part essay by Clive Dilnot, a design historian and critic. In "The State of Design History," Dilnot reviewed the existing design history literature.[2] In the absence of a clearly defined status as an academic discipline (the kind of status, for example, that art history enjoys), Dilnot confessed that it was "bafflingly difficult to survey or define design history in its present state."[3] In place of a single, comprehensive definition of the field, he attempted to clarify what he described as the "forms and varieties of design history,"[4] and he argued for the relevance of design history to the larger intellectual project of exploring the significance of design as a fundamental human activity rather than just a particular form of professional practice.

Although the status of design history as an academic discipline in the United States may have changed little in the intervening years, the body of design history literature has grown in size and sophistication. This anthology collects the best of the design history articles published in the first ten volumes of *Design Issues* (1984–1994). It offers readers the opportunity to assess and reflect on the scope of recent design history and the insights generated by design historians. This process of reflection should begin with a discussion of the peculiar nature of anthologies because the anthology makes a different claim to our attention than other possible formats for design history. This is not a collection of documents, archival materials, or interviews that historians could treat as primary source materials. Beyond simply presenting design materials, all of the authors included here are interested in identifying and interpreting the significance of their subject matter. Nor can this anthology pretend to produce a unified, comprehensive narrative account of design history. Rather than outlining a single editorial line or defining concept of the proper subject matter and appropriate methodologies for design history, this collection demonstrates the varied interests and approaches of the contributors to *Design Issues*. The voice of history here is choral, and the reader is reminded of Dilnot's observation regarding the multiple forms and themes of design history.

1 Victor Margolin, "Editorial," *Design Issues* 1/1 (Spring 1984): 3.

2 Clive Dilnot, "The State of Design History, Part I: Mapping the Field," *Design Issues* 1/1 (Spring 1984): 4–23; Clive Dilnot, "The State of Design History, Part II: Problems and Possibilities," *Design Issues* 1/2 (Fall 1984): 3–20. Dilnot's essays are reprinted in Victor Margolin, ed., *Design Discourse: History, Theory, Criticism* (Chicago: University of Chicago Press, 1989), 213–50.

3 Dilnot, "State of Design History, Part I," p. 12.

4 In "The State of Design History, Part I," Dilnot identified four major varieties of design history: (1) as a continuation of the traditional histories of the decorative and minor arts applied to manufactured articles of the nineteenth and twentieth centuries; (2) as an aspect of the history of Modernism; (3) as the study of design organization in industrial systems; and (4) as the study of the social relations that arise from design activities.

The choral nature of an anthology such as this is especially appealing in light of critical arguments advanced by feminist and poststructuralist writers. Criticisms of the manner in which widely disseminated narrative histories tend to reinforce the hegemonic status of national, class, or gender-based systems of authority and legitimacy have left many wary of the single authorial voice.[5] In their introduction to an anthology entitled *Remaking History*, Barbara Kruger and Phil Mariani compared historians to ventriloquists putting words into the mouths of people unable to speak for themselves. More often than not, they argued, there has been only one history: "a bulky encapsulation of singularity, a univocal voice-over, an instructor of origin, power, and mastery. . . . If traditional history has been in a sense a process of collecting, it has also been a process of marginalizing, omitting."[6] In place of histories that marginalize or omit the contributions of people outside the traditional centers of cultural or political power, Kruger and Mariani argue for the development of "alternate histories" dedicated to the recovery of the heritage of neglected groups or forgotten individuals.

As this anthology demonstrates, *Design Issues* can certainly claim to contribute to such a project of recovery. Ellen Mazur Thomson's article, "Alms for Oblivion: The History of Women in Early American Graphic Design," for example, is a major contribution to our understanding of the role of women in American graphic design between 1850 and 1920. Her description of the presence, status, and role of women in graphic design demonstrates the way in which uncovering the story of forgotten or neglected groups can refine our understanding of the history of an entire design area like graphic design. In a similar manner, Matthew Turner's "Early Modern Design in Hong Kong" and Shou Zhi Wang's "Chinese Modern Design: A Retrospective" extend the geographic boundaries of design history to include areas missing from American and Eurocentric historical accounts of design.[7]

It would misrepresent the purpose and scope of this anthology to interpret it primarily as a concentrated effort to produce a history of marginalized design experiences and groups. The cast of characters the reader will encounter in this anthology ranges from the anonymous to the charismatic. Design personalities like Arthur Mackmurdo, John Ruskin, Norman Bel Geddes, Walter Dorwin Teague, and Harley Earl, along with well-known corporate and industrial leaders like Henry Ford, Alfred Sloan, and William Paley, command our attention here, just as they do in the standard design histories familiar to students and scholars alike. In addition to accounts of design in parts of the world distant from the traditional centers of historical interest, readers will find themselves on familiar ground in the British Isles, Central Europe, and North America.

Over the course of the past decade, the composition of the staff, editorial board, and advisory board of *Design Issues* has varied as new faces join the effort and others retire, resign, or pass away.[8]

5 For an insightful feminist critique of design literature see: Cheryl Buckley, "Made in Patriarchy: Toward a Feminist Analysis of Women and Design," *Design Issues* 3/2 (Fall 1986): 3–14. Buckley's article is reprinted in Victor Margolin, ed., *Design Discourse*, 251–62.

6 Barbara Kruger and Phil Mariani, "Introduction," in Barbara Kruger and Phil Mariani, eds., *Remaking History. DIA Art Foundation Discussions in Contemporary Culture, Number 4* (Seattle: Bay Press, 1989), ix–x.

7 It is worth noting here the lacunae in this anthology. Historical accounts of African and South American design experiences, for example, are missing not because these stories lack value, but because, to date, they have lacked historians. *Design Issues* remains committed to publishing a range of historical material as it becomes available.

8 Along with changes in the composition of the editorial board and staff, the institutional home of *Design Issues* has changed. Volumes 1 through 9 (1984–1993) were published by the University of Illinois at Chicago. The journal recently relocated to the Department of Design at Carnegie Mellon University and, beginning with volume 10 (1994), is published by The MIT Press.

One thing that has remained constant, however, is the original commitment to publishing a journal that can serve as "a place for ongoing deliberation." The journal's editors have preferred articles that pose provocative questions, rather than offer tidy answers or neat definitions, in the belief that such questions are the most effective way to promote a critical discourse about design. What is the subject matter of design history? How has design represented ideological values? What are the economic, political, and social factors that together constitute the matrix within which design efforts unfold? What have designers been asked to do by those who commission design? How has design shaped fundamental aspects of cognitive experiences in the modern era? This list could be extended. One way to approach this anthology is to treat it as a catalog of such questions compiled by historians as they endeavor to trace the connections in the modern era among images, objects, services, and systems brought into being through design.

In his 1984 review of the literature, Clive Dilnot characterized the field of design history as being plagued by "unresolved issues" and "fundamental ambiguities" concerning its scope and purpose. A decade later, Victor Margolin, one of the journal's editors, expressed his concern that "design history has not developed a self-conscious process of questioning its subject matter and asking why the particular objects that constitute the bulk of historical research should be the primary ones studied by the field."[9] In light of such comments, we must ask whether this anthology-as-catalog can claim to be exhaustive in its treatment of design history. It seems equally necessary to answer, "Certainly not." This need not be considered a sign of failure on the part of design historians. The field of design history continues to be enriched by new discoveries, fresh insights, and provocative questions. Historians and critics continue to refine the scope of their activities and develop more sophisticated methodologies for examining the history of design. It is important to recognize, in this regard, the way in which accounts of the past are linked to the present. History is the concerns of the present projected onto the past. As our present evolves, so too do the questions we ask of the past. Historians have always shaped their work in ways that reflect and illuminate the concerns of the present. They have long recognized this "presentness" of history as an integral part of their discipline. In the words of the eminent French historian Fernand Braudel, "History, in its essence and through all its permutations, has always been dependent on concrete social conditions. 'History is the child of its time.' So its preoccupations are the same as those which weigh on our hearts and minds. And should its methods, its projects, those answers which only yesterday seemed so rigorous and dependable, should all its concepts suddenly collapse, it would be from the weight of our own thinking, our own study, and, most of all, the experiences we have undergone."[10] Design history, like other areas of historical

9 Victor Margolin, "A Reply to Adrian Forty," *Design Issues* 11/1 (Spring 1995): 19. This issue of *Design Issues* was devoted entirely to the theme of design history.

10 Fernand Braudel, "The Situation of History in 1950," in *On History* (Chicago: University of Chicago Press, 1980), 6.

inquiry, is constantly reconfiguring itself, reformulating its subject matter, and redefining its methods in order to contribute in a vital way to the discussion of contemporary issues and opportunities.

The body of work presented here demonstrates that design history is no longer an inchoate endeavor trapped in the shadows of more established disciplines like art or architectural history. Considered individually, each essay in this anthology offers specific insights into particular topics, but the importance of this anthology extends beyond the individual merits of the essays. The act of collecting these articles together in one place focuses the collective insights of the contributors in a way that reinforces and amplifies their significance for design history as a whole. The significance of this anthology has little to do with the establishment of a canon—a set of paradigmatic objects, figures, and texts—for design history. Instead, these essays, considered in aggregate, ask the kinds of questions and offer the type of critical self-reflection that Margolin called on design historians to pursue. Rather than describe each essay separately, it is worthwhile to consider the threads that run throughout the collection. Beyond the specific themes of each essay, it is possible to identify three metathemes that pervade this anthology: place, vision, and time. These metathemes do not arise in each and every essay but they occur often enough to suggest their overarching significance for contemporary design history.

The concept of place in design history should not be confused with the sense of place encountered in architectural discourse. Architects and architectural historians often seek to identify the formative role played by the distinctive natural features and cultural traditions of specific locales in the design of cities and buildings. Place, in the context of this anthology, embraces more than cultural geography. One set of essays is collected under the heading "Design in the Context of National Experiences" in an effort to fill the gap between monographic treatments of individual designers and sweeping international surveys of design in the modern era. Even in an era of internationalism, the specific economic, political, social, and historical contexts of a particular country inevitably influence design efforts in ways that reflect local conditions and shape distinctive personal and communal identities. As the articles collected here under the heading "Design in the American Corporate Milieu" reveal, the constituent elements of place need not be defined by national or regional borders alone. The concept of place suggested here embraces the social setting as well as the physical locale in which design occurs. The automotive industry considered by David Gartman in his essay, "Harley Earl and the Arts and Color Section: The Birth of Styling at General Motors," or the milieu of broadcasting described in my essay, "Design at CBS," are as significant as the locus for design as the English factories surveyed by James Schmeichen in "Reconsidering the Factory, Art-Labor, and the Schools of Design in Nineteenth-

Century Britain." Historians, like designers, need to recognize that the influence the place of design exercises on the process of design.

The concept of vision that emerges from this anthology deals not so much with *what* one sees but *how* one sees it. The problems and achievements associated with the visualization of knowledge, the visual communication of information, the creation of images that signal identity, and the recording of experience and thought in nonverbal formats pervade the material collected here. David Brett's "Drawing and the Ideology of Industrialization," for example, explores how the codification of developments in descriptive drawing reveals a profound epistemological shift from metaphorical to instrumental thought in the early nineteenth century. In "Evolutionary Affinity in Arthur Mackmurdo's Botanical Design," Larry Lutchmansingh argues that Mackmurdo's drawing style—his way of seeing nature—should be recognized as a thoughtful and informed reflection on evolutionary theory as described in the work of Victorian scientist Herbert Spencer. For Lutchmansingh, decisions concerning drawing styles reflect more than aesthetic preferences, they reveal fundamentally different forms of intellectual engagement with the pressing scientific issues of the day.

The concept of time explores the temporal dimensions of designed objects and human experience. For example, what are the significant spans of time in the lives of men and women, of cultures, and of objects? For certain classes of designed objects, planned obsolescence is part of their very definition. Yet other things are conceived as enduring for long periods of time and become obsolete for reasons never anticipated by their makers. A history of design that fails to pay attention to the effects of time misses a crucial dimension of experience. The ephemeral is as much a constituent part of our sense of time and experience as the enduring. How are we to assess the relative weight of each in design history? World Fairs, for example, are, by their very nature temporary events that combine entertainment, education, and salesmanship in an ebullient mixture. Yet, as David Marchand argues in his two-part article "The Designers go to the Fair," out of the planning for the great fairs of the 1930s in Chicago and New York emerged a new relationship between designers and their corporate patrons and a new set of themes and strategies for corporate planning in America.

One of the revisionist arguments that emerges from this anthology deals with the lingering, negative effects of a particular conception of time encountered in earlier design literature. One of the persistent arguments advanced by the cultural avant-garde in the early twentieth century involved the claim that the present was irrevocably separated from the past. "We stand on the last promontory of the centuries!" wrote F.T. Marinetti, the founder of Italian Futurism, "Why should we look back?"[11] Yet more than once in this anthology, the reader is advised to beware of accepting too quickly the avant-garde claim of a definitive break between earlier periods and the radi-

11 F.T. Marinetti, "The Founding and Manifesto of Futurism" (1909), in Umbro Apollonio, ed., *Futurist Manifestos* (New York: Viking Press, 1973), 21–22.

cal new machine age. In "Imre Kner and the Revival of Hungarian Printing," for example, György Haiman focuses on the desire to employ design in ways that suggest the importance of threads of continuity within a culture. Kner's work would find little place in a history of design structured to conform to a concept of the radical disjuncture between the twentieth century and preceding periods. When modernist shibboleths are called into question, a different, richer, and more complex version of the history of design emerges.

It is important to remember that the past is as complex as the present. At any given moment in the past, multiple possible futures existed; nothing was preordained, and nothing is the inevitable outcome of a given set of circumstances. Historians do their readers a disservice when the simplify the past by constructing uncomplicated cause-and-effect chains to account for the emergence, development, and fate of the varied phenomena that constitute the domain of design history. In various ways, the authors included in this anthology point out the distortions caused by the creation of simplistic narratives predicated on inadequate theoretical and interpretive frameworks describing the triumphant rise of modern design. Mitchell Schwarzer, for example, begins his article, "The Design Prototype as Artistic Boundary," by arguing that in their desire to produce linear and monolithic treatments of early modern design, historians amalgamated groups (such as the British Arts and Crafts Movement and the German Werkbund) with contrasting philosophies in a manner that obscures a more complex set of historical experiences.

The authors anthologized here ask the reader to consider what people have found persuasive in civil and social discourse. Have societies adopted certain courses of action because they were drawn to the future or were fleeing the past? How have people weighed the relative merits of enduring cultural values versus the liberative potential of new ways? What design strategies have proved effective in attempts to create economic markets, social identities, and confident, independent nations? *Design Issues* was founded to provide "a place for ongoing deliberation" concerning design. By asking probing questions of the sort evident throughout this anthology, design history constitutes one important form of deliberation on the artifacts, events, issues, and themes intrinsic to design in the modern era.

Dennis P. Doordan

Section I

Graphic Design

Drawing and the Ideology of Industrialization

David Brett

Drawing is an activity fundamental to human action. It belongs with counting and speaking as being a primary form of cognition. A people that did not draw would be as unimaginable as one that did not count or speak, and, if not too pedantic about how drawing is defined, we may assert that the activity of making lines is a mode of thought. A line, as it extends, takes in the world, and because drawing may be both descriptive and prescriptive, lines can model possible worlds. The form used to represent the worlds (the objects) we seek to make is, preeminently, drawing.

The first industrial revolution required new graphic conventions to communicate its need for precision, and, therefore, many books and pamphlets on drawing were written in the first decades of the nineteenth century. Some of these were fundamental textbooks in isometric projection; others were useful manuals for tradesmen and apprentices. Still others were for the general education of young people and amateur artists or for the developing profession of "designer." (In British usage, this term meant those who drew designs for applied ornament and was distinguished from mechanical drawing.) The majority of these books attempted to treat drawing in a systematic manner, and a smaller number treated it as a science, presenting sets of axioms to use to analyze a drawing problem. The latter now encroach on the territory occupied by teaching machines and computer-driven drafting tables.[1] Most taught a dry, linear style of drawing.

Literature is part of the process of mass education that any newly industrialized society demands; it was the earliest example of the process still under way in Third World countries. The process entails a profound epistemological upheaval, a shift from metaphorical to instrumental thought, and the teaching of drawing at such a juncture is obviously part of an ideological struggle to transform human understandings.

Descriptive drawings of machines, mines, and buildings are, of course, very ancient types of drawing; but industrial production at that time demanded a prescriptive clarity that could convey unambiguous instructions in a universally comprehensible code. This was equally true in both decorative and mechanical design.

In the preface to his description of the building of the Eddystone lighthouse (1786), John Smeaton found it necessary to write about his plates as such: "They are little more than geometric lines, drawn to explain geometric and mechanical subjects. If any of

1 Typical titles in these categories include *Geometrical and Graphical Essays*, by George Adams (1791), *The Practice of Isometrical Perspective*, by Joshua Jopling (1833), *Treatise on Isometrical Drawing*, by Peter Sopwith (1834), *The Carpenter's Guide: a Complete Book of Lines for Carpenters* (8th ed. 1828), *Rudiments of Drawing Cabinet and Upholstery Furniture*, by R. Brown (1822), *An Essay in Ornamental Design*, by D. R. Hay (1844), *A Manual for Teaching Model Drawing from Solid Models*, by B. Williams (1843), *The Science of Drawing Simplified, or the Elements of Form Demonstrated by Models*, by B. W. Hawkins (1843), *The Oxford Drawing Book*, etc., by N. H. Whittock (1825 several eds.), *Elements of Perspective Drawing*, by A. O. Deacon (1841), *Drawing for Young Children*, by H. Grant (1833), *First Exercises for Children in Light, Shade and Colour*, by H. Cole (1840), *The Lessons in Art*, by J. D. Harding (1835, etc. many eds.). I am indebted in some points to an unpublished thesis by David Jeremiah entitled "Drawing and Design: Theory and Practice, 1830–1870," University of Reading, 1971. Accompanying these texts are many manuals on drawing instruments and their use and a spate of inventions to assist the draftsman, culminating in the camera. Machines were devised for drawing elipses and parabolas, for enlarging or contracting drawings, and so forth. Beam and telescopic compasses came into regular use, as did "geometrical pens," complex dividers, proportional compasses, and innumerable forms of rulers. The modern T-square and protractor were first illustrated in 1830. The primary instrument of all, the humble pencil, was also coded for the first time, and by 1830, HH for engineers, H for architects, F for sketching, and B for shading were recorded. The combination of drawing instrument and hard pencil was devised to provide exactly that determinate line that the drawing manuals demanded and mechanical drawing required. See: P. J. Booker, *A History of Engineering Drawing*, (1963), K. Baynes, *The Art of the Engineer* (1983) and *Drawing Instruments* R.I.B.A. catalog. (1982).

them put on the appearance of anything further, it is to render it more explanatory and descriptive. They are, in reality, not meant as pictures. . . ."[2] The plates, splendid large engravings, are a mix of mechanical drawing and picturesque detail—some distance from modern engineering drawing. For that style to be achieved, a uniform industrial practice was essential so that a uniform graphic convention could both mirror and create it.

This codification took place in naval dockyards and the workshops of engine designers and railway builders,[3] creating a new professional group with its own self-conscious values and powers. In 1836, George Stephenson complained, "They have no sooner come into an office, and become acquainted in every detail with our plans, than they leave and carry away what has cost us a great deal of money and more thought."[4]

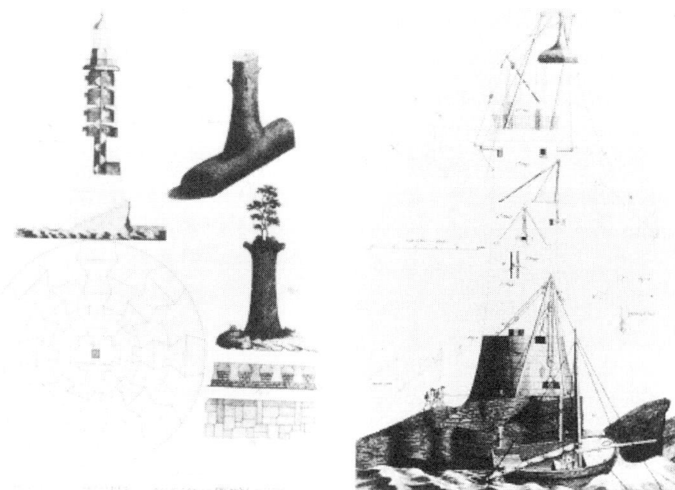

Figures 1a and 1b
Two plates from John Smeaton's *A narrative . . . of the building of the Eddystone light . . . etc.* 2nd ed. (1813). Graphic conventions poised between picturing and diagrammatic explanation.

The prescriptive nature of such drawing indicates a change in the nature and flow of information; it is the visual language of experts instructing operatives. This operational necessity is also the creation of a social function. "An engineer is a mediator between the philosopher and the working mechanic, and like an interpreter between two foreigners, must understand the language of both. . . . Hence the absolute necessity of his possessing both practical and theoretical knowledge."[5] Engineering drawing is the language of such mediation, as have been the innumerable other forms of diagram, chart, map, and instructional sheet developed since the 1820s. The tacit understanding of the craft-based ship- or millwright is being replaced by the explicit science of the industrial manager and technologist. A recent writer observed, "If we divest ourselves of any notion of instrumental rationality as a Geist-like disembodied wraith, and see it instead as a part of the occupational culture of experts and technicians who constitute a specific status group, with status interests they wish to protect and advance, and for which they require political allies, and which, in turn, require an ideology acceptable to these allies,

2 J . Smeaton, *A narrative...of the building of the Eddystone light...etc.* 2nd ed. (1813).

3 The role of military and naval requirements in the long war years has clearly some part to play in this, especially in France, where the organization of the polytechnics created the first real engineering education. The preponderance of books in English indicates the lack of regular schooling; Nicholson's *The Carpenter's Guide* (see note 1) has to begin with a short course on Euclid to do the work of a school class. It was not until the 1830s and 1840s that the mechanics institutes became numerous enough to supply the want of instruction.

4 See K. Baynes, "Drawing as Design Method," in *Design and Industry: the Effects of Industrialization and Technical Change on Design*, ed. N. Hamilton. (London: The Design Council, 1980), 46–47.

5 H. R. Palmer of the newly formed Institute of Civil Engineers (1818) as quoted in W.H.G. Armytage, *A Social History of Engineering* (London: Faber and Faber, 1961), 22.

then it becomes clear: technicians and experts are forced to go beyond instrumental rationality, and to generate a larger morality."[6]

In the domain of decorative design, a similar process of codification took place, and two determinants can be identified. The first was the technical constraints of designing motifs and patterns capable of production by mechanical means; the second involves intellectual and esthetic factors, being a theory of what was appropriately beautiful for the new age.[7]

Technical constraints hampered the design of patterns for the newly mechanized textile trades, notably printed cottons. The use of engraved or punched copper rollers, printing on an evenly stretched continuous belt of cloth, demanded a certain simplification of drawing and the abandonment of shading. A writer suggested, "The combination of the cylindrical, never-ending surface, with the small mill and die, tended to produce overall patterns, minute florals, geometric and optical effects. The pervasiveness of the small repeat, in texture and motif, is so widespread that textile students today, when asked to produce a dress print, often instinctively produce designs of this sort."[8]

However, this tendency to linear simplicity, flatness, and close repeat remained a stylistic desideratum even when no longer technically necessary. These qualities were approved by Augustus Pugin, the writers in the *Journal of Design and Manufacture,* and Richard Redgrave, Owen Jones, and Christopher Dresser,[9] but to describe the patterns merely as contemporary taste avoids interpretation. D. Greysmith observed, "Despite the many factors at work bringing design into being, the new machine-produced patterns can be seen, anthropologically, as the sign language of a people changing from a predominantly rural to an increasingly urban culture."[10]

This linearity and flatness did not simply appear; it had to be taught in the design schools. Redgrave later described the instructions "a method wholly new." When viewing nature, the trainee designer had to perform an "ornamental analysis . . . displaying each part separately according to its normal law of growth, not as viewed perspectively, but diagrammatically flat to the eye . . . this flat display was specially suitable to the requirements of the manufacturer, to reproduction by painting, weaving, stamping, etc., to which naturalistic renderings do not readily lend themselves."[11] Dresser developed the same idea still further, arguing that "for ornamental purposes we deem literal copies altogether insufficient; representations of a more rigid character and analytic nature being necessary . . . ," and asserted that plant drawing for decorative purposes must "generally . . . coincide with the architect's plans of the building . . . a series of drawings which shall convey a perfect knowledge of every part."[12] The expected manner of drawing was always hard, clear, unshaded pencil work.

This approach to drawing, which by mid-century became known as "conventional art," was given its first full expression in

6 A. W. Goulden, *The Dialectic of Ideology and Technology* (London: Macmillan, 1976), 269.

7 To treat the technical constraints first does not imply their logical priority. Monocausal explanations of culturally complex realities should be rejected as a naive idealism. In studying design, we need to be careful not to confuse different orders of explanation. Technical constraints seems to belong to one such order and nexus of causality, and esthetic and intellectual assumptions, to another. Design occurs at the meeting place of several such trains of implication. I have found useful an article by P. G. Dickens, entitled "Social Science and Design Theory," *Environment and Planning B* Vol. 7 (1980), 353–360, which discusses the interacbon between production and ideology.

8 D. Greysmith, contribution to *Design and Industry,* ed. Hamilton (see note 4), 62–65.

9 For a very interesting discussion of "flatness" see J. Maschek, "The Carpet Paradigm: Critical Prolegomena to a Theory of Flatness," *Arts Magazine* (September 1976): 82–106.

10 D. Greysmith, *Design and Industry.*

11 S. and R. Redgrave, *A Century of Painters* (London: Smith, Elder, 1866), 564–5. See also Macdonald, *The History and Pbilosophy of Art Education* (London: University of London Press, 1970), Ch.12.

12 C. Dresser, "Botany as adapted to the arts and Art Manufacture," *Art Journal* (December 1,1858): 362.

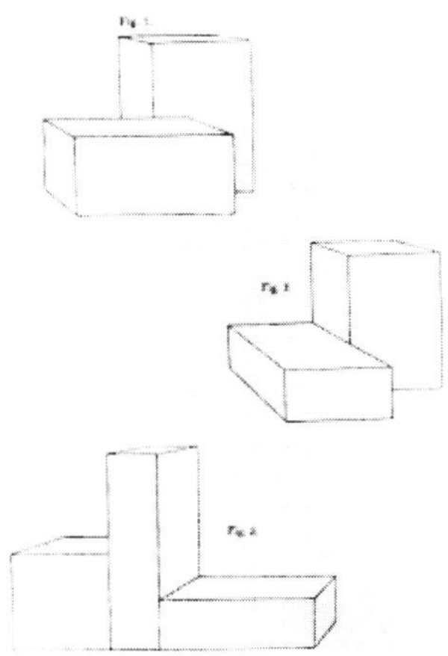

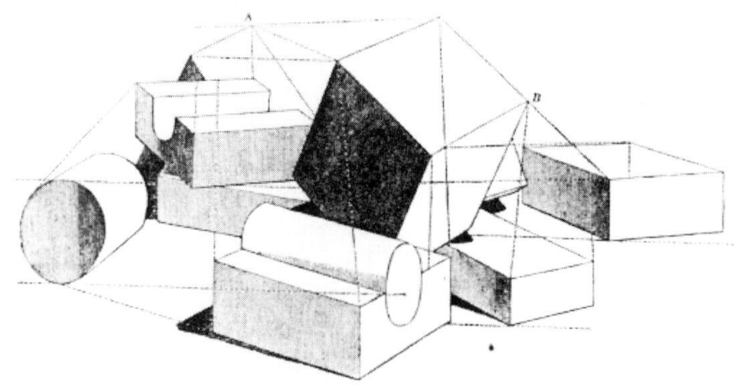

Figures 2a, 2b, and 2c
Three plates from J. D. Harding's The Guide and Companion to The Lessons in Art (1854) illustrating the use of wooden blocks for self-instruction. Harding wrote several "how to draw" manuals, mainly for amateur artists: *The Lessons in Art* (t835, t849, etc.) was his most pedagogical. See also his Drawing Models and Their Uses (1854).

The Drawing Book of the Government Schools of Design, produced by William Dyce in 1842–43.[13] This book followed a progression, familiar to all who have studied these drawing manuals, from simple linear elements to increasingly complex ornamental forms abstracted from botanical study. It was intended to teach young people to be designers. "Beauty," wrote Dyce, "is a quality separable from nature's objects . . . . [The designer] makes the separation in order to impress the cosmetic of nature on the productions of human industry. Works of industry thus molded into shape are not imitations of nature because they are covered with pictures or sculptured resemblances of natural objects, but because they are adorned on the same principles as the works of nature themselves." The purpose of drawing was to study nature and its "operating and governing laws" to form "abstractions . . . beauties of form and color [which] . . . by the very fact that they are abstractions, assume, in relation to the whole progress of art, the character of principles or facts, that tend by accumulation to bring it to perfection."[14] By these means, ornamental design was to become "a kind of practical science, which, like other kinds, investigates the phenomena of nature for the purposes of applying natural principles and results to some new end."[15]

13 William Dyce's intellectual biography included a scientific education and lengthy experience of German artistic life and design training. He had some association with D. R. Hay and the circles in Edinburgh in which the relationship between science and art was discussed (see note 14 below).

14 William Dyce, *The Drawing Book of the Government Schools of Design* (London: Chapman and Hall, 1842), Introduction. A full unpacking of the concepts carried in this passage would be most revealing. See also Dickens's lampoon of it in *Hard Times* (1854), Ch 11.

15 In *The Journal of Design and Manufacture,* Vol. I (March–August 1849).

Figure 3

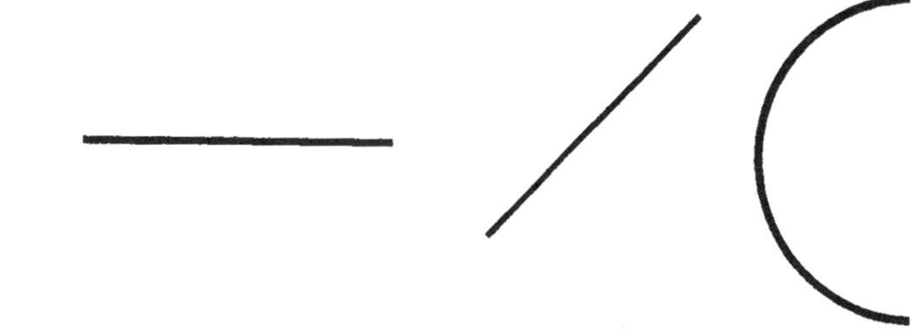

To understand this highly cognitive and positivist concept of drawing, the pedagogical and philosophical assumptions that preceded it need review. These assumptions were broadly shared by Dyce, Redgrave, Dresser, David Hay, Jones, Cole, Pugin, and, indeed, all the major British decorative designers and theorists of the early and mid-century, with the exception of Ruskin and his followers.

The drawing manuals published in Britain during the first 30 years of the century were based on the assumption that all drawing is founded upon a set of primary or elementary lines. The ability to form these lines must be imparted before any attempt is made to produce images, because the linear elements have priority. They are, indeed, the *a priori* conditions of any kind of drawing. A characteristic formulation can be found in the pages of William Robson's *Grammigraphia* (1799): "Lines are four; perpendicular, horizontal, oblique, and curve. All the variety of appearance in nature are presented by a combination of these four lines placed agreeably to proportion and position." The production of a line should be considered as "properly the continuation of a point. A point can proceed in four ways only . . . and from these we derive a mathematical account of all the common figures: angle, square, circle, ellipsis, oval, pyramid, serpentine, weaving, and spiral." The student was expected to use a line as distinct and determinate as possible.[16]

Robson's scheme of four lines is similar in kind to that of George Field, for whom "from the direct, reflect, and inflect motions of a point are generated the three primary figures: the right line, the angle, the curve."

Figure 4

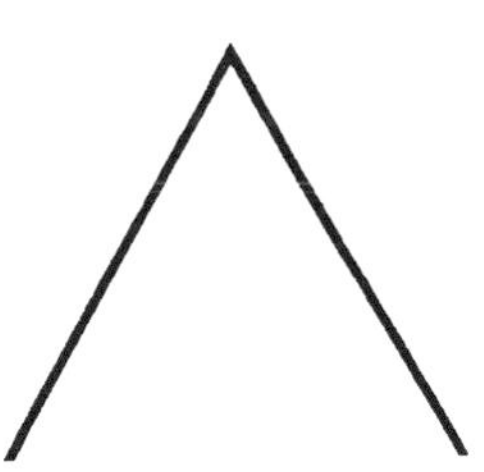

16 William Robson, *Grammigraphia; or the Grammar of Drawing* (London: Wilson, 1799). An interesting little book that contains evidence for most of the themes discussed here. It was recently mentioned by Stafford (1979) (see below).

From these, "all possible figures constituted of lines, surfaces, and solids [are produced] by the variation and composition of the three primary figures. It follows that all graphic art, and that of drawing in particular, consists elementarily in the ability to form the three primary lines—straight, angular, and curve—in all their variations of position, gradation, and composition."[17]

From such beginnings—though not all manuals were so axiomatically organized—students were expected to progress to the drawing of regular solids, simple perspective, and, finally, effects of light and shade. Some authors encouraged students to draw from wood or plaster "models" of cubes, cylinders, and tetrahedrons, and some manuals were published with sets of such wooden blocks provided.[18] Dyce's *Drawing Book* (which was, significantly, usually called the "Outlines") may be regarded as the summary of this pedagogy, which had both this native British element and one much indebted to German ideas.

In Germany, this approach had been incorporated by Pestalozzi and his followers, notably J. C. Buss, into part of all elementary education. It was known there as *pedagogische Zeichnen* and was held to be quite distinct from expressive or *Kunstzeichnen.* Inasmuch as in the philosophy of Kant space and form are *a priori,* the activity of drawing should begin with exercises that enlarged and developed a child's existing understanding of space and form. Drawing based on empirical observation came a decided second.[19]

Buss, in an account of Pestalozzi's methods published in 1828, wrote that "Angles, parallels, and arcs comprise the whole art of drawing. Everything that can possibly be drawn is only a definite application of these three primary forms. We can imagine a perfectly simple series arising out of these primary forms, within which an absolute standard is to be found for all drawing; and the esthetic beauty of all forms can be evolved from the nature of these primary forms." He went on to elaborate an "ABC of Form," which built exercises from the simple to the complex and linked them with the development of measuring and mathematical skills. He remarked, significantly, "This is a new art that should precede the usual, old-fashioned, well-known ideas of art culture."[20]

Pestalozzian ideas were first favorably reported in England in 1814, and the first school using these principles was founded in London in 1836, where Hermann Krusi taught the ABC of Form as an algorithmic method for the production of decorative motifs through the combination and permutation of simple elements. The evidence presented to the Parliamentary Committee in Arts and Manufactures (1835–36) reflected this German teaching, as well as the native British element.[21]

Similar ideas were in circulation in the United States, where there was a considerable publishing effort by a educationalists such as J.G. Chapman, W.B. Fowle, and Rembrandt Peale. Peale's "Graphics" (2nd ed. 1838) quotes extensively from Pestalozzi. These

17 The interesting figure of George Field touches on these topics at several points. The leading color chemist of his day, he was the author of a standard work on color, *Chromatography* (1835: several eds.), and a number of highly theoretical writings in which he developed an analogical philosophy whereby primary forms and colors were construed as part of a logical system of universal analogy that linked written and spoken language, and even machine pans, with the fundamental constituents of the universe. See D. Brett, "The Aesthetical Science: George Field and the 'Science of Beauty', " *Art History* Vol. 9, No. 3 (September, 1986): 336–350.

18 Clive Ashwin has written, "The progressive adoption of geometric models at all levels of art teaching, including the art schools and academies, is a subject . . . worthy of further research." In what follows I am particularly indebted to C. Ashwin, *Drawing and Education in German-speaking Europe, 1800–1900* (Ann Arbor, MI: UMI, 1981), and for other writings by Ashwin.

19 See C. Ashwin, "Pestalozzi and the Origins of Pedagogical Drawing," *The British Journal of Educational Studies* Vol. XXIX No. 2 (June 1981): 138–151. Also G. Sutton, *Artisan or Artist: a History of the Teaching of Arts and* Crafts *in English Schools* (London: Pergamon, 1967).

20 Quoted by Sutton, *Artisan or Artist*, 30.

21 See *Parliamentary Papers. Select Committee* (1836) Pt. 1., p.vii. "Such elementary instruction should be based on an extension of the knowledge of form, by the adoption of a bold style of geometrical and outline drawing, such as is practiced in the national schools of Bavaria." See also D. R Hay, *The Laws of Harmonious Colouring* (4th ed. 1836) for a discussion of the evidence. *In the Parliamentary Report on Foreign Schools of Design for Manufacture* (1840), Dyce describes himself as "looking for something constituted out of both. "

ideas were tried out by A.B. Alcott in his experimental schools in Boston between 1834 and 1839; but the appeal of the drawing manual was very strong in a country in which the education system was still in an early stage. W.B. Fowle's self-teaching handbooks were written to supply the want of teachers.[22] However, the main force of the Anglo-German pedagogical tradition reached the United States through the work of Horace Mann, the secretary of the Massachusetts State Board of Education; Mann was responsible, on one hand, for bringing over Walter Smith of the Leeds School of Design to teach the South Kensington system in the Massachusetts Normal Art School (in 1873) and, on the other, for introducing Peter Schmid's system of Naturzeichnen through the pages of the *Common School Journal*.[23] Smith wrote of the Normal Art School that "it is intended as a training school for the purpose of qualifying teachers and masters of industrial drawing. In the future it may be necessary to provide for high skill in technical drawing and art culture, but the immediate pressing demand is for teachers who know the elementary subjects thoroughly." He had written earlier, "To do this, [the teacher] must first learn the alphabet of the subject and know by name and at sight any feature of form from the dot to the most subtle compound curve, and from the simplest geometric form to the last problem in perspective."[24]

Ideas similar to Pestalozzi's were also developed by Friedrich Froebel, who envisaged an *a priori* perceptual grid, or network, in which "The vertical and horizontal directions mediate our apprehension of all forms . . . in our imagination we constantly draw these lines across our field of vision, we see and think according to these, and thus there grows in our consciousness a network of lines keeping pace in clearness and distinction, without consideration of the form of things." His drawing exercises, as described in *The Education of Man* (1828), consisted of linear adventures within this network.

22 I am here indebted to Diane Korzenik, whose collection of early drawing books is very useful. Her *Drawn to Art: A Nineteenth-Century American Dream* (Hanover, N.H.: University Press of New England, 1986) contains much interesting material. For A. B. Alcott, see F. M. Logan, *The Growth of Art in American Schools* (New York: Harper, 1955), 16–19.

23 For a detailed description and discussion of Schmid's work, see C. Ashwin, "Peter Schmid and Das Naturzeichnen: An Experiment in the Teaching of Drawing," *Art History* Vol. 5, No. 2 (June 1982): 154–165. Schmid produced a huge book supported by a kit of wooden models (1828–32). Ashwin observed that "What Schmid had devised was a primitive teaching machine, complete with self-checking mechanism in the form of the plates which represented what the learner should be producing, and, like all well-designed teaching machines, it had the great advantage that the learner could progress at hls own pace even when working in a class context." A number of simplified versions of Schmid's system appeared in Germany in the 1830s; in Britain, A . O. Deacon's *Elements of Perspective Drawing, or The Science of Delineating Real Objects* (1841) came accompanied by a box containing 57 wooden elements. Also see Logan, *The Growth of Art in American Schools,* 19.

24 See Logan, *The Growth of Art in American Schools,* 66 et. seq. Smith's *Teacher's Manual of Freehand Drawing and Designing* (Boston: L. Prang, 1873) set out to do for American pupils what Dyce's *Outlines* were intended to do for British, 30 years earlier: to take the student from simple squared lines and polygons to curves, complex curves, scrolls, ornaments, symmetries, and botanical analyses to snow crystals and beyond. All drawing was to be done in a clear style with hard pencils. Smith's book was preceded by R. Demcker's A *Course of Systematic and Progressive Drawing* (Cincinnati: Ehrgott, Forbriger, 1868); it was a Schmid-based manual.

From this network developed his notion of "gifts"—sets of blocks and other materials in which the child can explore simple spatial and volumetric experience.[25]

Other systems of pedagogical drawing came into existence in both Britain and Germany, but discussing the fine distinctions that contemporaries perceived among them is not necessary. Worthy of note, however, is dictation drawing, devised by Platz in 1818. Every child was provided with a matrix of dots, each one numerable. A relatively complex design could be converted into a code and then dictated at regular speed to the class, which drew it in unison. "It is clear that in this way the full attention of the little draughtsman is demanded. The slightest inattention to the word of the teacher leads unavoidably to mistakes."[26] Such is one first step toward the computer-driven drafting table.

Neither in Britain nor in Germany was conventional art or pedagogical drawing regarded as an attempt at art education. Influential writers regarded such drawing as a useful mechanical skill, attainable by all. A typical apologia was provided by the *Encyclopaedia Mancuniensis* (Manchester, 1813), which under "Drawing" stated, "It should be learned by every person as answering the same purposes with writing . . . we are convinced that it is of the utmost importance to society that this should always form part of common school education, in the same manner as writing."[27] In the 1840s, Dyce was fond of pointing out to recalcitrant staff of the British Schools of Design that the regulations stated that "no person making Art his profession should be eligible as a student." Many similar examples might be given.

These schemes were justified in both idealistic and narrowly utilitarian terms. For Froebel, "Form . . . reveals in various ways inner spiritual energy. To recognize this inner energy is part of man's destiny. . . . It is therefore an essential part of human education to teach the human being, not only how to apprehend but also how to represent form; and inasmuch as the perpendicular relations (of the vertical and horizontal) aid the development of form consciousness, the external representation of these relations as a means for study and representation of form is based on the very nature of man, and of the subject of instruction." However, "The use of this instruction would supply one of the greatest wants of our schools in town and country; . . . it teaches the eye a knowledge of form and symmetry and trains the hand in representing them; and these find much to do in all relations and activities of practical life."[28] Logan noted, "Widespread approval of this kind of drawing was based on its value in the manual training of a population (employed) in industry and the skilled crafts."[29]

That these arguments should be both idealistic and utilitarian is a consequence of the intellectual tradition that brought them into being, as well as the ideological process of which they were a part. The first argument is clearly a combination of lore and assumptions embedded in the academic tradition, both of which were reinforced by eighteenth-century natural philosophy, with its as-

25 Writers on Frank Lloyd Wright have noticed the importance he attached to the Froebel education he received. We should probably think of Wright and Sullivan before him as the direct inheritors of this tradition of decorative design. The role of Frank Furness is probablv seminal in this transmission of precepts. Furness had access to both Jones's and Dresser's ideas directly and to those of Jones's French associates, Cesar Daly and Labrouste. Furness's decorative interiors seem to be what Owen Jones and Dresser were wanting to achieve.

26 See Ashwin, *Drawing and Education in German-speaking Europe, 1800–1900,* 124.

27 The argument that writing and drawing are somehow congruent with one another is very common in this literature; its most complete statement is in the pages of Field's *Analogy of Logic* (1850). Robson, *Grammigraphia; or the Grammar of Drawing,* also thought that drawing could be taught "with nearly as much truth and certainty as a sum in arithmetic" and that "Musick is a science founded on the same principle of quantity as drawing." Horace Mann was another who thought that "Drawing is a form of writing and should be taught with it." (See Logan, *The Growth of Art in American Schools,* 21.)

28 See F. Froebel, *The Education of Man* (1828) trans. W. N. Hailman (New York: Appleton-Century Co., 1887), 278–299. See also Sutton, *Artisan or Artist,* 35–44.

29 Logan, *The Growh of Art in American Schools,* 19.

sumptions about the regularity and inexorable precision of the functioning Universe.

In the pages of Rosicrucian writers such as John Dee or Robert Fludd, the expansion of the point to line, plane, and solid was given a mystical significance as being emblematic of the unfolding of the manifold creation. The capacity to "frame" lines and geometrical diagrams was part of the natural magic that accompanied this occult philosophy, a body of ideas that many writers have shown to be germinal of the academic tradition. The magical framing was not perfectly distinguishable from the utilitarian drawing of masons, architects, and carpenters. An important feature of Dee's *Praeface to Euclid* (1577) is the separation it attempts between practical workman and learned architect, through the instrumental skill of drawing. "The hand of the carpenter is the architect's instrument . . . the whole feate of architecture in building consisteth of lineaments and in framing. And the whole power and skill of lineaments tendeth to this; that a right and absolute way may be had of coapting and joining lines, by which the face of the building, or frame, may be comprehended and concluded. . . . the form and figure of the building may rest in the very lineaments, etc. And we may prescribe in mind and imagination the whole forms, all material stuff being secluded."—the immateriality of perfect architecture.[30] The frame for these writers meant both the elevation of the building and its abstract and mathematical scheme as depicted in "lineaments." Thus, when they spoke of the frame of the Universe, they meant its geometrical configuration expressed in number and line.

At such points, the Neoplatonic mysticism of the Renaissance blended with the artificer's theology of the "argument from design," which perceived the Creator as supernal Designer of the Universe. The theological point is not easily grasped today but has considerable import. The combination of Neoplatonism and orthodox belief preserved the idea of divinity in the mechanistic world-picture; it was thus the linch pin of the orderly ideology constructed upon Newtonian philosophy throughout the Enlightenment. The esthetic precepts of this were best described by Galileo and Wren.

For the former, "Philosophy is written in this grandest of all books, forever open to our eyes (I mean the Universe), but which cannot be understood if we do not learn first to understand the language and interpret the letters in which it is written. It is written in mathematical language; the characters are triangles, circles, and other geometrical figures, without which it is impossible to understand a single world: without these there is only aimless wandering in a dark labyrinth."[31] For the latter, "There are two causes of beauty, natural is from geometry, consisting in uniformity (that is, equality) and proportion. Customary beauty is begotten by the use of our senses, as familiarity breeds a love to things not in themselves lovely. Here lies the great occasion of error, here is tried the architect's judgment; but the true test is always natural or geometrical

30 John Dee, *The Mathematical Preface to Euclid* (1577) (New York: reprinted by Science History Publications, 1977). I have simplified his erratic spelling. Dee is an early example mystical idealism and utilitarian intentions .

31 G. Galilei, *Opere* VI trans. Brophy and Paolucci, (New Yok: Burnes and MacEachern, 1962), 232.

beauty. Geometrical figures are naturally more beautiful than other irregular; in this all consent as to a law of nature. Of geometrical figures, the square and circle are most beautiful, next the parallelogram and oval. Strait lines are more beautiful than curve, next to strait lines equal and geometrical flexures. There are only two beautiful positions of a strait line, perpendicular and horizontal; this is from nature and consequently necessity, no other than upright being firm. Oblique positions are a discord. . . ."[32]

Figure 5
Illustration from *Syllabus of Drawing for Elementary Scbools, Standard Three* (Dept. of Science and Art, London, 1886 ed.). The South Kensington System in full operation.

In this intellectual complex, simple geometrical form was esthetically desirable, epistemologically necessary, and magically effective. These disparate (and to us irreconcilable) components were tied together in a theological natural philosophy. Although these matters require further study, it seems that the pedagogical drawing of the early nineteenth century recorded a movement of thought away from this complex natural philosophy and toward scientism. The platonic simplicities of the linear and solid elements no longer carried with them any metaphorical significance. They were, as it were, shorn of affect.

And yet, not entirely, for there remained a theory of the beautiful as a whispering ghost in the positivist machine. "Beauty," for Dyce, "is a quality separable from natural objects." It was to be

32 *Parentalia* (1750). For discussion, see J. A. Bennett, "Christopher Wren: the natural causes of beauty," *Architectural History* Vol. XV (1972), 5–22.

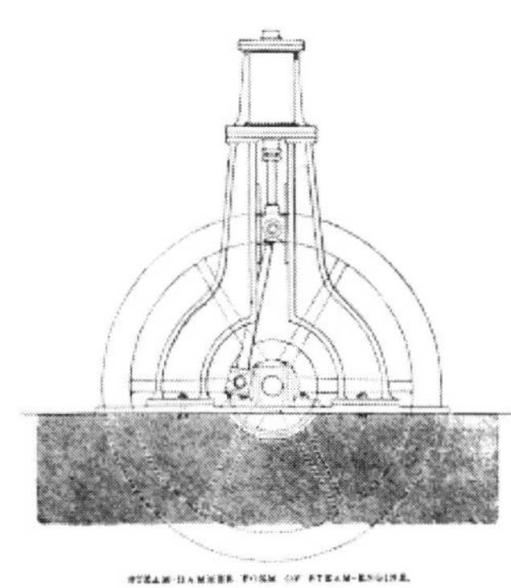

Figure 6

found through what Dyce called "abstraction" and others "conventionalization," that is, through the creation of typical forms or motifs. For the decorative artist, the ornamental type was created by ornamental analysis of botanical and other types. It was therefore necessary to study the natural sciences.[33]

For the designer of machines, the mechanical necessities of power generation and transmission (as understood through Galileo's geometrical characters) were not only necessities, but also stylistic desiderata. "In mechanical structures and contrivances I have always endeavored to attain the desired purpose by the employment of the fewest parts, casting aside every detail not absolutely necessary, and guarding carefully against the intrusion of mere traditional forms and arrangements. The latter are apt to insinuate themselves and to interfere with that simplicity and directness of action which is in all cases so desirable a quality in mechanical structures. Plain common sense should be apparent in the general design . . . and a general character of severe utility pervade the whole."[34] John Nasmyth further wrote, "Viewing abstractedly the forms of the various details of which every machine is composed, we shall find that they consist of certain combinations of six primitive or elementary geometrical figures, namely, the line, the plane, the circle, the cylinder, the cone, and the sphere; and that, however complex the arrangement and vast the number of parts of which a machine consists, we shall find that all may be, as it were, decomposed and classed under these six forms; and that, in short, every machine, whatever be its purpose, simply consists of a combination of these forms. . . ."[35]

Although this statement addressed the practical problems of precision machining, it was also a statement of esthetic intention (evidenced by Nasmyth's own designs and by much of early nineteenth-century machine design) and a commentary upon the teaching of drawing. Nasmyth was concerned with the *visual grammar suited to precision technology*.

In such an intellectual culture, for there to be an interest in the mathematics of form, closely linked with questions of design and ideas of harmonic proportion, is not surprising. For Richard Reinagle explained, "All elegant forms are derived from curvilinear ones . . . radiation is the first arrangement of lines which presents anything like the appearance of an agreeable form . . . I have discovered the ruling law of the Greeks to be in thirds, that two and one always constitute varieties of the most agreeable character, as do three and five, two and five, etc. . . ."[36] Hay (heavily influenced by George Field's "analogical philosophy") believed he had created a "Science of Beauty," and his "harmonic analyses" of Greek vases, the human form, and color relationships helped form a considerable literature in the later part of the century. Hay, through his association with the anatomist John Goodsir in the Aesthetic Club of Edinburgh, was able to link these interests with the latest discoveries in mathematical

33 Lectures on scientific topics were a standard part of the South Kensington system. Leading botanists, such as John Lindley, and the zoologist Edward Forbes appear on the curriculum. Christopher Dresser was a leading botanist, with several books on plant morphology. The roots of art nouveau and organic design theories can be found here.

34 James Nasmyth, "James Nasmyth, Engineer: An Autobiography" (New York Harper, 1883), as quoted in H. Schaefer, *The Roots of Modern Design* (London Studio vista, 1970), 28. Nasmyth was the leading machine designer of his day; he was also fully acquainted with the Edinburgh circles in which the relationship between science and art were discussed.

35 James Nasmyth in Robertson Buchanan's *Practical Essays on Mill Work and Other Machinery etc.* 3rd ed. (London John Weale, 1841), 394–5.

36 Evidence given to the Parliamentary Committee on Arts and Manufactures, June 17, 1836. Reinagle was a subscriber to Field's principal works. This evidence was reprinted in George Phillips's *Rudiments of Curvilinear Design* (1839), one of the first books to discuss the decorative arts in relation to industry. His evidence appears, in the Parliamentary Papers, next to evidence on automatic routers and carvers for the wood and stone trades.

morphology.[37] For Field, an analogical system of [drawing] extended all the way from the primary elements of drawing, to the primary elements of machine design.[38] This was an idealist esthetic, a late development of absolute rather than associational theories of beauty; however, it was an idealism in scientistic dress. It may be thought of *as a transformation of elements of the academic tradition,* rather than as its rejection.

The proponents of conventional drawing of course regarded their work as a refutation of academic teaching. It was to be "a method wholly new," a "new art that should precede the usual old-fashioned, well-known ideas of art-culture." It would guard against "mere traditional forms and arrangements." For Dyce, it was part of making design into a "practical science" and, for Dresser, part of the "scientific study of art" and would "express our secular knowledge of nature, as revealed through the sciences," just as earlier decorative conventions revealed religious faith.[39]

In the disputes of the 1830s, in which modern design education was first considered, the academic tradition was represented by Benjamin Haydon, who argued with force that "if any school of design, though exclusively devoted to manufacture be founded, without provision in its code of instruction for the knowledge of the human figure, the very elements of taste and beauty in manufacture will be omitted in the basis." He proposed a course in which students began by drawing from casts of the antique figure, plaster details of anatomy, and "the best books on Art, Anatomy and Design. . . . No student should be admitted (to the study of ornament) but by a drawing where at least a decent knowledge of the figure should be apparent." He argued that "the same principle regulated the milk jug and the limb, and it is not by separating the inferior from the superior you attain excellence in both; but it is by combining the two; as the Greeks did, the Italians, and the French at present do."[40]

Later in the century, when conventional art had become the orthodoxy of British design education, it was once again opposed, by

---

37 David Ramsay Hay was a leading interior designer and the author of several rather repetitious but interesting books heavily influenced by George Field. I am aware of 15 main titles, of which the most interesting are *The Laws of Harmonious Colouring* (1828), *An Essay on Ornamental Design* (1844), *The Natural Principles of Beauty etc.* (1852), and *The Harmonic Laws of Nature applied to Architectural Design* (1855). These and his other titles were summarized in *The Science of Beauty* (1856). In it he argues that the science of beauty "must be founded on fixed principles after the manner of natural science." For the Aesthetic Club, see the *Anatomical Memoirs of John Goodsir*, ed. William Turner (Edinburgh: A. and C. Black, 1868), and Brett, "The Aesthetical Science: George Field and the 'Science of Beauty'" (1986). The club has also been noted by Phillip Steadman in *The Evolution of Designs* (Cambridge: Cambridge University Press, 1979). Hay's studies of the mathematics of the forms of Greek vases, the human body, and the Parthenon were taken up later in the century by Cook, Colman, Hambidge, and other writers on "the hidden geometry of art and nature." Goodsir and Hay believed that the logarithmic spiral and systems of proportion derived from it were the key to both natural growth and the beauty of artifacts. Hay argued against Zeising's notion of "golden sections." There is a strongly masonic flavor to the Aesthetic Club.

38 See Brett, "The Aesthetical Science: George Field and the 'Science of Beauty.'"

39 Christopher Dresser, *The Builder* (March 15, 1862): 185–6.

40 And also "The perfection of design in manufactures depends on the perfection of design and position and encouragement of the poetical and elevated branches." B. Haydon, "Lectures on painting and Design" Lect. 1. Vol I (London: London, Brown, Green, and Longmars, 1846). See also Macdonald *The History and Philosophy of Art Education* (1970), Ch. 5 for a useful summary.

Ruskin, most notably in his lecture on "The Deteriorative Power of Conventional Art over the Nations," which was given at the South Kensington Museum in January, 1858 (as if in the lion's den). It was based upon the rejection of "natural facts" and the belief that no great school "ever yet existed which had not for primal aim the representation of some natural fact as truly as possible . . ."[41] The consequence and the cause of geometrical simplicity was held to be "savagery." This attack on the normative teaching of conventional antinaturalism was pressed with great clarity and force of example. In addition, just as pedagogical drawing pointed toward an industrial future and the cult of the machine, so natural drawing pointed toward a natural handcrafted past and the cult of the vernacular. At the same time, Ruskin's intuitive ascription of savagery to conventional art was an insight into the de-cultured, de-historicized world of positivism.

Pedagogical drawing, claiming to be based upon the *a priori* of all depiction, could not act as the transmitter of existing culture. Geometry was held to be factual, positive, and, therefore, modern. Its analytic/synthetic manner was perceived to be scientific, and was capable of axiomatic expression. These qualities, without doubt, commended it to liberal politicians and industrial management. This was certainly the reason for its adoption and formulation in the British Schools of Design, urged on by a government bent on electoral and educational reform, and headed by an industrialist (Sir Robert Peel) whose fortune had been made in the very trade of printed cottons in which conventional linearity and flatness had been explored by a new class of designer-artists. The Parliamentary Enquiry that began design education in Britain was promoted by the Board of Trade, and its chairman, William Ewart, conducted it in such a way to make its findings exactly what he required. The same interests were evident in Henry Cole's *Journal of Design and Manufacture* and the preparation of the Great Exhibition of 1851. They received informed support from the Prince Consort, whose German education may well have included a similar drawing curriculum.[42]

In the German states, *pedagogische Zeichnen* was introduced in the period of national reconstruction and resurgence after the Napoleonic wars. Every German state was willing to consider elementary drawing instruction in schools. The Prussian state led the way; Wilhelm von Humboldt, a friend of Goethe and Schiller appointed (1809) Alois Hirt to prepare a drawing program for the entire school system. Hirt adopted the Pestalozzian "alphabet," beginning with simple geometric figures. However, after the Year of Revolutions (1848) and the conservative reaction, pedagogical drawing fell into disfavor, along with all liberal educational thought. The new conservative regimes reintroduced drawing from prints and casts. Geometry returned to favor in the reforms following German unification in 1872. Though this matter is complex and always subject to local variation, reintroduction of drawing from antique casts and prints had an ideological significance.

41 Printed in George Allen's *The Two Paths: Being Lectures on Art and Its Application to Decoration and Manufacture* (1884 edition). A comparison of the dates of this lecture with those of published lectures by Dresser suggest strongly that the dispute was carefully timed. Ruskin's approach to drawing had been exemplified in *The Elements of Drawing* published the previous year. This book set forth an alternative teaching: tonal and impressionistic, antilinear and antigeometry. There is not space here to discuss the extent and consequences of the dispute.

42 For a discussion of the Prince Consort's role in the definition of the idealogy of industrialization and normative design education, see my unpublished doctoral thesis entitled "Quantities and Qualitites, Arts and Manufactures 1830–1930: A Study in the Philosophy and Ideology of Design Reform" (London: Royal College of Art, 1984).

In Ruskin's opposition through "natural drawing" a different significance can be discerned. The natural can no more be a carrier of the traditional culture than the *a priori,* and though Ruskin and Morris were much preoccupied with local association and historical memory, they could not evade the dialectical consequences of evoking nature. Apparently, the pursuit of the natural leads back beyond the pastoral toward the barbaric in industrial culture. This is the goal pursued in Morris's de-christianized romantic materialism and in the imaginative world of Richard Wagner, with whom Morris had much in common.

Instrumental rationality, although necessary to industrial production, evokes an equal and opposite reaction of irrational antimodernism. A study of drawing discloses this and further indicates the continuing uncertainty about what sort of drawing is appropriate in design education, as well as the relation between the fine and the decorative arts. This vagueness is a consequence of an undertheorized and de-historicized understanding, which is itself a problem disclosed by cultural criticism.

The decay of theological natural philosophy released fractions of transforming power: positivism and irrationality. Neither of these forces can tolerate or make coherent critique of each other. Positivism, by making metaphorical thought into a marginal activity, represses older philosophical traditions. It cuts off access to mythical forms of representation, meanwhile creating its own mystique. As Habermas said, it "monopolizes the self-understanding of the sciences" such that "the meaning of knowledge itself becomes irrational."[43] Utilitarian positivism—of which the drawing we have studied was the graphic expression—carried with it an absolutist and universalizing ambition, an intention to transform the world toward "that great end, to which indeed, all history points—the realization of the unity of mankind."[44] That unity was to be achieved through the trinity of science, industry, and art. This was the larger morality, the ideological rationale, to which the designers of the early nineteenth century made appeal; it was the justification of their theory of drawing.

43 See J. Habermas, *Knowledge and Human Interests,* trans. J. Shapiro, 2nd ed. (London: Heinemann, 1978), 68–69.

44 As quoted in the *Illustrated London News,* October 11, 1849. (See also R. R. James, "Albert, Prince Consort" (London: Hamish Hamilton, 1983),194–200.) The Prince's speech deserves to be studied as a classical statement of mystical futurism at the service of capital and technology; significantly, it refers to "immutable laws of beauty and symmetry," which art discloses to be "standards of action" for industry. See Brett, "Quantities and Qualities, Arts and Manufactures 1830–1930: A Study in the Philosophy and Ideology of Design Reform."

The Poster as Art; Jules Chéret and the Struggle for the Equality of the Arts in Late Nineteenth-Century France

Bradford R. Collins

At the end of the nineteenth century in France, the poster enjoyed high-art status.[1] The process by which it rose from mere commercial device to fineart print did not, as has been claimed, revolve around the sudden vogue for prints that occurred in the early 1890s;[2] its rise through the hierarchy of media was a long, complicated process dating from the 1830s. The crucial phase began in the third quarter of the century with a two-pronged attack on the centuries-old academic principle of a qualitative hierarchy of the arts. At the top were the fine arts: painting, sculpture, and architecture. The decorative or applied arts, such as furniture design, were below them, and the popular arts—caricature and the various arts for mass consumption—were at the bottom. On the one hand, Realists and their naturalist heirs advocated an end to all attempts to rank the arts. On the other, decorative-art reformers sought to elevate those arts to the level of painting and sculpture. The poster became involved in these related but very different crusades—and thus shared in their eventual victory over academic dogma—as the result of the exceptional poster work of one man: Jules Chéret (1836–1932).

Materials discussed here are largely drawn from my doctoral dissertation, "Jules Chéret and the Nineteenth-Century French Poster," Yale University, 1980. This essay is dedicated to my adviser, Robert L. Herbert because of his scholarly and humane assistance in that ordeal. I wish, also, to thank my former colleagues at the University of Illinois at Chicago, Peter B. Hales, Victor Margolin, and Laurel Bradley for their help in the preparation of this manuscript.

1 Posters, often unlettered and printed on high-quality paper, were sold by a number of Paris print dealers. The best known of these, Sagot's Librairie de nouveautés et librairie artistique (established in 1881), began selling posters in 1886. Sagot's 1891 catalog offered 2,233 posters. For more on the subject, see Phillip Dennis Cate and Sinclair Hamilton Hitchings, *The Color Revolution: Color Lithography in France 1890-1900* (Santa Barbara: Peregrine Smith, 1978), 12. For an account of poster prices at the time, see Jane Abdy, Chéret to Cappiello (London: Studio Vista, 1969), 25–26. Two periodicals were founded to cater to collectors and enthusiasts: *Les Maîtres de l'Affiche*, begun in 1896, and *L'Estampe et l'Affiche*, which commenced publication a year later.

2 Robert Koch, "The Poster Movement and 'Art Nouveau,'" *Gazette des Beaux-Arts 50* (1957): 285. A stronger case can be made for the view that the vogue for posters was the major factor in the print renaissance of the 1890s. The revival fostered by Cadard in the 1860s and early 1870s waned after his death in 1875. Despite some notable individual achievements and various collective efforts in the 1880s (see Cate and Hitchings, The Color Revolution, 13–14), the revitalization of the print dates from the early 1890s. The rising popularity of poster collecting, discussed bdow, was the prelude to the vogue for the print. The attention given the poster in the 1880s by collectors and critics did much to stimulate artists' enthusiasm for lithography, in particular, color lithography. That this medium was the mainstay of the print movement in the 1890s is revealing. The first prints by the men most identified with the renaissance, Bonnard and Lautrec, are posters, "France-Champagne" (1891) and "Moulin Rouge" (1891) (figures 11 and 12, respectively). Furthermore, eleven of the first fifteen lithographs by Lautrec were posters. André Mellerio, the first historian of the lithographic revival of the 1890s, said "posters opened up a new path—a path which the print happily followed." "La Lithographie originale en couleurs," 1898, translated in Cate and Hitchings, *The Color Revolution*, 94.

1

2

3

4

Chéret enjoyed a good entrance: economic and artistic conditions in Second Empire France (1852–1870) favored a talented, ambitious poster designer. By the late 1850s, when Chéret's career began, the lithographic poster was established as the main promotional device for the rapidly expanding French economy. Moreover, the illustrated poster had a legitimate, if modest, place in the arts. It was first associated with graphic art during the 1830s as a result of the vogue for illustrated books. Both frontispieces and text illustrations, enlarged and sometimes elaborated, were placed in shop windows to promote the sale of these books. Tony Johannot's frontispiece for the 1844 edition of Goethe's *Werther* (figure 1), for example, was the basis for his more complete poster image (figure 2). As is typical of such work, this poster is unsigned. Signatures first appeared regularly on posters promoting the new illustrated almanacs of the 1840s.[3] The designers of these posters, Cham (figure 3) and Charles Vernier chief among them, were the popular and respected caricaturists whose works appeared in these periodicals. Evidence of the status that the poster thereby gained can be found not only in the

3 Adolphe Lalance, a specialist in sensational-novel posters during the 1830s, was the first to sign his work regularly, but his colleagues did not follow his lead.

5

6

7

proud attention paid by minor illustrators of the 1850s and 1860s to the design and execution of posters advertising sensational novels,[4] but also in the fact that Gustave Dore, a leading illustrator and sculptor, contributed to the genre in this period (figure 4).

Chéret became a poster designer as a consequence of his decision to be a lithographic illustrator. After the completion of his lithographic apprenticeship in 1852 and a very brief course of study at the École nationale de dessin, Chéret worked as a technician for various Paris lithography firms, including Lemercier.[5] He also sought more creative assignments, but with limited success. The only documented work from the period before 1860 is the poster *Orphée aux Enters* (1858) (figure 5), which presents a rather romantic interpretation of Offenbach's light-hearted parody of Napoleon III's court. The importance of the commission suggests that Chéret had some reputation, at least. Despite favorable responses to the poster, *Orphée* did not create a significant demand for his services, which is apparently why he decided to leave Paris.[6]

In 1859, Chéret moved to London where he found a more receptive environment for his ambitions.[7] During his seven-year exile, he became the principal illustrator for one of England's major sheet-music publishers, Cramer and Company. Although his music covers included a range of moods and styles, his specialty was romantic effects. *The King's Butterfly* (1864) (figure 6) and *Hero to Leander* (1865) (figure 7) are typical. The dramatic content and broad graphic style have little to do with contemporary English standards in the genre;[8] Chéret's techniques were those of the French Romantic illustrators of the 1830s and 1840s, and his subjects were derived from Romantic painting. *The King's Butterfly* seems generally inspired by Gericault's *Wounded Cuirassier;* and *Hero to Leander* depends on the English tradition of sublime landscape established by Turner and John "Mad" Martin. That Chéret was looking at high art for his inspiration may say much about his artistic aspirations.

4 Horace Castelli, Charles Devrits, Auguste Belin, and A. Bellogua were the Icading poster designers in this area during the Second Empire.

5 Chéret claimed that he studied under Lecoq de Boisbaudran at the École Nationale de Dessin. Camille Mauclair, *Jules Chéret* (Paris: M. Le Garrec, 1930), 8. As Chéret was at the school less than six months and Boisbaudran only taught upper level courses, this is highly unlikely, although he may have been impressed with Boisbaudran's methods as discussed in the context of the school. Boisbaudran's course of drawing emphasized memory and speed of execution in the capture of scenes from daily life. Horace Locoq de Boisboudran, *Education de la mémoire pittoresque* (Paris: Bance, 1862). Lemercier was the leading lithography firm in Paris at midcentury. Michad Twyman, *Lithography, 1800-1850* (London: Oxford University Press, 1970), 235. Chéret's earliest known poster, "Orphee aux Enfers" (1858), discussed below, was printed at Lemercier (figure 5).

6 Gavami, the famous caricaturist, was one of those impressed by the poster. Mauclair, *Jules Chéret*, 8.

7 This was Chéret's second trip to London. In 1854, he had spent six months there looking for work. Mauclair, *Jules Chéret,* 8.

8 English covers are almost without exception more descriptive and quieter. See Doreen and Sidney Spellman, *Victorian Music Covers* (London: Evelyn, Adams, and Mackay, 1969).

8

9

The most important aspect of Chéret's stay in London was his relationship with Eugene Rimmel, a perfume manufacturer and member of the Royal Society of Arts.[9] The Society was committed to the encouragement of industrial art under the vigorous leadership of Prince Albert. To determine how English production fared in comparison with that of other nations, the Society organized the great Crystal Palace Exhibition of 1851. The results were disappointing and distressing to Albert's circle, and they therefore decided on a broad plan of reform.[10]

Rimmel's contribution to the nationalistic aims of the Royal Society of Arts, ironically enough, was to aid the young French lithographer Chéret. Rimmel not only hired Chéret to design his perfume labels and took him to various European art centers, but he also gave him the funds to open printing establishments in London and Paris.[11] Equally important, he taught Chéret the design principles established by the Royal Society of Arts. One of these principles was that design should fit the object's purpose.[12]

By applying this principle to a series of commissions from Offenbach, which he received after returning to Paris in 1866, Chéret established himself as one of France's leading poster designers.[13] In the first of the series, *La Vie Parisienne* (1866) (figure 8), for example, Chéret stifled his romantic inclinations and attended strictly to the spirit of the operetta. The exaggerated gestures and the brisk, angular configurations of line and shadow effectively capture and convey the frenetic mood of Offenbach's happy hymn to Second Empire social life.

The adjustable approach to poster design that characterized Chéret's work until about 1885 is evident in a comparison of *La Vie Parisienne* with *La Fée* (1869) (figure 9). Rather than happy and excited, the woman in *La Fée* is relaxed and peaceful, almost reflective. Although there are vital passages of line in her costume, these are subservient to the fluid rhythms of her pose. Her elongated proportions add to the languid effect. Chéret created a completely relaxed figure, implying that this product reduced, if not eliminated, the effort involved in sewing; this machine released its user from the drudgery of work.[14]

---

9 Chéret met Rimmel around 1860 as a result of a commission from another French expatriate, Auguste Le Maout, who had written two epic poems celebrating Rimmel's life. Chéret provided illustrations.

10 See Nikolaus Pevsner, *Matthew Digby Wyatt* (Cambridge: Cambridge University Press, 1950).

11 Mauclair, *Jules Chéret*, 8. The London firm closed sometime before 1869.

12 For the others, see Pevsner, *Matthew Digby Wyatt*, 14–15. That Rimmel shared the ideas of the society and spread them is revealed in his book, *Recollections of the Paris Exhibition of 1867* (London: Chapman & Hall, 1868) 70 and 83–84.

13 Chéret's printing establishment was probably the first to specialize in posters. Two printers soon followed his lead: Charles Lévy, who labeled his work "Affiches Americaines," and Emile Lévy, who frequently used the phrase "Affiches Françaises." The relationship between the two has never been determined. The three men shared the bulk of the poster design in France in the 1870s and early 1880s.

14 The differences of relative scale and text legibility can be explaned largely in terms of where each would have been posted. The smaller theater poster (68 x 51 cm.) would have been either in a theater lobby or on a nearby kiosk. The larger commercial poster (112 x 84 cm.) would have been on a wall space where it would have had to compete more vigorously for the viewer's attention. Rigorous guidelines for poster hangers were not introduced in France until 1881.

10

During the 1870s, Chéret's artistic ambitions resurfaced, but now in the form of a desire to solidify the poster's historical connections with caricature and, thereby, to draw his own medium deeper into the arena of accepted art forms. This goal is not evident in either his theater or commercial posters, wherein he seems to have been content with the status quo; it is evident, however, in his posters for music halls and other popular entertainments, that is, precisely in the areas where his work coincided with that of the caricaturists. Here Chéret invested considerable inventive energies. Moreover, the bizarre figural contortions and formal exaggerations of work such as *Les Majiltons* (1876) (figure 10) are consistent with a major development in contemporary French caricature. That Chéret came to identify with these artists is also manifest in the fact that in 1882 he was a founding member of Les Incohérents, an iconoclastic exhibition society composed almost entirely of caricaturists.[15]

Chéret's strategy of focusing on popular entertainment posters was rewarded when the art critic and novelist Joris-Karl Huysmans, then making a study of these diversions, mentioned him in Salon reviews of 1879 and 1880.[16] Chéret and the poster were thereby thrust into the sphere of high art. Huysmans first mentioned Chéret and the poster as a means of abusing the "official" painters. Following the example of his mentor, Zola, Huysmans distinguished the artists of the École des Beaux-Arts, who painted historical themes according to "all the old formulas," from "the independants," devoted to what he considered the more relevant and exciting task of painting modern life.[17] His "Salon de 1879" ends with the following indictment:

"Of the 3,040 catalogued paintings, there are not one hundred worth examining. The rest certainly do not measure up to the commercial posters on view on street walls and boulevard kiosques, these small pictures representing the corners of Parisian existence, the vaults of the ballet, the work of clowns, the English pantomimists, the interiors of the hippodromes and circuses.

Personally, I would prefer all the exhibition rooms hung with the colored lithographs of Chéret ... than to see them blemished like this by a mass of sad works."[18]

In this review then, Chéret warrants praise for his subjects; Huysmans wished to encourage painters to follow Degas's lead in accepting popular culture as suitable material for high art.[19]

Huysmans's appreciation for Chéret was stated positively in his Salon review of the following year, and the last two paragraphs of "Le Salon de 1880" were dedicated to the poster artist:

"I can only counsel people sickened . . . by this cheap and insulting display of prints and paintings to cleanse their eyes by directing them outdoors . . . where shine the astonishing fantasies of Chéret, these fantasies in colors so quickly drawn and so spiritedly

15 Members of the group included Adolphe Willette, Caran d'Ache, Somm, and De Sta. Annual exhibitions were held 1882–1891. A final exhibit and ball were held at the Folies-Bergère in 1891. Jules Lévy, a journalist and later a publisher who organized the group, stated that its aim was to promote gaiety in the face of the dourness of the naturalists and pretentions of the academics. Lévy's ideas were a major factor in the development of Chéret's mature esthetic. For more on the group, see Jules Lévy, "L'Incoherence," *Le Courrier Français* (March 12, 1885), and Philippe Roberts-Jones, "Les Incohérents et leurs Expositions," *Gazette des Beaux-Arts* 52 (1958): 231–236.

16 The first two essays in his collection *Croquis parisiens* (Paris: H. Vaton, 1886) deal with the Bal de la Brasserie Europeene and the Folies-Bergére.

17 J.-K. Huysmans, *Oeuvres complètes de J.-K. Huysmans*, 18 vols. (Paris: G. Cres, 1928–34), VI: 16.

18 Huysmans, Oeuvres VI: 14.

19 Huysmans says of Degas in his review of 1879: ". . . one of the first, he dared to grapple with artificial lighting, the bursts of the footlights before which bawling, barenecked, the cafe singers, or frolicking, pirouetting, the dancers dressed in gas." Huysmans, *Oeuvres* VI: 12.

painted. There is a thousand times more talent in the smallest of these posters than in the majority of the paintings that I have had the sad opportunity to review."[20]

In championing Chéret, Huysmans was contributing to a democratizing strain of thought that emerged in the context of the Revolution of 1848. Egalitarian sociopolitical sentiments had inspired writers such as Champfleury and Baudelaire to reject the academic hierarchy of the arts; instead, they attributed an absolute artistic value to the arts of the people, caricature, and folk arts.[21] Among the artists, Courbet led the way in incorporating into "high art" both the styles and subjects of the "low arts."[22] One of the major figures to attempt this in the 1880s, Seurat, was undoubtedly inspired by Huysmans's writings: Chéret's posters were Seurat's major source material.[23]

Those who participated in this tradition of thought and action aimed to bring the fine arts down from their lofty heights to engage life as the popular arts did. Their objections to the traditional ranking of the arts were liberal, and democratic; for them, art for a privileged elite only consolidated class distinctions and antagonisms.

The academic notion of a hierarchy of the arts was also opposed at this time by advocates of the decorative arts, but they wanted to elevate the designers of these arts to the rank of the painter and sculptor. Their aristocratic aims were rooted in the Rococo revival inaugurated in the 1830s by Theophile Gautier and his circle on the rue du Doyenne. Members of the *petit cenacle* were greatly impressed by the eighteenth century's respect for the minor arts, especially its devotion to the concept of *decor:* the principle that all aspects of art are important because they contribute to the beauty of one's surroundings.[24]

---

20 Huysmans, *Oeuvres* VI, 12.

21 Baudelaire's contributions were his three articles on caricature: "De l'Essence du rire" (1855), "Quelques Caricaturistes étrangers" (1857), and "Quelques Caricaturistes français" (1857), as well as his essay on Constantin Guys, in *Le Peintre de la vie moderne* (1863). Champfleury [Jules Fleury] wrote *Histoire de l'imagerie populaire* (Paris: E. Dentu, 1869) and a five-part Histoire de la caricature (Paris: E. Dentu, 1865?–1880). For the definitive discussion of the formation of this tradition of thought around the events of 1848, see Meyer Schapiro, "Courbet and Popular Imagery: An Essay on Realism and Naiveté," *Journal of the Warburg and Courtauld Institutes* IV (1941): 165–191.

22 Schapiro, "Courbet and Popular Imagery." Realist respect for popular art was responsible for Edouard Mann's sole contribution to poster art, the advertisement for Champfleury's *Les Chats* (1870). Although Manet's contribution to the genre was unprecedented, it was but an extension of Courbet's pioneering work in the area of popular art. Courbet produced his first popular image in 1850, a portrait of the Fourierist missionary, Jean Journet, for a broadside. For this and similar images, see Schapiro, "Courbet and Popular Imagery": 167–168. Moreover, Manet's poster was a manifestation of the same general climate of critical opinion responsible for Courbet's work. Both Baudelaire and Champfleury were close friends of Manet's in the 1860s and no doubt encouraged the liberal view that permitted him to allow one of his lithographs to be used for a poster. That an artist of Manet's stature was willing to contribute to the genre must have been flattering and encouraging to poster designers, but the incident was isolated and had no immediate repercussions.

23 See Robert L. Herbert, "Seurat and Jules Chéret," *The Art Bulletin* 60 (1958): 156–158.

24 Gautier lauded the century for making everything from ceilings to fans beautiful. He admired Boucher and Watteau for considering the painting of snuff boxes worthy of their talents. (Carol Green Duncan, *The Pursuit of Pleasure: The Rococo Revival in French Romantic Art* (New York: Garland Press, 1976), 172 and 229. Théodore de Banville, a poet and disciple of Gautier's, noted approvingly in a discussion of Rococo an that "the desire for harmony between man and that which surrounds him is the very soul of art." Carol Green Duncan, "The Persistance and Re-Emergence of the Rococo in French Romantic Painting," (Ph.D. diss., Columbia University, 1969), 172.

The ideas of Gautier and his friends were carried to a larger audience not only in their individual writings, but also in *L'Artiste*, which a founding member of the group, Arsène Houssaye, purchased in 1843. From the mid-1830s, the periodical devoted a fair amount of space to the applied arts. In the 1850s, it regularly featured articles such as that by Philibert Audebrand in which an applied artist announced to a sculptor that "I am worth more than you, I am useful to man . . . ".[25]

Articles in *L'Artiste* and comments by Gautier's Doyenné circle laid the groundwork for the French industrial art reform movement that began in the 1860s. French industrialists and their critics had also perceived the shoddy design at the Crystal Palace Exhibition of 1851, but they did nothing about it because observers agreed that French products, although faulty, were superior to others.[26] These industrialists were finally stirred to action by London's 1862 World's Fair; here the French saw the results of the reforms initiated by the Royal Society of Arts in the 1850s, and they feared the end of their preeminence in the design field.[27]

By 1864, two professional associations modeled after the Royal Society of Arts had been founded in France: the short-lived Société de l'art industriel and the Union Centrale des Beaux-Arts appliquè á l'Industrie. The work of the Union Centrale, especially in its early years, was greatly aided by the staff of the *Gazette des Beaux-Arts*,[28] whose keen interest in the decorative arts was the direct result of values maintained and spread by Gautier's circle. Arsène Houssaye's younger brother, Edouard, co-founded the magazine in 1859 and served as its first managing editor. For the three years prior to his publishing venture with Charles Blanc, Edouard had been coeditor of *L'Artiste*.

As with the Royal Society of Arts, the Union Centrale devoted considerable attention to the quality of technical school instruction and to promoting a better appreciation of good design principles. But its chief concern was to raise the professional standing of the decorative designer to the level of the painter and sculptor by establishing the principle of the equality of the arts. They believed that an improved status would attract a higher caliber of talent to the field.[29]

Precisely what equality of the arts meant to these men is revealed in Ernest Chesneau's *Dessins de Décorations des principaux Maîtres* (1881), one of the many books published with Union support. The book, ending with a lengthy plea for more public recognition of the decorative artist, states, "These painters, these sculptors, these draftsmen, these authors of patterns have, from the middle ages to the present, produced so many art objects and are artists of the same rank as the maker of statues and the painter of pictures."[30]

Chesneau did not challenge the painter's or sculptor's lofty reputation, nor did he question the notion of absolute standards; he

25 "L'Art appliqué à la vie intime," *L'Artiste* 16 (1855): 134.

26 Count de Laborde, the official French observer at the exhibition, noted the general decline in the decorative arts in his 1853 report, but said "In effect, the jury of the fine arts stated, and all intelligent visitors had to admit, that we had a general superiority. . ." Cited in Marius Vachon, "La Situation actuelle des industries d'art en France," *Gazette des Beaux-Arts* 25 (1882): 154.

27 Prosper Mérimée in his official report on the exhibition said, "English industry ... far behind from the point of view of art, has made since the Exposition of 1851 prodigious progress, and if they continue to proceed at that rate, we will soon be passed." Cited in Charles Blanc, "L'Union Centrale des Beaux-Arts appliqué à l'industrie," *Gazette des Beaux-Arts* 29 (1865): 194.

28 Besides devoting an unusually large number of articles to the Union in the mid-1860s—thirteen in 1865 alone—writers for the periodical, apparently as a result of a policy decision, lent their assistance to its actual work. The special commission established to advise the organization on various matters was composed of twenty men, three of whom were members of the *Gazette*'s staff: Philippe Burty, Paul Mantz, and Emile Galichon. And of the ten men given the responsibility of realizing the society's ambition of establishing a French counterpart to the R.S.A.'s South Kensington Museum (now the Victoria and Albert), four were colleagues at the magazine: Galichon, Louvrier de Lajolais, Albert Jacquemart, and Alfred Darcel. Blanc, "L'Union Centrale des Beaux-Arts": 195 and 200.

29 De Laborde, in his 1853 government report, first argued that the lower reputation of the decorative artist discourages the more talented men from considering such a career. Vachon, "La Situation actuelle": 154–155.

30 Ernest Chesneau, *Dessins de Décorations des principaux Maîtres* (Pans: A. Quantin, 1881), 160.

wished only to elevate the decorative artist to the same rank as the painter and sculptor. This was the ambition that stood behind French decorative-art reformers' condemnation of the academic hierarchy of arts. Victor Champier, the editor of the *Revue des arts décoratifs,* the official organ of the Union Centrale, condemned the "absurd hierarchy manifested in art" while insisting that the decorative arts deserve a place in the art world "equal to that of painting."[31] Although the principle of the equality of the arts for which these men fought suggests the leveling aims of the artistic liberals, their goal was quite different. "The arts" included only those officially sanctioned, only those taught at legitimate schools. And in their ideal artistic society, all art forms would be aristocrats, as with the characters in the Doyénne's vision of eighteenth-century France.

The naturalists and the decorative-art reformers often gave the appearance of a united front because of their shared antagonism to an established dogma. That the inheritors of the Realists of 1848 must be distinguished from the advocates of the applied artist is most evident, perhaps, in their respective attitudes to Salon practice. Whereas the former wished to eliminate it, the latter wished only to alter it. In May 1894, Renoir, an "indépendant," wrote to his dealer Durand-Ruel that he planned to organize a new exhibition association, La Société des Irregularistes, which would give the decorative arts a place equal to painting. And in the summer of that year the newly formed Société des Artistes Indépendants, formed by Seurat's circle, resolved that their exhibitions would embrace all branches of art equally.[32] "Les Indépendants" fought for the principle of the equality of the arts as one facet of their wholesale attack on the authority of the Academy's conservative value system. The decorative-art reformers, on the other hand, did not want to destroy that system; they wanted to be accepted within it. In 1882, for example, the Salon des Arts décoratifs—organized by the Union Centrale—was held at the same time as the official Salon in an adjoining building to dramatize what its organizers considered their unjust exclusion from the latter.[33]

The attempts to "democratize" the fine arts and those to "aristocratize" the applied arts together fueled the poster events of the 1880s and 1890s. In general, the naturalists' promotion of the popular arts, Huysmans's efforts in particular, launched the vogue for poster collecting that began around 1880, but the decorative-art movement provided the bulk of the rhetoric that sustained it.[34] The two factors are evident in the first essay dedicated specifically to the illustrated poster, Ernest Maindron's two-part history that appeared in the *Gazette des Beaux-Arts* in 1884.

Maindron was neither a professional critic nor an historian; he was an employee of the French Institute whose only connection with the world of art was as a poster collector.[35] That collecting prompted him to write is clear from his opening sentence: "Collectors are very respectable men." This declaration is followed by a brief discussion of

31 "Les Arts décoratifs au salon de 1889," *Revue des arts décoratifs* IX (1888–1889): 348349.

32 Sven Löevgren, *The Genesis of Modernism* (Bloomington: Indiana University Press, 1971),12–13 and 54–55.

33 Alfred Darcel, "Le Salon des arts décoratifs," *Gazette des Beaux-Arts*, 25 (1882): 583.

34 Decorative-art reformers, on the other hand, made no mention of the poster or of Chéret. They were not trying to raise all the lower arts to the top. Although the poster was a form of industrial art, it could also be considered a popular art and, therefore, beneath the area of their concern.

35 Maindron reorganized the archives of the Academy of Science. Henri Béraldi said he was a "passionate collector of posters: (he possesses more than ten thousand of them)." *Les Graveurs du XIXe siècle*, vol. IV (Paris: L. Conquet, 1886) 203.

the then recent phenomenon of poster collecting.[36] Maindron's book, *Les Affiches Illustrés* (1886), which resulted from the article, begins with a longer description of the joys and sorrows visiting the growing ranks of men who haunted the streets in search of the best examples of advertising art.

After Maindron discusses poster collecting in his 1884 article, he mildly reproves the increasingly conservative Champfleury for pronouncing that "the epoch which follows this will be astonished, perhaps, by the excessive importance now attached to the lesser arts." Maindron claimed that "the future will be more equitable and will applaud us. They will say that we have sought perfection in all the branches of art. . . ."[38]

Maindron then sketches the history of the poster from ancient times. The critical voice is absent until the early nineteenth century. At this point in the historical narrative, this thesis is clear: French poster designers had been slowly perfecting the art since about 1830. Of Johannot's poster for Topffer's *Voyages en Zigzag* (1840s) he exclaims, "It's nearly high art."[39]

In the second installment, Maindron discusses both the poster's brief decline during the Second Empire and the work of Manet and Doré, which signals the genre's modern era. As these artists were only marginally committed to the poster, it fell to a dedicated group of young men "to promote poster art to the elevated place which it has occupied for the last twenty years." Emile Lévy, Charles Lévy, Léon Choubrac, Appel, and a host of now forgotten men are briefly noted before Maindron concludes with four pages praising Chéret. In a passage reminiscent of Chesneau's claims for the decorative artist, Maindron calls Chéret a genuine artist, one of equal stature with the best painters and sculptors of the era.[40]

The next important writing on Chéret, a short monograph in the fourth volume of Henri Béraldi's *Les Graveurs du XIXe siècle* (1886), belongs to the democratic current of thought. After outlining Chéret's career and stating that he and others consider the illustrated poster a fine-art print, Béraldi concludes by emphatically rejecting any ranking of the arts: "Let us set aside the question of high and low art; the ideal is to have art in everything, even the most ordinary objects."[41]

Maindron's and Béraldi's writings contributed to Chéret's growing popularity in the late 1880s and shaped the critical acclaim that he received in the popular press.[42] Old attitudes were difficult to change, of course, and the positions of Chéret and the poster remained somewhat unclear. In March of 1889, one critic summed up the situation by stating, "The name of this man (Chéret) . . . has not yet been inscribed in the golden book of artists, or at least his works have not been admitted to the category of art work. Today no one hesitates to recognize that Mr. J. Chéret is an artist 'in his genre'. . . ."[43]

36 "Les Affiches Illustrées," *Gazette des Beaux-Arts* 30 (1884):419–420.

37 Ernest Maindron, *Les Affiches Illustrées*, (Paris: Launette, 1886), vi–viii.

38 Maindron, *Les Affiches Illustrées*, 420.

39 Maindron, *Les Affiches Illustrées*, 432–33.

40 Maindron, *Les Affiches Ilustrées*, 544–-47.

41 Béraldi, Les Graveurs, 169–170.

42 See, for example, Boyer d'Agen, "L'Art dans la rue: M. Jules Chéret," *La Revue Blanche* (May 19, 1888); Felicien Champsur, " L'Imagerie parisienne," *Figaro* (May 16, 1885); and "Les Affiches estampes," *Le Temps* (May 3, 1886). These and the other reviews referred to below are in the three volumes of *Coupures de journaux relatives à Jules Chéret données par M. René Bordeau* at the Cabinet des Estampes of the Bibliothèque Nationale, Paris.

43 Alfred de Lostalot, "Expositions divers,"

11

12

An exhibition at the Theatre d'Application later that year rescued Chéret from this limbo and inscribed his name in that golden book.[44] The one-man show included posters, lithographs, drawings, sketches, and pastels. Roger Marx, a respected critic associated with the causes of decorative art and printmaking, wrote the catalog introduction. His essay, following Maindron's lead, insists that Chéret raised the poster to high art.[45]

The exhibition created a considerable stir in artistic circles. Jean Frollo in *Le Petit Parisien* reflected the general surprise with his statement that "Who would have guessed that a poster exposition would become a sensational artistic event .... "[46] One indication of the phenomenal attention given the show is the petition signed by a large number of artists, including Degas and Rodin, which successfully demanded a decoration of the Legion of Honor for Chéret.[47]

Chéret was not the only beneficiary of the Théâtre d'Application exhibition. Georges Frappier's review in *Le Petit Caporal* makes clear how much all poster designers had gained: "Chéret, in effect, and several others have succeeded in raising to the serene regions of Art (sic) these productions which until recently did not go beyond the banal realm of industry."[48]

Frappier's reference to "several others" was purposefully vague because none of Chéret's fellow poster designers were of his calibre. Of the great names now associated with poster art at the end of the century, only Eugene Grasset was then working in the field, and the two works that he had produced had commanded no notice.

Gazette des Beaux-Arts 1 (1889): 238.

44 Earlier in the year, a number of his works had been included in the first large-scale exhibition of posters held at the world's fair, and a variety of his work (three sketches for posters, a decorated fan, a pastel, and two colored lithographs) was included in a print show at Durand-Ruel's Gallery, January 23 through February 14. Lostalot's review, above, was of that exhibition.

45 *Jules Chéret* (Paris: Théatre d'Application, 1889) ii. Dec. 24, 1889 to January 1890, were the exhibition dates.

46 Exposition des oeuvres de Jules Chéret, " in *Coupures de journaux.*

47 Mauclair, *Jules Chéret*, 12.

48 "De l'Exposition Chéret," Dec. 31, 1889.

In the late 1880s, Chéret was a one-man movement, "the king of the poster."[49] Chéret set the stage for the famous poster designers of the 1890s. Bonnard's first poster, *France Champagne* (1891) (figure 11), a pastiche of Chéret, demonstrates the master's powerful influence. And when Toulouse-Lautrec decided to make his first poster in the same year, he sought Chéret's advice and instruction. As acknowledgment of his debt and esteem, Lautrec sent Chéret a copy of every poster he produced.[50]

Chéret was the focal point for Bonnard and Lautrec, but the master and his students belonged to different theoretical camps. Bonnard, Lautrec, and others, such as the socialist Theophile, were, in effect, following Huysmans's advice to the artists of 1879–1880 to direct their attention to popular sources and subjects. Their poster work was the logical conclusion to Realist efforts at midcentury to undermine the absolute distinction between fine and popular arts.

Chéret's endeavour, on the other hand, paralleled that of the decorative-art reformers. Having brought the poster to the level of caricature around 1880, he then sought to raise it to the realm of high art. The best evidence of this aspiration is his mature sources: Watteau and Tiepolo. Chéret's posters of the late 1880s and 1890s were transpositions of the Rococo ideal of femininity and ease into contemporary situations. Works such as *Bal au Moulin Rouge* (1889) (figure 12) elevated middle-class persons and pastimes into an aristocratic sphere.[51] The skill with which this illusion was accomplished forged an identification of the poster with its art sources.

Developments in late nineteenth-century France had a definitive effect on the poster elsewhere in time and place. Because Paris was the art capital of the Western world, its verdict was considered conclusive. Thus, *fin-de-siècle* poster artists in countries such as Germany, England, and the United States did not have to concern themselves with their artistic legitimacy; they were free to focus entirely on design issues. In the twentieth century, with the question of the equality of the arts still in some doubt,[52] the status of the poster as fine-art print remains secure—potentially, at least—because of what Chéret and his immediate heirs, Lautrec in particular, accomplished. It also remains secure because the two struggles against the academic hierarchy of the arts established a theoretical climate in which they could thrive.

49 References to Chéret as "le roi de l'affiche" were commonplace in poster criticism of the 1890s.

50 Chéret's heirs claim that they had occasion several years ago to purchase a letter in which Lautrec admitted learning color lithography from Chéret. This claim is supported by the inscription signed by Chéret on the back of a copy of Lautrec's "Jane Avril" (1893): "This proof has been colored in my presence by Lautrec." *Exposition de Cent Ans de Théatre, Music-Hall et Cirque* at the offices of Bernheim-Jeune, May 25–July 13, 1936, no. 105. I am indebted to the collector and dealer, Walter Hoving of Toulouse and Co., Chicago, for this information.

51 In 1892, Chéret referred to Watteau as "my master." "M. Chéret," *La Revue Blanche* (March 26, 1892). The connection between Chéret and Watteau was widely acknowledged in the 1890s. Degas, for example, referred to Chéret as "le Watteau de la rue." (Abdy, *Chéret to Cappiello*, 32). Tiepolo seems to have been the major influence in Chéret's predilection for airborn figures.

52 That a hierarchy of the arts persists is everywhere evident: in the small mount of attention given to the applied arts in journals, in the small amount and quality of space given them in museums and in the small number of colleges and universities offering courses in their history.

Tradition and Innovation: The Design Work of Willian Addison Dwiggins

Paul Shaw

In February, 1929, the American Institute of Graphic Arts (AIGA) presented its ninth gold medal to William Addison Dwiggins. In retrospect, the timing of the award seems unusual, as such honors are traditionally bestowed at the end of long and glorious careers, not at the outset or in midstream, as in the case of the 48-year-old Dwiggins. In Dwiggins's case, the aspects of his career for which he is best known today still lay before him: his work as a book designer for Alfred A. Knopf, Inc. had begun just three years earlier, and his association with Mergenthaler Linotype as a type designer and consultant was still a few months away. However, to the members of the AIGA, there was no question that Dwiggins fully deserved the medal. He had already spent over twenty years amassing a considerable reputation as an advertising designer and lettering artist, and it was for these efforts that Dwiggins was honored.

W. A. Dwiggins was the first individual to promote himself as a "graphic designer," yet he occupies an anomalous place in the brief history of American graphic design. His early associations with Frederic W. Goudy and Daniel Berkeley Updike, together with his subsequent work in book design, have led many persons to identify him as just another member of the Arts and Crafts inspired fine printing movement in America. However, his work in book and type design was almost completely outside the realm of private presses, letterpress printing, and handset type. In fact, Dwiggins criticized the advocates of fine printing and their philosophy, urging a rapproachment with the new printing and typesetting technology. His pronouncements on such matters as machine versus handcraft, and "designing for purpose" often sound similar to the ideas expressed by the European Modernists of the time, but he was equally vociferous in his criticism of their position.

He considered himself a Modernist, but not in the Bauhaus vein. As was the case with his fellow midwesterner Frank Lloyd Wright, Dwiggins outgrew the Arts and Crafts movement only to find that he was at odds with those in the succeeding movement. His Modernism was of an independent and eccentric nature, both pragmatic and whimsical, exotic and sober.

Dwiggins's career as an advertising designer, despite its longevity and success, was more the result of necessity than of choice. Born in 1880, Dwiggins came of age during the height of the influence on the turn-of-the-century Arts and Crafts movement on fine printing typified by William Morris and his Kelmscott Press. At nineteen, Dwiggins left his home in Cambridge, Ohio, to attend the Frank Holme School of Illustration in Chicago. There he studied lettering under a young Frederic W. Goudy, who had recently taken his own first tentative steps toward becoming a type designer. At that time, Goudy was deeply immersed in the private press aspect of the Arts and Crafts movement, an enthusiasm which he transmitted to Dwiggins. Beginning with the establishment of the Booklet Press in 1894, Goudy had made several attempts to emulate Morris's success with the Kelmscott Press, culminating in the founding of the Village Press in 1903. When the Frank Holme School folded, also in 1903, Dwiggins worked briefly for Goudy before returning to Cambridge, where he established his own private press, the Guernsey Shop, with the intention of producing illustrated books. The Guernsey Shop failed to attract an audience, and the following year Dwiggins accepted Goudy's invitation to join him at his Village Press, which had recently relocated in Hingham, Massachusetts, a small town outside Boston. But the Village Press fared little better than the Guernsey Shop, and in 1906 Goudy moved again, this time to New York, leaving Dwiggins behind. In search of a new source of income, Dwiggins soon found himself doing advertising design.

For the next fifteen years, Dwiggins devoted most of his energies to advertising. His work ranged from direct advertising mailers and brochures to "potboilers," small drawings of furniture for newspaper advertisements. In addition to several leading advertising agencies in Boston, his principal clients during this time included New England Telephone, Filene's Department Store, the Paine Furniture Company, several paper mills, principally Strathmore and S. D. Warren, and *Direct Advertising,* the organ of the Paper Makers Advertising Club. These commissions provided Dwiggins with an excellent opportunity to sharpen his skills and experiment with new design ideas.

Dwiggins's work for *Direct Advertising* and the paper mills was probably the most important of all. His designs for the latter allowed him to experiment with different paper stock and various color combinations of ink, and the development of Dwiggins's famed stencil method of illustration can be traced in these designs and decoration, as well as his increasing fondness for unusual color harmonies. Dwiggins's early work, such as the portrait of General Joffre done for Liberty Covers in 1917, was primarily pen and ink or woodcut illustration. Parallel-line shading was frequently employed. His later work, especially "The Pageant of Color" series for the Hampshire Paper Company in 1921, forsook this approach in favor of a simpler and more abstract style. Stencil illustrations, with their large areas of flat color, had taken over. This evolution may have been aided by the desire of many of the mills to display their colored papers as an integral element of the design. Strathmore used the slogan "Strathmore is part of the picture" in several of its advertisements. Likewise, the mills encouraged the use of odd colors in their advertisements as a means of indicating the ability of their papers to print under adverse conditions. Consequently, Dwiggins's designs employed such unusual color combinations as peach and powder blue on goldenrod or vermilion and forest green on turquoise. These colors were a far cry from the red and black on cream white that typified the private press movement!

Initially Dwiggins had drifted into advertising because of his abilities as a lettering artist rather than as an illustrator. Handlettering was extensively used in advertising of the day, not only for logos and headlines, but frequently for body copy as well. Dwiggins's tutelage under Goudy, who was considered by many to be the foremost lettering artist of the time, had prepared him well for such work and he quickly made a name for himself.[1] As early as 1912, Will Bradley, the famed poster artist, had noted that Dwiggins's work had brought taste and skill "back into a branch of artistic endeavor which had sunk to the lowest possible depths"[2]. Dwiggins had eschewed the debased letterforms of the Victorian era and the fanciful ones of the Art Nouveau practitioners in favor of the classical letterforms associated with the Roman Empire and, later, the Renaissance and 16th-century France. The simplicity and grace of his roman letters made them stand out not only from the average lettering of the day, but also from that of his great contemporaries Oswald Cooper, Fred G. Cooper, Walt Harris, and even Bradley and Goudy.[3] His letters, to use a Dwigginsian phrase, have "the fat sweated off them." A good example of these slimmed down roman capitals can be seen on the covers of *Direct Advertising.*

Despite his enormous success as an advertising designer, Dwiggins had never felt fully at ease doing such work, as he grew older his dissatification increased. Although in 1916, in a pseudonymous article in *The Printing Art*, he was still able to discourse dispassionately on the ability of "drawings to sell goods" and to praise Goudy for introducing "correct design to advertising," four years later he found himself sharply increasing his rates to discourage advertising commissions.[4] Thus, when he learned in 1922 that he, like his father before him, had diabetes—at that time a disease very difficult to control—he took the opportunity to quit the advertising field. He wrote, "I am a happy invalid and it has revolutionized my whole attack. My back is turned on the more banal kind of advertising, and I have cancelled all commissions and am resolutely set on starving. I shall undertake only the simple childish little things that call for compromise with the universal twelve-year-old mind of the purchasing public and I will produce art on paper and wood after my own heart with no heed to any market. Revolution, stark and brutal."[5]

It was not "revolution, stark and brutal", as Dwiggins continued to produce advertising design in the following years, but 1922

1 Raymond F. DaBoll, "An Appreciation of O.B.C.," in *The Book of Oz* (Chicago: The Society for Typographic Arts, 1949), 1. DaBoll quotes Oswald Cooper, himself a noted lettering artist and type designer, as crediting Goudy with initiating the revival in handlettering in America at the turn of the century.

2 Dorothy Abbe, *William Addison Dwiggins* (Boston: The Boston Public Library, 1974) 9.

3 Fred G. Cooper, Walt Harns, and Will Bradley were prominent lettering artists of the time. Cooper's work can be found in *American Alphabets* (New York: Harper Brothers, 1930); Harris's in numerous issues of *Direct Advertising;* Bradley's in *Will Bradley: His Chap Book* (New York: Toe Typophiles, 1955).

4 Hermann Puterschein [W.A. Dwiggins], "Drawings That Sell Goods." *The Printing Art* 28 (October 1916): 98; W.A. Dwiggins to Carl P. Rollins, June 16, 1920, Carl Purington Rollins Papers, Yale University, New Haven, CT.

5 W.A. Dwiggins to Carl P. Rollins, June 6, 1923, Rollins Papers.

was a watershed year in his career nonetheless. Having privately declared his independence from advertising, Dwiggins set out to do so publicly. Responding to a "call for controversy" from the editor of *Direct Advertising,* he wrote an article entitled "Advertising Uses Seduction to Exploit Weaknesses of Mankind." In it he differentiated between informative advertising and associative or atmospheric advertising. The former contributes to human happiness by openly and honestly telling consumers about a product. It is a necessary part of commerce. The latter is strictly concerned with selling a product and exploits man's weaknesses in order to do so. Dwiggins was appalled by the extensive research behind such advertising that had sprung up after World War I. With a nod to the horrors that the war had introduced to civilization, he likened associative, advertising to "gas ammunition," labeling it a "whiff of chlorine." It was the sharp increase in advertising gas following the war that convinced Dwiggins he should direct his design activities elsewhere.[6]

Having aired his criticisms of seductive advertising, Dwiggins followed his defense of informative advertising by writing *Layout in Advertising* (in 1928),[7] a summation of all that he had learned in his nearly twenty-five years of the business. One of his most enduring achievements, *Layout in Advertising* was considered by many to be the standard book in its field well into the 1950s, and it still can be read with profit. Its title to the contrary, the book deals with almost all aspects of graphic design for print, not simply with advertising layout. In a characteristically logical and comprehensive manner, Dwiggins discussed the apparatus of design paper, type, lettering, ornament, and illustrations—and the technique of design, concluding with brief discussions of almost every conceivable form of advertising and graphic design from broadsides and brochures to blotters and billboards. His discussions were accompanied not by actual advertisements and designs, as one would expect, but by illustrations designed specifically for the book. As a result, Dwiggins was able to explain his points simply and precisely.

Layout in Advertising is important not only for its comprehensiveness and unique method of presentation, but also its attitude toward design process. Reacting to contemporary efforts to standardize design and scientifically prescribe esthetics, the most notable being Jay Hambridge's theory of dynamic symmetry which sought to establish laws of natural design based on the symmetry of growth in plants and in man, Dwiggins stated, "The practitioner in any art is obliged to build up his own equipment of standards and to evolve and perfect his own technique. He cannot lift a method of procedure, ready made, out of a handbook."[8] He stressed that a book such as *Layout in Advertising* could do no more than offer a method of solving a problem. It could not provide actual solutions. This attitude, which we, conditioned by the teachings of the Bauhaus, take for granted, was unusual for its time, especially as it ran counter to the American penchant for quick and easy solutions.

6 W. A. Dwiggins, "Advertising Uses Seduction to Exploit Weaknesses of Mankind," *Direct Advertising* 11 (1922): 25–26.

7 W. A. Dwiggins, *Layout in Advertising* (New York: Harper Brothers, 1928).

8 Dwiggins, *Layout in Advertising,* ix. Hambridge's theory of dynamic symmetry was originally published in *The Diagonal* (1919) and later gathered into book form as *The Elements of Dynamic Symmary* (New York: Brentano's, 1926). Dwiggins parodied Hambridge in "Standardized Art: A Movement Toward Quantity Production," *Direct Advertising* 8, (1921): 4–8, in which he created a theory of design based on the Purple Sexagon.

When Dwiggins resolved to abandon all banal advertising commissions, he turned his attention to book design, in effect picking up where he and Goudy had left off in 1906. Although most of his work during the intervening years had been for advertising, he continued to do some work in printing and publishing, primarily for Alfred Bartlett, a publisher of greeting cards, calendars and catalogs, and for the Merrymount Press of Daniel Berkeley Updike. However all of this work, with one exception, consisted of lettering either for title pages and bindings or for illustrations and decorations. The typography—the heart of book design—was done by others. The lone exception was *Sonnets and Other Lyrics* by Robert Silliman Hillyer (1917), published during the period when Dwiggins was serving as acting director of the Harvard University Press during World War 1.[9]

This latter experience, brief as it was, coupled with his close association with such outstanding printers as Updike, Rollins, and Goudy, provided Dwiggins with a basic understanding of book design and how it differed from advertising. Thus, when Dwiggins, through the efforts of Chester Lane of the Harvard University Press and Frederic Melcher of R.R. Bowker & Co., was introduced to the publisher Alfred. A. Knopf in 1923, he was not a total neophyte in this field.[10]

Although the two men hit it off almost immediately, it was three years before Dwiggins designed his first book for Knopf—*My Mortal Enemy* by Willa Cather, one of Knopf's most prized authors, and it was not until 1928, when he designed six books, that he became the firm's principal designer. His association with Knopf continued until his death in 1956. During those three decades he designed 280 books for the firm and it is for this work that he is probably best known as a graphic designer.

The association between Dwiggins and Knopf was mutually beneficial. Dwiggins, through his designs, caused Knopf's Borzoi Books to be "regarded with overwhelming respect, even awe, both in and out of the trade."[11] And Knopf, for his part, promoted Dwiggins in writings, advertisements, and, most noticeably, through the colophons that have distinguished all Borzoi Books.[12] The colophon, headed "A Note on the Type in Which this Book is Set," was a device adapted at Dwiggins's instigation from private press books as a means of calling the reading public's attention to a book's design and manufacturing background. Initially ridiculed by other trade publishers as an affectation, it has since been copied to varying degrees by many of them. Its introduction was only one manifestation of the private press concept of book design that Dwiggins brought to trade books through his work for Knopf.

When Dwiggins joined Knopf, whereas the design of books had changed very little from the days of Gutenberg, the quality of book production had declined drastically. Most of the decline had occurred during the nineteenth century as the Industrial Revolution overtook publishing. Technological innovations in printing, type-

9 Chester C. Lane, director of the Harvard University Press, hired Dwiggins to serve as his replacement when he entered the service during World War I. See Chester C. Lane, "Early Years in Hingham," in Paul A. Bennett, editor, *Postscripts on Dwiggins*, vol. 2, *Typophile Chap Book* 36 (New York: The Typophiles, 1960), 158.

10 Alfred A. Knopf established himself as a publisher in 1915. By the time he met Dwiggins he had already gained a considerable reputation for the literary excellence of his books. With Dwiggins's help, Knopf books quickly became equally renowned for their physical excellence. See Paul A. Bennett, editor, *Portrait of a Publisher*, 2 vols., *Typophile Chap Book* 18 (New York: The Typophiles, 1948).

11 John Tebbel, *A Histoy of Book Publishing in the United States*, vol. 4 (New York: R.R. Bowker & Company, 197481), 115.

12 Blanche W. and Alfred A. Knopf, advertisement in the *Times Literary Supplement* 17 (September 1, 1954): 44. "We point with special pride to thirty years' association with W. A. Dwiggins of Hingham, Massachusetts. We do not believe that any publisher in the English-speaking world can match for general quality of design and infinite variety the hundreds of volumes for which Mr. Dwiggins has been responsible."

setting, papermaking, binding, and the reproduction of illustrations enabled publishers to print books more quickly and cheaply, but the product was made more shoddily. The perfection of the cylinder press, with its need for thinner inks, led to "greyer" pages; the substitution of wood pulp for cotton and linen fiber in papermaking resulted in paper that quickly yellowed and became brittle; the replacement of sewing in the pages with casing them in, of hand-tooling with stamping, and of leather with cloth as the principal binding material resulted in flimsier books; the increased emphasis on halftones required the shiny-coated papers that failed to produce crisply the effeminate old-style typefaces then in favor.[13] Moreover, the design of books was still largely left to the printer.

Dwiggins's book designs for Knopf stressed the importance of unity and harmony of all the elements that comprise a book: paper, type, ornament, illustration, binding and endpapers, stamping, and, if possible, the jacket. His insistence on the importance of paper and type was a revelation to those many publishers who believed a beautiful book could be achieved simply by adding illustrations and a deluxe binding. In "The Structure of a Book," written as the introduction to the 1926 AIGA *Fifty Books of the Year* exhibition catalog, Dwiggins stated, "The text of the book is the thing for which everything else exists. In it are involved all the questions of paper, type, and page design. The design of the book begins here and works outward to the cover."[14] Dwiggins's emphasis on the importance of paper and type derived from his advertising experience, especially his work for the New England paper mills, while his concept of designing a book from the inside out was a result of his fine printing experience with Updike and Rollins. They, and all those who followed the example of William Morris, saw the need for a book's appearance to reflect the design sensibility of a single individual, preferably that of the printer. This was in contrast to the prevalent practice in trade book publishing of the time whereby all design decisions were divided between the printer and, if there was one, the illustrator. The printer was responsible for all typography and composition, as well as printing and binding, and the illustrator was responsible for any special lettering or decoration that was needed in addition to the illustrations. There was no book designer as such. Dwiggins was one of the first professional book designers to work almost exclusively with trade editions. In that capacity he took on all of the design duties of the fine printer, but none of the production duties. He handled the typography (or, as he called it, page design), ornamentation, illustration, binding design, and jacket design, and left the printing and manufacturing to others. Thus, the books that Dwiggins designed for Knopf exhibited a harmonious appearance throughout.

Dwiggins adapted private press ideals to trade book design, but he refused to mimic private press practices. He had no patience with those who insisted on retaining hand processes in printing and

13 Peter Beilenson, "The Nineteenth Century" in *A History of the Printed Book: Being the Third Number of "The Dolphin"*, edited by Lawrence C. Wroth (New York: The Limited Editions Club, 1938), 245–60.

14 W.A. Dwiggins, "The Structure of a Book," "Mss. by WAD," *Typophile Chapbook 17* (New York: The Typophiles, 1947), 58.

publishing in the belief that they were inherently superior to machine processes. "Fabrication of a book is a machine process," he wrote, "[It] Properly has no traceback to the standards of hand work. Just as silly to try to keep handcraft values in a machine made book as to put fake hammer marks on a machine-stamped spoon." The maintenance of handcraft values in twentieth-century publishing was not only silly but also phony, and Dwiggins detested phoniness in all areas of design and craftsmanship. He was in basic agreement with the Bauhaus slogan "Art and Technology, a New Unity," and the Modernist dictum "form follows function." Unlike the other leading figures of the American fine printing revival, Dwiggins was willing, even eager at times, to accept machines and work with them. "Design starts with the fact of machine-made," he argued. "Trys to use the machine as a tool. *Conventional* design derives from handcraft standards, so we've got to find a new way and new standards. The modern masters of the book (BR) [Bruce Rogers] have made their books *imitations* of handmade books. Not a competition between hand-made and machine-made imitations of handmade books—for the trade-result is shabby genteel—desperate effort to keep up handmade appearances without funds to go on. Better way—to accept the conditions and materials and work out an aesthetic on that basis."[15]

Figure 1
Binding designs from *Stephen Crane: An Omnibus* (NewYork: Alfred A. Knopf, Inc., 1952) illustrating both Dwiggin's handlettering and geometric, Art Deco stencil ornaments.

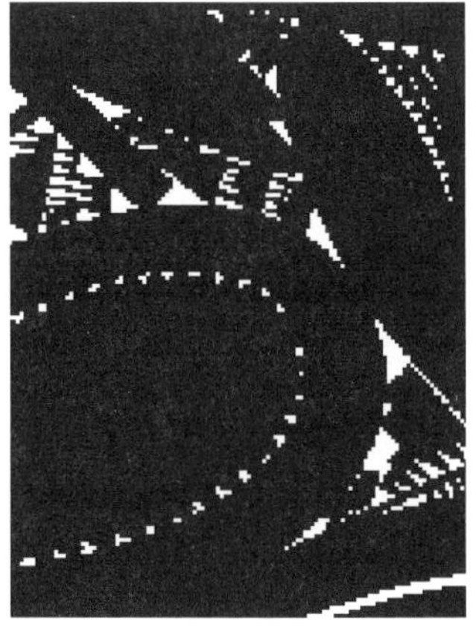

Figure 2
Stencil design from the cover of H.G. Wells's *The Time Machine.*

However, despite their rhetorical similarity, no one would mistake a Dwiggins-designed book for one by the European Modernists, for Dwiggins's interpretation of these catchphrases differed markedly from that of the young Jan Tschichold or El Lissitzky. From Dwiggins's point of view, most of the traditional elements of a book's structure, from jacket to colophon, served a function. It was the exact form that each took which he questioned. For instance, while he agreed with the Modernist movement that Renaissance ornament was inappropriate in a twentieth-century book, he did so not because he found ornament *per se* out of place but because such ornament was not contemporary or fresh. He objected to modern art on the same grounds. "*Imitation* seems to be the obnoxious element," he stated, whether it is imitation of the Renaissance or of "the Papuan savage and the pre-Cretan child mind."[16] Although not necessary to all books, ornament was acceptable to Dwiggins—and perhaps inevitable because "Man is an ornamenting animal"—if it was indigenous and natural rather than transplanted from somewhere else.[17]

Consequently, it is not surprising to find that ornament is the most distinctive element in a Dwiggins-designed book. The trade books he designed for Knopf achieved the rich elegance of limited-edition books, not by the use of luxurious papers and bindings, but through the judicious application of bold and idiosyncratic ornamentation. His style of ornamentation was unique, though partially inspired by the French *pochoir* (stencil) tradition. Using home-made tools, Dwiggins cut hundreds of "elements," geometric and organic

15 W.A. Dwiggins, "The Book-Fancier", William A. Dwiggins Collection, Box 105, The Boston Public Library, Boston; W. A. Dwiggins to Sidney Jacobs, 6 September 1939, Alfred A. Knopf Papers, The University of Texas, Austin. Dwiggins commonly used this telegraphic essay style in his letters to Jacobs and Knopf.
16 Dwiggins, Structure of a Book," 63.
17 Dwiggins, "Structure of a Book," 62, 64.

shapes, from transparent celluloid which he then combined and stenciled to produce highly original ornaments (see fig. 5).

Several divergent influences can be discerned in Dwiggins's many stencil ornaments and designs. The geometric patterns are similar to contemporary Art Deco and Art Moderne designs, though Arab and Moorish tilework was more likely Dwiggins's source of inspiration. His striking floral designs have an affinity with Chinese and Japanese renderings of plants. And his odd color harmonies, such as red, green, yellow, and lavender, owed much to Chinese and Persian art. He described such color combinations as "a chutney-sauce effect with lots of pepper and mustard and spices."[18] Often criticized by other book designers at the time as garish or ugly, such color combinations are increasingly common today. Dwiggins's ornaments, both in their structure and color, often screamed for attention; and in that respect they were a far cry from the intricate and classically ordered type ornament "pictures" designed by Bruce Rogers and T. M. Cleland, to which they are sometimes compared.

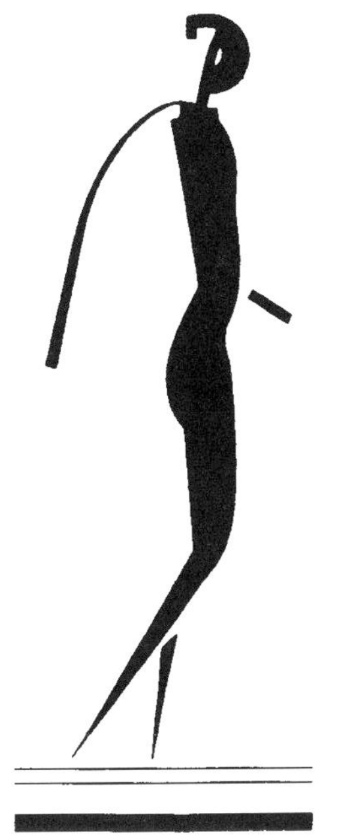

Figure 3
Stencil figure from *One More Spring*, by Robert Nathan (Stamford: The Overbrook Press, 1935).

Dwiggins's unwillingness to accept traditional book design blindly led him to reassess its individual components rather than to advocate an entirely new construct geared to the twentieth century. A number of his letters to Alfred Knopf were thinly disguised essays on means of adapting books to changes in manufacturing processes and in reading habits. He advocated plastic book covers, the substitution of pasted labels for ink stamping on bindings, standardized book sizes and formats, the imposition of a house style, paperback covers, and two-column formats for lengthy manuscripts.[19] Most of these ideas, first expressed in the mid-1930's, have eventually become reality. Not only are paperback books ubiquitous today, but many are in series with standardized sizes and formats. House styles, pioneered by Knopf, are more common; books are routinely designed with two, or even three, column formats *à la* magazines and newspapers. In endorsing these innovations, Dwiggins sought a "new way of styling books.... Something simpler [than currently exists], and more closely related to the *process of reading*—something not so aloof and mechanically perfect as the regular thing—not starched collars and neckties, but the loose polo-shirt kind of thing we all take to when we can.... "[20] His principal concern ultimately centered on readers and their reading needs, esthetic as well as financial. Dwiggins's goal was to make books that were beautiful, functional, and inexpensive. With Knopf he often succeeded.

Although Knopf was his principal employer, Dwiggins also designed books for other publishers, usually in the limited edition or fine printing vein. Much of this work was done for George Macy and The Limited Editions Club. The collaboration between Dwiggins and Macy began in early 1929 and, as with the relationship with Knopf, lasted the remainder of Dwiggins's life. Of the seven books Dwiggins designed for The Limited Editions Club, two were AIGA Fifty Books of the Year selections: Balzac's *Droll Stories*

18 W.A. Dwiggins quoted in *Bookbinding* (April 1936): "I like Far East color combinations; a chutney-sauce effect with lots of pepper and mustard and spices, odd harmonies that make you sit up. I think many neutral harmonies are extremely smart.... I think the Chinese were the greatest color manipulators, and after them the Persians of the miniatures. I like black as a part of the color-scheme."

19 W.A. Dwiggins to Sidney R. Jacobs, various letters 1936–1942, Knopf Papers; Paul A. Bennett, ed., *Postscripts on Dwiggins*, vol. 2, *Typophile Chap Book* 36 (New York: The Typophiles, 1960), 50–51.

20 W.A. Dwiggins to Sidney R. Jacobs titled: "Obiter Dicta," Knopf Papers.

Figure 4
Double-page title spread from *The Time Machine,* by H.G. Wells (New York: Random House, 1931), using handlettering and stencil ornaments.

(1932) and Rabelais's *Gargantua and Pantagruel* (1936). Both are noteworthy for their excellent stencil illustrations, especially the one that runs across the spines of all five volumes of *Gargantua and Pantagruel.* This innovative use of stencils is only one example of the greater freedom of design that Dwiggins enjoyed in his work for The Limited Editions Club and other publishers of deluxe books. His stencil illustrations graced a number of his other award-winning books, most notably *The Travels of Marco Polo* (The Printing House of Leo Hart, 1933) and Robert Nathan's *One More Spring* (The Overbrook Press, 1935). The illustrations for the latter make outstanding use of paper as part of the picture, deftly balancing blank space with abstract geometrical shapes to imply figures and scenes. In addition to extensive use of stencil illustrations in his book designs for limited editions, Dwiggins introduced other design innovations, among them the double page title spread for H. G. Well's *Time Machine* (Random House, 1931), which was included in the 1951 Books for Our Time exhibition of modern book design.[21] *The Time Machine* also boasts a text printed in two colors.

Through his work, especially for Knopf, and his writings, Dwiggins is responsible more than any other designer, including Bruce Rogers, for the increased quality of American trade book design since World War I. His writings on the subject of bookmaking and book design have been as influential as his actual designs. As a matter of fact, the notorious *"Extracts from an Investigation into the Physical Properties of Books as They Are at Present Published,"* written anonymously for the fictitious Society of Calligraphers, appeared seven years before Dwiggins designed his first book for Knopf. And yet, the effect it had on the publishing industry was electric. The Society's "unanimous" conslusion that "All books of the present day are badly made" received wide attention, much of it indignant, in the publishing industry.[22] Publishers were excoriated in the tract

21 Marshall Lee, editor, *Books for Our Time* (New York: Oxford University Press). This seminal exhibition and catalogue, sponsored by the Trade Book Clinic of the American Institute of Graphic Arts, sought to document the modern approach to book design that had gradually taken place since the mid-1920's.

22 Hermann Puterschein [W.A. Dwiggins] and Jacob Putershein [Laurance B. Siegfried], "Extracts from an Investigation into the Physical Properties of Books as They are at Present Published," "Mss. by WAD," *Typophile Chap Book* 17 (New York: The Typophiles, 1947), 13.

for selling books as if they were soap, indiscriminately using illustrations and gold-stamped bindings to create the impression of luxury, bulking books, and wholly ignoring design in book production.

Although the Society's case was deliberately overstated, it proved effective. In the ensuing two decades American book design and production improved dramatically, despite the Depression, a fact that Dwiggins duly noted in "Twenty Years After," a follow-up piece to *Extracts* which was commissioned by *The Publishers' Weekly*. Evidence of the change can be seen in the AIGA Fifty Books of the Year exhibitions, intitially established in 1923 and still being held. The AIGA's recognition of the importance of design in the production of books, and its advocacy of book design as a profession, was most cogently expressed by Dwiggins himself in "The Structure of a Book," the introduction to the 1926 exhibition catalog.

Dwiggins's oeuvre as a writer went beyond these essays and the aforementioned *Layout in Advertising* to include other articles and treatises on design, short stories, and plays. In *Towards a Reform of the Paper Currency, Particularly in Point of Its Design*,[23] he urged a thorough reevaluation of the design of all American paper money, stamps, revenue labels, and cancellation devices. Accompanying his argument was a series of such designs executed for the mythical country of The Antipodes. Although the immediate response to Dwiggins's critique was hostile and often facetious (many reviewers remarked that they would be glad to own a $5 bill, regardless of its design), many of his suggestions, particularly concerning stamp design, have come to pass. Dwiggins's admonition to focus on color rather than on linear detail as the key element is reflected in most contemporary stamp designs, as is his preference for simplified, more graphic shapes. Elsewhere, Dwiggins counseled clients on how to best deal with artists, explained his unique system of marionette articulation and motion (which influenced his ideas on the design of newspaper typefaces),[24] and discussed the process of type design.

Dwiggins's background as a lettering artist/calligrapher was at the heart of his three major design activities: advertising, book design, and type design. He entered advertising by hand-lettering ephemera for Alfred Bartlett and the Paine Furniture Company; he captured the attention of the publishing industry through the publications of his fictitious Society of Calligraphers; and he became a type designer because of a remark he made about sans serif typefaces in his discussion on lettering in *Layout in Advertising*. However, his success in these areas has obscured his importance as a lettering artist/calligrapher. Beginning with his studies under Goudy at the Frank Holme School, he was one of the pioneers of the twentieth-century revival of calligraphy. He was quick to recognize the importance of *writing* the letters with the broad-edged pen rather than *drawing* them with the pointed pen. And he was equally quick to point out the need to use calligraphy as an underpinning for hand lettering and text typefaces. Dwiggins's work in this area evolved

23 Dwiggins's suggestions for redesigning currency echo the work done by Herbert Bayer in redesigning Germany currency for the State Bank of Thuringia in 1923. Bayer's designs were motivated by the need for notes of large denomination occasioned by Germany's rampant postwar inflation. They are distinguished by the substitution of sans serif type for the traditional fraktur, the absence of all decorative scrollwork, and the judicious use of large areas of white space and flat color. These changes are almost identical to those advocated by Dwiggins for the improvement of U.S. currency. See Arthur Cohen, *Herbert Bayer* (Cambridge: MIT Press, 1984) for a detailed discussion of Bayer's currency design.

24 For the relationship between Dwiggins's marionette designs and his thinking on the design of newspaper type see Gerard Unger, "Experimental No. 223, A Newspaper Face, Designed by W.A. Dwiggins," *Quarendo* 11(1981): 4.

Figure 5
Illustration from *Reform of the Currency.*

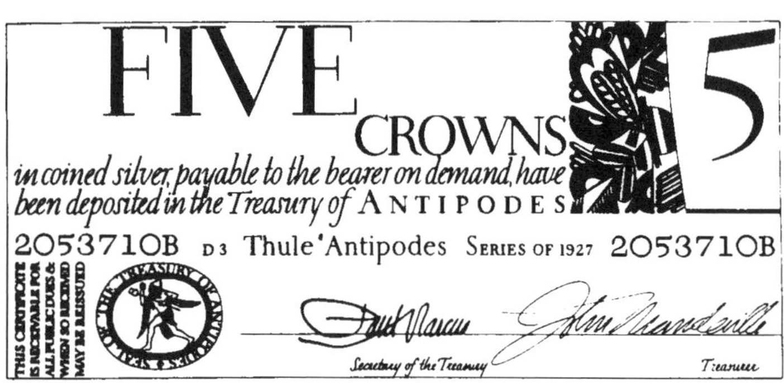

independently of the great European calligraphic pioneers, Edward Johnston in England, Rudolf Koch in Germany, and Rudolf von Larisch in Austria. As a matter of fact, although Johnston's seminal *Writing and Illuminating and Lettering* was published in 1906, it was not until a year later that word of it began to filter through the American design community, and by that time Dwiggins had already become immersed in calligraphy on a commercial basis.[25]

Dwiggins's asessment of the role of calligraphy in contemporary design was as pragmatic and unromantic as his notions on handcrafts in bookmaking. Calligraphy, instead of being rendered superfluous and obsolete by technological advances in printing and typesetting, had become increasingly feasible in his view. He envisioned a postmanuscript calligraphy in which advances in photoengraving and offset lithography would make it possible to produce hand-written books economically on a mass scale.[26] In addition to his early efforts for Alfred Bartlett, Dwiggins himself produced several such manuscripts, most notably *The Drums of Kalkapan* (1935), *WAD to RR* (1940), and *The History of Susanna* (1947).[27]

"The Shapes of Roman Letters" (1919), an article initially written for *Direct Advertising* and later incorporated into *Layout in Advertising*, represents Dwiggins's most significant commentary on calligraphy and its relationship to lettering and type. In it he argued that an understanding of the "Suitable Motions of Manufacture" was essential to the construction of letters having the desirable qualities of order, simplicity and grace. Thus the motion and nature of

25 The first citation of *Writing and Illuminating and Lettering* by Edward Johnston in the United States that I know of occurs in *The Printing Art,* 9 (April 1907), in which extracts from the book are quoted and attributed to Edwin [sic] Johnston.

26 Philip Hofer, "Towards a Renaissance of the Manuscript Tradition," *Postscripts on Dwiggins,* vol. 1; Paul Shaw, "Pattern and Motion: WAD as Lettering Artist," in *A Tribute to William Addison Dwiggins 1880–1956,* edited by Vincent Torre (New York: The Inkwell Press, 1980); Frederic Fairchild Sherman, "Modern Hand-Lettered Books," *The Printing Art* 10 (February 1908): 373–79.

27 *WAD to RR: A Letter About Designing Type* (Cambridge: Harvard College Library Department of Printing and Graphic Arts, 1940); *History of Susanna, From the Apocrypha of the Hebrew Bible According to the King James Version* (New York: Archway Press, 1947); *Drums of Kalkapan,* published by The Limited Editions Club, New York, as an insert to *The Dolphin: A Journal of the Making of Books,* 2 (1935).

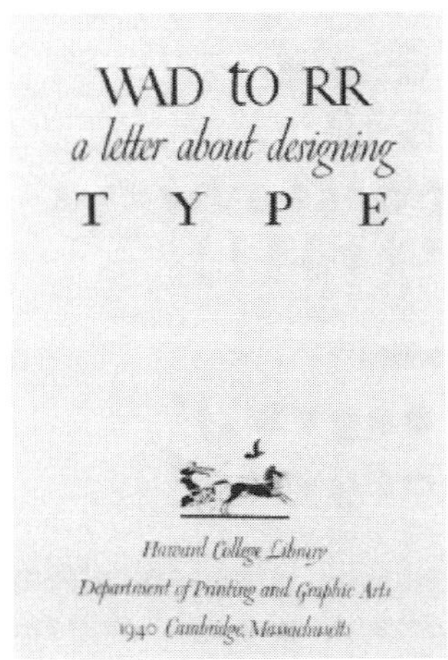

Figure 6
Title page from *WAD to RR: A Letter About Designing Type* (Cambridge: Harvard College Library Department of Printing and Graphic Arts, 1940) Although the letter is concerned with Dwiggins's method of designing type, the book is entirely handwritten, including the title page.

the pen, whether broad-edged or pointed, must be taken into account when creating letters. The pen is responsible for the detail of serifs, the "snap" and style of a letter, and the shape of curves and arches. The importance of the pen in the creation of letters extends beyond calligraphy and handlettering to type. But Dwiggins, while stressing the historical and structural affinity between broad-pen letters and classic typefaces, did not lose sight of the fact that type letters were composed of metal, not paper. The type designer "does not attempt to copy *exactly* the form of his pen-written model," Dwiggins concluded, "but modifies the pen form to a shape suitable to its final state—that of a metal punch."[28] Dwiggins's recognition of the role of the graver, file, and punch in type designing kept him from falling into the romantic trap so common to calligraphers of viewing type as no more than frozen calligraphy.[29]

"Gothic—the newspaper standby—in its various manifestations has little to commend it except simplicity; it is not overly legible, it has no grace," Dwiggins wrote in *Layout in Advertising*. He went on to say, "Gothic capitals are indispensable, but there are no good Gothic capitals. The typefounders will do a service to advertising if they will provide a Gothic of good design."[30] Dwiggins's challenge to the typefounders was immediately taken up by Harry Gage, assistant typographic director at Mergenthaler Linotype. In February, 1929, Gage invited Dwiggins to attempt the design of a good Gothic or sans serif face for Mergenthaler. The offer was accepted. The immediate result was the design of Metro, a sans serif that was closer in style to Gill Sans or Edward Johnston's type for the London Underground than to the pure geometry of Erbar or Paul Renner's Futura. More important, the long-term result was Mergenthaler's decision to hire Dwiggins as a typographic consultant. Designed to capitalize on the new interest in sans serif faces in the 1920s, Metro arrived too late and failed to supplant Futura or Gill Sans, the best of the faces created at the time. Eventually Mergenthaler replaced it with Spartan, a Futura look-alike. That Metro's design closely paralleled that of Gill Sans and the London Underground type is not surprising as all three were designed by calligraphers with a sense of classical, Trajan's column, proportions and forms. Although a failure in the marketplace, despite the redesign of several letters such as the *a* and *g*, Metro was an impressive first effort, revealing Dwiggins as a type designer willing to take risks.[31]

Metro's failure did not surprise Dwiggins. (Upon completing the design he remarked, "A hellish letter when you really stop and look at it.") Nor did it shake Mergenthaler's confidence in Dwiggins.[32] Dwiggins's association at Mergenthaler, especially with Chauncey H. Griffith, the typographic director, proved as close and enduring as his relationship with Knopf. In the ensuing two and one-half decades, Dwiggins designed eleven faces for Mergenthaler (of which only five, including Metro, were issued), and provided advice on the design and development of numerous other faces. The four additional faces Mergenthaler issued were Electra (1935),

28 W.A. Dwiggins, "The Shapes of Roman Letters," "Mss. by WAD," 39, 42 and 50; *Layout in Advertising*, 20.
29 See Robert Saunders, "Calligraphy into Type," *Scripsit* (July/August, 1981).
30 *Layout in Advertising*, 23–4.
31 The alternate characters shown in Fig. 11 are those that Dwiggins redesigned in an attempt to satisfy Mergenthaler customers who wanted a face that would rival Futura.
32 W.A. Dwiggins to Harry Gage, November 28, 1929, Dwiggins Collection.

Figure 7
Metroblack and Metrothin

METROBLACK AND METROLITE

ABCDEFGHIJKLMNOPQRSTUV
WXYZ&ÆŒæœ
1234567890
abcdefghijklmnopqrstuvwxyz
[($£,.:;'-'?!*†‡§¶)]

ABCDEFGHIJKLMNOPQRSTUV
WXYZ&ÆŒæœ
1234567890
abcdefghijklmnopqrstuvwxyz
[($£,.:;'-'?!*†‡§¶)]

Alternative Characters

AGJMNVWWaegvw,;'
AGJMNVWWaegvw,;'

* designed 1944, issued posthumously in 1961 to celebrate Mergenthaler Linotype's 75th anniversary.

Caledonia (1939), Falcon (1962)* and Eldorado (1953). Dwiggins also designed a suite of 29 border ornaments called Caravan (1941). The remaining faces were all experimental efforts in which he attempted to solve various self-imposed problems.

Of these efforts, Electra and Caledonia are the most significant. Both are of enduring quality, easily able to hold their own with the classic book faces of the past. Electra is the more original of the two. Whereas Caledonia is a frank adaption of Scotch, there is no single discernible model for Electra. The inspiration for it was ostensibly derived from a dream Dwiggins had in which the famed Japanese scribe Kobodaishi instructed him to avoid the recreation of classic faces and, instead, to design a face that reflected the twentieth century, a face that was full of electricity, "sparks, energy—high-speed steel—metal shavings coming off a lathe—precise, positive." The letters were expected to have snap, achieved by streamlining the curves. And that is exactly what Electra has. By weighting the "top serifs of the straight letters of the lower-case" and letting the "curves get away from the straight stems" in a flat way, Dwiggins injected energy into the face.[33] Yet despite the energetic nature of Electra, it retains a warm, human look. Dwiggins managed a coup by successfully marrying the best qualities of old and new style faces; in essence, Electra is Garamond wedded to Bodoni. Electra is also notable because it originally had an italic companion that was actually a sloped or oblique roman. This innovation of Dwiggins's, sparked by Stanley Morison's *Fleuron* article "Toward an Ideal

33 See W.A. Dwiggins, *Emblems and Electra* (Brooklyn: The Mergenthaler Linotype Company, 1935).

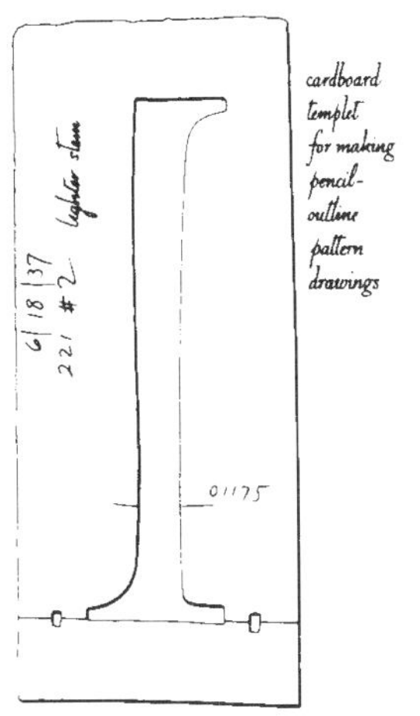

Figure 8
This illustration, from *WAD to RR,* shows how Dwiggins adapted his stencil process to thc problem of designing type. This large-scale template is intended for use in the creation of all lowercase letters with ascending stems: b, d, h, k, and 1.

Type," proved a failure, and Electra Cursive was later designed as a more traditional counterpart.[34]

Unlike Goudy, who claimed to have designed some 144 faces, or Morris Fuller Benton, who is credited with designing more than 100 faces (each with innumberable variations of weight, width, and slant), Dwiggins was not a prolific type designer. He had no desire to crank out design after design simply for the sake of novelty. His interest lay not in display faces but in text faces. With the exception of Metro, all of his faces, both issued and unissued, were designed for extended reading. Legibility and fluidity took precedence over novelty. Furthermore, as in his book design work, Dwiggins approached each typeface as a problem-solving exercise. Just as Metro was designed to fill a perceived need for a good advertising sans serif, other faces were designed to fill other specific needs. That is why so much of Dwiggins's meager output as a type designer was in the form of experimental faces that were never issued to the public. Among them were attempts to create a typeface suited to the peculiar linguistic nature of the English language; an upright script for use in legal and financial documents; a more legible, and yet esthetically pleasing, newspaper face; and a modelled sans serif that anticipated Hermann Zapf's Optima by some twenty years.[35] Dwiggins's approach to designing typefaces was often as unorthodox as the faces themselves. Much of his inspiration for the design of Hingham, a newspaper face, was derived from his hobby of carving marionettes; Winchester, an Anglo-Saxon typeface, was based on eighth-century calligraphic letters; and several faces were designed with the aid of celluloid stencils. This eclectic attitude was simultaneously Dwiggins's greatest asset and his major defect as a type designer. It led him down many a blind alley, but it also resulted in the design of Electra and Caledonia, the two types that ensure Dwiggins's continuing stature as a type designer of the first rank.[36]

Of Dwiggins, Dorothy Abbe, his long-time colleague, has written, "His innate talent found expression along many lines: calligraphy, type design, advertising layout, book typography, typographical ornament via stencils, illustration; wood carving and marionettes; the writing of books and essays; occasional excursions into architecture, furniture design, mural painting, kite-flying and weathervane making; stencil and woodcut prints, watercolor painting; and the making of his own tools."[37] It is a formidable list of accomplishments for one man, even if one dismisses several of the activities as no more than hobbies or the efforts of an amateur. But it is more comprehensible when one remembers that such a set of achievements was typical of many who came under the sway of William Morris and the Arts and Crafts movement. Persons as diverse as Frank Lloyd Wright, Koloman Moser, and Rudolf Koch are proof that the age of specialization in design had not yet set in. These men, Dwiggins included, readily accepted the notion that an esthetically sensitive individual could and should take an active role in re-

34 Dwiggins, "Twenty Years After," in "Mss. by WAD," 67–69. W.A. Dwiggins to C.H. Griffith, June 14, 1932 and August 22, 1932, Chauncey H. Griffith Papers, University of Kentucky, Lexington.

35 See Paul A. Bennett, "WAD and Linotype," *Postscripts on Dwiggins,* vol. 2, and Griffith Papers for further details of experimental type designs.

36 Dwiggins, *WAD to RR,* and Gerard Unger, "Experimental No. 223," *Quaerendo* 11 (1981).

37 Abbe, *Dwiggins,* 5–6

Figure 9
William Addison Dwiggins. Photograph by Dorothy Abbe from *WAD: . . . to celebrate a life . . .* (Boston: The Society of Printers, 1957).

designing or beautifying all aspects of life. The design of diverse elements by a single person was encouraged to achieve an harmonious unity. In Dwiggins's case, this unity was effectively accomplished. His many and diverse activities, both professional and amateur, were intricately interrelated. His lettering and calligraphy were integral components of his advertising and book design; his typefaces were often created for use in the books he designed; his marionettes provided insights into type design, as did his stencils; his writings were frequently lettered, illustrated, and designed by him; and so on. Dwiggins integrated his art with his life.

In 1960 George Salter wrote, "Today, Dwiggins is history."[38] Dwiggins's reputations, at its zenith in 1937, dropped precipitately after World War II, as the influence of the Bauhaus and the Swiss School increasingly dominated American graphic design. Since then, his reputation has slid even further as more and more of his work has receded from memory. Yet, as Salter stated in defense of Dwiggins, "greatness is absolute and does not depend on recognition. It can go unseen and unheard unaffectedly. Recognition and appeal are but the transitory image reflected in the mirror." Perhaps this summary of his work will restore some permanence to that image, reminding us that we have a rich, and largely unexplored, design heritage.

38 George Salter, "Is Dwiggins Good?" *Postscripts on Dwiggins,* vol. 2, 198.

Super Veloz: A Typographic System for the Small Printer
Enric Satué

for George Tscherny, Hubert Leckie, Ivan Chermayeff, and Rafael Moneo.

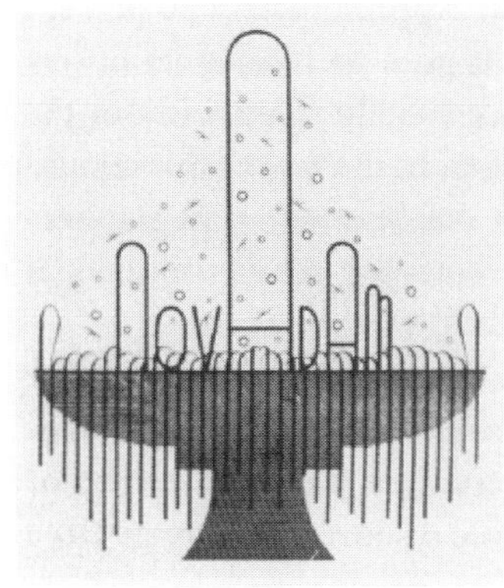

Figure 1
Brilliant exercise in colors, published in the catalogs of NOVADAM, a Joan Trochut original, completely built with combinable pieces of Super Veloz.

The development of an industrially advanced type design such as Super Veloz, which was designed by Joan Trochut in 1942, in so tragic a time for Spaniards as the early 1940s, seems amazing from today's perspective. The historical period in which this type is located, the brutal period following the Spanish Civil War in its most impure and stentorian years of Francoism, must be considered accidental. In reality, the process started much earlier, in the 1930s. This decade was a particularly significant time for the Spaniards, who were joyfully beginning an inspired and moving collective adventure, having been shaken by 100 years of traditional rulers: kings, cardinals, or generals.

During Spain's republican decade, all intellectual activities developed in an extraordinary way, fomented by a euphoric social spirit which generated a spate of work that was profoundly Spanish, despite its universality. Works by Federico Garcia Lorca, Jose Ortega y Gasset, Manuel de Falla, Pau Casals, Luis Bunuel, Josep Lluís Sert, and others are examples.

In the 1930s, graphic design reached a peak that has yet to be surpassed. The Spanish poster reached its apogee in the midst of the Spanish Civil War, an epic struggle for freedom that was passionately defended by the leading design professionals in the country. The civil war posters are the best-known products of those years. The quality of the new designers had already been recognized by the most reputable European critics. Some of these young designers were already on their way to becoming models of their epoch: the poster artist and master of photomontage Josep Renau, whom exile took to Mexico and East Germany before he returned to Spain in the body of a scarcely recognized mythical character; the poster artist Antoni Clavé, exiled in Paris and happily transformed at present into a successful painter; and the typographer Enric Crous Vidal, transplanted from his warm birthplace of Lleida to a gray and gloomy Paris where he tried to find a common denominator for his Latin roots, searching for the typeface Mediterranean in a succession of celebrated designs.

In the 1930s, Joan Trochut was a teenager with a solid base of typographic knowledge received from his father. He inhaled the

Figure 2
ADAM colored logo developed with typographic geometrical forms by E. Trochut Bachmann for ADAM, no. 3.

healthy creative air of those years while nurturing the hope for his new type design. Unfortunately, the Spanish typographic industry lagged far behind the rest of the country's culture, and its pitiful reality was appropriately denounced by Trochut. At the begining of the 1930s, the typographic industry consisted of extremely modest autonomous print shops that lacked such complimentary services as photoengraving, mechanical text composition, and the mechanical manipulation of paper stock. The concentration of industrial equipment in the largest cities made the development of these small industries extremely difficult. This situation has changed very little: A few years ago, many Spanish cities of more than 50,000 people did not even have a photoengraving shop.

On the other hand, design is a relatively recent phenomenon in Spain and is still of minor importance. Approximately 50 percent of the Spanish printing industry continues to receive its orders directly from the client, and these are usually filled without the intervention of the professional designer. In the face of this regular dilettantism to which the printer is condemned, typographers have overcome the obstacle of differentiating small commercial printed pieces from each other in the best way they can.

In the midst of this uncontrolled situation, some of the master printers of the 1930s—a time when Spanish advertising underwent important changes—discovered a second problem, as serious or more so than the first: the lack of artistic resources to help modern printers complete their orders with some originality.[1]

The rationalization of typographic art

Esteban Trochut Bachmann, father of Joan Trochut and a printer of some prestige in Barcelona, was absorbed with the idea of planning a freer and more flexible system for the small typographic shops that created printed ephemera. In 1930, he began publishing a series of deluxe albums of typographic models that were based on the study of the letter as the principal decorative element.

Centuries behind in competitive type design, Spain was particularly flattered by the warm international reception given to Esteban Trochut's editorial project. Printers in Germany, Belgium, Holland, Switzerland, France, and the United States were enthusiastic about his unusual albums, which were published in Spanish and

1 Since the time of Gutenberg, artisans have sought to overcome the limitations of the type case. Toward the end of the nineteenth century, typographers were surprised by the freedom and speed with which lithography produced forms but they strongly resisted it as they thought lithography would eventually eliminate the need for typographers. But in fewer than 50 years, they created more new typefaces and ornaments than in all previous history. Examples are Helvetica, Gill Sans, Futura (with the various series of Venus, Akzidenz, and Grotesk), Times Roman, Clarendon, Menhart, and Weiss. A. M. Cassandre's experiments with Deberny and Peignot and ultimately, in a maddened dynamic of consumerism, the appearance of a famous series of geometrical figures also occurred in this period.

Figure 3
Logo designed with typographic geometrical forms by E. Trochut Bachmann for ADAM, no. 2.

French. Alternating with models of typographic printing, which were combined with photoengraving, the publications of Trochut, entitled ADAM (Archivo Documentario de Arte Moderno/Documentary Archives of Modern Art), included some strictly typographic designs whose purpose was to multiply the possibilities of typography for printers.

In spite of the indubitable Bauhaus resonances of his publication's motto ("For the Study and Rational Modernization of Typographic Art"), Esteban Trochut's goal was not theoretical grandiloquence but useful and progressive pragmatism. He asserted the artisan's will to overcome the limitations of type with fantasy and imagination in a touching, permanent, and anonymous historic process.

During the previous century, type design in Spain was a widespread custom and typographers themselves undertook design exercises that consisted of modifying commercial types with file and knife, thus creating new forms that scarcely differed from the foundry types. This operation prospered in Europe to such a point that, toward the end of the 1920s, manufacturers put the famous geometrical figures (moveable and combinable, circular, triangular, square, and rectangular pieces) on the market. This action allowed, on the one hand, a greater number of possibilities in print ornamentation and, on the other, the somewhat clumsy construction of new letters. The popular success of these figures was enormous, and there is no doubt that Super Veloz derives from this antecedent. Many artisans shared the desire to escape the limitations of an excessively rigid system of typography, and these geometric designs pointed the way. Esteban Trochut, with his ADAM albums, extended his initial experiments and, armed with file and knife, began to manipulate the geometric forms of commercial type with the hope of finding new expressive possibilities from which he could recover the imagination missing in most printed ephemera.

First Collection

Second Collection

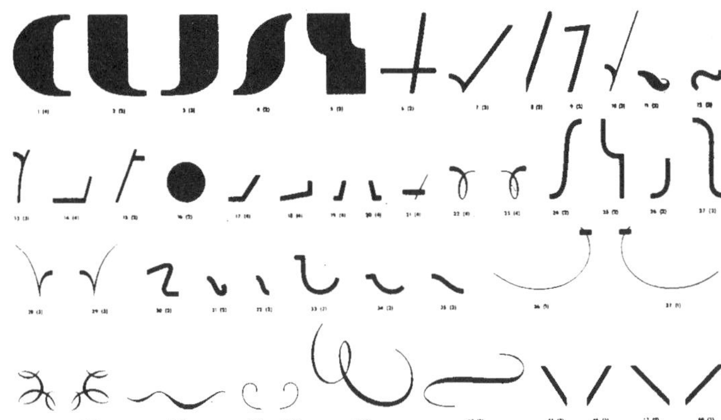

Third Collection

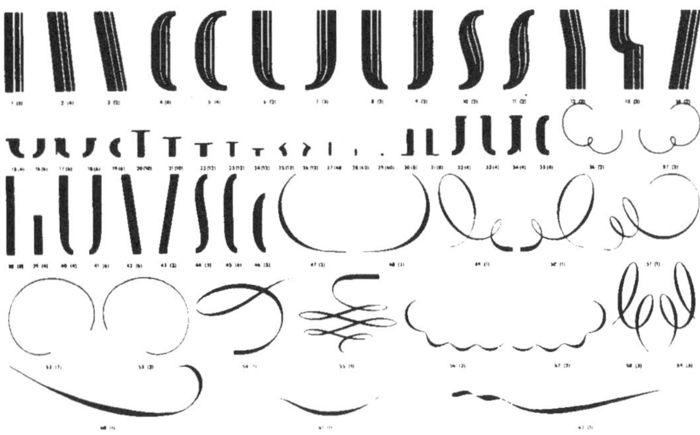

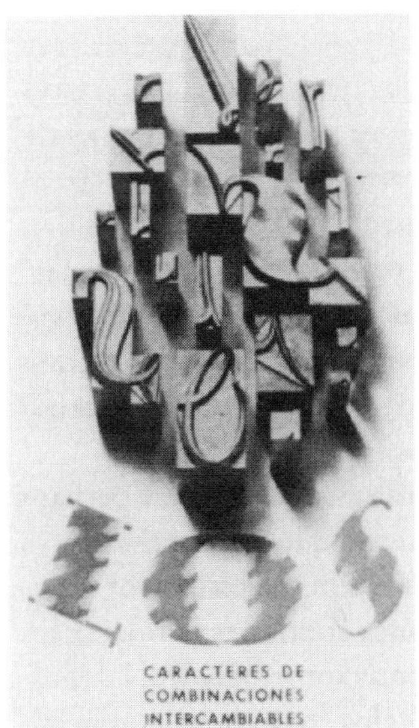

Figure 4
Display of foundry pieces of Super Veloz, exemplifying the physical possibilities typographic adaptation and combination of these interchangeable elements.

Super Veloz

The formal chaos that resulted from these operations on existing typography also corresponds to a more general phenomenon of communication common in the transmission of cultural ideas, at least in the West. In general terms, it is something like the voice that loses clarity with distance until, finally, something different from what was actually said is heard. Likewise, these naive typographic exercises corresponded, without too much sense, to what less illustrious professionals learned in quite a clumsy way in general from the radical directions of the new typography and from the typographic avant-garde of the 1920s: Lissitzky, Moholy-Nagy, and Tschichold. In such a way, the postulates of the European avant-garde were understood in the most humble print shops, far from where they were first invented. Thus, the dogma of handling type without ornamentation and, at times, without capitals created a notable confusion that could be seen in the small commercial pamphlets that were becoming impoverished by the economic crisis of the 1930s.

From a strictly typographic pointof view, Joan Trochut grew up in a propitious atmosphere. In this critical professional environment, he struggled to return "the joy and the beauty" to the unim-

Figure 5
Elements of Super Veloz from the First, Second, and Third Collections as well as the Complements no. 1 and no. 2.

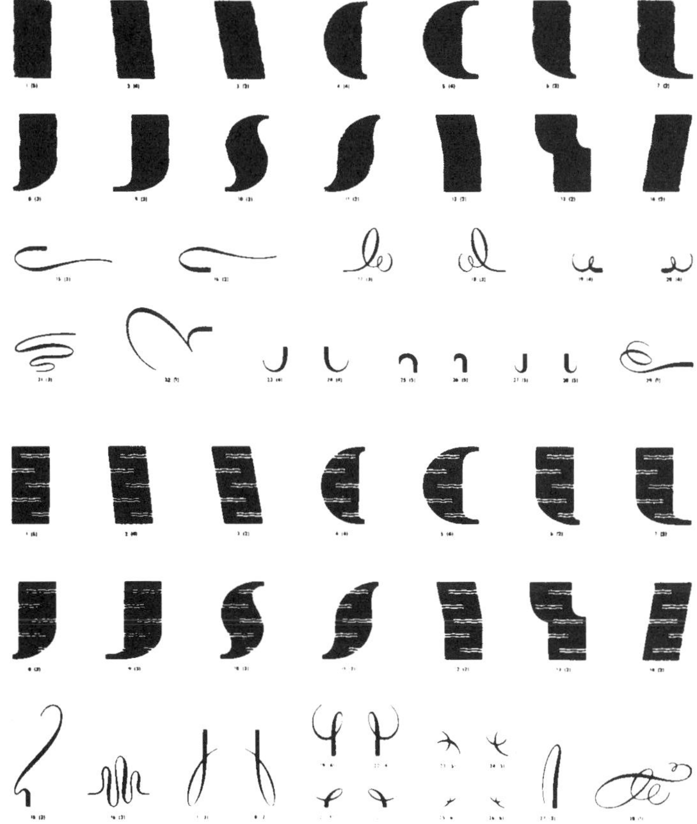

Complement No. 1

Complement No. 2

portant ephemeral, though enormously common, small pamphlets that were habitually "designed" by the Spanish printers in their own small shops. He knew their "needs and miseries" more than well enough as he pointed out in one of the promotional statements for Super Veloz, published in the new albums NOVADAM (Nuevos Archivos de Arte Tipografico Moderno/New Archives of Modern Typographic Art).

Joan Trochut's concern for the needs of small printers perhaps partially excuses the nostalgia that he seemed to feel for the loss of ornamentation in typography. Once more in the history of typographic design, the unfinished appearance continues to float in his design, which impedes its consideration as something truly definitive. Therefore, this analysis of Super Veloz focuses on its conceptual achievement and content, which seemed to be the most rigorous and opportune in its time. Super Veloz certainly derives from the mediocre circumstance's of its creator, but the essential idea still holds enormous interest.

Trochut was led by an extremely pure concept to develop Super Veloz. "From the invention of printing," he said in another of his publicity texts, "there have been few innovations in the fundamental principles of printing type. Only the designs of the letters have been changed frequently and often not very well. To admire the most beautiful creations of foundry types, we always have to return to the origins of our history." No doubt he was referring to such classic types as Jenson, Manutius, Garamond, Baskerville, and Bodoni, but in spite of the above statement, Trochut never wanted to compete with the classics. In truth, Super Veloz poses two exclusively formal problems: the ornamental or typographic solution for small pamphlets, and the construction of loose words (logotypes,

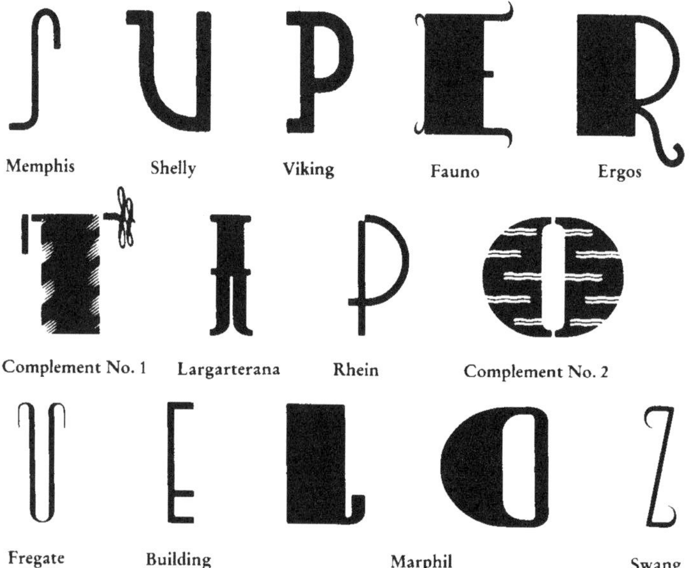

Figure 6
Display of different letters and the name of the type in which each is composed.

commercial names) or capital letters to accompany, underline, or differentiate other texts composed in columnar types.

For the first time, this "rigorously integral" typography, as it was depicted in its time, accepted the challenge of freely drawing and titling with the typographic element itself. This was resolved with an ingenious compositional system whose simplicity and variance allowed it to be used by any worker in the typographic industry.

Figure 7
Composition of letter and image built with combinable pieces of Super Veloz; work by Joan Trochut, published in the catalogs of NOVADAM.

A rigorously integral typography

Antoine Seyl, director of the Belgian magazine *Chronique Graphique* said of Super Veloz that it "constitutes in the field of typography a novelty of considerable importance; in reality it is not a matter of types, but of *elements of combinable types* in a very large variety of different forms, according to the needs determined by each application."

The combinable elements are reduced to the amazing quantity of 14 designs that constitute the foundation of the system. These elements are "the trunks of the letters to which are added all secondary forms," to use the precise words of Joan Trochut. Beginning with the 14 modules, a spectacular variety of more than 200 secondary forms that allow almost infinite combinations can be generated. For example, letters of diverse morphology can be constructed to then form more than 50 different alphabets.[2]

In addition, gathering the artisan's experiences in modifying type with file and knife, the basic modules are converted into new formal orders by treating the stem of the character with unusual veins. After these modules, the possibilities of connecting the thick stems with the fine ones and semiblacks again multiply the prospects of creating different typographic effects as a third group, which finally comes forth from the simple operation of ornamenting the type legs with the minor elements of the extensive variety of secondary forms.

Furthermore, the straight and curved segments that make up the extensive catalog of basic and secondary forms can be armed with all kinds of designs: figurative or abstract, filled in, linear, or mixed. In addition, color transforms the elements in a new way, as was suggested in the deluxe albums of NOVADAM which were given to buyers of Super Veloz sets. In these catalogs, exemplary ideas for using this rigorously integral typography can be counted by the hundreds.

Up to this point, the description of Super Veloz corresponds perfectly to the history of many unachieved experimental projects that, no doubt, must have been designed in various places in Europe and America. But it is most surprising that Super Veloz was a fabulous commercial success in that distant and confused year of 1942. Its commercialization by the type foundry of José Iranzo has neither a precedent, nor an epilogue, either in Spain or probably elsewhere.

In the precarious situation of the typographic industry after the Spanish Civil War, when producing a simple pamphlet was

2 The typefaces Ergos, Building, Fauno, Shelley, Marfil, Viking, Memfis, Rhein, Fregate, Swang, and Legarterana can be found in the catalogs. They are in simple, engraved, or channeled versions, which means a choice of 48 different alphabets. If the extended and condensed versions of each version are added to this list, the quantity triples!

slower than a century before, the printing industry developed that avant-garde product, Super Veloz, which was intended to resolve the two major problems of typography: speed and quality. From the viewpoint of industrial profit, the integral typography of Joan Trochut eliminated the use of photoengraving, the main obstacle of the small commercial pamphlet.

In effect, this modular system made the production of simple drawings possible. For such an end, the third volume of NOVADAM (1948) and the fourth and last volume (1952) promoted Super Veloz exclusively. The editorials in both volumes addressed to the printers stated that "neither the letters nor the vignettes have been drawn, but instead were manufactured with typographic pieces. This systematic material advantageously replaces the illustrations and woodcuts of the previous albums."

Figure 8
Three drawings made with pieces from the Super Veloz collections by Joan Trochut, published in the catalogs of NOVADAM.

These albums presented a series of printed examples that were constructed according to a previous drawing, built up with selected elements from the enormous repertoire of Super Veloz according to the personal creativity of the typesetter or designer. The functionalism of these catalogs, in which each illustration was published with the modules for its construction, was similar to needlework catalogs that stimulated the imagination of housewives.

Super Veloz was sold in modules of 14 primary collections or forms to which were added the secondary and complementary elements that each client selected freely. Its economy justified the euphoria with which the national market (and an important part of the European market, especially France and Belgium) received this project which its producers placed at the service of "the ingenuity and the creative spirit of good typographers; and concerning limits, it only has those of good taste."

In a world that has stopped considering typographic procedures as an industrial alternative for the future, Super Veloz has today lost all usefulness. And if in this exact moment the review of this project leads to contemplating it with curiosity, there are lessons that may still be derived from a conceptual approach that, beyond the formal reservations, would, no doubt, come from a rigorous examination of its pieces (fortunately useless today).

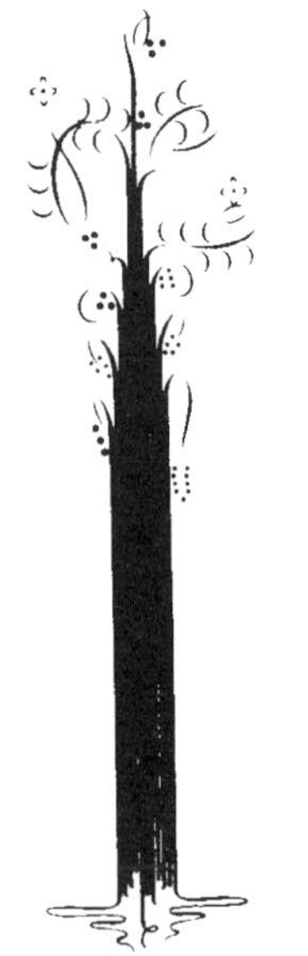

Figure 9
Virtuoso display in the handling of Super Veloz pieces. Work in color original by Joan Trochut, published it the catalogs of NOVADAM.

The new typefaces created with the help of computers and imposed by the force of audiovisual methods suffer much more serious formal defects. To throw overboard 500 years of alphabetic models and force the world to codify new forms for old meanings is, first and above all else, an insult to cultural society and, second, the gratuitous and overpowering loss of iconic identity, the design of extraterrestrial colonies foreign to the preexisting cultures of humanity.

The seven-segmented system, for instance, and all present electronic systems in general, are unavoidably produced through rigid geometrical structures that impoverish the visual aspect of some of the alphabet signs and numbers, which were so laboriously

Figure 10
The necessary pieces to build the previous floral design in figure 9.

improved during five centuries of formal exercises directed by rationality and esthetics. In this context, Super Veloz comes forth again, transparent and warm, splendidly incomplete, as an inspiring transposition of the literary theory known as the open work, which emphasizes the reader's participation in completing a text.

As the writer Juan Benet points out, this type of work ends up "carrying that kind of damnation of all unfinished things." However, it may be a utopian nourishment for which we hunger in these times when Jurgen Habermas and others lucidly observe the signs of a loss of Western culture's self-confidence. Faced with this, as Habermas said during a recent visit to Spain, one must try again in the measure of the impossible to "reunite the two forms of thought, characteristic of she Western world since the eighteenth century, which modern culture had aspired to unite: historical and utopian thought."

And here lies the lesson of Super Veloz, designed in the epigenesis of modern times. Understood in its masterly ambivalence, Super Veloz was able to conciliate Habermas's historical thought, "saturated, in effect with experience" (thanks to the empirical professional knowledge of its creator and to pragmatic objective goals that he proposed himself: to renew a decaying professional activity) with his overflowing utopian thought, "with its function of illuminating spaces of possibility which go beyond historical continuity." (In effect as already indicated, the essence of this project, the intellectual basis of its concept, points with all evidence to this possibility.)

Rarely has the substance survived the form so long and been so ignored. The latter, innocent victim of its own temporality, has died too young. Its partner, faithful and resigned, has remained ignored—like a good Latin—and marginal to a ravenous and gossipy actuality in order to appear fortuitously at present, with enviable health and an indispensable charismatic image. Super Veloz is adored by the moral and cultural survivRiors of modernity, due, no doubt, to the cult of reason, and equally venerated by the new, postmodern generations, enamored with the naiveté of its slightly irrational and spontaneous forms. And both, presumably, are dominated by the snobbism of the novelty that implies the rediscovery of a graphic language of this type and quality.

Translated from the Spanish by Manuel Blanco-Gonzalez

Imre Kner and the Revival of Hungarian Printing

György Haiman

Figure 1
Imre Kner, book cover composed of typographic elements, 1907.

Due to a number of publications and exhibitions, we have learned a good deal in recent years about the Hungarian avantgarde. Names like Lajos Kassák and László Moholy-Nágy are internationally known, but we know considerably less about other Hungarian artists and designers. Of these, one of the most important is Imre Kner, who is primarily responsible for the revival of Hungarian printing beginning in the early 1920s. Kner was born a hundred years ago, on February 3, 1890, in Gyoma, where his father, Izidor Kner, a very poor but talented young man, had set up a one-man printing shop in 1882. Gyoma was a small Hungarian market town which at the most had agricultural traditions but was very far from all forms of bourgeois culture that would have ensured the existence of a printing house. At the time of Imre Kner's birth, his father's printing shop had only a few employees, but by 1904, when his father sent him to Leipzig to study, the shop was already operating in a new building with modern machines and more than one hundred workers. All this was the result of Izidor Kner's outstanding ability, sense of quality, and up-to-date knowledge of printing.

As a student in the Julius Mäser Technikum für Buchdrucker, the 14-year-old Imre not only learned printing technology but also studied typographical design in the spirit of the Jugendstil, which had spread its tendrils everywhere by that time. Imre proved to be a talented designer and also drew, modeled, and showed a passionate interest in all branches of the arts. On his return home, at the age of 17, he became the artistic and technical manager of his father's printing house, as well as the designer of numerous books and printed materials (*figure 1*).

Imre was attracted to the progressive trend of the artists grouped in the German Werkbund, especially the new approach to design adopted by Peter Behrens in architecture, products, and graphics. Imre became more and more convinced that Hungarian book printing was in a deep crisis because the industrial revolution, which occurred in Hungary in the second half of the nineteenth century, "had broken the personal bond that tied the old worker, the old craftsman to his work."[1] Imre Kner believed that "the feeling for quality has been completely lost and as a result the market is swamped with a flood of cheap imitations in industrial, artistic, decorative arts . . . production."[2] These were the thoughts of a William Morris in a Hungarian context. However, Imre Kner did not seek a simple return to tradition nor did he wish to follow foreign

1 *Kner Almanach* (Gyoma, 1919), a yearbook produced by the Kner Printing House.

2 Imre Kner, *Industrial Education and the Applied Arts*, (Gyoma, 1919), p.g.

MÁJUS

KL

NAP		RÓM. KATH.	PROTEST.	IZRAELITA
1	Cs	Fülöp és Jak. ap	Fül. és Jak.	1 Ijar R. Ch.
2	P	Atanáz pk.	Atanáz	2
3	Sz	Sz. Kereszt megt.	Ker. föltalál.	**3 S. Kedos.**
4	**V**	**E 2 Misericordia**	**E 2** Flórián	4
5	H	V. Pius p.	Gotthárd	5
6	K	Olajba t. János	Dam. János	6
7	Sz	József oltalma	Szaniszló	7
8	Cs	Mihály föa. mj.	Arzén	8
9	P	Naz. Gerg. ea.	N. Gergely	9
10	Sz	Antonin pk. hv.	Antonin	**10 S. Emor.**
11	**V**	**E 3 Jubilate**	**E 3** Mamert	11
12	H	Pongrácz vt.	Pongrácz	12
13	K	Szervácz pk.	Szervácz	13
14	Sz	Bonifácz vt.	Bonifácz	14
15	Cs	De la S. János hv.	Mózes	15
16	P	Nep. János hv.	Peregrin	16
17	Sz	Paskal hv	Paskál	**17 S. Behar**
18	**V**	**E 4 Cantate**	**E 4** Erik	18
19	H	Cölesztin p. hv.	Ivo	19
20	K	Szién. Bernar. hv.	Bernardin	20
21	Sz	Timót vt.	Ilona	21
22	Cs	Julia sz.	Júlia	22
23	P	Dezsö pk. vt.	Dezsö	23
24	Sz	Már. ker. segit.	Eszter	**24 S. Bekh.**
25	**V**	**E 5 Rogate**	**E 5** Orbán	25
26	H	N. Fül. hv.	Béda	26
27	K	Béda et	Lucián	27
28	Sz	Ágost pk.	Emil	28
29	**Cs**	**Áldozó csüt.**	**Áld. csütörtök**	29
30	P	Sz. Jobb. tel.	Nándor	1 **Sziv.** R. Ch
31	Sz	Angela Mer. sz	Petronella	**2 S. Bamid.**

Figure 2

Kner's first experiment in a new book style, 1918.

examples. "We do not want to copy the foreign examples, we do not want to achieve outwardly showy successes . . . by copying old books and old techniques. We believe that a truly artistic solution can be found for modern, mass-produced, machine-made books too, and that this can be linked with the noble tradition of the finest ages of the book."[3]

Since the 1910s Imre Kner had sought a form of book design that was more objective, in harmony with the technology and materials of his day. He was firmly convinced of this by World War I, which he regarded as a senseless destruction of values. He considered that when the war was over, a better age, giving reason its place, would dawn on mankind. As he stated, "Now . . . the problems of the future are coming forcefully into the spotlight. In all fields it is the revival of life which most interests people."[4] And he added, "Our generation has been given the possibility to cut off the past behind it and to step straight into the future, to travel on different paths."[5] He wrote these words in 1916, when Lajos Kassák, the avant-garde artist and cultural organizer, was addressing the Hungarian avant-garde in the columns of the journals *Tett* and *Ma*, although with a different attitude; when Béla Bartók composed his ballet *The Wooden Prince* (Kner published the libretto of Béla Balázs for the ballet); and when Endre Ady, the great twentieth-century Hungarian poet, was leading the protests of the Hungarian people in his anti-war poems.

To destroy and rebuild—this was a constant refrain of the Hungarian avant-garde artists at that time. But Kner thought differently: he believed it was important to know the past and to establish a continuity between it and the future. What he had in mind, however, was not the past distorted through the spectacles of the present; he wanted to draw from what Béla Bartók called the "pure source."

Others were also thinking along the same lines. Kner made the acquaintance of Lajos Kozma, an architect who decorated his buildings with distinctive ornaments of folk inspiration. He also made a name for himself as a graphic artist with his outstanding draftsmanship. The two men spent the summer of 1918 together in Selmecbánya, a traditional bourgeois town in what was then Upper Hungary. There they coordinated their plans. Both considered that in the interest of developing Hungarian fine printing there was a need to rediscover and revive the esthetic values embodied in old Hungarian books (*figure 2*). As an experiment they began working together on a yearbook. Kner had a trial page set in one of the local printing shops, and Kozma sketched the heading for the month that they later cut in wood. The result of the experiment was a publicity yearbook, the *Kner Almanach* for 1919, with ornaments by Kozma.

By then the two had already decided to design, following a pattern similar to the yearbook, a series of books by classical Hungarian poets. However, their plans were upset by the revolu-

3 *Kner Almanach.*

4 Imre Kner, "On the Present and Future of the Hungarian Book," *Library Review* (1916): 105–22.

5 *Ibid.*

AZ
MIASSZONYUNK SZÍZ MÁRIA CSODÁIRÓL
való
HÉT LEGENDA
mellyeket
EGYNIHÁNY SZENTEKNEK ÉLETEKNEK
RÖVID
HISTÓRIÁJÁVAL
egyetemben
TÖBB RÉGI MAGYAR MANUSKRIPTUMOKBÓL
KISZEDEGETETT
KIRÁLY GYÖRGY
deák
NYOMTATTA
KNER IZIDOR KÖNYVNYOMTATÓ GYOMÁN
1920. esztendőben

Figure 3
Title page of one of the *Three Tiny Books*, 1920.

Figure 4
Kozma's illustration of an old Hungarian legend, woodcut, 1920.

tions of 1918–19. From April 1919 Gyoma was under Rumanian occupation for almost a year. Imre Kner was stranded in Budapest and unable to return home until the summer of 1920. However, the time spent in Budapest was not fruitless. Kner studied hundreds of old Hungarian books in the University Library and acquired understanding of the typesetting customs and layouts used by the best Hungarian printing presses of past centuries. He proved to be an excellent partner for Lajos Kozma in this field, and as a result their attempt to recast Hungarian tradition continued as a joint effort. They were joined by the literary historian György Király, an expert on old Hungarian literature, who collected brief histories, legends, and humorous anecdotes of famous and anonymous authors of Hungarian Renaissance and Baroque literature. The men published the collection in three small volumes. A critical review by a leading literary historian gave the series the name, *Three Tiny Books*.

The typography for this project was jointly designed by Kner and Kozma, who decided to accompany the text with ornaments and illustrations (*figure 3*). Until that time, ornaments and borders used in Hungary, mostly from German type foundries, were unsuitable for this purpose because they were poorly designed. Kner and Kozma therefore decided to create a stock of special Kner ornaments. Kozma designed headlines, vignettes, and initials. For the execution of Kozma's pencil sketches, which were done on transparent paper, Kner sought out experienced woodcutters who were not only familiar with the woodcutting technique but could also reproduce Kozma's style. For the first time in decades, after working mainly on dull advertising illustrations and price lists of little importance, the woodcutters were given a task fitting their ability. The same method was also used for Kozma's illustrations, which were printed from woodcuts and then colored by hand (*figure 4*).

The *Three Tiny Books* were ready for Christmas 1920. They had title pages of Baroque complexity, the first of the Kozma decorations, with a series of initials and two woodcut printer's devices. One depicted the printer's griffin holding the Kner shield, and the other an itinerant bookseller (*figure 5*). The latter was particularly appropriate because Kner's ancestors had been bookbinders and itinerant booksellers who went from fair to fair in the eighteenth century. Albert Kner, Imre's brother, prepared the covering paper, set with Kozma borders, for the slipcase containing the volumes bound in vellum and leather; he also designed the marbled paper and the paste paper for those with paper covers.[6]

Kner and Kozma also began to build up a collection of borders (*figure 6*). Kner "scored" Kozma's drawings to typographical sizes as required for the setting of borders. At that time there were still two Hungarian punchcutters alive, and they undertook the cutting of the punches; hence, the matrices were prepared and then cast at the First Hungarian Type Foundry. The creation of the border series continued from 1920 to around 1927.[7]

6 In 1940, Albert Kner came to Chicago, where he eventually headed the packaging lab at the Container Corporation of America.

7 By 1942 the Kner type specimen book contained 455 different ornaments. This enormous stock was the exclusive property of the Kner Printing House and no one else was authorized to use it. On two occasions Kner ornaments were used without permission. In one case, the First Hungarian Type Foundry showed some of the copper lines as its own in one of its brochures. Then, in England the *Manchester Guardian* used line blocks made from several Kozma ornaments. When approached by the Kner family, the *Guardian* admitted its infraction and sent the blocks to the family. (A record of the incident can be found in the family archives.)

Figure 5
One of Kner's early printer's devices, woodcut by Kozma, 1920.

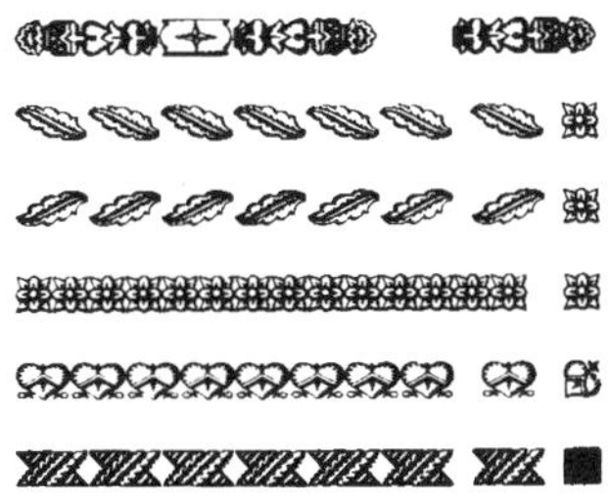

Figure 6
Kozma's borders for Kner, from the early 1920s.

In his writings, Imre Kner gave a precise, detailed, and convincing theory of the rediscovery and revival of traditions and the restoration of the continuity between the new and the old culture. He also addressed the questions of transplanting the old forms into the new technical framework, but paid little attention to the period or the books in which he considered this "pure source" to be found. In one place he contrasted the serious artistic errors of the nineteenth and the early twentieth century with the beautiful books of the sixteenth to eighteenth centuries.

Kozma, in detailing how he perceived this return to tradition, went back not to Gutenberg but to the Baroque, which he called the last good period (*figure 7*). Kozma believed that the valuable traditions from this age survived in folk art too, and he drew on these traditions not only for book design but also as an architect and interior designer, producing distinctive designs known as "Kozma Baroque." On the subject of the contemporary ornaments he produced, Kozma wrote: "Rather than animation, restlessness and what is finished, it is preparation, the growth of life, fever, driving force which finds delight as much in flashes of lightning as in the burgeoning growth of fleshy tendrils, in short the dynamic power of portrayal which is fundamentally related to Baroque ornament."[8] The Kozma-Kner ornaments were, in fact, splendid decorative material fully in keeping with the spirit of the book (*figure 8*). Kozma produced very conscious typography when he designed ornaments. "I strove to advance among the printing types that represent the world, among the hard lead soldiers," he wrote.[9] He was, for example, fully aware of the function of his borders and said that "the borders must merge in different associations with their fellows from those of the letters, which must be interesting in themselves, but even in its closed nature the form must be able to show a link with its neighbors!"[10] Kozma believed that "the basic condition for a good ornament is the same as that for a good type: while building up its own character to the utmost degree, it must adapt to its fellows, the type. If the ornament wishes to blend with the type it must renounce all the fortuities of handwriting and must concentrate all its message in the hard, characteristic language of engraving."[11]

There is only one error in Kozma's argument. He thought that each of the older printing presses had its own designer who drew the characteristic ornaments. In reality, this was the case in only a very few places. It was the woodcutters, about whom we still know very little, who designed—or, occasionally, had them designed by artists—and executed these ornaments and sold them to numerous printing presses in Hungary and abroad.[12]

But Kozma was not entirely wrong either. For in the Hungarian book and the Hungarian typographical environment, these ornaments with an international past became, metaphorically speaking, Hungarian because their users selected them according to

8 Lajos Kozma, "Individuality and Traditions," in *Kner Almansh* (Gyoma, 1922), 68–79.
9 *Ibid.*
10 *Ibid.*
11 *Ibid.*
12 As a result, the woodcut ornaments and initials, or their close relatives, used by Hungarian printers in the seventeenth and eighteenth centuries are also found in Vienna, Graz, Prague, Venice, Livorno, Torino, Halle, Augsburg, Ulm, and elsewhere. The list is far from complete, and as yet very little research has been done to determine the origin and route of the woodcuts.

Hungarian taste, and the setting of the Hungarian text made the entire composition with all its elements Hungarian.

On the subject of this "metaphorical Hungarianness" it is worth noting one of Imre Kner's suppositions: if someone were to make a thorough study of the history and development of the typographical composition and structure of the title pages of many thousands of old Hungarian books, they would find that the Hungarian way of thinking and the Hungarian word order had shaped the nation's style of typography. It is also due to the internal rules of the Hungarian language that only certain kinds of type are suitable for setting Hungarian. Kner had in mind here that the Hungarian reader traditionally insists on certain print types; he also had in mind that one in six letters in the Hungarian language has an accent, which means that the overall appearance of the text differs greatly from that of Latin or English, for example.

Imre Kner, in his substantial theoretical work and vast body of correspondence, did not denote "the last good period" in the history of Hungarian printing, whereas Kozma specified the Baroque period. However, we can deduce from Kner's intellectual legacy that this period could only have been the eighteenth century, following the liberation from Turkish rule that had held back Hungarian book printing. At that time the printing press of the Jesuit Academy in Nagyszombat, commonly known as the University Printing Press, was the leading press in the country. It is probable that woodcut ornaments of the University Printing Press were one of Kozma's main sources; indeed, as he himself wrote, he revived some of them, although he modified them slightly to his own taste (*figure 9*).

Kner followed the *Three Tiny Books* with the series of works by Hungarian poets that he had planned earlier (*figure 10*). Under the title *Kner Classics*, 12 volumes in this series appeared in 1921. These contained the selected verses of the most important Hungarian poets of the sixteenth to nineteenth centuries. The elegant narrow form of the books was adapted to the structure of the verses. The coordinated typography varied slightly from volume to volume and discreetly reflected the book design customs of the periods in which the poems were written. Kozma designed the ornaments, initials, and borders for the books, as well as the vignettes that decorated the title pages of the different volumes and referred to their contents.

Imre Kner's biggest project, which can now be regarded as a true classic, the *Monumenta Literarum* series, was produced during 1921–22 (*figures 11 and 12*). This series contained a selection of old and modern masterpieces of world literature in 24 large-format quarto volumes. Typographically, each work reflected the spirit of its age. They made abundant use of the large stock of Kozma ornaments, and only the common printing type and uniform concept linked them together (*figure 13*). Kner obviously regarded the series

Figure 7
Kozma's vignettes in woodcut, 1920–23.

Figure 8
Kozma's woodcut letters, 1920–21.

Figure 9
Eighteenth-century Nagyszombat University Press flower basket (above) and a similar shape by Kozma (below), 1921.

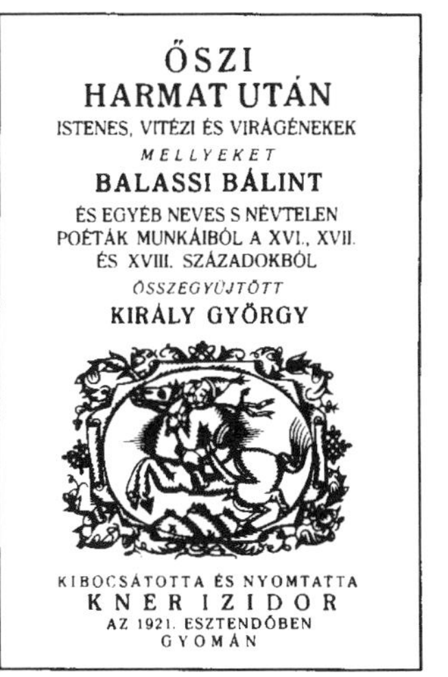

ŐSZI
HARMAT UTÁN
ISTENES, VITÉZI ÉS VIRÁGÉNEKEK
MELLYEKET
BALASSI BÁLINT
ÉS EGYÉB NEVES S NÉVTELEN
POÉTÁK MUNKÁIBÓL A XVI., XVII.
ÉS XVIII. SZÁZADOKBÓL
ÖSSZEGYÜJTÖTT
KIRÁLY GYÖRGY

KIBOCSÁTOTTA ÉS NYOMTATTA
KNER IZIDOR
AZ 1921. ESZTENDŐBEN
GYOMÁN

Flgure 10
Title page from the *Kner Classics* by Imre Kner with Kozma's woodcut vignette.

Az Szent
BARLÁM ÉS SZENT JOZAFÁT KIRÁLFI
ÉLETÉRŐL VALÓ IGÖN SZÉP
LEGENDA
mellyet
KILÖMB-KILÖMB RÉGI SZENT KÖNYVEKBŐL
szeretettel öszveszedögetött és görögül
megirt vala az tisztölletös
DAMASCENUS JÁNOS
doktor,
OZTÁN GÖRÖGBÜL DEÁKRA FORDITTATOTT,
deákbul kegyiglen magyar nyelvre, az
Legenda Aurea szerént
NÉVTELEN AUTHOR
által.

NYOMTATTA ÉS KIBOCSÁTOTTA
KNER IZIDOR KÖNYVNYOMTATÓ, GYOMÁN,
MCMXXII.

Figure 11
Title page from the *Monumenta Literarum* by Imre liner with Kozma's woodcut vignette.

as his main work because this was the only occasion in his career when he indicated in the colophone that he designed the layouts.

All that Kner and Kozma wrote on their theory and practice of reviving tradition and that appeared in the *Kner Almanach* of 1922 was unique in its own way, but it was not without precedent. "I strove to advance, but if the path was difficult, I was not ashamed to look back," wrote Kozma.[13] We cannot deny the similarity here to what the British typographer and historian Stanley Morison wrote concerning his revival of historical printing type beginning in 1922: "The original twentieth-century book type might come in due course. But certain lessons had first to be learnt and much necessary knowledge discovered and recovered. The way to learn to go forward was to make a step backward."[14]

"The last good period"—this was Kner's pragmatic rather than theoretical choice of a source. And as Morison put it: "The new programme was not romantic in either direction. It looked neither forward nor backward. The fact was that there were on the pages of books printed in the long and recent past several magnificent founts, engraved in periods when the art flourished, which had no present-day equivalent in point of nobility or utility, and had been rendered unobtainable by the effects of great changes in taste and technique that swept over typography, as so much else, after the eighteenth century."[15]

What did Kner and his associates have to restore and revive after it had been "swept over" in the eighteenth century? What were the new quality requirements for books produced by the Kner Printing House after 1920? We can list these as follows:

13 Lajos Kozma, "Individuality and Tradition."
14 Stanley Morison, *A Tally of Types* (Cambridge: Cambridge University Press, 1973), 38.
15 *Ibid*, 35.

4 AZ SZENT BARLÁMNAK ÉS

got eltávoztatnám, az te testödet ingyen majd tűzre vettetném. Kelj fel azért hamar és fuss el az én szömeimnek elöle, hogy tégöd továbbá ne lássalak és gonoszúl el ne veszesselek. ¶ Az istennek embőre kegyiglen nagy szomorúsággal mene el az királnak elöle azért, hogy martiromságot nem szenvedhete.

zönközbe mikoron az királnak magzatja nem vóna, szilettetek ö neki egy igön szép férfiu-magzat, kit Jozafátnak neveztete. Öszvegyitvén kegyek az királ örömében nagy sok népet, hogy az szilетött gyermökért az istenöknek áldoznának, ötven égbenéző böcseket és hivata hozjá, hogy mint lenne jövendöbe az ö magzatjának dolga, szeretettel megtudakoznák és ö neki megjelöntenék. Sokan azért közölök mondák az gyermököt jövendöben nagynak lenni hatalmasságban és kazdagságban; de egy, ki az többinél böcsebb vala, az királnak im ezt felelé: Ez gyermök, ki teneköd szilettetött, ó királ, nem leszen az te országodba királ, de az te országodnál hasonhatatlan jobba; mert az körösztyén hitnek, melyet te háborgatsz, ez gyermök jövendöbe tisztöllöje leszön. Ezt kegyiglen ez böcs ö magátul nem mondá, hanem isteni ihlésböl. ¶ Hallván kegyék ezt az királ, igön megrettene rajta. Az városban magának egy igön szép palotát rakattata, és az gyermököt az palotába behelhözteté. Szörze kegyék ö mellé nömös ifjakat szolgálatra, és parancsolá ö nekik, hogy az gyermök elött se kórságot, se vénségöt, se halált, se kegyiglen szegénségöt ne emlötenének, se egyebet valamit, ki ö neki valami szomorúságot hozhatna; de mindönöket gyönyörüségösöket mondanának ö elötte, hogy az ö elméje gyönyörüségökben foglaltatván, semmit az jövendökröl ne gondolhatna. ¶ Ez ifjak közöl kegyéglen, ha valamelliknek történik vala megkórúlnia, az királ azt onnétan ottan kiviteti vala és más ifjat állat vala helébe. Parancsolá továbbá az királ, hogy ez gyermöknek elötte valami emléközetöt Urunk Krisztusról ne tennének.

zon idöben az királnak udvarába vala egy vitéz, ki titkon körösztyén vala. Ez az királnak nagy szeretetibe vala és az ö udvarába elsö vala. Ez egy idöben, mikoron az királlal vadásznia ment volna, talála egy szegén embört az födön fekvén, ki az ö lábába bestyétöl megsértettetött vala. Ki kezdé az vitézt kérnie, hogy ötet felvétetné, házához vitetné és gondját viselné, és netalámtán ö neki idö jártába valamibe használhatna. Kinek monda a vitéz: Én tégedet örömest felvétetlek; de mibe használhatnál én neköm, nem gondolhatom. Az szegén embör kegyik mondá: Én beszédnek urvosa vagyok. Ha valaki azért beszéddel megbánttatik, alkalmas urvosságot tudok ö neki adnom. Az vitéz ke-

gyig-

Figure 12

A page from a legend of J. Damascenus; layout by Imre Kner, woodcut letters by Kozma, 1922.

Aucasin és Nicolete.

Ófrancia széphistória.

Fordította

Tóth Árpád.

Nyomtatta

Kner Izidor könyvnyomtató

Gyomán 1921-ben.

Figure 13

A cover from the *Monumenta Literatum* by Imre Kner.

- The quality of composition deteriorated from the second half of the nineteenth century. The spaces between words grew out of all proportion and became irregular. Out of a false respect for authority, the rules of composition of the Leipzig Typographic Society (1883) were widely followed in the printing houses. These contained contradictory and irrational prescriptions listed within 47 principles; in the final analysis, these contributed to the widening of the word spaces.

  Imre Kner considered that the "texture" of the text had to be restored so that the line was not broken into fragments but remained a single unit, and that the page should have an even tone value. To this end, he defined the ideal value of the average word space as one-third of the emquadrat, and abolished the restricting rules of division of the Leipzig Typographic Society.
- Kner made it a rule that the spaces between lines should be identical within a book; that is, great attention should be paid to the back-up register, to the proportions of the page and the margin. He established a series of rules for layout, always emphasizing that in concrete cases the designer had to make a creative decision, also taking into account the wishes of the author and the publisher.
- Kner devoted special care to the title page. He said: "The title page is actually the face of the book; the development of the style of the title page provides the material for the most interesting studies in art history. . . . The given text can be varied in a thousand ways, merely by means of typographical spatial proportions, by changing the size of the type, and in forming it a role can be played by artistic expression, by rational spacing, by the publisher's advertising concerns and by many other considerations."[16]
- Kner paid special attention to clear, sharp, easily legible, and evenly inked printing, which required a careful choice of suitable paper. Printing ink was also produced for him according to a special formula.
- To achieve this even inking, Kner developed his own quality requirements for the paper to be used in his books. This paper was produced for the Kner Printing House with its own watermark, mainly in the Diósgyör Paper Mill. When using handmade papers, if necessary, Kner employed the old method of printing on dampened sheets.
- Imre Kner regarded a text free of errors as a typographical requirement. To achieve this, books were generally proofread five times, and the control was generally carried out on four of these occasions by Kner himself.

Kner never regarded the layout of a book or an important printed piece as something sacred, conceived in a

16 Imre Kner, 'Limits of Typography and Book Art," in *Yearbook of the Hungarian Biblgophile Society* (Budapest, 1928),20-39.

A férfi Goethe

1777 – 1800

Antológia
a költő férfikorának
műveiből

Fordította
Szabó Lőrinc
és
Turóczi-Trostler
József

Gyoma, 1932
Kner Izidor könyvnyomtató
kiadása

Figure 14
One of Title pages from *The Eternal Goethe*, layout by Imre Kner with Bodoni types.

precise form guaranteed to be successful. It was only practice and trials that could confirm the quality of something for him. He made a number of trial compositions for books and title pages of books, which he continued to modify and correct with his colleagues until he judged that they were ready for execution.

- When the books were stitched or bound, Kner insisted that the margins, which the typographer designed, and other rules be respected precisely. He demanded the highest quality of craftsmanship; machines played only a limited role in binding the Kner books because of the small number of copies.

Kner's position on printing types was largely theoretical since he produced his finest books in the difficult years following World War I, after two-thirds of his equipment had been plundered from the printing house by Rumanian troops. At that time he had only one printing type available for use, the Leipzig University Antiqua, a rather neutral type first produced in 1911. The lack of supplies had one advantage: Imre Kner demonstrated that five centuries of literature could be printed with a single typeface while at the same time reflecting the typographical styles of the periods concerned. These books, like all the later publications of the press, were composed by hand. Precisely because of the hand setting, the firm never acquired an Old Style type. Kner liked only the Monotype Company's Garamond type, but there were many obstacles to adoption of the Monotype system.

The period of Kner-Kozma ornaments came to an end in the second half of the 1920s. Kner became acquainted with the American Type Founder's Bodoni type in 1923 when he presented a paper at the International Congress of Master Printers in Göteborg, Sweden. But it was not until 1928 that Bodoni became available in Hungary. The Kner Printing House purchased a large quantity of it, and Kner switched his design to the unadorned modern typography. This step made such an impact that many printing houses in the country followed his example.

Under the new conditions, the emphasis shifted from ornamentation to proportions, to the extremely precise alternation of sizes, and to spatial layout. The emphasis was placed on logic and rationality in typographical structure. Imre Kner was highly expert at this. His finest publication of this period was the three-volume set, *The Eternal Goethe*, which appeared in 1932 for the centenary of the poet's death (*figure 14*).

Imre Kner's commitment to the Bodoni type and modern typography may seem odd to Anglo-Saxon taste. However, the popular masses in Hungary became readers in the 1820s and 1830s, when the Modern type was widely used, and as a result this type became inseparably identified with the reforms that paved the way for the bourgeois revolution of 1848 and with Hungarian national ideals.

It was not by chance that Imre's father also considered the Modern type to be the "Hungarian" type, and that the son adopted this view. This attitude is illustrated by the fact that when, on the eve of World War II, the forces opposing German influence launched a new daily paper in Budapest, they set the headline of the paper in the type used for the "National Song" in 1848—the public understood the message hidden in its choice.

In 1937 the Fifth International Congress of Master Printers was held in Budapest, and Imre Kner presented a paper on "Contemporary Problems of Typographic Style." Here he made the acquaintance of Beatrice Warde, his co-reporter on this theme. In their later correspondence Kner expounded the essence of his views on typography, which he summed up in a few basic principles.

- I strive to use the fewest possible sizes of a given type family within the same layout. Each size has been cut on a different optical scale and is located in a different optical plane. This means that if the sizes alternate too frequently and too many sizes are used in a composition it easily disintegrates and the different parts appear not to be located in the same plane.
- I try to use type that is not too large. Emphasis can be given to something not only by using a very large size line, but also by surrounding the line with a white space. I do sometimes use very marked differences in size, but I always emphasize these with the spatial distribution.
- I always strive to combine the text in groups. An upper-case line or one that is to be strongly emphasized always stands out better against a background of uniform, unarticulated gray text. This can be achieved the way I described it in the above two points.
- I am convinced that we must be cautious of the "horror vacui." It is sometimes attractive if the text covers the surface like a carpet and only a single line or a few lines rise out of the composition. However, a large white surface which is well-balanced and rhythmically coordinated is just as valuable a part of the composition. A friend of mine has said: the proof of a printed border is when the white spaces between the ornaments themselves form pleasing ornaments. I have long held the view that the typogrpaher receives everything from others: the text, the types, the paper and so on. He adds only one thing to the composition: the white spaces. And it is precisely here that the secret is to be found! Empty space is just as important as the type itself.[17]

The principles of the major experiment conducted in the early 1920s in the revival of tradition were summed up by Imre Kner, Lajos Kozma, and György Király in the 1922 *Kner Almanach*.

17 Imre Kner, letter to Beatrice Warde, October 27, 1937. Kner Printing House Documents in the Békés County Archive, Gyula, Hungary.

Figure 15
From Imre Kner's manifesto, "Our Aspirations," 1922.

TÁRSADALMI ÉS EGYÉNI KULTURA
A KÖNYVKIADÁS FELADATAIRÓL
IRTA KNER IMRE

HÁROM esztendeje épen, hogy legelső almanachunkat kibocsátottuk. Mikor kiadását elhatároztuk, az volt a célunk, hogy általa közvetlenebb és szorosabb érintkezést teremtsünk kiadóvállalatunk és könyveink barátai között. Úgy gondoltuk, hogy majd minden esztendőben összefoglaljuk benne az esztendő munkáját, ismertetjük jövendő terveinket, programmunkat, s közvetlenebb formában, mint ez könyveinken keresztül lehetséges, megvilágitjuk törekvéseinket. Amikor az első évfolyamot sajtó alá rendeztük, már közeledett a nagy háboru vége, azt hittük nemsokára elkövetkezik az intenziv munka, az újjáépités ideje, s hogy ezzel hozzáfoghatunk régi terveink megvalósitásához, és hogy első almanachunkat majd sok-sok évfolyam megszakitatlan sora követheti. Mire azonban az első kötet kikerült a könyvpiacra, kitört a forradalom, s már előrevetették árnyukat azok a későbbi események, amelyek fiatal kiadóvállalatunk és majd negyvenéves könyvnyom-

NEUE
BAHNEN
UNGARISCHER BUCHKUNST

EMERICH KNER
ÜBER DIE AUFGABEN
DES VERLEGERS

LUDWIG KOZMA
RANDBEMERKUNGEN
EINES UNGARISCHEN
BUCHKÜNSTLERS

BEILAGE
ZUM ARCHIV FÜR BUCHGEWERBE
UND GEBRAUCHSGRAPHIK

BUCHDRUCKEREI ISIDOR KNER
GYOMA, UNGARN
1922

Figure 16
"New courses of Hungarian book art," Imre Kner's manifesto in German, Leipzig, 1922.

"Our Aspirations," which also appeared in the Leipzig *Archiv für Buchgewerbe und Gebrauchsgraphik* in German in the Christmas 1922 issue, could even be regarded as the manifesto of their movement (*figures 15 and 16*).

In subsequent years, too, Kner strove to analyze his practical experiences and formulate them in theory—or the reverse, to try out his theoretical notions in practice.[18]

Imre Kner opposed the typographical avant-garde, especially in the 1920s. He thought that its practitioners were imposing a form on books and printed materials that was foreign to the technique and spirit of typography. He argued with Jan Tschichold (at the time Tschichold was espousing his principles of "elementary typography"), Lajos Kassák, Imre Reiner, and others. Documents preserved in the Kner archive show that, despite differences of views, those on the other side respected and acknowledged Kner's achievements. Tschichold described the works of the Kner Printing House as a "good cause," and László Moholy-Nagy declared that he "gained inspiration" from the typographical aspirations of the Kner books.

It is interesting that these diametrically opposed positions later drew closer together. A time came when Kner and Tschichold were very close to each other in the use of classical typography. In the mid-1930s the rationality of both men met on the common ground of Tschichold's motto that the task of typography was to present the essentials in a clear and ordered way. This principle was further developed by Paul Renner in his book *Die Kunst der Typographie* (*The Art of Typography*) in a manner with which Kner was able to agree. Although it never occurred to Kner to abandon the principles of classical typography in his books, he proved to be a skilled practitioner of "functional" typography in his advertising materials.

But, unfortunately, Kner died in a German concentration camp in April 1945, and his life work remained unfinished.

18 Kner did not have time to sum up his theoretical work in a book, and the task of collecting his writings on the esthetics and history of typography fell to the author of these lines. Kner's writings were published with the title *The Art of the Book* in two editions of 1957 and 1972..

Nonetheless, Imre Kner's theory and practice concerning the revival of tradition has been justified by his many publications between 1920 and 1944 that represent an almost uniformly high-standard oeuvre. Many of these documents are of lasting value in the history of typography. History, too, has justified Kner's work: his neo-classical period, in particular, has had a lasting influence on Hungarian typography, which today rests on the basic principles that he elaborated. Current achievements in Hungary occasionally fall below the standards of Imre Kner because even though many have learned from him, only a few have acquired his restless, critical spirit which was always in search of something new and was consumed by the fever of creation. This spirit that Imre Kner possessed has been given to few others in the 550-year history of printing.

Translated by Elayne Antalffy.

Alms for Oblivion: The History of Women in Early American Graphic Design

Ellen Mazur Thomson

Time hath, my Lord, a wallet at his back, Wherein he puts alms for oblivion, A great-siz'd monster of ingratitudes . . .
William Shakespeare, *Troilus and Cressida*

When Linda Nochlin's article "Why Have There Been No Great Women Artists?" appeared in 1971, it generated enormous interest in neglected work by women artists.[1] Nochlin challenged traditional art historians to analyze the institutional and ideological structures that distort what women have accomplished or were unable to achieve. She warned that women must "face up to the reality of their history and of their present situation, without making excuses or puffing mediocrity. Disadvantage may indeed be an excuse; it is not, however, an intellectual position."[2] Since then, feminist historians have explored the limitations placed on women in pursuing their artistic careers, as well as the representations of those women who did succeed.[3] Graphic design historians, however, have only recently faced the biases in their own field and begun to identify individual women and document their position in graphic design history.

Martha Scotford Lange began this process by showing that the major texts used to teach graphic design concentrate on the work of a limited number of "great men" and that, graphic design historians, either consciously or unconsciously, have created an unacknowledged canon that excludes women.[4] She suggests that cultural history, rather than art history, would provide a better model for historians to follow.

This essay is the result of preliminary research into the conditions that governed the role of women in early modern American graphic design. By concentrating on the period from approximately 1850 to 1920, the beginning of "professionalization," this essay explores the extent and character of women's participation in this development. While it is important to recover the names of individual designers, it is equally important to understand some of the conditions and attitudes that determined the fortunes of women graphic designers by examining their treatment in both literature of the time and later.

During this period, graphic design emerged as a profession, one that developed in response to social changes and technologies that generated an enormous amount of printed material for mass

1 Linda Nochlin, "Why Have There Been No Great Women Artists?" *Art News*, 69, 9 January 1971), 22–39, 67–71. This article also appeared as "Why Are There No Great Women Artists?" *Women in Sexist Society Studies in Power and Powerless*, ed. Vivian Gornick and Barbara Moran. (New York: Basic Books, 1971) and *Art and Sexual Politics*, ed. Thomas B. Hess and Elizabeth C. Baker (New York: Colliers, 1971).

2 Nochlin, *Art News*, 70.

3 Feminist art historians have expanded Nochlin's agenda considerably. For an overview of feminist art criticism and art history in the 1970s and 1980s, see Thalia Gouma-Peterson and Patricia Mathews, "The Feminist Critique of Art History," *Art Bulletin* LXIX, 3 (September 1987), 326–357.

4 Martha Scotford Lange, "Is There a Canon of Graphic Design History?" *AIGA Journal of Graphic Design*, IX, 2 (1991), 3–5, 9. Lange analyzed the contents of five well-known histories: James Craig and Bruce Barton's *Thirty Centuries of Graphic Design*, Alan Fern and Mildred Constantine's *Word and Image*, Steven Heller and Seymour Chwast's *Graphic Style*, Philip B. Meggs' *A History of Graphic Design* and Josef Mueller-Brockman's *A History of Visual Communication.*

consumption. The concept of graphic design and the professional graphic designer evolved in the United States during the second half of the 19th century.[5] Previously, compositors, printers, typographers, and artist-engravers designed as part of their craft. The revolution in press and paper technology, photography and photomechanical reproduction, and transportation and business practices encouraged specialization and professionalism. By 1900, art directors, commercial-art managers, layout artists, and illustrators, sometimes called "designer," were recognized professionals.[6] Those trained in printing, typography, engraving, and illustration moved into separate art departments of advertising agencies, book and magazine publishers, or worked as free-lance designers. Relying on basic texts of graphic design history one would assume that women were marginal if not absent in this transformation.[7]

In part, the omission of women from design history occurred because historians have emphasized graphic design's roots in relation to printing's history. By doing so, they remove graphic design from its cultural context, and thus tend to ignore or de-emphasize the impact of the advertising industry and new theories of art and education on visual communication.[8] Arguably, advances in transportation technology that linked the continent by rail and ship, and the advent of mass marketing and widespread literacy that spurred the growth of newspapers and magazine publications are as significant as the revolution in print technology that occurred at the same time. Unfortunately, advertising historians have ignored the visual aspects of advertising, concentrating instead on the work of advertising agents, copy writers, and agency heads.[9] Feminist art historians, even when they include illustrators in their histories, are

5 See Howard Leathlean, "The Archaeology of the Art Director?" Some Examples of Art Direction in Mid-Nineteenth-Century British Publishing," *Journal of Design History* VI,4 (1993), 229–45, and Ellen Mazur Thomson, "Early Graphic Design Periodicals in America," *Journal of Design History*, VII, 2 (1994), 113–126.

6 W. A. Dwiggins first used the term "graphic design" in 1922 to describe professions involved in the design of commercial printing, commercial illustration, type design, and advertising design. I have followed these general parameters. "New Kind of Printing Calls for New Design," *The Boston Evening Transcript*, (August 29,1922), Graphic Arts Section, Part III, 6.

7 See Lange, op. cit., for the omission of women designers from major graphic design texts.

8 The recognized "great men" of early graphic design were trained in a variety of fields and spent their professional lives in a wide range of activities that now constitute professional design practice. They are, nonetheless, first identified as "printers" in the literature. For example, William Addison Dwiggins (1880–1956) worked in advertising for twenty years, and in a long and success career was a calligrapher, illustrator, prolific writer, and master puppeteer, as well as a typographer and book designer.

9 The classic histories, Henry Sampson's *A History of Advertising fnom the Earliest Times* (London: Chatto, 1874. Reprint. Detroit: Gale Research, 1974) and Frank Presbrey's *The History and Development of Advertising* (Garden City, NY: Doubleday, Duran, 1929. Reprint. Westport: Greenwood Press, 1968) ignore advertising artists, although Presbrey does include some information on the development of art departments in agencies. Daniel Pope in *The Making of Modern Advertising* (New York: Basic Books, 1983) describes the increased use of illustration in advertising but not the illustrators themselves. More surprising, given the authors' abundant use of illustration, is *Advertising in America* by Charles Goodrum and Helen Dalrymple (New York: Harry N. Abrams, 1990).

There is a brief discussion of advertising art in one chapter "Art, Artists, and Illustrators," but both text and pictures feature the work of James Montgomery Flagg, J.C. Leyendecker and Norman Rockwell. Jessie Willcox Smith is the only woman mentioned and she is represented by a small black and white reproduction. A perfect example of Lange's canon.

inclined to ignore the commercial aspects of their work.[10] Art historical models, as noted above, are often based on the great men and monuments model and fail to go beyond narrations of lives, assessments of influence, and progressions of styles.

In describing women's experiences in the printing and advertising industries, and in commercial illustration, I hope to highlight the areas in which women participated in graphic design, as well as show how their experiences reveal the profession's ties to other aspects of American culture.[11]

In a pioneering article, Cheryl Buckley argues that women's roles in all aspects of the design field have been defined by "the sexual division of labor, assumptions about femininity, and the hierarchy that exists in design."[12] During the second half of the nineteenth century many women worked in the printing industry, but in limited capacities. They were gradually forced out of the printing trades because male-dominated unions argued that the work was too physically demanding even as technology made it less so. Women also worked in the advertising industry but are absent from its history because they were unable to reach higher levels of management where their names would be associated with particular campaigns.

The women's movement, identified with the fight for voting rights, grew in power and foreed the nation to confront "the woman question." The number of schools and colleges, including schools of fine and applied art open to women, increased dramatically.[13] This

10 Nonetheless, the two most useful biographical references in graphic design are concerned with women artists. See Chris Petteys, *Dictionary of Women Artists: An International Dictionary of Women Artists Born Before 1900* (Boston: G.K. Hall, 1985), and Charlotte Steifer Rubinstein, *American Women Artists from Early Indian Times to the Present* (Boston: G.K. Hall, l982).

One of the problems encountered in any attempt track women is that of multiple surnames and cross-references are not always used. Also, many women and men signed their work with initials instead of first names and some first names are gender neutral—a problem in identifying signatures in published work in cases when it is signed. And most advertisements and magazine illustrtions were not signed.

11 This paper does not, for example, address issues of class or ethnicity as it was manifest in different aspects of the profession. African-Americans, Native Americans and European immigrant groups were involved in the printing industry and produced material for their own communities. Both Anthea Callen and Roger B. Stein have examined the effect of the Arts and Crafts movement on upper class women, or women whose economic status gave them a great deal of leisure time. See Anthea Callen, *Women Artists of the Arts and Crafts Movement 1870–1914* (NewYork: Pantheon, 1979) and "Sexual Division of Labor in The Arts and Crafts Movement." *Woman's Art Journal,* V (Fall/Winter 1984–1985), 1–6. And Roger B. Stein, "Artifact as Ideology: The Aesthetic Movement in Its American Cultural Context," *In Pursuit of Beauty* (New York: Metropolitan Museum. 1986), 22–51. The advertising profession was dominated by white Protestant males from rural backgrounds. For a sophisticated analysis of advertising as a cultural phenomena, see T.J. Jackson Lears, "Some Versions of Fantasy: Toward a Cultural History of American Advertising.1880–1930" *Prospects* Vol. 9 (Cambridge: Cambridge University Press, 1984), 349–405, especially page 356.

12 Cheryl Buckley, "Made in Patriarchy: Toward a Feminist Analysis of Women and Design," *Design Discourse: History Theory Criticism,* ed. Victor Margolin (Chicago: Chicago University Press, 1989), 262.

13 The National Academy of Design began in 1826 in New York City. It was joined by: Cooper Union for the Advancement of Science and Art, including a School of Design for Women (1859), the Art Students League (1875), the Society of American Artists (1877), the Society of Decorative Art (1877), and the Metropolitan Museum of Art School (1880). The Massachusetts State Normal School in Boston was established in 1873 and the Lowell Free School of Industrial Design, allied with the Boston Institute of Technology was opened to women. The Rhode Island School of Design was founded in 1877. Other include: the University of Cincinnati School of Design, the St. Louis Art Academy, the Art Institute of Chicago, the School of Drawing and Painting at the Museum of Art in Boston, the School of Design in San Francisco (1873), the Indianapolis School of Art, and in Philadelphia: the Pennsylvania Academy of Fine Art, the Philadelphia School of Design, The School of Industrial Art. In Baltimore, the School of Design of the Maryland Institute and the Decorative Art Society.

Illustration 1
"Rocky Mountains," Frances Flora Bond Palmer (1812–1876)
(From the Prints and Photographs Division, Library of Congress. Reprinted here with permission.)

was in part a result of theories expounded by John Ruskin and William Morris, and their influence in the American Aesthetic and Arts and Crafts movements.[14] Changing attitudes towards the applied arts and women's education gave women illustrators new opportunities, but often encouraged them to work on domestic subjects and in a decorative style.

At the same time, women were ignored in the literature. A good example of this can be seen in the case of Frances Flora Bond Palmer (1812–1876), known as Fanny Palmer. Palmer was one of three full-time lithographers on the staff of Currier & Ives. All but forgotten since her death, modern feminist art historians have revived her memory.[15] Born and trained in England, she emigrated to New York in the 1840s. Palmer was responsible for over 200 Currier & Ives lithographs; she made the original drawings and transferred them to the stone. She worked in a tremendous range of subject matter: landscapes, cityscapes, hunting scenes, still lifes. She made prints of trains, steamships, buildings, and dramatic battles from the Civil War, subjects not defined as "feminine." Her "Rocky Mountains, Emigrants Crossing the Plains" (1866) was one of the company's most popular prints and was found in homes throughout the country. She contributed to the technical aspects of commercial lithography. She developed a method of printing a background tone and, with Charles Currier, improved lithographic crayons. Although she was unusually gifted and productive, her historical fate is, nonetheless, typical. Palmer was an employee, so her work was not recognized as that of an individual but subsumed under the Currier & Ives imprint. She supported an alcoholic husband and her children, yet in her obituary she is identified only as her husband's wife, or in the less than felicitous terms of that day, "a relict of Edmund S. Palmer of Leicester, England." She is mentioned only as a part of Currier & Ives history until feminist art historians became interested in her work.

14 See Callen, *Women Artists of the Arts and Crafts Movement* and "Sexual Division of Labor," and Stein, "Artifact as Ideology," op cit.

15 Basic information on Fanny Palmer can be found in Henry T. Peters' *Currier & Ives: Printmakers to the American People* (Garden City, NY Doubleday, Doran, 1942), 26–29. Peters summarizes her life and identifies the prints known to be hers. Otherwise she is absent from graphic history until Mary Bartlett Cowdrey's "Fanny Palmer, An American Lithographer," *Prints: Thirteen Illustrated Essays on the Art of the Print* (New York: Holt, Rinehart and Winston, 1962), 219–234 and her entry in *Notable American* Women (Cambridge: Belknap Press, 1971), 111, 10–11. Charlotte Steifer Rubinstein included Palmer in *American* Women *Artists* (Boston: G.K. Hall, 1982), 68–70 and wrote in depth about her in "The Early Career of Frances Flora Bond Palmer (1812—1876), " *The American Art Journal*, XVII, 4 Autumn 1985), 71–88.

To understand the positions women found in the graphic design profession, we must turn to documentary sources that provide a broader picture of the profession and its history.

Documentation

Literature outside the usual scope of design history often illuminates important aspects of the graphic design profession. The relationship between the struggling printers' unions and women who worked in the printing trade was discussed in union journals and the popular press of the period. Modern histories of women workers also document the conditions of women in the trades.[16] Trade unionism developed early in the printing industry, which saw itself as progressive and open to new ideas and technologies. However, the ambivalence union members felt toward female workers explains as much about the situation women faced in the design profession as it does about the precarious situation of trade unionism itself.

Histories of the women's movement, either by participants or by modern feminist writers, are excellent sources because many suffragettes published and edited newspapers and magazines as part of their activities.[17] Susan B. Anthony and Amelia Jenks Bloomer were allied with women trying to find jobs in the printing trades and their confrontations with local and national printing unions are well documented.

During the second half of the 19th century a tremendous number of art and design schools opened throughout the country and many of them accepted women students. The published histories, original charters, and early annual reports of these institutions describe the ideological basis for education in the applied arts and explain why women were encouraged to pursue careers in design.

If women's presence in the work place generated heated arguments about trade unionism and women's rights, it also attracted the attention of statisticians and economists.[18] Unfortunately,

16 For bibliographical information, see Martha Jane Soltow and Mary K. Wery, *American Women and the Labor Movement 1825–1974.* (Metuchen, N.J.: Scarecrow, 1976). Especially useful histories on women in the printers' union include: Elizabeth F. Baker, *Technology and Women's Work* (New York: Columbia University Press, 1964); Mary Biggs, "Neither Printer's Wife Nor Widow," *The Library Quarterly*, L, 4 (1980); Eleanor Flexner, *Century of Struggle* (Cambridge: Belnap Press, 159); Philip Sheldon Foner, *Women and the American Labor Movement* (New York: Free Press, 1979); George A. Stevens, *New York Typographical Union* No.6 (Albany: J B. Lyon, 1913), 421–440; Barbara Mayer Wertheimer, *We Were There* (New York: Pantheon Books, 1977).

17 For guides to women's periodicals see Maureen E. Hady, *Womens Periodicals and Newspapers From the 18th Century to 1981* (Boston: G. K. Hall, 1982); Nancy K. Humphreys, *American Women's Magazines* (New York: Garland, 1989); Mary Ellen Zuckerman, Sources on the History of Women's Magazines, 1792–1960 (New York: Greenwood Press, 1991). On the history of the suffragette press see Lynne Masel-Walters, "To Hustle with the Rowdies," *Journal of American Culture*, III,1(Spring 1980).

18 A fine example is the work of Carroll D. Wright, chief of the Bureau of Statistics of Labor, whose study appeared in 1889 as *The Working Girls of Boston* (Boston: Wright & Potter, 1889. Reprint. New York: Arno, 1969). It was undertaken "to ascertain the moral, sanitary, physical and economic conditions of the working girls of Boston," including those in the printing trades. [p. 1] Wright concluded that, "the working girls are as respectable, as moral, and as virtuous as any class of women in our community; that they are making as heroic a struggle for existence as any class is a fact which all the statistics prove." [p.120] And in case anyone missed the point, he spelled it out: "...girls cannot work hard all day and be prostitutes too." [p.121] See also Edith Abbott and Sophonisba P. Breckinridge, "Employment of Women in Industries," *Journal of*

most statistics on the nineteenth century American work force defy easy interpretation. Compilers defined categories broadly and changed their definitions over time. The umbrella category of "printing and related professions," for example, included printers, typographers, compositors, and bindery workers.[19] The category "engravers" included those who worked on precious stones and metals, e.g., silversmiths, as well as those who copied illustrations onto metal plates for mechanical reproduction. Within these limitations, however, statistics describe the position of women workers in the larger picture of economic development.

Trade magazines for printers, typographers, and advertisers first appeared in the 1850s; by 1880 their numbers had increased dramatically.[20] They reflect the prevailing attitudes of their professions towards women and only unintentionally reveal women's participation. Unfortunately, as will be seen in the discussions that follow, these journals often preferred to ignore them.

Histories of art, particularly of American graphics illustration and biographies of American women artists, contain information on women who worked as illustrators for magazines, books, and posters. They continue to emphasize painters, sculptors, and "fine" printmakers untainted by commercialism, although women art historians have written about individual women illustrators.[21] By concentrating on broader cultural issues rather than individual artists, a few art historians have shown how particular movements, such as the Aesthetic and the Arts and Crafts, have influenced educational and professional opportunities for women.[22]

Printers

A significant number of men associated with the beginning of graphic design began their careers in printing establishments and so it is logical to look for women there as well.[23] From the colonial period on, women were well represented in the American printing

Political Economy, 14 (January 1906), 14–40; John R. Commons, *Documentary History of American Industrial Society* (Cleveland: 1910–1911); United States Women's Bureau, *Women at Work: A Century of Change,* no. 161, (Washington: Government Printing Office. 1933).

19 Women also worked in printing establishments as typesetters or operators on hand presses, but there is insufficient information to determine who designed type or page layouts. We know that binderies employed women in significant numbers, see Abbott and Breckinridge.

20 Thomson, op.cit.

21 See citations in "illustrators" section below. It should be noted, however, that many of these monographs are narratives of "the life and work." An notable exceptions is Ann Barton Brown's *Alice Barber Stephens: A Pioneer Woman Illustrator* (Chadds Ford, Pa., Brandywine River Museum, 1984). Barton puts Stephens career in context by discussing educational and professional opportunities for women, the treatment of women illustrators by the popular press, and the struggle of women to be taken seriously as professionals.

22 Anthea Callen in her studies of the Arts and Crafts has demonstrated that despite its iconoclastic theories, the movement reinforced patriarchal ideology even as it opened opportunities for women in the arts. See Callen *Women Artists of the Arts and Crafts Movement,* op. cit. and "Sexual Division of Labor in The Arts and Crafts Movement," op. cit. In Roger B. Stein's essay on the Aesthetic Movement, he examined its intellectual and cultural implications showing how it dealt with the "women question," by encouraging middle-class women to pursue an arts education that would not threaten the status quo. See "Artifact as Ideology," op. cit.

23 This does not modify my contention that exclusive concentration on printing history is unfortunate.

Illustration 2
Woman Printer cut. (From the General Collection, Library of Congress. Reprinted here with permission.)

Earnings in Boston, 1831

687 men earned	**$1.50/day**
395 women earned	**$.50/day**
215 boys earned	**$.50/day**

industry.[24] Several presses, including the first press in North America, the Cambridge Press established in 1639, were run by women.[25] It is often argued that women only became printers because it was their family's trade, but this was just as true for male printers. Girls, however, were trained in the printshop at home in contrast to boys who often learned their craft during a period of apprenticeship. The issue of apprenticeship, became a critical one for women professionals. There is no doubt that some women printers attained the respect of their profession. For example, *The Typographic Advertiser* (1869) carried an obituary for Lydia R. Bailey, a widow, who took over her husband's printing establishment. It noted that from 1808 to 1861:

> [h]er office was one of the largest in Philadelphia. She instructed forty-two boys into the mysteries of typography; and some of our present prosperous master-printers served their apprenticeship under her. For a considerable period she was elected City Printer by the Councils; and her imprint was well known. She had great energy and decision of character. [26]

Moreover, the editor saw Bailey's achievements in the wider context of political and economic rights:

> Of late days we hear much talk about women's rights. Something may probably come of it to women's advantage: how we may not forecast. There is certainly room enough for improvement in the condition of many women; but will the privilege of suffrage bring it about?[27]

Women not linked by family ties to printing were interested in the printing trade because it was relatively open to them and offered higher wages.[28] Nonetheless, women earned considerably less than men. In Boston in 1831, for example, men earned three times as much as women and boys in the printing industry.[29]

24 Leona M. Hudak, *Early American Women Printers and Publishers 1639–1820* (Metuchen, NJ: Scarecrow Press, 1978), 2.
25 Elizabeth Harris Glover established the Cambridge Press, the first press in North America, in 1639. Her husband, Jose Glover, wishing to set up a printing business, boarded a ship from England with his family, a press, and printing supplies. He died en route. See Hudak, op. cit., 9–19.
26 *Typographic Advertiser* XIV, 3 (April 1869), 1.
27 Ibid.
28 Edith Abbott, "Harriet Martineau and the Employment of Women in 1836," *Journal of Political Economy*, XIV (1906), 615.
29 Wertheimer, op. cit., 92.

Table 1: Number and pereentalle distribution of female gainful workers in printing and allied industries, 1870–1930

	1870	1880	1890	1900	1910	1920
Printing, and Allied Industries	4,233	8,947	23,771	31,613	45,090	45,274
Percent of Women Workers	40.8	39.1	51.6	53.8	59.4	55.8
Engravers	29	103	303	453	538	561
Percent of Women Workers	0.3	0.4	0.7	0.8	0.7	0.7

By 1880, the average weekly earnings for women in all trades was $6.03, whereas in printing and publishing earned $6.61, or over 9% more.[30]

In 1853, the suffragette and dress reformer, Amelia Jenks Bloomer, began publication of *The Lily: A Ladies' Journal Devoted to Temperance and Literature*. In 1854, she tried to hire a woman apprentice but the printers refused to work under this condition and struck both her paper and that of her husband. Bloomer persisted and finally found three women and three men to publish both papers; she paid them equal wages.

By the end of the Civil War, the number of women in printing had increased. For example, in 1868 there were 200 women typesetters in New York City, constituting 15–20% of printing trade workers.[31] The printing trades attracted an increasingly larger percentage of women workers as shown in Table 1.[32] Despite the introduction of new technologies that raised worker productivity, an increase in demand for printed matter allowed the total number of workers in printing to expand.[33] Women workers continued to be concentrated in typesetting. In 1870, 3.7% of compositors were women; in 1880, 4.7%; in 1890, 9.9%; and in 1900, 10.3%.[34]

The local printing unions that had existed during the first half of the 19th century, eventually formed a national organization, the United Typographical Union in 1852. In contrast to the union's tradition of progressivism, these all-male organizations exhibited great ambivalence towards unionizing women workers. Many printers hired women at lower wages under the guise of giving them an opportunity to learn the trade and women worked as scab labor during strikes. The unions had two options, either fight for equal wages and unionize women, or ban them from the industry.

The attitude of the printing trade journals of the period reflect these contradictions. In 1884, the editor of the *The Inland Printer* wrote:

> The printers employed on the *Evening Wisconsin*, of Milwaukee, twenty-three in number, are on a strike because the manager of that sheet insisted, after several remon-

30 Wright, op. cit., 82 83.

31 Foner, op. cit., 145.

32 H. Dewey Anderson and Percy E. Davidson, *Occupational Trends in the United States*, (Stanford: Stanford University Press, 1940), 300.

33 Ibid., 301. While printing material increased by more than 760% from 1899 to 1929, only 120% more workers were employed. Ibid., 309.

34 Lois Rather, *Women As Printers*, (Oakland, Ca.: Rather Press, 1970), 25.

strances, on paying the female compositors, members of the Cream City Typographical Union, twenty-eight cents instead of thirty-three cents per thousand ems—the union scale—as paid to the male compositors; and this, too, in the face of the admission that the women did better work than a majority of the men. The action of the union in making the cause of the girls its own is worthy of all commendation. Of course, no protective organization could tolerate, for a moment, a sliding scale arrangement, all its members, irrespective of sex, age or nationality, being required to observe the *minimum* rate of wages. Any other policy would be suicidal. The standard raised—"equal pay for equal work"—is one which will command the sympathy of every right-minded citizen; and it is needless to add that those now engaged in this struggle have our warmest wishes for their success.[35]

Despite these sentiments, the very same editors advocated barring female students from trade schools and accused any woman who wanted such training—or indeed worked in the trades—of being selfish by taking jobs away from men with families to support. Although they did not all subscribe to the idea that women were incapable or less hard working, editors argued that the printing trades required a greater amount of time to develop skills and that many women workers left as soon as they married. Some of the arguments appeared in the form of patriarchal sermons on the need to protect women from the dangers of the trade: their exposure to materials dangerous to health, women's supposed frailty and inability to carry heavy forms, and their proximity to "unsuitable" printed matter.[36] Other argued that women lacked training, that they were incapable of doing anything but the most straightforward jobs because few had served an appenticeship. Women, indeed, accounted for only 9.7% of all apprentice typesetters.[37] But the most troubling issue, and the primary focus of the opposition, was that women worked for lower wages and were used by employers to fight unionization. It was on this issue that the suffragette leader, Susan B. Anthony, entered the fray.

Anthony encouraged women to learn typesetting by taking jobs they were offered by printers, even during strikes. It is unclear if she really lacked an understanding of the need for worker solidarity as some writers charge, or if she, unlike women unionists, considered male workers so unsympathetic that they would never voluntarily integrate their shops. In a report of her fight for admittance to a union convention, printed in the *Workingman's Advocate* in August 1869, Anthony said she represented:

. . . a class of women that had no husbands, and who were on the street penniless, homeless and without shelter. Now, I ask you what we are to do with these girls? Shall we tell

35 *The Inland Printer* I, 6 (March 1884), 10.

36 The rhetoric used by both sides is fascinating. A printshop owner recommended hiring women typesetters and wood engravers because they were more obedient, did not use foul language, and cost considerably less. He concluded:

At least let women have a fair opportunity to do something else besides get married. What man is there who would not resent being told that his chief ambition in life should be to be a father? Yet women are told daily that they should devote twenty years of a lifetime in the preparing for motherhood, at least ten years in bearing children, and the rest of their lives in recovering from the effects. If they prefer to think that the world is populated sufficiently, or that to bear a child does not call for sacrifice of a lifetime, they are snubbed, and especially so when they show any inclination to compete with men in trades. "Male Versus Female Labor," *Art Age*, 111, 25 (August 1885), 14.

37 Riggs, op. cit., 438. Riggs notes that the percent of women apprentices in printing was high compared to women in other skilled trades and that there is some neason to believe the percentage of men who actually underwent a six-year apprenticeship was also relatively small. Certainly the trade journals complained of this and supported technical education for boys to make up the deficiency.

them to starve in the garrets because the printers, by their own necessities, open their doors and give a slight training to a few girls for a few weeks? Shall I say to the girls, "Do not go in, but starve?" or shall I say, "Go in, and get a little skill into your hands, and fit yourselves to work side by side with men?" I want to ask the Cooperative Union of New York how many girls they have taken to learn the type-setting business? How many women have you ordered each department or establishment to take as apprentices, and to train in the art of type-setting?[38]

Union leader Augusta Lewis clashed with Anthony over these tactics. Lewis (c.1848–1920), a journalist and typesetter, believed that by preserving union solidarity and by foregoing the immediate advantage of work, women would eventually find an equal place in union shops. Lewis founded the Women's Typographic Union No. 1 in October 8, 1968 and urged women members not to accept nonunion work. A year later, the United Typographical Union became the first national union to admit women, and in 1870, Lewis was elected corresponding secretary of the national organization. Yet Lewis was shortly disillusioned by the union's treatment of its women members:

> [We] have never obtained a situation that we could not have obtained had we never heard of a union. We refuse to take the men's situations when they are on strike, and when there is no strike if we ask for work in union offices we are told by union foremen 'that there are no conveniences for us.' We are ostracized in many offices because we are members of the union; and although the principle is right, disadvantages are so many that we cannot much longer hold together.[39]

The continued resistance to women in printing is evident in the attention they received in the trade joumals. In the 1880s and 90s, the *Inland Printer* attacked women in the printshop, using a series of arguments to disparage their competence.[40] The catch, of course, was that when women did succeed they were derided as unfeminine and grotesque. In describing an itinerant printer he met in western Ohio, one writer claimed: She was dressed plainly but neatly in what might be called a cross between a traveling and office suit of brown color. The toughened expression on her face indicated that she was familiar with the tricks of the profession, versed in the study of vulgarity. No tender, trusting female was she, but a hardened, suspicious, masculine woman.[41]

When the journals were not questioning women's abilities, they ignored them. However, they were quick to take umbrage at similar treatment from women. For example, the *Inland Printer* (1883) reprinted an article from a British trade journal reporting that women compositors in Boston published a journal called *Elle*:

38 "Proceedings, National Labor Union. August 1869," *Workingman's Advocate* VI, 5 September 4, 1869) and reprinted in *America's Working Women*, ed. by R. Baxandall, L. Gordan, and S. Reverdy (New York: Random House, 1976), 112–113.

39 From a report given by Lewis at the international Typographers convention in 1871 and cited by Stevens, op. cit., 437.

40 *Inland Printer* 1, 1 October 1883),1; VII (October 1889),108–09; VII, (June 1890) 819–20; IX (July 1892), 875–876; X, 5 (February 1893).195; X, 6 (March 1893) 501.

41 F. M. Cole. "Lady Compositors," *Inland Printer*, VII, 2 (November 1889)109.

Illustration 3
Woman typesetter cut.
(From the General Collection, Library of Congress. Reprinted here with permission.)

Brown's Patent Type-setting machine was introduced during the 1860's by Oren L. Brown

> This paper is veritable man-hater; not the slightest mention of man in any shape or form is to be found in its columns, neither is the genus homo allowed to hawk it![42]

The notice is doubly significant. *Elle* does not appear in any of the standard sources on magazine literature and it is possible that no copies have survived. We know of its existence now only because it irritated the editors of a mainstream journal.

The introduction of new technology, particularly the Mergenthaler Linotype, beginning in the 1880s, might have increased opportunities for women. The typographer's union admitted that women learned to work with the system more quickly, but also charged that they lacked endurance. In the end the union insisted that only fully qualified (i.e., male printers), should be allowed to use them.[43] In typesetting, traditionally the one printing profession in which women significantly competed for work, they lost ground. By 1900, only 8% of women belonged to unions, compared with 32% of men. Only 10% of compositors were women, while only 700, or 5.8%, operated typesetting machines.[44] Barred from the apprentice system and trade schools and betrayed by the trade unions ostensibly representing them, working class women rarely followed men who made the transition from the printshop into the design of printed material.[45]

The private press movement, with its emphasis on the highest standards of presswork, was based on William Morris' Kelmscott Press and the English Arts and Crafts tradition. It inspired American printers and designers from Boston to San Francisco. But women are excluded almost completely from its history although from fragmentary records we know that their presses existed.[46] In San Francisco, the Women's Cooperative Printing Union was founded in 1868 and survived until 1880. In 1873, two sisters, trained designers and wood engravers, founded Crane and Curtis Company there. Women ran the Chemith Press in Minneapolis in 1902 and the

42 "Woman as Compositors," *Inland Printer*, VII, 8 (May 1890), 820.

43 Baker, op. cit., 44. Employers also preferred to retrained male typesetters already working in their shops, see Harry Kelber and Carl Schlesinger *Union Printers and Controlled Automation* (New York: The Free Press, 1967), 8.

44 Baker, op. cit., 45.

45 The experience of women printers in the territories and states in the West was somewhat different. In a pictorial study of frontier journalism, numerous photographs from state archives show women working as editors, printers and compositors. See Robert F. Karolevitz, Newspapering in the *Old West* (Seattle: Superior Publishing, 1965), especially "Printers in Petticoats," pp. 173–180. Karolevitz also includes photographs of women in printing classes in state universities as well as in a special school for Native Americans.

46 Edna Martin Parrat, "Women Printers," *Bulletin of the New York Public Library*, LVI, 1(January 1952), 42–43. Often cited, this was only a brief reply to an item on women printers. The names of other women printers can be found in Rather, op. cit.

Unlike are we, unlike, O princely Heart!
Unlike our uses and our destinies.
Our ministering two angels look surprise
On one another, as they strike athwart
Their wings in passing. Thou, bethink thee, art
A guest for queens to social pageantries,
With gages from a hundred brighter eyes
Than tears even can make mine, to play thy part
Of chief musician. What hast thou to do
With looking from the lattice-lights at me,
A poor, tired, wandering singer, singing through
The dark, and leaning up a cypress tree?
The chrism is on thine head,—on mine, the dew,—
And Death must dig the level where these agree.

Thou hast thy calling to some palace-floor,
Most gracious singer of high poems! where
The dancers will break footing, from the care
Of watching up thy pregnant lips for more.
And dost thou lift this house's latch too poor
For hand of thine? and canst thou think and bear
To let thy music drop here unaware
In folds of golden fulness at my door?
Look up and see the casement broken in,
The bats and owlets builders in the roof!
My cricket chirps against thy mandolin.
Hush, call no echo up in further proof
Of desolation! there's a voice within
That weeps . . . as thou must sing . . . alone, aloof.

Illustration 4
Double page from "Sonnets from the Portuguese."
(From the General Collection, Library of Congress. Reprinted here with permission.)

Butterfly Press from 1907 to 1909 in Philadelphia.[47] Bertha Goudy, who operated the Village Press with her husband, Frederic Goudy, is fulsomely praised only in studies of her husband's life and work.[48]

Women book designers gained opportunities and recognition as the private press movement grew. In 1901, *The Craftsman* devoted a whole issue to book binding and printing. Women wrote the articles and it featured women's binderies along with the work of presses inspired again by Morris' Kelmscott Press. Helen Marguerite O'Kane designed books for the Elston Press, owned by her husband. She also worked for commercial presses. Ellen Gates Starr, a colleague of the social worker Jane Addams, was also a disciple of William Morris and shared his beliefs on art and socialism. Starr studied book design in England with T. Cobdon-Sanderson at the Doves Press and returned to Chicago to establish a bookbindery in the 1890s.[49] Helena De Kay Gilder is now remembered for one book cover: a gold peacock feather on a plain blue ground that captures the essence of the Aesthetic style.[50]

Modern historians regard the relative openness of the Arts and Crafts movement to women's participation in applied arts for their success in this field, but contemporary observers, even participants, ascribed their abilities to gender-specific skills. T. J. Cobden-Sanderson, Starr's teacher, is quoted as saying:

> [w]omen ought to do the best work in book-binding, for they possess all the essential qualifications of success: patience for detail, lightness of touch, and dexterous fingers.[51]

Alice C. Morse, an accomplished book cover designer, also claimed that women possessed an inherent ability:

47 Butterfly Press publishers were Margaret Hunter Scow, Alice Rogers Smith, Amy Margaret Smith, and George Wolfe. They edited *The Butterfly Quarterly* from 1907 to 1909. See Susan Otis Thompson, *American Book Design* and *William Morris*, (New York: R. R. Bowker, 1977), 206.

48 The exception is a profile in an exhibition catalog published by Women in Design, Chicago. *Ten Years: Women in Design Chicago Anniversary Exhibition 1988.* It is clear, however, that the authors were unable to determine the extent of Bertha Goudy's contribution to the design of books issued by the press.

49 Eventually her political commitment led Starr to abandon design for political activism. "If I had thought it through, I would have realized that I would be using my hands to create books that only the rich could buy." *Notable American Women*, op. cit., 352.

50 For a biographical sketch and extensive bibliography on De Kay, see *In Pursuit of Beauty*, op. cit., 418–419.

51 *The Craftsman*, 11,1 (April 1902), 33–34.

Women seem to have a remarkable faculty for designing. Their intuitive sense of decoration, their feeling for beauty of line and harmony of color, insures them a high degree of success."[52]

It is no coincidence that the Arts and Crafts Societies, that began in 1897, in Boston and New York, and spread to cities and towns in other parts of the country, were one of the few clubs to include women.[53] However, when the prestigious Society of Printers was founded in 1905 in Boston, no women were members. In 1911 fourteen men began "The Graphic Group" in New York, dedicated to the "highest in the art of printing." They later formed the nucleus of what became, in 1914, the American Institute of Graphic Arts.

Advertising Artists

Although women were immediately recognized as important targets for advertisers' messages, they were rarely mentioned in the early advertising journals as practitioners and are absent from advertising histories until the 1920s.[54] Information about women in the advertising industry appears fortuitously in advertising trade journals that were not sympathetic to them, but intermittently championed the work of individual women. More frustrating to the researcher are journal reports on design contests in which women's names appear regularly as winners, suggesting that there must have been a significant number of trained and employed women in the field.

With its very first issue in 1891, *Profitable Advertising* sounded the derisive note that it sustained throughout. Although somewhat incoherent, the ridicule and warning were impossible to ignore:

> *The Boston Globe* is encouraging women to become "writers on business," female "Powers," as it were; scientific experts, etc. O. General Taylor, this is too much. And offering prizes for advertisements, too, written by women! Great guns! there are about 6,946 male scientific advertising experts in the United States who will soon with Othello raise the very devil about their flown occupation. The result will be more disastrous than the female typewriter craze. Of course the women will cut rates. Boys, get together, formulate a union and boycott *The Globe*. Or start the women off on writing advertisements for pants. Would they succeed? Well, *would* they? They would find virtues in pants us poor males never dreamt of.[55]

Women's participation on the editorial staff of any trade journal was extremely rare and, given prevailing attitudes, even when they were present, editorial policy was not enlightened.[56] Kate E. Griswold began at *Profitable Advertising* as manager and became editor in October 1893. In June of that year, an article appeared that she may have written. Signed "Miss Progress," it was a diatribe against uniform wage scales. The writer acknowledges that women

52 Alice C. Morse, "Women Illustrators," *Art and Handicrafts in the Woman's Building of the World's Colombian Exposition.* Chicago 1893, ed. Maud Howe Elliot (Paris and New York: Goupil and Company, 1893), 75. There are several examples of work by women in Susan Otis Thompson's "The Arts and Crafts Book," *The Arts and Crafts Movement in America 1876–1916*, ed. Robert Judson Clark. (Princeton University Press, 1972), 93–116 and her *American Book Design*, op. cit. See also Wendy Kaplan. "The Art That Is Life" *The Arts and Crafts Movement in America, 1875–1920* (Boston: Little, Brown for the Museum of Fine Arts, 1987) for reproductions of work by women with extensive captions by Thompson.

53 For a history of the Boston group, see Mary Spain, *The Society of Arts and Crafts,1897–1924*, (Boston and New York: The Society, 1924).

54 Library terminology can also present difficulties. The subject heading "Women in advertising" retrieves material on women as subjects/objects of advertisements. "Women as professionals in advertising" is the relevant heading, but it pulls up very little material at present.

55 "Editorial Squibs," *Profitable Advertising* I,1 (June 1891), 9.

56 In addition to Kate Griswold, who eventually became publisher of *Advertising Experience*, several other women gained prominence in advertising management and journalism at the turn of the century. See "No Sex in Success?" *The Ad-School. A Practical Advertiser* I, 7 (July 1901), 11.

Illustration 5
Advertising designs by Beatrice Tonnesen. (From the General Collection, Library of Congress. Reprinted here with permission.)

have been limited in their professional opportunities in the past "but that day has gone."

> Oh, no, we are not ranting "women's righters" in the common acceptance of the term. We have no fondness for women who disgust men, as well as members of their own sex, by their arbitrary methods of attempting to secure what they are pleased to sum up as their "rights."[57]

Even when women's work was noticed, their achievements were attributed to their femininity. *Advertising Experience*'s February 1898 issue featured advertising photographers, Beatrice Tonnesen and her sister, Clara Tonnesen Kirkpatrick. In praising their work, the editors claimed: "[t]he fact that the Tonnesens are women photographers has no doubt made it possible for them to secure a better class and a larger selection of models that could be secured by a male photographer."[58]

Indeed, photography may have provided an entry for some women into advertising although there is very little research in this area. Photography was a fad in the 1890s and many of the women who began at the time preferred to remain "amateurs" devoted to personal artistic expression. We do know of some who did become professionals and worked in portraiture and photojournalism.[59] In a study from a feminist perspective, C. Jane Gover shows that from 1890 to 1920 photography was a profession adopted by economically secure women who found in it a measure of personal freedom and yet remained firmly tied to Victorian gender definitions:

> The camera provided women with the means of stepping beyond the private, domestic space. At the same time, the women's lifestyles and imagery sustained middle class ideology as it celebrated the domestic ideal and woman's place as nurturers.[60]

Unfortunately, Gover, like most photography historians, does not consider advertising photography, although she does mention Beatrice Tonnesen in other contexts.

Advertising posters also provided work for many illustrators, including a significant number of women. Ethel Reed is per-

57 "Women in the Business World," *Profitable Advertising,* III,1 (June 15, 1893), 37.

58 "Photography in Advertising," *Advertising Experience,* VI, 4 (February 1898), 24.

59 Clarence Bloomfied Moore,"Women Experts in Photography," *Cosmopolitan,* XIV, 5 (March 1893), 580–90. Although he was more interested in their aesthetics and most of the women appear to consider themselves "amateurs," some were involved in commercial photography. The best known, Frances Benjamin Johnston (1864–1952) sold her architectural and portrait work to magazines and periodicals. Moore coyly notes that "Cornelia J. Needles has been offered substantial sums 'by a prominent firm dealing in soap'"

60 C. Jane Gover. *The Positive Image. Women Photographers in Turn of the Century America* (Albany, NY: SUNY. 1988), xvii.

Illustration 6
"Folly or Saintliness," by Ethel Reed. (From the Prints and Photographs Division, Library of Congress. Reprinted here with permission.)

haps the most famous. For a short period, she designed book posters for the publisher Lamson, Wolffe and Company of Boston. She was the only woman to be the subject of a profile in *The Poster* magazine. Its author began this article with a lengthy dissertation of women's limited abilities in general and women artists' lack of artistry in particular.[61] He then praised Reed, because, she:

> knows well the marvelous secret of design and colours, and while she executes pictures with clever hands, she sees with her own and not masculine eyes; her work has feminine qualities, one sees in it a woman, full of sweetness and delicacy, and this is the greatest praise one can bestow upon a woman.[62]

Several other women first gained recognition as poster artists. Florence Lundborg of San Francisco designed a series of advertisements for *The Lark* as well as book illustrations and murals, Blanche McManus designed posters and illustrations for books and magazines and, in 1911, became art editor of *American Motorist*.[63] Helen Dryden designed posters, stage scenery, illustrated for magazine and worked as an industrial designer, including automobile designs for the 1937 Studebaker.[64]

Advertising art was rarely signed and, therefore it is difficult to identify the artist. Jessie Wilcox Smith, was an exception; her name appeared prominently on all of her work. She produced advertisements throughout her career for Campbell Soup, Eastman Kodak, and Ivory Soap. [Illustration 8: Kodak Advertisement] Helen Elna Hokinson, who later became famous for her *New Yorker* cartoons, designed advertisements for department stores in Chicago and New York.[65]

Graphic Arts, begun in 1911, profiled leading printers, designers, and advertising artists. In 1913, Elizabeth Colwell was the first and only woman to be featured.[66] Colwell, a Chicago designer, did publicity for Marshall Fields and for Cowan Company. She designed

61 S. C de Soissons, "Ethel Reed and her Art," *The Poster*, (November I898). 199–202.

One can understand that women have no originality of thought, and that literature and music have no feminine character, but surely women know how to observe, and what they see is quite different from that which men see, and the art which they put in their gestures, in their dresses, in the decoration of their environments is sufficient to give us the idea of an instinctive and peculiar genius which each of them possess. [199–200] It is interesting to compare this to another writer of the period who began his essay on women illustrators by claiming that until recently women only showed "intellectual achievement" in "the direction of literature, and the governing of kingdoms." Samuel G. W. Benjamin. *Our American Artist* (Boston: D. Lothrop, 1881. Reprint. New York: Garland, 1977). There was no agreement, apparently, on the exact nature and extent of female ability.

62 Ibid., 202.

63 Peneys, op. cit. For biographical material and examples of work by women poster artists, see Victor Margolin, *The American Poster Renaissance: The Great Age of Poster Design*, (New York: Watson-Guptill Publications, 1975), and Carolyn Keay, *American Posters of the Turn of the Century* (New York: St. Martins Press, 1975).

64 Ibid.

65 See *Notable American Women*, op. cit.. 201–202. The article about Hokinson also mentions her friend, Alice Harvey Ramsey, another designer and cartoonist. Edwina Dumm (1893–?) was the only syndicated female cartoonist of the period. She was responsible for "Cap Stubbs and Tippee," "Tippee," and "Alec the Great" and is included in Martin Sheridan, *Comics and Their Creators* (New York: Luna Press, 1944). See also Maurice Horn, *The World Encyclopedia of Comics* (New York: Chelsea House, 1976).

66 Alice Rouillier, "The Work of Elizabeth Colwell," *The Graphic Arts*, IV,4 (March 1913), 237–248.

Illustration 7
"The Lark," by Florence Lundborg.
(From the Prints and Photographs Collections, Library of Congress. Reprinted here with permission.)

Illustration 8
Kodak advertisement by Jessie Wilcox Smith.

bookplates and was known for her lettering and her work as a book designer. The editor, Henry Lewis Johnson, acknowledged:

> [i]t has been an axiom among designers, although just why it is hard to say, that women cannot do good lettering. Miss Colwell with many other women designers, offers direct proof to the contrary.[67]

From other sources we know that Colwell was a also a typographer and that she designed "Colwell Hand Letter."[68]

Helen Rosen Woodward, a pioneer in advertising, wrote an autobiography that gives an overview of the practice of advertising, as well as the sexism and anti-Semitism encountered by workers at the turn of the century.[69] When Woodward began in New York in 1903, agents were not only expected to plan campaigns, but to

67 Ibid., 237.

68 Petteys, op. cit.

69 Helen Woodward, *Through Many Windows*, (New York: Harper and Brothers, 1926. Reprint. New York: Garland, 1986).

Small Things
of the highest distinction at *small prices* are better than large things of no distinction. The moral–
Shop at
COWAN'S
Four floors full of the world's most notable objects of *Beauty and Usefulness*–the prices a marvel of moderation and sanity.
See for yourself.
W. K. Cowan & Co.
203-207 Michigan Ave.
The Fine Arts Building

Illustration 9
Examples of work by Elizabeth Colwell. (From the Prints and Photographs Division, Library of Congress. Reprinted here with permission.)

design ads, write copy, as well as hire and direct illustrators. At that time women earned $18 a week, men $25.[70] In 1926 she wrote:

> [t]he difference between the pay of men and women for the same work has largely disappeared in the advertising business but it is still hard for women to get positions where the bigger money lies.[71]

This was corroborated by Taylor Adams, who began his advertising career in the 1920s:

> Women began flowering in the creative departments of agencies in the '20s, but you could hardly have said they were prevalent. With a single outstanding exception, then were either temporary tokenists hired for specific tasks (such as "influencing" decision makers of client or prospect) or more often anonymous foot-sloggers who rarely made it to title or stockholder.[72]

In fact, the work of most advertising artists, male and female, was unsigned and ephemeral. And although trade magazines encouraged higher standards of composition, drawing, and typography, little is known about the people who created professional advertisements.

Illustrators

To the degree that the proponents of the Aesthetic movement and the Arts and Crafts movement broke down barriers between fine and applied art, they raised many of the crafts traditionally associ-

70 Ibid., 147. On this subject, Woodward, who initially resisted the suffragette message, wrote: "About 1909 the women began to change. In a few years the desire for the vote was nearly universal with them. That desire was focused by the suffrage propaganda, but it grew exactly as grew the self-respect of the women who worked. Their wages went up before the wish for suffrage came, not afterward."

71 Ibid., 102–103.

72 Taylor Adams, "Early Women in Advertising— All Uphill," *How It Was In Advertising 1776–1976* (Chicago: Cain, 1 976), 30.

ated with women to a new legitimacy. They also encouraged the establishment of schools to train women in the arts, although their motives here were not straightforward. Walter Smith, an English Arts and Crafts proponent who became Massachusetts State Director of Art Education, saw the arts as a way to divert women from their struggle to gain political power:

> We have a fancy that our lack of art schools and other institutions where women can learn to employ themselves usefully and profitably at work which is in itself interesting and beautiful, is one of the causes which drives them to so unsex themselves as to seek to engage in men's affairs. Give our American women the same art facilities as their European sisters, and they will flock to the studios and let the ballot-box alone.[73]

In the United States, the first applied art school for women began in Philadelphia at the behest of Sarah Peter, a wealthy philanthropist, under the auspices of the Franklin Institute. The School of Design for Women opened on December 3, 1850 with a class of 94 students and expanded rapidly.[74] The arguments for its establishment, found in the Franklin Institute proceedings, reflect the ideology of the Aesthetic movement: the legitimacy of the applied arts and women's contribution to them, the development of women's "natural" ability as related to her domestic life, and the non-threatening nature of women's contribution. Peter was very explicit. She wanted "to enlarge the sphere of female occupation" without endangering male employment and or upsetting women's traditional sphere:

> I selected this department of industry, not only because it presents a wide field, as yet unoccupied by our country men, but also because these arts can be practiced at home, without materially interfering with the routine of domestic duty, which is the peculiar province of women.[75]

The Institute's chairman expanded Peter's argument. Women are especially adept at decoration and, therefore this would not cause an economic problem:

> their quick perceptions of form and their delicacy of hand very especially fit them; while even should they, in these and similar branches of labor, finally supplant men entirely, no evil could occur, especially in a country like ours, where such broad fields for male labor lie entirely unoccupied. [76]

A large number of art schools for women, or open to women, were founded in the United States beginning in the 1870s.[77] Although women were allowed greater opportunities in art education, they were blocked from membership in artist clubs. Perhaps because illustrators did much of their work in isolation, they formed a large number of these groups and their importance cannot be

73 Walter Smith. *The Masterpieces of the Centennial International Exhibition Illustrated*, vol. 2 (Philadelphia: Gebbie & Barrie, 1877), 95–96. In this catalog of works appearing in the 1877 Centennial International Exhibition, Walter Smith praised Englishwomen for their expertise in needlework, a skill learned at new schools of applied design. I am indebted for this citation to Roger B. Stein, op. cit. 28–30. See also works by Callen, op. cit

74 *First Annual Report of the Committee on the School of Design for Women* (Philadelphia: The School, 1852). 2–4. A complete early history of the school can be found in T. C. Knauff, *An Experiment Training for the Useful and Beautiful* (Philadelphia: The School, 1922). The curriculum was divided into three departments: drawing (a basic course for all students), industrial design (including textile, wallpaper, oil clothe, carpet, and furniture design), and wood engraving and lithography (illustration for the arts, sciences and natural history). From its first year in existence, students obtained patents and sold their work to manufacturers and publishers.

75 *Proceedings of the Franklin Institute of the State of Pennsylvania, for the Promotions of the Mechanic Arts. Relative to the Establishment of a School of Design for Women* (Philadelphia: The Institute, 1850), 1.

76 Ibid., 5.

77 The importance of these institutions in graphic design education remains to be explored. The best sources I have found on early design education for women are Arthur D. Efland, *A History of Art Education: Intellectual and Social Currents in Teaching the Visual Arts* (New York: Teachers College Press, 1990), and Thomas Woody, *A History of Women's Education in the United States,* 2v. (New York: The Science Press, 1919) II, 75–80.

overestimated.[78] Many began as informal sessions for sharing work and evolved into social occasions for editors, printers, publishers, and other potential employers to meet with artists. In short, they provided opportunities for professional advancement. Although not specifically barred, women were not members. The Society of Illustrators, founded in 1901, had 96 members by 1911, all male, and four associate members, the most successful women illustrators of the time: Elizabeth Shippen Green, Violet Oakley, May Wilson Preston, and Jessie Wilcox Smith.[79] One of the few clubs for professional women artists was founded in 1897 in Philadelphia. Led by Alice Barber Stephens, an illustrator and teacher at the School of Design, and by Emily Sartain, an artist and director of the School, the Plastic Club provided the same kind of community and publicity that male illustrators had found so useful.[80]

In the 1880s and 1890s, the need for illustrations, for magazine covers and stories, outdoor advertisements, and popular fiction swelled as the number of periodicals, newspapers, and advertising posters grew. Technological developments such as steel-line engravings, the half-tone printing process, and four-color printing, combined with the growth of literacy to create a huge market for the mass circulation magazine and advertisings.[81]

Historians celebrated these decades as the Golden Age of Illustration. Three notable chroniclers of the time, Hopkinson Smith, Frank Weitenkampf, and Henry Pitz, included women illustrators in their discussions, but always grouped them together and then selected two or three for praise.

Hopkinson Smith was an illustrator and his *American Illustrators* was a dramatized account of the activities in New York illustrator clubs he frequented. In it he reviewed and praised American male illustrators and showed their work in beautiful reproductions. Since women were not members of the clubs, Smith mentioned them only in a review of the annual Water Color Society exhibition. While he made fun of most women artists ("their devotion to mild-eyed daisy and the familiar golden-rod standing erect in a ginger jar of Chinese blue...."), he allowed exceptions: Rosina

78 In New York City alone the following clubs were in operation: The Century, Lotus, Grolier, the Society of Illustrators, the Salmagundi Club (1871), the Tile Club 1877), and the New York Etching Club Many clubs and societies published their charters, constitutions, and membership lists. The only discussion I have found on the importance of illustrator's club occurs in James Best's *American Popular Illustration* (Westport, Conn.: Greenwood Press, 1984), chapter 5, "The Social and Artistic Context of Illustration."

79 Ibid., 120

80 Ann Barton Brown, Alice Barber Stephens, op. cit., 24–25. Stephens (1858–1932) studied at the Pennsylvania Academy of the Fine Arts and the Philadelphia School of Design for Women and began as a wood-engraver for Scribner's. For a contemporary view, see Julius Moritzen, "Alice Barber Stephens," *The Twentieth Century Home,* II, 5 (December 1904), 45–46.

Emily Sartain (1841–1927), also began as an engraver. See Ellen Goodman, "Emily Sartain: Her Career," *Arts Magazine* (May 1987), 61–65; Phyllis Peet, "Emily Sartain, America's First Woman Mezzotint Engraver," *Imprint* (Autumn 1984), 19–26; Phyllis Peet, "The Art Education of Emily Sartain," *Women's Art Journal* (Spring/Summer 1990), 9–15.

81 Conway is the subject of *That Red Head Gal: Fashions and Design of Gordon Conway 1916–1936,* (Washington, *D. C.:* American Institute of Architecture Foundation, 1980).

Emmett, Mary Hallock Foote, and Alice Barber Stephens.[82] Although they are praised, their work is not discussed or shown.

In American Graphic Art (1912), Weitenkampf also placed women illustrators in a separate category. Indeed, he remarked that the disruption of his chronological organization was "brought about by the convenient classification by sex."[83] And he, too, commended the work of Foote and Stephens. Weitenkampf believed that the illustrations of Howard Pyle's women design students "exemplify various possibilities resulting from the application of the female temperament to illustration"[84]

Many women illustrators did specialize in domestic subjects, and some, though not all, worked in a decidedly decorative style. Howard Pyle was not only a famous illustrator, but an equally important as a teacher at the Drexel Institute in Philadelphia and at his own school for professional illustrators at Chadds Ford, Pennsylvania. A third of his students at Chadds Ford were women.[85] Pyle himself used a dramatic, realistic approach to illustrating, as did many of his male students. Henry Pitz, in *The Brandywine Tradition* (1968), concluded that women were naturally drawn to another style and subject matter:

> The women artists, with a few exceptions, give the impression that they formed a consistent school some-what different from the men....Their almost unfailing sense of the decorative, a shared technique and their natural inclination toward feminine, homely, reposeful subjects are there in almost every picture.[86]

To what degree Pyle was responsible for the separate style and technique of his female students is uncertain. Oakley, Shippen, and Smith were all advanced pupils before they studied with Pyle,

82 Hopkinson Smith. *American Illustrators,* (New York: Scribner's, 1892). Rosina Emmett (Sherwood), once so popular, is now forgotten. Examples of her work are reproduced in Morse, op. cit. Mary A. Hallock Foote (1847–1938) was singled out for praise by almost every illustration historian but has received little serious attention. Foote, like Stephens, began her career in engraving and transferred to illustration; she studied with William J. Linton, the famous wood-engraver, at Cooper Union Institute of Design for Women. Although she spent most of her adult life in remote areas of the American West raising a family (her husband was a mining engineer), Foote wrote and illustrated 16 novels and contributed illustrations regularly to popular magazines on Western subjects. She is not, however, included among the *Fifty Western Illustrators,* a widely respected bibliographic reference by Jeff Dykes (Flagstaff, Ariz.: Northland. 1975). See *Notable American Women,* op. cit., 643–-645 and her autobiography. A *Victorian Gentlewoman in the Far West* (San Marino, Ca.: The Huntington Library, 1972), an astonishing document of hardship and disappointments told as a cheerful adventure.

83 Frank Weitenkampf, *American Graphic Art,* (NewYork: Holt, 1912. Reprint. Johnson Reprint, 1970), 189–90.

84 Ibid. Even modern references treat male and female illustrators differently. Walt and Roger Reed's *The Illustrator in America,* 1880–1980 (New York: Madison Square Press, 1984) is organized in a series of brief biographical sketches arranged by decade. Women are included, but their marital status and children, if any, are always mentioned. The men's entries, on the other hand, contain only professional information.

85 Rubinstein, *American Women Artists,* op cit., 159. Feminist art historians have written on the women artists of this area. See: Christine Jones Huber, *The Pennsylvania Academy and Its Women, 1850–1920* (Philadelphia: The Academy, 1974); Helen Goodman. "Women Illustrators of the Golden Age of American Illustration," *Woman's Art Journal,* (Spring/Summer 1987), 13–22; Charlotte Herzog, "A Rose by Any Other Name: Violet Oakley Jessie Wilcox Smith and Elizabeth Shippen Green," *Woman's Art Journal* (Fall 1993/Winter l994), 11–16.

86 Henry Pitz, *The Brandywine Tradition* (Boston: Houghton Mifflin, l969), 178.

Illustration 10
"Looking for Camp." by Mary Hailock Foote. (From the General Collection, Library of Congress. Reprinted here with permission.)

and they worked in proximity and supported each other professionally throughout their lives. One can also imagine that art directors encouraged a particular subject matter; illustrators then, as now, were classed as specialists in a particular genre.

Women illustrators from 1890 to 1910 were successful by any standards. Their work was published widely, they were known by name to the public in an age when popular illustrators were celebrities, and they supported themselves and their families. But in a 1912 newspaper article, "Qualities That make for Success in Women Illustrator," the author is clear what qualities gained women illustrators adherents:

> The field of illustration has been steadily widening for women since those days in the early 70s when Addie Ledyard's pictures of ideally pretty children with sweeping eyelashes won our young hearts and Mary Hallock Foote, whose quality of exquisite tenderness, rather than the strength of her drawing, brought her ardent admirers, was illustrating her own and other people's stories.[87]

Conclusion

Women graphic designers were allowed to work at jobs that took advantage of their culturally defined sex-specific skills. Since they had smaller hands, they were thought to be able typesetters. Their supposed affinity with the decorative and domesticity made them illustrators of women and children. They were encouraged to participate in those careers in which they did not threaten male economic advantage. When they ventured beyond those limits they were belittled, vilified, or "disappeared" from history.

It is clear that women participated in significant though not overwhelming numbers in all aspects of graphic design. Art and design schools were open to women or established specifically to train women. The prevailing ideologies during these periods, the

87 F. R Marshall, "Qualities That Make for Success in Women Illustrators," *Public Ledger*, Philadelphia, (December 15, 1912).

Aesthetic Movement and the Arts and Crafts Movement, elevated the status of applied arts, including the decorative and domestic arts, and allowed women to participate more fully. Nonetheless, women were still seen as having specific abilities associated with their gender. The exceptions proved the rule; historians who praised a chosen few were justified in ignoring the majority.

Since the graphic design process is a collective effort, and since women rarely headed advertising agencies, publishing houses, or magazines, their contributions are hard to document. The record of women's participation in early graphic design is meager unless the researcher goes beyond standard design histories to statistical studies, suffragette histories, documents and institutional histories of art and design schools and artists' clubs, and to the trade journals. A definitive history of women in graphic design, including the biographies and work of poorly known women, would right the balance. It would also provide a realistic view of the cultural, political, social and economic conditions in which graphic design began.

The author is grateful to Victor Margolin for his criticisms and advice on an earlier draft of this paper.

Section II

Design in the American Corporate Milieu

The Designers go to the Fair, I: Walter Dorwin Teague and the Professionalization of Corporate Industrial Exhibits, 1933–1940

Roland Marchand

The organizers of the 1933 Century of Progress Exposition in Chicago, recalling the tremendous attention that Henry Ford's operating assembly-line exhibit had commanded at the 1915 Panama Pacific Exposition, counted heavily on Ford's participation. And Ford fully intended to rejuvenate his assembly line for a triumphant 1933 encore. But Ford was preoccupied with other things in 1930 and 1931, including his own programs to end the depression and to enable industrial workers to regain the security of partial subsistence on the land. By the time he made up his mind to submit a proposal to the exposition board, General Motors had stolen a march on him and had gained approval for its own assembly-line exhibit. "Ford was furious," reports David Lewis, historian of Ford's public relations. In a fit of moral outrage at the theft of his idea, Ford walked out on the fair and launched his own, highly successful "Ford Exposition of Progress" in Detroit and New York City.[1]

When Chicago's Century of Progress reopened in 1934, however, the Ford Motor Company contributed the fair's biggest news stories. With an expenditure of over $2.5 million, the largest sum ever invested in a fair exhibit, Ford turned his delayed entrance into a grand gesture. The critics agreed that he "stole the show" in 1934, attracting 76.9 percent of all fair visitors to his exhibit and outdrawing the previous attendance leader, General Motors, by a two-to-one margin.[2]

Ford's grand entrance at Chicago marked a significant moment in the transformation of the corporate industrial exhibit. In place of an operating assembly line, Ford offered a massive "fair within a fair" of diverse features. That such an unlikely approach should have gained such media acclaim and made so striking an impact on observers was widely attributed to the man who had infused dramatic showmanship and a stylistic unity into this eclectic display—the industrial designer Walter Dorwin Teague. The Ford exhibit in 1934 ushered in a period of striking convergence between an increasing corporate sensitivity to public relations and the application of designers' expertise to display strategies. More than ever before, the great fairs became arenas for the public dramatization of corporate identities. By the time of the 1939 World's Fair in New York City, the advanced "production qualities" of the indus-

1 David L. Lewis, *The Public Image of Henry Ford* (Detroit: Wayne State University Press, 1976), 297; "The Reminiscences of Fred L. Black," 197 typescript of interview, 1954, Oral History Section, Ford Motor Company Archives, Edison Institute Dearborn, Michigan.

2 Lewis, *Public Image*, 298–301; F. L Black to Fred Campsall, June 30, 1934, Acc. 285, Box 1540, Ford Archives.

trial exhibits of the major corporations enabled them to overshadow both the amusement zone and the thematic exhibits as the "hit shows" of the fair.[3]

The expression "hit shows," liberally employed by Teague and his design firm as well as by the media, alerts us to an infrequently noted aspect of the convergence between designers and corporate executives in the 1930s and 1940s. Studies of the incorporation of high art and modern design into corporate identity campaigns and accounts of the enthusiastic corporate adoption of industrial design during this era often focus on three central issues in this merger: (1) the motives behind, and the extent of authenticity in, the aspirations of corporate leaders toward esthetic uplift; (2) the appropriateness of artistic modernism to corporate imagery; and (3) the threats to the artistic integrity of designers created by corporate imperatives.[4]

A focus on the rapid expansion of the designer's role in corporate industrial exhibits in the 1930s, however, reveals that their advocacy of esthetic modernism was not the only influence that they exerted upon big business. In their emergence as the producers of "hit shows" for industrial corporations, designers often promoted an orientation toward the cultural tastes of the masses as much as they did an adoption of the esthetic standards of high art. In this respect, they were already beginning to assert a role within the corporation that would later emerge as a central theme in the promotion of corporate design: the claim to having expertise on the "expectations and sensibilities" of ultimate consumers.[5] A very modest suggestion of such a claim had appeared in the late 1920s and early 1930s as designers exhorted manufacturers to overcome saturated markets through new designs that would stimulate consumer desires.[6] But the significant emergence of designers as experts on, and avowed spokespersons for, the needs and tastes of the masses stemmed from their involvement in the profusion of regional, national, and world's fairs that ensued between 1933 and 1940.

The starring role in fair design, ever since the mid-nineteenth-century origins of the great world's fairs, had been enjoyed by the architects. And even with the entrance of the professional designer in Chicago in 1933–34, it was the architect Albert Kahn, long noted for his modern, functional factory architecture, who designed and reaped the credit for the symbolic, gear-shaped Ford building (*figure 1*). But Walter Dorwin Teague, with full responsibility for the building's interior and the design of the exhibits, stepped forward to promote himself and his emerging profession. He reaped widespread publicity for his role in bringing drama and coherence to the Ford exhibit and was soon able to boast that "the guiding hand of the industrial designer" had transformed older exhibits of a "static conventional character" into "compelling displays that drew increased thousands on whom they left indelible impressions." He insisted again and again that it was the "internal exhibits," not the

3 The corporation exhibits, by some calculations, outpulled the Amusement Zone by an astounding margin of seven to one. See Market Analysis, Inc., "Third Attendance Survey of New York World's Fair," November 13,1939, 28–29, Box GA-2, folder 19, BF Goodrich Archives, University of Akron; "World's Fair - A Study of Circulation and Reactions," Acc. 146, Box 16, Ford Archives. For the use of the phrase "hit shows," see Martin Dodge to Edward Stettinius Jr., November 3,1939, reel 16:30A, Walter Dorwin Teague Papers, George Arents Research Library, Syracuse University.

4 James Sloan Allen, *The Romance of Commerce and Culture: Capitalism, Modernism and the Chicago-Aspen Crusade for Cultural Reform* (Chicago: University of Chicago Press, 1983), 23–24, 268–79;Jeffrey L. Meikle, *Twentieth Century Limited Industrial Design in America, 1925–1939* (Philadelphia: Temple University Press, 1979): *passim;* Arthur J. Pulos, *American Design Ethic: A History of Industrial Design to 1940* (Cambridge, Mass.: The MIT Press, 1983), 316–33, 396–411; Neil Harris, "Designs on Demand: Art and the Modern Corporation," in National Museum for American Art, *Art, Design and the Modern Corporation* (Washington, D.C.: Smithsonian Institution, 1985), *passim.* In his conclusion to *Twentieth Century Limited* (209–10), Meikle notes how closely designers came to approach advertising agents in their orientation.

5 See John Heskett, *Philips: A Study of the Corporate Management of Design* (New York: Rizzoli, 1989), 28, 43,155; and Jeffrey L. Meikle, *Design in the Contemporary World* (Stanford, Cal.: Pentagram Design, 1989),17, 65.

6 Meikle, *Twentieth Century Limited,* 14–18, 68–77.

architectural facades, that most significantly conveyed corporate messages to fairgoers. By 1937, the ascendance of exhibit over architecture found expression in this advertising agency description of the role of the industrial designer in corporate fair exhibits: "he first plans the exhibit and then clothes it in an appropriate building."[7]

For corporations, several significant transformations and quandaries accompanied this distinct shift from a predominant emphasis on fair architecture to an accent on the industrial displays themselves. The expression of corporate image through architecture had largely defied any calculated assessment; virtually the only measures of the effects of architectural "statements" were the responses of art and architecture critics and the comments of the cultural peers of corporate executives. Since the effects of architecture upon the public could be theorized but not measured, only the standards of high culture critics served as a check upon the personal tastes of corporate leaders. But the impact of specific industrial displays upon the public could be subjected to rough quantitative assessments. With the expensive corporate investments in such exhibits in 1933–34, attempts at such appraisals began in earnest. Not only did companies and survey associations keep careful counts of attendance at the major corporate displays, they also began to keep statistics on the sex and age of visitors, on the length of their stay at each feature of an exhibit, and even on elements of their behavior and conversations.[8]

As a result of such changes, the industrial designers who came into prominence in the creation of corporate displays proffered their services on the promise of providing two distinct qualities which were not entirely congruent. On the one hand, they asserted their authoritative understanding of the cardinal esthetic principles of proper line, proportion, color-harmony, and stylistic unity. But at the same time, in deference to the corporations' interests in measurable results, they also cast themselves as experts on public tastes and behaviors. From their rapidly accumulating experience, they claimed to know exactly what would attract and hold the attention of the public.[9] Whether the validity of eternal esthetic principles would find corroboration in stopwatch measures of the average attention spans of distracted fairgoers remained to be determined.

Thus, when Teague proclaimed in 1936 that a modern consciousness dictated that not merely the fair buildings, but the "industrial exhibits themselves . . . be works of art," it remained unclear what *manner* of "art" this would be.[10] In several exhibits at Chicago in 1933 and 1934, Teague and other designers had combined elegance, monumentality, and modernistic motifs to bestow an image of high-toned technological progressiveness upon companies such as the Norge Corporation and Bausch and Lomb.[11] But in exhibits like those Teague created for Ford in 1934—and for Ford and Du Pont at the Texas Centennial Exposition at Dallas in 1936—designers aspiring to their own conceptions of beauty and

7 Walter Dorwin Teague, "Designing Ford's Exhibit at a Century of Progress," *Product Engineering* (August 1934): 282, clipping in Acc. 450, Box 2, Ford Archives; "A Realist in Industrial Design," *Arts and Decoration* 41 (October 1934): 44–48; Walter Dorwin Teague, "Memo for Du Pont Presentation," (November 1936), n.p., reel 16:21A, Teague Papers. On Teague's emphasis on internal exhibits see Teague to William A. Hart, June 11, 1936, reel 16:32A and Teague to Robert Gregg, April 5,1937, reel 16:30A, Teague Papers. On the advertising agency comment, see BBDO Bulletin, May 19,1937, BBDO House Organs file, BBDO Archives, New York, N.Y.

8 A.W. Page, "Memorandum," November 14,1933, "The Bell System at A Century of Progress," 16–17; and S. L. Andre to A. W. Page, March 15, 1934, Box 1061, AT&T Archives, Warren, N.J.; Fred Black to Edsel Ford, June 9,1934, Acc. 285, Box 1540, Ford Archives; Rohe Walker, "Twenty-Two Million Gold Fish," Minutes of the Creative Staff Meeting January 3, 1934, 1–2, J. Walter Thompson Company Archives, New York (now located at Duke University); Ford Motor Company, "1934 Report on the Fair, "passim, Acc. 544, Box 4, Ford Archives; "Case History and Final Report, Texas Exhibit," Series II, part 2, Box 51, E. I. Du Pont de Nemours & Company Papers, Hagley Museum and Library.

9 For examples of these distinct claims to expertise, see Walter Dorwin Teague to Edsel Ford, June 14,1934, Acc. 6, Box 167, Ford Archives and Teague to William Hart, December 3,1935, Acc. 500, Series II, Box 53, Du Pont Papers.

10 Walter Dorwin Teague, "Industrial Art and Its Future," 3, typescript of address at School of Architecture and Allied Arts, New York, N.Y., November 18,1936, Box 79, Teague Papers.

11 *Advertising Arts* 4 (July 1933): 15, 18.

Figure 1
The gear motif of the 1934 Ford exhibit building evoked a sense of machine-age design and exemplified Teague's insistence on thematic unity. From the Collections of Henry Ford Museum and Greenfield Village Museum, Dearborn, Michigan.

Figure 2
Teague rendered the theme of Ford's 1934 exhibit in striking pictorial form without sacrificing its didactic intent. A Century of Progress Collection, Special Collections, The University Library, University of Illinois at Chicago.

Figures 4 & 5
Close-ups in the 1934 Ford photomurals worked to visualize employee dedication and "humanize" production. Repeated images estheticized the process and connoted a modernist sensibility. From the Collections of Henry Ford Museum and Greenfield Village.

Figure 3
Henry Ford cherished his River Rouge plant and the complex and monumental production it symbolized. In 1934 Teague employed the new technique of the photomural to attempt to bring the aura of Ford's factory to the fair. From the Collections of Henry Ford Museum and Greenfield Village.

Figures 6 & 7
While Teague strove for simplification and dramatic lighting in the 1936 Du Pont display in Dallas, he was still constrained to show the factories and instruct the audience. Hagley Museum and Library.

Figure 8
Ford's "animated mural" towered over visitors. Its gyrating and pulsating mechanisms and flashing lights sought to convey the aura of the factory and the dynamic power of the V-8 engine. From the Collections of Henry Ford Museum and Greenfield Village.

Figure 9
In Ford's 1939–40 "Cycle of Production" the old attempt to instruct visitors in the wonders of production was now animated in cartoon-like simplicity. (cp. figure 2). From the Collections of Henry Ford Museum and Greenfield Village.

Figures 10 & 11
Teague sought to retain the didactic impulse behind Ford exhibits while reaching the lowest common denominator of the audience with animated, Disney-like figures. From the Collections of Henry Ford Museum and Greenfield Village

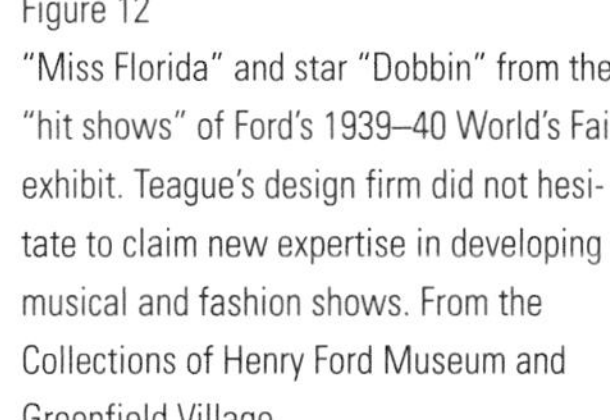

Figure 12
"Miss Florida" and star "Dobbin" from the "hit shows" of Ford's 1939–40 World's Fair exhibit. Teague's design firm did not hesitate to claim new expertise in developing musical and fashion shows. From the Collections of Henry Ford Museum and Greenfield Village.

Figure 13
Ever straining for simplicity and audience attention, Teague not only sought to eliminate "all technical details not familiar to the public" from Du Pont's 1939–40 "Wonder World of Chemistry" display, but added a puppet show. Hagley Museum and Library.

effectiveness in industrial displays had to contend with the limits placed on them by a variety of internal company tensions and by the powerful but prosaic notions of educational service held by some corporate leaders. It would offer a tidy conclusion to say that through successive adaptations between 1934 and 1939, the corporations and the designers developed a unified esthetic through which corporate identities were canonized in industrial exhibits. But the reality is that by 1939 several disparate and quite incongruous modes of presentation had merged. Even the most successful of these, General Motors's Futurama, gained its impact by providing an experiential adventure that transcended its educational thrust and esthetic impulses.

To examine the diverse strategies that emerged in the efforts to disseminate corporate identities through exhibit design, it is best first to return to Ford and Teague in 1934. What was Teague's challenge? How did he proceed in his attempt to impose the values of the designer on the exhibit of a company headed by a man so little attuned to artistic modernism? Unquestionably, Teague's major challenge was to work successfully within the conditions set by two of Henry Ford's preoccupations: his enchantment with his massive River Rouge factory, with all it symbolized of the production ethic; and his conception of himself as a model for, and educator of, the mechanically minded common man.

Henry Ford attributed the inspiration underlying his development of an internal combustion engine to his experience as a young man at the Columbian World's Exposition of 1893, when he had observed several small gasoline-powered water pump motors in operation. It gratified his sense of paternalism and public service to view his company's industrial exhibits as providing similar stimulation to deserving young men of the next generations.[12] Thus Ford's guidelines for his 1934 extravaganza were simple. "I want an exhibit that is educational and will show people how we do things." He added, "Make plenty of places for people to rest."[13]

Ford's son Edsel, to whom he relegated most of the authority over exhibit planning, was far more esthetically inclined and attuned to artistic modernism than Ford. But, in his more sophisticated way, Edsel also welcomed public recognition as an educator and could not ignore the accolades that he (and, mostly, his father) received from such publications as the *Literary Digest* and the *New York Times* for playing "schoolmaster" to the millions at the 1934 fair. (One of Ford's suppliers, the Aluminum Company of America, was so taken with the education imagery that it declared the 1934 Ford exhibit a "great schoolroom where the textbooks are to be the machines, ores, and men who produce the materials for the Ford car.") Through 1939, both father and son continued to emphasize the educational qualities of all the Ford exhibits.[14]

The 1934 Ford exhibit contained five major elements: (1) an immense rotunda which told the "Ford drama of transportation"

12 "Young Henry Ford went to the Fair," brochure, 1939, Acc. 544, Box 21, Ford Papers; Black, "Reminiscences," 198. The conventional exclusion of young women from this vision coincided with the assumption by Ford, and nearly every other industrial exhibitor, that fair exhibits could be more "serious" than many advertisements because the industrial display was a form of "man-to-man" communication.

13 Black, "Reminiscences," 193.

14 *Literary Digest,* August 18,1934, 6; Lewis, *Public Image,* 299; *New York Times,* May 16, 1934, 14; *New Outlook,* 164 (September 1934): 56; Fred Black to Frank Campsall, July 23,1934, August 25, 1934, August 29, 1934, Acc. 285, Box 1540, Ford Archives; *The Alcoa News,* May 28 1934, 4; San Francisco *Chronicle,* February 26,1939, A4.

through a striking photomural and a display of 67 vehicles from the times of ancient Egypt to the present; (2) an Industrial Hall, with exhibits of manufacturing processes by many of Ford's suppliers; (3) an Industrial Barn, with a soybean processing display; (4) a Ford Museum, which included Ford's original Bagley Avenue workshop; and (5) the Ford Gardens, including a symphony terrace and amphitheater and a "Roads of the World" feature where visitors could be driven over replicas of 100-foot segments of nineteen famous highways of the past and present. Teague also designed a private, second-floor lounge in the building for Ford executives, winning kudos from *Arts and Decoration* magazine for developing a "(b)ackground for masculine hospitality," an atmosphere of comfort, rationality, and "workability" where Ford's managers could escape the noise and overstimulation of the "glorified factory atmosphere conveyed by the Ford exhibits below."[15]

Reflecting his increasing fixation on restoring the worker's links with the land as a way of preventing the ills of economic depressions and his continuing cultivation of a rural constituency for his products and ideas, Henry Ford decreed that the central precept of his exhibit must be: "Man must go to the Earth for all Materials" (*figure 2*). This theme not only incorporated the major lesson of the "industrial barn"—the promise of soybeans as a crop through which farmers could prosper by supplying materials for auto production—it also dictated that the displays would conform to a well-developed convention that corporations could best win public favor by impressing fair visitors with the scope, difficulty, efficiency, and almost-miraculous results of their processes of production. Although Ford had been thwarted in his intention to display again an operating assembly line, as he had at San Francisco in 1915, his new theme bolstered a penchant that he shared with many other industrial exhibitors: the instinct to use the fair exhibit as a substitute for a time-honored public relations stratagem—the visit to the factory.[16]

Given these directives and constraints, Teague labored to infuse dramatic impact and an aura of modernity into the displays. He lectured Edsel Ford that unity was central to "all good design" and, through patterns of spatial organization, graphic and visual consistency, and color coordination, he claimed to have brought a "great number of varied elements . . . into harmony." In the Industrial Hall, a wing of the exhibit estimated by one reporter to be "the size of two football fields," Teague organized exhibits of production processes from scores of suppliers of basic materials to Ford. He selected only those processes of each that could most dramatically be displayed through dioramas, photographic montages, miniature models, and, above all, full-scale working displays.[17]

For the circular wall on the inside of the immense entrance rotunda, Teague developed the world's largest photomural to depict

15 *Literary Digest*, August 18,1934, 6; Lewis, *Public Image*, 299; *Arts and Decoration* 41 (October 1934): 35, 44, 47–48.

16 Walter Dorwin Teague, "Designing Ford's Exhibit at a Century of Progress," 282; "Out of the Earth," (pamphlet) and "Man must go to the Earth for all Materials," souvenir box for mailing, folder 16-269, Century of Progress Papers, University of Illinois, Chicago.

17 Walter Dorwin Teague to Edsel Ford, June 14,1934, Acc. 6, Box 167, Ford Archives; *New Outlook* 164 (September 1934): 59.

production activities at Ford's River Rouge factory plant *(figure 3)*. *Literary Digest* characterized it as "representing a trip through a modern automobile plant." Of "astounding size and technical perfection," this two-story, 600-foot-long selective representation of the dynamism, worker dedication, and modernistic beauty of the Ford plant set the tone and established the context for all the subsidiary exhibits. Interspersed between the huge panels of the mural, in large chromium letters, appeared a series of maxims that conveyed moral and political messages. "The recovery we need is of our American spirit of independence," read one. "With one foot on the land and one in industry, America is safe," another announced reassuringly. The combined effect of the "greatest photographic panorama ever built" and these "ringing aphorisms, below which no signature appears and for which none is needed," according to observers, was "that of Gibraltar giving voice to a battery of guns."[18]

An emphasis on production and on the factory characterized even the most frivolous element of the Ford exhibit: a film entitled *Rhapsody in Steel.* Although Ford publicity brochures frankly characterized this cartoon movie as "an amusing fantasy" in which a whimsical "Ford imp" cast a magical spell over "a staid collection of parts," inducing them to engage in supernatural pranks and carry out a "dance of the connecting rods," the brochures also noted that the film provided viewers a clear impression of the magnitude of the company and its plans and an appreciation for the various operations in the construction of a Ford car. The imp carried out its pranks "(a)gainst the serious background of the drafting room, . . . the laboratories, foundries and shops" the company solemnly announced, and the musical score, which sought to reproduce "sound effects incident to the building of the Ford V-8 car," had actually been composed in the River Rouge plant.[19]

If such an appeal to the visitors' simple thirst for entertainment did not harmonize esthetically with Teague's larger unities of design, still it exemplified a different "unity" noted by observers of the Ford display. This was the absence of "selling pressure" at any point in the exhibit. Sensing, as did an increasing number of other major corporations, that exhibits at major fairs might better be employed for broad public relations purposes than as magnified selling booths, Ford created an atmosphere in which, according to *New Outlook*, "the usual ballyhoo of salesmanship is strangely and satisfyingly missing." As its representatives at the fair, the company employed neither its own plant personnel nor experienced salespeople, but college students. They were enthusiastic and personable but would not exert "selling pressure," and were therefore best for dealing with the public.[20]

Such an approach coincided with the tone of service and high educational seriousness that characterized the "glorified factory atmosphere" of most of the Ford exhibit. Visitors were even encouraged to disseminate the exhibit's production-oriented theme

18 *Literary Digest,* August 18, 1934, 6; *New Outlook* 164 (September 1934): 59; H. D. Morrow, "The Ford Proposition," (1934), Acc. 450, Box 2, Ford Papers.

19 Ford Motor Company, "Ford at the Fair," (booklet, 1934), folder 16-269, Century of Progress Papers.

20 *New Outlook* 164 (September 1934): 56; Black, "Reminiscences," 194.

of "going to the earth for all materials" by taking home or mailing small-sectioned boxes, covered with cellophane, in which tiny samples of a dozen of the earth's basic materials—from iron ore and bauxite to cork and soybeans—were neatly compartmentalized and labeled for the collector's edification.[21] Ford handouts stressed the artistic beauty of the dioramas, but they also dutifully explained that wherever it had not been possible to show the actual manufacturing processes mechanically, photographs, dioramas, and lectures had been developed to bridge these gaps and provide visitors with a full explanation.[22]

In such an exhibit, where selective and partial demonstrations of productions processes had replaced the full assembly line, graphic artists like Teague emerged as important figures in simplifying and romanticizing the processes of manufacture (*figures 4 and 5*). The power and virtuosity of their designs aimed at enfolding the company image within a high-toned aura of quality and service. As consultants to the corporations, the new professional designers almost invariably found themselves on the side of the head office and its interests in a unified image as opposed to the more diffuse and insular concerns of the product and geographical divisions.[23] They also invariably lined up on the side of the public relations department, with its long-range concern for corporate reputation, as against the sales department, with its concern for quick results. The concurrent appearance at Ford of a professional design consultant and a de-emphasis on sales pressure at the fair was no mere coincidence.

A series of major regional fairs ensued in the wake of the Century of Progress Exposition: at San Diego in 1935, at Dallas in 1936, and at Cleveland in 1936. Meanwhile, preparations had begun in earnest for world's fairs in New York and San Francisco in 1939. Teague designed the Ford exhibits for all of these fairs, as well as for the Texaco exhibit at Dallas, the Du Pont exhibits at Dallas and New York, and the United States Steel, Eastman Kodak, National Cash Register, and Consolidated Edison exhibits in New York. He also served on the official Design Board for the New York World's Fair. Other designers joined the exhibit bandwagon, but Teague dominated the field and aggressively solicited new contracts on the basis of his rapidly acquired experience.

Teague's firm increasingly described the nature of its expertise with such terms as "visual dramatization" and "industrial showmanship." In soliciting the business of United States Steel, Teague proposed that he should not only specify the details of the company's exhibit, but should be engaged in "the fundamental work of determining what your exhibit should be." In this initiative, he moved energetically to establish a more responsible position for the designer than he had attained, for example, with Bausch and Lomb in 1933, when he had been appointed simply "to work out the details . . . from the artistic point of view." Teague's design firm claimed in 1936 that it had already devised methods of dramatizing a company's message

21 *Arts and Decoration* 41 (October 1934): 35; "Man must go to the Earth for all Materials," folder 16-269 Century of Progress Papers.

22 "Ford at the Fair," folder 162–69, Century of Progress Papers; H. D. Morrow, "The Ford Exposition," Acc. 450, Box 2, Ford Archives; Teague, "Designing Ford's Exhibit," 282–83.

23 In 1937, Teague called attention of United States Steel to its potential mistake in attributing one of its proposed displays at the 1939 New York World's Fair to the American Bridge Company simply because that subsidiary had made all the contracts for the display. United States Steel, not one of its subsidiaries, should take the public relations' credit, Teague advised. Teague to J. C. MacDonald, August 2,1937, reel 16:30A, Teague Papers.

visually in such a way "that the average visitor cannot escape its import." Like others who had carefully studied visitors' reactions at the 1933–34 fair, Teague had quickly concluded that more exhibits must include animation and some form of visitor participation. He also explored the effects of interior lighting, proposing to Edsel Ford the use of dimly lit halls for the entrance to Ford's Dallas exhibit so that the main exhibition hall and its dioramas would seem "brilliantly lighted" by comparison. Above all, Teague preached the message of greater unity and radical simplicity.[24]

But despite his aspirations to enhance design esthetics and effectiveness through simplification, Teague often still found himself constrained by the pressures from a company's decentralized divisions. At the Texas Centennial Exposition in 1936, all of the divisions of the Du Pont Company insisted on being represented in the display. Teague reluctantly included aerial depictions of all of the Du Pont factories and found himself compelled to tell more numerous and complex stories of product development than he wished *(figure 6)*. Teague took pride in having "systematized" the Du Pont story for the public, but urged that future Du Pont exhibits "carry the process of simplification still further" and completely abandon the idea of telling the entire story of Du Pont activities. The route toward even greater public impact, he insisted, involved the "complete elimination of technical details not familiar to the public, with the whole complex process reduced to a few dramatic steps."[25]

Contrary to the entrenched assumptions of the production-minded executives at Du Pont, Teague implied, the central purpose of corporate fair exhibits was not the technical education of the masses. Rather, their purpose was to "educate" visitors in the beneficial social and economic services performed for them by Du Pont. Chaplin Tyler, rapidly emerging as Du Pont's in-house expert on exhibits, concurred that the 1936 experience had confirmed the idea that "the object of the exhibit is to educate the public regarding the company as an institution." For that kind of education, Teague argued, simple dramatic gestures would serve better than detailed explanations. Moreover, Teague suggested to Du Pont in 1937, emphasis on the processes on which past achievements had been based would appeal less to the average citizen's thirst for glamour and novelty than would visions of the potential marvels of chemical research.[26]

The official theme of the 1939–40 New York World's Fair, the "World of Tomorrow," further promoted this futuristic emphasis and encouraged the promulgation of corporate identity through the dramatic, symbolic gestures that Teague favored. Initially, Teague had envisioned a "key statement" at the Du Pont exhibit entrance in the form of "a mounted Crusader, displaying the Du Pont oval as his shield . . . strikingly painted." The crucial element of motion could be injected through "flashing electric effects, the object being to create an impression of onward invincible action." Ultimately,

24 M. Poser to John Stephen Sewell, July 5, 1932, folder 1-1426, Century of Progress Papers; Walter Dorwin Teague to Robert Gregg, April 5,1937, reel 16:30A, Teague, "Memo for Du Pont Presentation," reel 16:21A, Teague Papers; Teague to Edsel Ford, December 28,1935, November 25, 1936, Acc. 6, Box 337, Ford Archives; Oversized Scrapbook, Acc. 77.242, Du Pont Photographic Archives, Hagley Library; "Suggestions for Rebuilding 'The March of Chemistry'," 7, Series 11, part 2, Box 51, Du Pont Papers.

25 Walter Dorwin Teague to Carl J. Hasbrouck, June 22, 1936, Teague to William A. Hart, June 22, 1936, reel 16:21A, Teague Papers; Teague Drawings, Series 11, pt. 2, Box 55 Du Pont Papers; Oversized Scrapbook, Acc. 77.242, Du Pont Photographic Archives.

26 Walter Dorwin Teague to William A. Hart, June 22, 1936, January 4, 1937, Teague to Carl J. Hasbrouck, June 22, 1936; Teague, "Memo on Du Pont Presentation," reel 16:21A, Teague Papers; Chaplin Tyler, "Visit to Texas Centennial Exposition," in Tyler to Charles K. Weston, July 1936, 2, Box 51, Series 11, part 2, Du Pont Papers.

Teague would devise more futuristic ways for the corporation to make a dramatic gesture. Entrance murals, composed entirely of Du Pont materials, depicted the story of an "ever-expanding frontier opened up by research" while a symbolic tower of dramatic height called attention to the Du Pont building from a wide area of the fairgrounds (*figure 7*). Dubbed the "Tower of Research" by Teague, this 100-foot-high structure, composed of abstract forms representing the apparatus for chemical reduction, sought to give colossal iconic status to shapes that symbolized chemistry in action and linked research to futuristic images. Teague added the crucial element of motion through pulsing lights and rising bubbles.[27]

The concept of a striking, symbolic entrance exhibit also governed Teague's design for the 1939 Ford exhibit. Visitors to the Ford building were greeted by what the company's advertising agency called "the crowning feature of the whole exhibit," an immense, 70-foot-high "activated" mural. Constructed in three dimensions, with pistons, crankshafts, and connecting rods protruding, this mural featured whirling gears, pumping pistons, and flashing lights (*figure 8*). Its purposes, as variously described by its creator and Ford press releases, were to give visitors a "vivid picture" of the operations of Ford factories and to symbolize the relationships between mass production, modern technology, and pure science. According to Henry Billings, the mural's creator, it was intended "not to instruct but to impress." On some visitors, at least, that was its effect. So awed was the fair's director of science and education that he hailed it as an "altarpiece of science."[28]

For all of this impulse toward artistic abstraction and symbolic unity, however, Teague's displays for Ford and Du Pont were highly eclectic; their only significant "unity" lay in their public relations intent. Teague was quite accurate in forecasting, late in 1938, that the corporations would virtually abandon direct selling at the New York World's Fair and "throw the entire emphasis of their shows upon the social and economic services they perform for the country." But these corporate "shows," which Teague characterized as "spectacular almost to the point of solemnity," did not necessarily depend upon fundamental esthetic principles for their effect. And what Teague chose to call their "solemnity" lay less in any educational seriousness than in their efforts to evoke awe and gratitude by conveying the great efforts the companies had expended in creating them.[29]

At Ford, for instance, Teague applied his strategy of radical simplification while ostensibly complying with the insistence of Henry and Edsel Ford on an exhibit with educational qualities. The theme of the exhibit was still the almost-miraculous processes by which Ford produced cars from diverse natural materials. But many of the earlier full-scale working models were eliminated in favor of the use of a massive, animated cyclorama to depict manufacturing processes. Dubbed the "Cycle of Production," the Ford cyclorama

27 *Du Pont Magazine* 32 (November 1938): 11; *Life,* August 7, 1939, 4; Walter Dorwin Teague, typescript of essay "to be submitted to NY. Times, Vogue, WHC . . .": circa April 3,1940, reel 16:34A, Teague Papers; Outline for Extension of "Wonder World of Chemistry" (1939), Acc. 77.242, Du Pont Photographic Archives. Teague assured Du Pont's director of public relations that there were "scientific rules" that could be embodied in the use of color and form for shaping the opinion of the vast "uninitiated" public, for whom chemistry was "a subtle and mysterious science." Teague to Theodore Joslin, May 23, 1939, reel 16:21A, Teague Papers.

28 *Ayer News File,* February 10, 1939, 1–2; April 12,1939, 2; N. W. Ayer & Son Archives, New York; "Beauty of its Whirling Gears Attracts Throngs to World's First Mobile Mural," press release, May 13,1939, Acc. 544, Box 14; Henry Billings, "Report on Mural Decorations for Entrance Hall," typescript, n.d., Acc. 544, Box 1, Ford Archives.

29 *Advertising* and *Selling* 31 (October 1939): 32.

consisted of a 30-foot-high, rotating turntable (likened by one observer to a huge wedding cake) which displayed 87 groups of animated carved figures of men and animals with "humorous details . . . added through plastic noses, eyes, horns, and tails" (*figure 9*). While a recorded sound track intoned ponderous messages about the wonders of mass production at Ford, these figures (workers supplemented by other "amusing" human interest characters to achieve "an emotional effect") demonstrated the processes of production from raw materials through their animated motions. (Examples included "a cowboy riding a horse and throwing a lariat; cotton picking, with little pickaninnies playing among the bales . . . a miner trying to get a stubborn donkey down a steep hill" *[figures 10 and 11]*.)[30] In such form did"education" and esthetic unity persist in the face of Teague's increasing sensitivity to presumed audience tastes and capacities and his drive for radical simplification and abstraction.

Even more divergent from any central esthetic harmony were the theatrical shows and movies that constituted central elements in the Ford exhibits at New York in 1939 and 1940. In a technicolor movie (*Melody in F*), the animated figures of the Ford Cycle of Production came to life and told the story of Ford production in cartoon form. Meanwhile, Teague turned to a live musical drama and ballet to recount the history of transportation, as seen through the eyes of "Dobbin," the droll, obsolescent horse (*figure 12*). Visitors to the Ford exhibit were thus able to place the development of auto technology in context; its history "unfolded hilariously" in a show that Teague himself described as having "a fantastic, Walt Disney quality."[31]

At Du Pont, also, Teague implemented the strategy of an eclectic variety of displays to maximize the possibilities for gaining and holding the attention of undiscerning and distracted fairgoers. Warning Du Pont executives against "(s)tuffiness in either policy or appearance," he supplemented the more "solemn" and artistic symbols of corporate identity and the demonstrations of chemical processes with such light entertainment features as a marionette show (to show off Du Pont textiles through fashions) and a magic trick in which Miss Chemistry of 1940, "clothed from head to foot in the products of chemical research," was "made to appear from an apparently empty test tube of 'Lucite' plastic, as if she herself, in addition to her costume and accessories, had been created by chemistry" (*figure 13*). In 1940, Teague abandoned the marionette shows in favor of a "dramatic spectacle" with "innovations in stagecraft" never before employed. He thus helped to fulfill his own 1938 forecast that the fair would be characterized by specially designed theaters for single productions to be "staged with care and imagination that should make the best of Hollywood respectful."[32]

By 1940, Teague had come to describe the expertise that he offered corporations in the creation of industrial displays more in terms of showmanship than of design. He even established a new

30 Morton Eustis, "Big Show in Flushing Meadows," *Theatre Arts Monthly* 23 (August 1939), 576; Edward Mabley to Fred Black, September 23, 1938, Acc. 1109, Box 7, Ford Archives; N. W. Ayer & Son, "Ford Cycle of Production, 1940, revised," (enclosure to H. L. McClinton to Fred Black, June 18, 1940), Acc. 544, Box 21, Ford Archives.

31 W. H. Beatty to George Pierrot, April 3, 1939, Acc. 1109, Box 7, and "45 Minute Show Built for 1940 Fair," press release, Acc. 554, Box 21, Ford Archives; Edward Mabley, "Transportation Pageant," typescript, October 19, 1937, and Walter D. Teague, "Ford Exposition, 1940," reel 16:23A, Teague Papers.

32 Walter Dorwin Teague to Theodore Joslin, May 23, 1939, reel 16:21A, Teague Papers; "Du Pont Presents the Wonder World of Chemistry." Acc. 77.242, and 72.341.76, Du Pont Photographic Archives; Du Pont "The 1940 Wonder World of Chemistry," brochure, Box 1005, New York World's Fair Collection, New York Public Library; The Psychological Corporation, "A Study of Visitors' Reactions," Series 11, part 2, box 34, Du Pont Papers; *Advertising and Selling* 31 (October 1938): 32.

"Industrial Showmanship" department in his design firm to produce commercial films and "playlets" for such occasions. Although he continued to assume the existence of an esthetic "rightness" and to stress such fundamental esthetic principles as "balance and symmetry," "unity," and "rhythm of line and form" in his 1940 volume, *Design this Day*, Teague spoke a different language in his bids to design fair displays. There, Teague merchandised himself on the basis of his sensitivity to mass audiences and his capacity to provide them with the "visual dramatizations" they would enjoy.[33]

Teague was not alone in subsuming design within the category of showmanship at the 1939–40 New York World's Fair. Raymond Loewy designed Chrysler's bid for mass popularity as a "five star show" entitled "Sixty Minutes of Magic" and developed a simulated rocket trip to London as its central feature. Drawing upon his experience in stage design and his flair for theatricality, Norman Bel Geddes topped them all with his experiential "Futurama" ride for General Motors, in which visitors in moving chairs enjoyed a simulated airplane ride over an elaborate model of a superhighway system and a city of the future. And, despite the pretentiousness of his claim to have envisioned the United States of 1960 for fair visitors, Bel Geddes insisted that the Futurama was intended primarily as entertainment rather than for education.[34]

While the designers continued to refer occasionally to the esthetic qualities of certain features of their fair exhibits and some manufacturers, especially Henry and Edsel Ford, continued to assert the primacy of education in their displays, the major effect of the participation of industrial designers in creating fair exhibits had been to imbue them with the same concerns with, and attitudes toward, mass audiences that many producers for the mass media had earlier developed. They were impressed by the short attention spans of fairgoers, their seeming inability to comprehend or take an interest in any but the most simplified explanations, and their restless search for sensation, vicarious experience, and animated displays.

As many corporations during this era looked increasingly to their research laboratories rather than their factories to impress the public with their competence to serve the public in the future, the designers saw themselves challenged by the task of conveying an ever-more-complicated corporate reality to a seemingly more heterogeneous, less comprehending public. Too ambivalent in their purposes to choose either the symbolic abstractions of esthetic modernism or the trivialities of popular showmanship as a unified strategy, many designers gravitated pragmatically toward such eclectic displays as those of Teague for Ford and Du Pont in 1939.

In this arena, what had proved to be most "modern" by 1939–40 was not so much the artistic styles of the industrial designers but the imperatives to appeal to popular tastes that underlay the public relations efforts of major corporations. Baffled by what they perceived as public scorn and distrust during this depression

33 Walter Dorwin Teague, *Design This Day: The Technique of Order in the Machine Age* (New York: Harcourt Brace, 1940), vii, 5, 98–111, 162–74, 191–205 .

34 "What to See Today at the Chrysler 5-Star Show: 60 Minutes of Magic," flyer (May 1939), Vol. 330, T. J. Ross Scrapbooks, Ivy L. Lee Papers, Princeton University; *Chrysler Motors Magazine* 6 (June 1940): 6; Norman Bel Geddes, untitled memo beginning "The Proposed Exhibit . . .," *circa* April 7,1938,14, file 381 (correspondence), Norman Bel Geddes Papers, University of Texas, Austin.

decade and often engaged in expanding their offerings of consumer goods, the corporations were desperately seeking both the trade and the goodwill of the "common man." If designers could contribute a little to these causes through the design of new products and packages, they were pressed to fulfill these corporate needs even more when they were commissioned to design fair exhibits.

In that respect, the most "modern" thing designers could do in the 1930s was to educate themselves in public tastes, behaviors, and capacities in order to understand them and find ways to respond to them. If they sought to attune corporate executives to esthetic modernism and cultural uplift in some aspects of their service, the designers also, in their capacity as experts on exhibits, acted to wean manufacturers away from "stuffiness," technical education, tedious didacticism, and a fixation on their factories. Thus, in his rapid adoption of the credos of the "visual dramatization," the "key statement," the dramatic gesture, and the eclectic "hit show"—as well as in the style of his specific industrial designs—Walter Dorwin Teague exemplified a certain thrust toward the modern.

The Designers go to the Fair, II: Norman Bel Geddes, The General Motors "Futurama," and the Visit to the Factory Transformed

Roland Marchand

During the 1930s, the early flowering of the industrial design profession in the United States coincided with an intense concern with public relations on the part of many depression-chastened corporations.[1] Given this conjunction, it is not surprising that an increasingly well-funded and sophisticated corporate presence was evident at the many national and regional fairs that characterized the decade. Beginning with the depression-defying 1933–34 Century of Progress Exposition in Chicago, major corporations invested unprecedented funds in the industrial exhibits that also marked expositions in San Diego in 1935, in Dallas and Cleveland in 1936, in Miami in 1937, and in San Francisco in 1939. The decade's pattern of increasing investments in promotional display reached a climax with the 1939–40 World's Fair in New York City.

Leaders in the new field of industrial design took advantage of the escalating opportunities to devise corporate exhibits for these frequent expositions. Walter Dorwin Teague led the way with his designs for Bausch & Lomb, Eastman Kodak, and the Ford Motor Company for the 1933–34 exposition in Chicago. In 1936 he designed the Ford, Du Pont, and Texaco exhibits at Dallas and three years later claimed responsibility for seven major corporate exhibits at the New York World's Fair—those of Ford, Du Pont, United States Steel, National Cash Register, Kodak, Texaco, and Consolidated Edison. While Teague won an impressive number of design contracts for 1939 on the basis of his claim to have developed an ability to create "hit shows" for earlier fairs, the unrivaled "smash hit" among corporate displays at the 1939–40 fair was not one of Teague's creations. Rather, it was the "Futurama" of the General Motors Corporation, created by Norman Bel Geddes as his first corporate fair exhibit.[2]

Bel Geddes was unique among the major industrial designers of the 1930s in having entered the field from a background primarily devoted to theater design.[3] In contrast to Teague, whom one journalist characterized as "self-contained," "realistic," and thus a "comforting fellow to . . . practical-minded business men," Bel Geddes was often viewed as an "impractical visionary." Although Bel Geddes claimed to be the equal of other industrial designers in appreciating the values and decision-making processes of practical

1 I am indebted to the American Council of Learned Societies and the University of California-Davis Humanities institute for fellowship support during the time when much of the research for the two essays on "The Corporation Goes to the Fair" was completed. Ms. Edith Lutyens Bel Geddes kindly granted me permission to make use of the rich and copious Norman Bel Geddes Papers at the Harry Ransom Humanities Research Center at the University of Texas, Austin, where H. K. Crain, Prentiss Moore, and Melissa Miller-Quinlan provided me with valuable assistance in exploring the collection. I wish to thank Jeffrey Meikle and Michael L. Smith for their helpful critiques of an earlier draft of this essay.

2 On Teague's claim to have acquired the experience to produce "hit shows," see Martin Dodge to E. Stettinius Jr., November 3, 1939, reel 16:30A, Walter Dorwin Teague Papers, George Arents Research Library, Syracuse University. The accolade "smash hit" appeared in Morton Eustis, "Big Show in Flushing Meadows," *Theatre Arts Monthly* 23 (August 1939): 568 and in the *Reynoldsburg* (Ohio) *Press*, August 31, 1939, clipping file, Norman Bel Geddes Papers, Theatre Arts Collection, Harry *Ransom* Humanities Research Center, University of Texas, Austin, by permission of Edith Lutyens Bel Geddes, executrix.

3 The only other major industrial designer with significant experience in the theater was Henry Dreyfuss, who had worked under Bel Geddes when the latter was primarily a stage designer. For excellent, concise reviews of the careers of the major designers, see Jeffrey L. Meikle, *Twentieth Century Limited: Industrial Design in America, 1925–1939* (Philadelphia, 1975), Chapter 3.

businessmen, he avowed in retrospect that "my interest in everything in life has never been as a businessman." And, privately, he dismissed Teague as derivative and unimaginative.[4]

As the 1939 New York World's Fair approached, the contrasts and rivalry between Teague and Bel Geddes were accentuated by the long-standing competitive antagonism between their leading clients, Ford and General Motors. A year before the fair's opening, Teague remarked to a Ford official that he had been "relieved" to see the early General Motors exhibit plans since Bel Geddes had conceived a grandiose scheme having such "enormous difficulties" that it would probably never materialize as planned. He might have been further reassured if he could have witnessed the anxiety of several top GM executives as they fretted over their last-minute decision to entrust their image at the fair to the visionary Bel Geddes and then watched their exhibit costs mount to double, and then triple, Bel Geddes's initial estimate.[5]

But it would ultimately be Teague and Ford who had to reconcile themselves to running a very distant second in popularity to Bel Geddes's dramatic creation.[6] The General Motors Futurama exhibit in 1939 captured the fancy of the public and critics alike. Journalists competed to find adequate words to convey Bel Geddes's "ingenuity," "daring," "showmanship," and "genius." Each day of the fair, thousands of visitors waited for hours in lines up to a mile in length for the opportunity to experience the Futurama.[7] At a world's fair at which the industrial exhibits (for the first time) outpulled the amusement zone attractions, GM's Futurama reigned supreme among the elaborate and popular corporate displays. One neutral survey of 1,000 departing fairgoers (perhaps the nation's first "exit poll") awarded the GM exhibit 39.4 points to only 8.5 points for second-place Ford as the most interesting exhibit. When asked which fair exhibit they would most like to visit again, 47.5 percent of these respondents picked General Motors

4 *New Yorker*, February 8,1941, 25; *Arts and Decoration* 41 (October 1934): 44, 47–48; Norman Bel Geddes, Draft for Autobiography (hereafter cited as "Autobiog.,") AJ-13, Chapter 68, Bel Geddes Papers. (Since Bel Geddes's two manuscript autobiographies were typed from dictation and often not corrected, I have inserted in quotes what I assume to be the correct names and words in instances where there have been obvious misunderstandings by the typist—i.e., "Gegges" for Geddes, "Neustein" for (William) Knudsen, "Future Ami" for Futurama, etc.). The characterization of Bel Geddes as "impractical visionary" appears in Arthur J. Pulos, "Dynamic Showman," *Industrial Design* 17 (July–August 1970): 60. For Bel Geddes's view of Teague, see "Transcription of Interview between Mr. Geddes and Selma Robinson," January 27, 1942, file 937 (draft for Chapter 76), Bel Geddes Papers.

5 Walter D. Teague to Fred Black, April 29,1938, Acc. 544, Box 15, Ford Motor Company Archives, Edison Institute, Dearborn, Michigan. Bel Geddes was well aware of how "scared" the GM executives were. See Bel Geddes to Francis Waite Geddes, November 9, 1938, personal correspondence, Bel Geddes Papers.

6 Having acknowledged by May 1939 that "(t)here is unfortunately no question but that the GM exhibit is decidedly more popular than ours," Ford public relations men reconciled themselves to promoting their display as more beautiful, more dynamic and "sounder educationally." George F. Pierrot to H. G. McCoy, May 21,1939, Pierrot to Donald H. Long, et al., May 18, 1939, Acc. 56, Box 3, Ford Archives.

7 Paul Garrett, chief of GM's public relations, explained to the president of Du Pont that arranging opponunities for the corporation's "special friends" to experience the Futurama without standing in long lines was "about the biggest headache we have." Garrett to W. S. Carpenter, Jr., August 16,1939, Box 821, Series II, part 2, E. I. Du Pont de Nemours & Company Archives, Hagley Museum and Library.

as compared to 7.3 percent for second-place General Electric and only 3.8 percent for Ford.[8]

To estimate the triumph of General Motors over Ford in the popularity of their exhibits in 1939–40, and also the relative mastery of Bel Geddes over Teague and other leading designers in pleasing the crowd, is not to discount the general advance in display techniques that nearly all corporations had achieved by 1939. Teague's exhibits for Ford and Du Pont were far from failures; judged by the standards of only a few years before, they represented major breakthroughs in corporate showmanship, as did Raymond Loewy's exhibit for Chrysler. But Bel Geddes and General Motors had carried corporate public relations a significant step further than the rest.

Many corporations in the late 1930s were still only beginning to advance beyond the axiomatic notion that the way to win public understanding and respect was to (synthetically) put their factories on display through dioramas, working models, photo-murals, and actual working exhibits of segments of their production processes. The public's esteem and sympathy could best be cultivated, production-minded executives had assumed, by displays of their impressive processes of manufacture. General Motors itself had constructed an operating Chevrolet assembly line as its exhibit at Chicago in 1933–34. As they moved, often reluctantly, toward more crowd-pleasing displays during the 1930s, corporate exhibitors began to merge their factory-oriented "educational" efforts with elements of pure entertainment. Under the guidance of professional designers, many moved to simplify and enliven their stories of production, even resorting to stage comedies or cartoon-like animations.[9]

In the GM Futurama, Norman Bel Geddes fell in line with the trend toward making entertainment dominant—but with a significant difference. He discovered a way to involve visitors experientially with the corporation—not so much by urging them to witness the difficulties and triumphs of its processes of production, but rather by offering them a chance to share its wider social and technological vision. Guests at the GM Futurama found themselves thoroughly entertained even as they shared a serious look at the nation's future—through the eyes of General Motors. In the process, Bel Geddes helped revise what it would mean for fairgoers of the future to accept that time-honored invitation to "come visit our company." Bel Geddes's Futurama transformed that invitation. Corporations would henceforth entice visitors not to "tour our factory," but instead to "share our world."

Although General Motors proved adventurous enough to embrace Bel Geddes' plan, it was clearly the designer rather than GM executives who conceived this public relations breakthrough. Bel Geddes had essentially devised all the elements of the Futurama before he persuaded General Motors to adopt the scheme; in fact, as late as the beginning of 1938 he had nearly succeeded in peddling the idea to another corporation. And Bel

8 *New York Journal and American*, June 11, 1939, 3; *Variety*, April 26, 1939; *San Antonio Express*, n.d., clipping, file 381 (Publicity folder), Bel Geddes Papers. Statistics on the Futurama's popularity appear in Market Analysts, Inc. "Ratings of Exhibits," (enclosure to Sanford Griffith to C. E. O'Neil, March 14, 1940, Box 9, RG 3,J. Walter Thompson Company Papers, Duke University and Sales Management, July 1, 1939, 60). On a rating system of three points for first choice, two points for second, and one for third, the Market Analysts, Inc. survey arrived at a rating of 1659 for General Motors to only 347 for third-place Ford. General Electric ranked second at 514.

9 Roland Marchand, "The Designers Go to the Fair: Walter Dorwin Teague and the Professionalization of Corporate Industrial Exhibits, 1933–1940," *Design Issues*, Vol. VIII–I (Fall 1991): 4–17.

Geddes was so intent upon casting himself in the role of visionary planner that he may not have seen the full ramifications of his innovations in visitor involvement. To appreciate the elements of theater, crowd psychology, and social ideology that Bel Geddes managed to unite within the Futurama exhibit, we need first to examine Bel Geddes's vision for the project and the circumstances under which he devised its various elements.

In 1932, only a few years after announcing his transformation from stage designer to industrial designer, Bel Geddes had published a daring and prophetic book he titled *Horizons*. In addition to proclaiming the coming triumph of true streamlining in all modes of transportation, the book showcased designs for such ingenious proposals as a revolving, floating airport in New York harbor, an underwater restaurant, an expandable concentric-ring factory designed to enhance employee welfare, an auditorium for staging Dante's *Divine Comedy* with a cast of hundreds and an audience of five thousand, and an open-air cabaret with long runways that extended the stage to enable performers to "bring the entertainment into intimate contact with the audience." As he assumed a new identity as industrial designer, Bel Geddes derided what he considered the inhibiting traditions of the theater, confining his treatment of that field in *Horizons* to a single chapter which he titled, with inflammatory intent, "Industrializing the Theater." At every opportunity, Bel Geddes proclaimed the demise of the old "peep-show" relationship of the audience to the traditional proscenium stage in favor of "a sense of unity, intimacy, and audience-participation." It was precisely this zeal to remove all barriers between audience and performers that he had sought to embody in such designs as the open-air cabaret with stage runways (*figure 1*).[10]

In *Horizons* Bel Geddes also appropriated the role of urban planner by advocating that all the buildings on each 15-block segment of current cities be replaced by a single super-skyscraper occupying approximately one full block in width and depth and rising as much as 150 stories. The vacated 14 blocks could then be devoted to parks, allowing the city greater access to light and air. Even small towns, he suggested, would eventually discover the wisdom of consolidating all their little businesses into "one tower-type building in the center of the town."[11] Such a development would emerge naturally within a society increasingly streamlined for speed and efficiency. In such a world, no artificial horizons would limit the vision and work of the industrial designer.

As Bel Geddes continued to explore the potentialities of streamlining and speed in the 1930s, he began to pay attention to the limitations that the nation's antiquated highway system placed in the way of a rational, streamlined mode of transportation. The impetus for another grandiose Bel Geddes's project appeared in 1936 in the form of a commission from the J. Walter Thompson advertising agency to provide a number of sketches outlining possi-

10 Norman Bel Geddes, *Horizons* (Boston 1932), 3–5,100,140,143,146, 150, 152, 157, 178, 181, 186–90, 193, 206–18; Norman Bel Geddes, *Miracle in the Evening: An Autobiography*, ed. by William Kelley (Garden City, New York, 1960),147, 251.

11 Bel Geddes, *Horizons*, 282–85.

Figure 3
Norman Bel Geddes, Model "City of Tomorrow" for Shell Oil, 1937.

ble solutions for traffic congestion. The drawings would provide the basis for a Shell Oil Company advertising campaign in 1937.[12]

In his typical manner, Bel Geddes escalated the project both in scope and theatricality. He and his staff voraciously devoured data on population trends, auto registrations, highway conditions, and city planning. They consulted with Miller McClintock, director of Harvard University's Bureau of Street Traffic Research, and addressed some of the questions provoked by contemplations of the city of the future: how would water and elevator systems work for buildings of 150 floors; might skyscraper roofs be used for plane landings; would the movie houses of the future be located within the central skyscrapers; could poor people afford to exist in this transformed environment? As he took upon himself the serious task of devising a comprehensive scheme incorporating superhighways and city planning, Bel Geddes also convinced Shell and J. Walter Thompson to finance the building of an elaborate scale model of a city of the future to dramatize the grand plan. The model would introduce the public to this idealized, streamlined future through the pseudorealism of close-up photographs of his model of "transportation, architecture, [and] parkways as they could be in 1960."[13]

Bel Geddes's scale model, and the accompanying explanations in the Shell ads, adopted the super-skyscrapers plus the parks and playgrounds imagery of *Horizons* (*figure* 2). He linked these with a system of "metropolitan express highways" and elevated sidewalks to separate pedestrian and motor traffic. Controllers stationed in towers and atop bridges would employ radio control to monitor the flow of traffic. Bruce Bliven, who reviewed the Bel Geddes model for *New Republic*, marveled at the striking illusions of depth and distance obtained through the "masterful photography" of the model. "Vague plans," he suggested, were afoot to display Bel Geddes's alternatives to modern traffic systems at the coming New York World's Fair.[14]

Although much of his vision of a magnificent, rationalized, transcontinental highway system with lanes for speeds up to 100 miles per hour was not incorporated into the Shell advertising campaign, Bel Geddes had glimpsed himself as a designer and planner on a grand scale. He adopted the stance of an adversary to the irrationalities and resulting inefficiencies and dangers of present conventions in highway building and as the champion of rational engineering and mistake-proof technologies. A system of 14-lane highways, on which drivers would respond to messages from radio-control towers and find their way illuminated at night by an electric-eye controlled system of indirect lighting, would eliminate most of the accidents resulting from "human failure." A two-tiered system of city streets, with all pedestrians separated from auto traffic, would eliminate urban traffic congestion. A system of widely spaced, immense skyscrapers would allow for more health-promoting open space within the cities (*figure* 3) and the speed and effi-

12 An excellent interpretive study of Bel Geddes's role in this campaign appears in Jeffrey L. Meikle, *The City of Tomorrow: Model 1937* (London: Pentagram Design, 1984).

13 Meikle, *City of Tomorrow,* 7–19; "Minutes of Meeting, April 5,1938," file 389, "Notes Taken in Meeting with Mr. Bel Geddes, November 10,1939" and "Shell City of Future Questions," 15, 21, 23, file 356, Miller McClintock to Bel Geddes, August 9, 1937, file 951, Bel Geddes, "Autobiog.," AJ-17, Chapters 74–75, all Bel Geddes Papers.

14 *Flash,* November 5, 1937, 1, and *People,* September 1937,1–3, both J. Walter Thompson Co. Papers; Meikle, *The City of Tomorrow,* 11, 19–22; Bruce Bliven, "Metropolis: 1960 Style," *New Republic,* September 29, 1937, 211–12.

ciency of the highways into the city would allow more people to live in peripheral towns and suburbs, affording workers a more wholesome suburban life.[15]

Thus, Bel Geddes had already conceived and modeled the serious, substantive content—and much of the social-technological message—of what would become the GM Futurama well before the General Motors Corporation acquired any connection with the project. In fact, during 1937 Bel Geddes futilely attempted to interest both GM president William Knudsen and GM sales manager Richard Grant in having his scheme developed as a fair display, only to suffer repeated snubs and rejections.[16] This situation reflected Knudsen's conservative satisfaction with the operating Chevrolet assembly line exhibit that had been successful for GM (and for Knudsen, then head of the Chevrolet division) at Chicago in 1933 and 1934.[17]

Despite GM's early disinterest, late in 1937 Bel Geddes had begun to envisage the full theatrics and technologies of a display that would not only vastly expand the Shell model but would transform the exhibit into a dramatic new experiential mode of corporate public relations. It is not clear exactly when Bel Geddes conceived the idea of moving visitors over and through a model of the highways and cities of the future rather than having them observe the model from several fixed "overlooks" (undated "preliminary sketches" for the project indicate lookout platforms from which stationary observers would look down upon the model) and when he determined that chairs mounted on a moving conveyor belt would be technically feasible. But it is clear from one set of blueprints that he had formulated the plan well before he finally gained GM's sponsorship in early 1938.[18] In the wake of this conception, Bel Geddes raced forward in a rush of creative ingenuity to surround his model with the theatrics of visitor manipulation that would turn a serious, appropriate display idea for an auto manufacturer (but one distinctly lacking in potential sales effectiveness) into an entrancing corporate publics relations triumph.

By the beginning of 1938 Bel Geddes had persuaded the Goodyear Rubber Company to make a tentative commitment to employ some version of the highways-of-the-future display for its exhibit in New York in 1939. Suddenly, in February 1938, Goodyear decided not to participate at all in the New York World's Fair. At this eleventh hour, Bel Geddes mounted a desperate siege of General Motors in a campaign to salvage his exhibit idea.[19] It was now less than 15 months before the New York fair would open. General Motors had already decided to feature an updated model of the Chevrolet assembly line that it had used in Chicago in 1933–34. This focal exhibit would be supplemented by an expanded research display drawing upon the highly effective "Parade of Progress" road show that the GM Research Laboratories had sponsored on national tour during 1936 and 1937. These elements nicely reflected the

15 Norman Bel Geddes, *Magic Motorways* (New York, 1940), 4–5, 52, 56, 207–8, 211; "Sound Chair Script," 18, Futurama folder, file 381, Bel Geddes Papers.

16 *New Yorker,* February 22,1941, 28–29; Bel Geddes, "Autobiog.," AJ-20, Chapters 80–83, 1, AE-84, Chapter 77, 4–5, Chapter 80,1, Bel Geddes Papers.

17 Bel Geddes, "Autobiog.," AE-84, Chapter 80, 6, Bel Geddes Papers; Alfred P. Sloan, Jr. to F. B. Jewett, November 30,1937, New York 1937 folder, Charles F. Kettering Papers, GMI Alumni Foundation Collection of Industrial History, Flint, Michigan.

18 "Preliminary Sketches, Highways and Horizons," Box 319, "Spectator's Transportation System," file 381 (Production Specifications folder), Bel Geddes Papers.

19 Jeffrey L. Meikle, *Twentieth Century Limited,* 207; People J. Walter Thompson Company), September 1937, inside front cover; "Notes Taken in Meeting with Mr. Geddes," November 10, 1936 and "Notes of Meeting with Mr. Geddes," November 12,1936, file 356, Bel Geddes Papers. On the collapse of the Goodyear sponsorship, see Bel Geddes to J. W. Dineen, February 24,1938 and March 16,1938, file 381 (Correspondence folder) and Bel Geddes, "Autobiog.," AE-84, Chapter 80,1-2, Bel Geddes Papers.

special biases of production-minded GM president William Knudsen and of Charles Kettering, head of the GM Research Laboratories and the corporation's most heavily promoted public figure.[20]

In his unpublished autobiographical manuscript, Bel Geddes tells the story of his ultimate triumph in a desperate "mission impossible" against an already-approved plan at General Motors. During a dramatic hours-long showdown meeting with 40 GM executives, Bel Geddes later recalled, he faced down Knudsen and Kettering through a spontaneous display of wit, bluff, and quick-thinking.[21] Undoubtedly Bel Geddes's version of the story owes more to his extensive theatrical background and melodramatic imagination than to a realistic assessment of decision-making at GM. But what was most important was that he succeeded in persuading the corporation to commit itself to his exhibit at *so late a date* and that he did so primarily with *a negative argument*: did General Motors dare to spend $2 million on its planned recreation of the 1933–34 assembly line exhibit only to "admit that it hasn't had a new idea in five years"?[22]

In taunting and cajoling General Motors into this belated change of plans, Bel Geddes created severe time pressures for his project. But he also gained substantial autonomy in shaping the Futurama. It was already early in May of 1938 when General Motors signed a contract with Bel Geddes for a building and display that was to open in April 1939. Knudsen and Grant were so fearful that Bel Geddes's complex project would not be completed in time that they hesitated to interfere with his work. Moreover, as Bel Geddes later gloated, "the thing [the Futurama model] was so far outside their field, so foreign to their customary executive activities, that in the early stages about all they could do was stand around and hope for the best." Eventually, Bel Geddes's obsessive attention to every detail of construction seemed to win him Knudsen's empathy as a fellow "production man."[23]

Above all, Bel Geddes owed the extent of his autonomy to the fact that he had ultimately gained entry into GM by first persuading Paul Garrett, GM public relations director, and Alfred P. Sloan, Jr., past president of GM and chairman of the board, of the virtues of his adventuresome concept. According to Bel Geddes's account, Sloan liked the idea of "something to catch the public's imagination beyond mere merchandising."[24] Both Sloan and Garrett had viewed better public relations and the effective delivery of a subtle anti–New Deal political message as a major corporate priority since the mid-1930s. Their sponsorship of the Bel Geddes project within General Motors meant that Bel Geddes, in the process of gaining GM's formal approval, had already effectively overcome the fundamental resistance to his approach by the more sales-oriented and production-oriented among GM executives. He was thus free to concentrate on an exhibit that would cultivate goodwill and appreciation rather than promote current sales. Since goodwill was, in a

20 On GM's commitment to the assembly line and research-exhibit plan in late 1937 see "Technical Suggestions Relative to New York World's Fair—1939," World's Fair, New York, 1937 folder; Alfred P. Sloan, Jr. to F. B. Jewett, November 30, 1937, General Motors, New York, 1937 folder, Kettering Papers; Alice Marquis, *Hopes and Ashes: The Birth of Modern Times* (New York, 1986), 20–23.

21 Bel Geddes, "Autobiog.," AMI Series, Chapter 76,1–9, Chapter 77, 3–8, AE84, Chapter 80, 1–11, Bel Geddes Papers; Marquis, *Hopes and Ashes,* 203.

22 Bel Geddes, "Autobiog.," AE-84, Chapter 80, 5, AMI series, Chapter 76, 9, Bel Geddes Papers.

23 Norman Bel Geddes to Frances Waite Geddes, October 26, 1938, October 27, 1938, personal correspondence; Bel Geddes, "Autobiog.," AJ-20, Chapters 80–83, 2 and page titled "GM Officials," William Knudsen to Norman Bel Geddes, May 3,1938, in folder for AE-84, Chapter 80, untitled manuscript, 3, file 381 (GM Intersection folder), Bel Geddes Papers.

24 Bel Geddes, "Autobiog.," AJ-17, Chapter 80, 3–4, Bel Geddes Papers.

certain sense, "priceless" to a giant corporation, Bel Geddes gained an advantage in his pursuit of perfectionism in the execution of his design. The extent to which he managed to retain control and implement his own grand vision is best suggested by his success in bringing General Motors along in support of his ever-expanding budget. Originally contracted for a sum of $2 million, Bel Geddes's Futurama eventually cost General Motors over $7 million.

Figure 4
Norman Bel Geddes, GM Futurama exhibit, 1939

Bel Geddes easily aligned his conception for Futurama with General Motors's interests. An animated model of a scientific highway system of the future, he assured General Motors, could demonstrate the need for vastly expanded highway facilities, promote the sale of more automobiles, and display GM's concern for highway safety. It could convey the corporation's optimism about the capacity of private industry to promote prosperity and create new jobs, thus expressing, in a positive way, the bitter antagonism of GM leaders toward President Roosevelt and the New Deal. And it would suggest the modernity, benevolence, and forward-looking social vision of the corporation.[25]

With his own vision thus comfortably fused with GM's public relations needs, Bel Geddes proceeded with the detailed design and construction of his future world. His venturesome plan called for an immense, animated model, on a scale of one inch to 200 feet, of a major segment of the nation, as of 1960. The model would cover 35,738 square feet and contain several million structures and more than a million trees. When another exhibitor sent out a promotional brochure in November 1938 forecasting its completion for the fair of the "biggest model in the world" with "1,000 individually designed buildings," Bel Geddes wrote his wife in glee, "Wait until they hear about this job, which is ten times the area." "In our principal city alone," he added, "we have more than 2,000,000 individual buildings." Not only was the model to feature attention-grabbing motion through extensive animation, but the visitors themselves would move over and through the model rather than observing it from some static vantage point. Six hundred moving chairs on a conveyor belt would transport them on a "serpentine, up-and-down route" over the vast landscape and cityscape of the model at a height and speed that would simulate a low-level airplane flight. Thus, the persistent quest of fair designers to create a feeling of participation for their audiences found a new realization in this opportunity for visitors to seemingly *enter and experience* a world created for them by the corporation (*figure 4*).[26]

And it was nothing less than the experience of actually visiting a new "world" that Bel Geddes sought to create. Drawing upon the urge to immerse his audience in a total environment that had emerged during his years of theater design, he employed every stage technique of lighting, spatial organization, camouflage, surprise, and scenic trickery to induce in visitors the kind of emotional response that he had previously sought in theatrical

25 "Draft of Presentation," (with penciled corrections), March 30, 1938, file 381 (Specifications Buildings folder), Bel Geddes Papers; Paul Garrett, "Survey on World's Fair," typescript, December 15, 1939, Department of Public Relations Presentations, General Motors Public Relations Archives, Detroit; GM Folks 2 (March 1939): n.p.

26 Press Release, April 15–16,1939, file 384 (Correspondence folder), Press Release, April 29, 1939, file 381, Press Guide, 1940, typescript, 9–10, file 381, Chart of Specifications for Preliminary Model, file 381, Norman Bel Geddes to Frances Waite Geddes, November 9,1938, personal correspondence, all Bel Geddes Papers.

Figure 5
Norman Bel Geddes, Model for GM Futurama Pavilon, 1939

productions. Just as he had insisted upon completely refashioning a theater interior to convert it into a medieval cathedral for a production of the play *The Miracle* in the mid-1920s, so he carefully plotted the visitors' entrance into the 1939 Futurama so that they would feel the sense of having been transported into a different world—the America of 1960. And just as critics had recounted their awe at encountering the hush and majesty of the interior of Bel Geddes's theatrical cathedral ("I rubbed my eyes in amazement. Who was I, and where was I? . . . I was part of parcel of that triumphant medievalism"), so they were to marvel over the experience of finding themselves suddenly borne into Bel Geddes's future.[27]

In 1937 an advertising agency newsletter seeking to comment knowingly on current trends noted that industrial designers rather than architects had suddenly gained control over the design of fair buildings. "The industrial designer," it explained, "first plans the exhibit and then clothes it in an appropriate building."[28] Bel Geddes proceeded exactly along that line. With the design of his central exhibit in mind, he designed the GM building with imposing, unembellished, curved surfaces that would look up to convey "a sense of power" yet conceal the actual shape of the Futurama with its massive surprise ending.[29] The "stark simplicity and mystery of the building" and the lure of the winding ramps leading up to it would "intrigue" visitors into entering the exhibit, Bel Geddes predicted. As one of his staff observed, there was no way of guessing from the exterior of the building what it might contain. But it reached out with a giant curved "hook" to scoop in the passing throngs who made their way up gently curved ramps to disappear into a mysteriously dark slot of an entrance (*figure 5*).[30]

Once the visitors crossed from the bright outdoors through the almost-hidden entrance, they descended sloping ramps with a low level of illumination so as to accustom their eyes to darkness. Soon they found themselves immersed in the "subdued twilight" of the seemingly boundless "Map Lobby." Bel Geddes, renowned for his lighting innovations for the stage, designed this room with diverging walls and an immense, 60-by-100-foot map that curved back high over the spectator. Bel Geddes had remarked years earlier, with regard to stage design, that "lighting can produce a semihypnotic influence over an audience." In the Map Lobby he had sought to realize this effect. He surrounded the huge map with a misty "gray blue tone" of illumination that, together with the diverging walls, gave visitors the feeling of not being in a room at all but instead of simply gazing out into limitless space at a map suspended in the midst of the sky. As one reporter described the scene, the "thousands of pilgrims" descending the ramps looked "like creatures in a far-off land bound for some magic shrine." The masses of dark figures moving down these same "zig-zag luminous ramps" prompted another reporter to imagine a scene from Dante.[31]

As the visitor experienced the solemnity of the high ceilings,

27 Bel Geddes, *Miracle,* 167, 274, 282, 293, 299; Bel Geddes, *Horizons,* 182–84; Bel Geddes, "Autobiog.," AJ-16, Chapter 72, pp. 21, 36, 40, Bel Geddes Papers.

28 BBDO Bulletin, May 19,1937, n.p., BBDO House Organs folder, BBDO Archives, New York.

29 Norman Bel Geddes to Frances Waite Geddes, November 16,1938, personal correspondence, Bel Geddes Papers.

30 "Description of the General Motors Building and Exhibit for the New York World's Fair," typescript, September 8, 1939, 1–2, file 381 (General Motors Building folder), "Peter Schladermundt, "What is Design," 14, in Bel Geddes, "Autobiog., " AJ- 17, Chapters 74–75, Bel Geddes Papers; Robert Coombs, "Norman Bel Geddes' Highways and Horizons," *Perspecta* 13/14 (1971):12–13; Meikle, *Twentieth Century Limited,* 201.

31 *The Sun* (New York), April 29,1939, n.p.; *Syracuse* (New York) *Post Standard,* May 19,1939, n.p., clippings, file 381 (Publicity folder), *Christian Science Monitor,* July 8, 1939, 6, clipping, file 397, Bel Geddes Papers; Eustis, "Big Show," 571; Coombs, "Bel Geddes," 15–16; Bel Geddes, *Miracle,* 262.

the eerie blue-gray light, and the illusion of gazing out into limitless space beyond the great map, "a quiet, intimate voice—as though of a friend walking at his shoulder"—explained the meaning of the changing lights on the map. Superimposed over an illuminated map display of the nation's main cities and waterways, the first projection, in "red electric bands," highlighted the highway system of 1939. The lights then switched to reveal the projected traffic congestion by 1960, and then changed colors and configurations again to outline the solution—a future network of superhighways. At this point, suitably readied for the dramatic visualization of this solution, visitors were ushered into moving chairs that would carry them on a relaxed, 15-minute serpentine ride over a portion of the nation of the future. In the theory of Bel Geddes's design, they had acquired both the mood and the information that would prepare them for a dramatic opening curtain on a pageant in which they would ultimately play an active, participatory role.[32]

To complete the stratagem of providing the visitor with an intense, controlled experience, Bel Geddes arranged synchronized sound equipment for each chair through which "a quiet authoritative voice at his shoulder" served as a private guide and mentor for each individual spectator. This "soft-speaking," "intimate" voice was intended to augment the visitor's sense of having been invited to share the exciting world of a friendly and benevolent sovereign.[33] As the unseen voice invited each visitor to "come tour the future with General Motors," one reporter recounted, "you glide into a black tunnel, swing miraculously around a corner, and the World of 1960 is spread before you . . . in dazzling lights."[34] Even the truculent critic Stuart Chase was enthralled by the spectacle that Bel Geddes had designed to greet his audience at this "opening curtain" to the Futurama:

> [S]uddenly the world of 1960 opens before you, reaching over hill and dale, field and village, to a far horizon. You know that it is all a model . . . but the effect is very real. Cows are grazing in the pastures. Blossoming fruit trees in immaculate patterns cover whole hillsides. Crop lands are plowed on the contours . . . Barns and silos are streamlined.

Meanwhile, the voice of the visitor's "private guide" coached the appropriate response by intoning, "The world of tomorrow is a world of beauty."[35]

As visitors acclimated themselves to this new world of 1960, Bel Geddes introduced a narrative plot to guide their comprehension. The audacious technique of moving the audience through the exhibit provided, in itself, a major advance in solving one of the central problems in exposition displays—how to control the flow and attention of visitors so that they could be told the corporation's story in a focused and sequential way and at a pace determined by the company. To this particular structured control, Bel Geddes added a story-line, physical "blinders," and rotation of the chairs to

32 "Description of the General Motors Building and Exhibit for the New York World's Fair," typescript, September 8, 1939, 4–5; Press Guide, 1940, 10–2, file 381, Bel Geddes Papers; Coombs, "Bel Geddes," 15–16; Eustis, "Big Show" 572.

33 Press Guide, 1940, 13, "This Exhibit. . .," (untitled typescript), 10, file 381, (Correspondence folder), Bel Geddes, Autobiography", E-84, Chapter 77, 1; *New York Sun,* April 19, 1939 (clipping), file 381 (Publicity folder), Bel Geddes Papers; "A Comprehensive Description of the General Motors Highways and Horizons Exhibit," Kettering Papers.

34 Eustis, "Big Show," 571; "A Greeting to Our Guests," n.p., pamphlet, file 408, Bel Geddes Papers.

35 Press Guide, 1940, 13, "Sound Chair Script, Futurama," 1, file 381, Bel Geddes Papers; Stuart Chase, "Pattern for a Brave New World," *Cosmopolitan* (December 1939): 39.

shift the spectator's line of vision—all to insure the desired pattern of audience attention. By controls on the visitors' line of sight, by the eye-catching motion of a particular vehicle in the initial rural panorama, and by promptings by the unseen voice, spectators were induced to follow the progress of a certain truck as it pulled out of a farmyard, traveled a country road, and then entered the superhighway system.[36]

From this point, the moving chairs carried visitors over the route of the massive highway that such a truck would follow in the world of the future—on a 14-lane superhighway, with separated lanes for speeds of 100, 70, and 50 miles per hour, across valleys, mountains, and suburbs toward its destination in a spectacular city of tomorrow (*figure 6*). Along the way, as they experienced "the sensation of flying, now high, now low" over the panorama of the future, they spied huge airports of innovative design, futuristic farms and barns, and thousands of cars in motion on the highways. After nightfall (accomplished by lighting effects) they crossed over "a steel town with Bessemer furnaces firing and glowing in the sky" and an amusement park (with animated merry-go-round and huge Ferris wheel) from which they could hear "boys and girls shrieking with glee on a pretzel-like skyride." "There's fun and merriment in this world of tomorrow," declared the voice of the unseen guide (*figure 7*).[37]

Figure 6
Norman Bel Geddes, GM Futurama exhibit, 1939

Figure 7
Norman Bel Geddes, GM Futurama exhibit, 1939

With obsessive attention to detail, Bel Geddes sought verisimilitude in every detail of the model. He even contracted with Eddie Rickenbacker, famed World War I pilot, to fly a dozen of his staff members over a portion of western Pennsylvania (where, incidentally, construction was beginning on an innovative turnpike) so that they could observe exactly how certain features appeared and what level of detail was visible from a low-flying airplane at various heights. When staff members noted that from 500 feet they could see cows "lashing and swinging their tails" and a man throwing food to chickens, Bel Geddes insisted on including animations of such "human interest" details in his Futurama design. He developed the means to simulate the spray of waterfalls (by combining tiny water jets and air jets), to include airplanes in flight with their moving shadows visible on the ground, and, by using chemical vapors, to create low clouds that would "cling to mountain sides." To insure proper execution of his subtle lighting effects, he insisted that General Motors employ "the best theatrical illumination engineers" rather than regular Westinghouse or General Electric technicians.[38]

The success of the GM Futurama owed much to the way Bel Geddes combined a grand vision with scrupulous attention to realistic detail. But his design contribution to corporate public relations stemmed more fundamentally from his theater-derived strategies of audience manipulation. The 600 "easy chairs" on his serpentine conveyor belt were designed with wide "wings" extending forward from the back of each pair of chairs on each side to severely limit the

36 "Memo NG from Self," July 25, 1938, and "Technical Supplement," typescript, April 7, 1938, 2–5, file 381 (Production Specifications folder), Bel Geddes Papers.

37 Press Guide, 1939, 14–17, file 381, Bel Geddes Papers.

38 Worthen Paxton to Norman Bel Geddes, November 1, 1938 and Anon., "Notes on Airplane Trip, November 2,1938," folder P. file 381, Notes on Meeting, November 1,1938, file 381 (Production Specifications folder), untitled manuscript, file 381 (GM Intersection folder), Worthen Paxton to Richard Grant, July 12, 1938, file 381 (Correspondence folder), Norman Bel Geddes to Frances Waite Geddes, November 2,1938, personal correspondence, all Bel Geddes Papers, Eustis, "Big Show," 571; Marquis, *Hopes and Ashes*, 210.

Figure 8
Norman Bel Geddes. GM Futurama exhibit, 1929

visitor's peripheral vision and insure that his or her attention was focused within a narrow, rectangular field directly ahead (see *figure 10*).[39] To this stringent containment of audience attention Bel Geddes added both the gentle guidance of the unseen voice and the less discernable control of lighting effects. Bel Geddes had pioneered the use of quick shifts of lighting and visual diversions to accomplish scene changes without the closing of theater curtains.[40] Now he brought the same subtle visual *legerdemain* to the service of creating a total environment for the visitors to GM's future world and to the molding of the sequence and content of their perceptions.

But, above all else, he brought his audience *into* the drama of the future, emotionally and physically. In his tirades against the restrictions of the proscenium stage, he had even gone so far as to try to envision how actors could move "through the audience" or even pass over its head.[41] Eventually, he had discovered how to enable the audience to "move through the stage setting and participate in the "play" itself. Nowhere was this more dramatically accomplished than in the "surprise ending" that Bel Geddes provided as the climax to his propagandistic drama of the future, a climax that raised the entire occasion onto a whole new plane of experience.

After gliding over a massive city (modeled upon St. Louis), divided in such a way as to contrast the "old city" of 1939 with the spectacularly futuristic architecture and open space of the city of 1960, the spectators on the moving chairs were brought down closer to one small segment of the new city, a particular intersection toward which the narrator directed their attention. Here they could admire from on high, yet in full and explicit detail, a rational new mode of urban planning in which pedestrians and auto traffic were segregated onto different street levels. "On the elevated sidewalks," as Bel Geddes described the visitors' entrancing vision at this moment, "the city crowds are walking, gazing in the shop windows, lounging on the building roof gardens. Children are playing in the parks. Cars are moving in the streets" (*figure 8*).[42]

> Then came the climax of the ride. As Bel Geddes described it: Suddenly the spectator, in his chair, is swung about! He can scarcely believe his eyes. He is confronted with the full-sized street intersection he was just looking down on. He gets out of his chair and becomes part of the crowd.[43]

No longer "a spectator looking at an animated scale model," the visitor viewed "the city intersection again, this time as the real thing" and became a "pedestrian projected twenty years forward into the heart of a great city." As Folke Kihlstedt has effectively described the impact of this moment, the intersection was "more than a small-scale model; it was a full-scale fragment of the new reality . . . an embryonic cell for a yet unborn world." Visitors could walk across the elevated sidewalks, look down on a plethora of GM cars and trucks simulating traffic on the streets below, gaze into the

39 "Notes of Meeting, November 1, 1938," file 381 (Product Specifications folder); Worthen Paxton to Norman Bel Geddes and "BW," April 11, 1938, file 381 (GM Building folder), "Original Presentation to Sloan, Knudsen & Grant," n.p. and Press Release, April 15–16, 1939, file 384, all Bel Geddes Papers.

40 Bel Geddes, "Autobiog.," AJ-16, Chapter 72, pp. 21, 36, 43, Bel Geddes Papers.

41 Bel Geddes, *Miracle*, 147. Bel Geddes had also developed the scenario in the mid-1920s for a movie that would be filmed in such a way that "every member of the audience would be in the place of the protagonists.... Thus the audience would not merely see the events, it would experience them." Bel Geddes, *Miracle*, 324.

42 "Description of the General Motors Building and Exhibit for the New York World's Fair," typescript, September 8, 1939, 31, file 381 (General Motors Building folder), Bel Geddes Papers.

43 Norman Bel Geddes, "Description of the General Motors Building and Exhibit . . .," typescript, September 8, 1939, 31, file 381, Bel Geddes Papers.

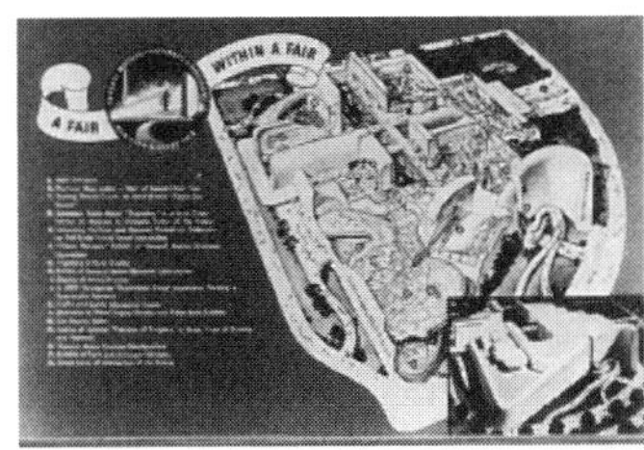

Figure 9
Diagram of GM Futurama exhibit, 1939

Figure 10
Norman Bel Geddes, GM Futurama exhibit, 1929

shop windows, and enter any of the large buildings on the four corners of the intersection to see additional General Motors exhibits. (GM's "A Fair Within a Fair" diagram (*figure 9*) cut away the roof of the building to reveal the path of the visitors through Futurama from point B, the surrealistic map lobby, to point E, where the visitor debarked from the moving chairs to enter the intersection of the future.) To commemorate this time-warp experience, all visitors received pins proclaiming "I have seen the future." The phrase was effective, but clearly it was too modest in its claim. They had not only seen GM's future, they had seen it "come to life" and had actually "*walked around in it*!"[44]

By imbuing the industrial exhibit with all of his theatrical imagination, Bel Geddes sought to realize for General Motors the premise that he had set forth seven years before in *Horizons*: "There is no more emphatic way of bringing an idea to the attention of a mass audience and doing it with great force and conviction than in the theater."[45] In this case, the "idea" was an amalgam of precepts and associations that embodied GM's strategic planning, ideology, and desired public image. General Motors was a supremely "modern" corporation, one in which an emphasis on scientific research obviously prepared it to plan intelligently for the future. Bel Geddes retained Charles Kettering's plan for an updated repeat of a marvels-of-science show and exhibit based upon the work of the General Motors Research Laboratory, positioning this "casino of science" in one of the buildings that visitors were encouraged to enter as they walked around the full-scale intersection of 1960 (*figure 10*). Now that many manufacturers wanted to emphasize their research laboratories as a way of associating themselves with modernity, science, and an orientation toward the future, the 1939–40 General Motors exhibit logically employed a magnificent vision of the future to lead visitors toward the display that would demonstrate how the GM research laboratory kept the company future-oriented.[46]

General Motors also counted on its display of benevolence and expertise—in placing an entertaining and educational vision of the future before the public—to confirm the principle that large private firms, not the federal government, were best suited to lead the public into an ideal future. In his initial presentation, Bel Geddes promised GM executives that the exhibit would offer "direct proof to the public" of "the needs of our industrial economic system" and GM's public relations director, Paul Garrett, concluded after the first year that the Futurama had served as "an object lesson in PROGRESS." The sound track's "authoritative personal guide" reminded visitors that the exciting future they were experiencing had been enriched not only by "new concepts in science and research" but also by "a new understanding of the true function of industry as an integral part of the nation's social and economic life." If that tribute to free enterprise was vague and muted, the GM Press Guide proudly

44 Bel Geddes, "Description of General Motors Building and Exhibit . . .," September 8,1939, 31–33, 'This Exhibit . . .," 22, file 381, Bel Geddes Papers; "A Comprehensive Description," Kettering Papers; Folke Kihlstedt, "Utopia Realized: the World's Fairs of the 1930s," 108, in Joseph J. Corn, ed., *Imagining Tomorrow: History, Technology and the American Future* (Cambridge, Massachusetts, 1986).

45 Bel Geddes, Horizons, 156.

46 New York Herald Tribune, October 28,1940, 28; Press Guide, 1939, 23–31, file 381, Bel Geddes Papers.

quoted the statement of GM chairman Alfred Sloan that for industry to move forward toward this future it was necessary to "destroy the economic barriers that now prevent the essential expansion of enterprise . . . and that repress the spirit of individual initiative."[47]

More concretely, the Futurama propagandized for public support of massive and expensive superhighways that would assure an expanding market for automobiles. As Garrett touted the exhibit to fellow GM executives, "It may well mark the beginning of a new era in road construction which will greatly stimulate the use and sale of cars, at a time when a saturation point may have been reached."[48] In fact, the creation of "a public enthusiasm for improved highways" was a more likely result of Futurama than the impact of its vague message about free enterprise. And the juxtaposition of these two messages, as Walter Lippman shrewdly pointed out, revealed certain ironies. Had not General Motors "spent a small fortune to convince the American public that if it wishes to enjoy the full benefit of private enterprise in motor manufacturing, it will have to rebuild its cities and highways by public enterprises"? Bel Geddes's vision of highway planning necessitated massive city planning and even regional planning. The scope of government planning and control involved in a project of this scale would undoubtedly have appalled the GM executives.[49]

Smaller ironies also emerged from Bel Geddes's compromises of his design principles in the service of popular theater. He carried his vision of rational streamlined future into the design of nearly every aspect of the Futurama, from the suggestive contours of the building to the shapes of individual model automobiles. The sound track exhorted visitors to "(s)ee how the beautiful landscaping and architectural features conform to the modern engineering of the highways." At one point Bel Geddes instructed his leading assistant to add more airports to the model to suggest the "tremendous air activity" of 20 years hence and insisted upon "complete and ultimate streamlining" in the models of all transportation vehicles.[50]

But the designer's principled rationale for streamlining had rested upon an esthetic and informational theory of visual candor: things should look exactly like what they were and should visually indicate the purpose they served. Trickery, camouflage, exaggeration, and visual deception seemed to have no place in such a commitment to forthrightness. Yet in Futurama, Bel Geddes concluded, the desired, emotional audience response must arise not only from the beauty of forms aligned with their purposes but also from the kinds of deception routinely justified in the theater to add to the spectators' pleasure. Bel Geddes and his staff, therefore, enthusiastically rejected "naturalism" as a standard and agreed to "increase the speed of everything" disproportionately in order to gain the effects of more strikingly visible motion.[51]

In a certain sense, of course, Bel Geddes was still applying the conventional modernist principle of form follows function.[52] The

47 Paul Garrett, "Survey of World's Fair Exhibit," December 15,1939, Public Relations Presentations Folders, General Motors Archives; Draft of Presentation, March 30, 1938, 29A–29B, file 381 (Specifications Buildings folder); Press Guide, 1939, 2,17, file 381, Alfred P. Sloan Jr. to Norman Bel Geddes, March 31, 1939, file 381 (Correspondence folder), "1960 Calling!" brochure, file 381 (Publicity folder), all Bel Geddes Papers.

48 GM Folks 2 (March 1939): n.p.; Garrett, "Survey," loc. cit.

49 Walter Lippman, "A Day at the World's Fair," *New York Herald Tribune*, June 6,1939, 25. Social critic Stuart Chase also needled General Motors in his review of the exhibit by observing: "Another major impression was that modern science and engineering had been given a free ticket to do their very best, unhampered by considerations of vested interest, property rights, dollar profit and loss." Chase, "Pattern for a Brave New World," 82. Rexford Tugwell made similar observations in his review of Bel Geddes's *Magic Motorways* in the *Saturday Review of Literature*, April 13,1940, 3–4. Even earlier, in reviewing the Shell Oil Company model, Bruce Bliven had observed in the *New Republic* (September 29, 1937: 212) that Bel Geddes's vision would require city, regional, and national planning and advertising agency copywriter William Day, as Jeffrey Meikle recounts, had momentarily piqued Bel Geddes's interest with an idea that had to be quickly discarded as inappropriate for Shell Oil sponsorship: "the simplest method of eliminating cars in New York City or elsewhere . . . would be to pass a law prohibiting private ownership." Meikle, *City of Tomorrow*, 7.

50 Bel Geddes to W. Paxton, memo, November 25, 1938, file 381 (Production Specifications folder), Bel Geddes Papers.

51 Press Guide, typescript, 1940,17, file 381, Norman Bel Geddes to Worthen Paxton, November 25,1938, file 381 (Production Specifications folder), "Notes on Meeting," November 1, 1938, file 381 (Production folder), all Bel Geddes Papers; Chase, "Pattern for a Brave New World," 83.

52 On Bel Geddes's theory of proper design principles, see *Horizons*, 18–20 and passim.

"function" of the Futurama was to give pleasure (especially esthetically) and to harness the "momentous power and inspiration" possible within theater to the public relations goals of General Motors and the vision of a modern national highway system.[53] All of the theatrical devices of visual deception, audience control, manipulation of attention, and exaggeration might thus be considered acceptable as contributions to those ultimate purposes. In that sense, Bel Geddes's industrial exhibit designs foreshadowed a more unreserved commitment of industrial designers to the incorporation of potential consumers' anticipated (or desired) emotional responses into product designs.[54]

Bel Geddes did acknowledge the costs to his ostensible ultimate goal of effective public education that his drive for maximum theatricality had incurred. From the outset, General Motors had worried about the 100 mile-per-hour lanes on Bel Geddes's highways. Wouldn't this feature open GM to charges of irresponsible disregard for highway safety? Bel Geddes was adamant in defense of his design. He counteracted the "supersensitivity" of the auto manufacturer by insisting, both privately to GM and publicly on the Futurama sound track, that his system would actually eliminate 98 percent of all accidents. Moreover, radio controllers would hold all motorists to within five miles per hour of the designated speed for their lane and the dangers created by the "Road Hog" and risky passing attempts would disappear.[55]

At one point Bel Geddes bemoaned the fact that the emphasis on speed "threw somewhat out of focus the main theme of the great undertaking" and at another that the pace of flow through the exhibit had been too rapid really to satisfy serious visitor interests. He acknowledged in his *Magic Motorways* book of 1940 that the Futurama ride had been far too superficial to convey the full substance of his highways vision. ("There was much more to see, and no time to see it. There was much more to explain, and no time to explain it.") But the compromises of pace and substance to serve entertainment and theatricality had been fully intentional. As Bel Geddes had counseled GM, the exhibit "although *scientific* and *educational*" would emphasize "the *entertainment* aspects." The tempo of the ride conformed to Bel Geddes's primary goal—to "provide the spectator with constant *thrills* and *entertainment* and *IN RESTFUL COMFORT*." And some of the choices in content stemmed from their promotional potential. As he confided to one interviewer, "If I had described the new highway as accommodating three lanes of traffic at 20, 30, and 40 miles per hour, it would have caused no indignation. It also would have caused no headlines."[56]

Within only a month of the fair's opening in April 1939, it was clear that Bel Geddes's Futurama qualified as the obvious "headline story" in any news about the fair. People stood in lines for hours to gain a place among the 28,000 visitors who could enter the Futurama each day.[57] Although the emphasis on speed may have

53 Bel Geddes, *Horizons,* 156.

54 Jeffrey Meikle, *Design in the Contemporary World* (Stanford, 1989), 65–66; John Hesket, *Philips: A Study of the Corporate Management of Design* (London, 1989), 51, 82–83,137; Richard Buchanan, "A Response to Klaus Krippendorff," *Design Issues* III-1 (Fall 1985): 73.

55 Paul Garrett, "Survey of World's Fair," loc. cit.; "Magic Motorways Presentation," typescript, n.d., 10, file 384, "The Proposed Exhibit," untitled memo, April 7, 1938, 5, file 381 (Correspondence folder), "Production Minutes," April 5,1938," as included in untitled typescript in file 381 (GM Intersection folder), Bel Geddes Papers.

56 Untitled manuscript, 33 in file 381 (Futurama Conveyor System folder), the *The Home Newspaper* (Detroit), June 18,1939, n.p., clipping, file 381 (Publicity folder), Bel Geddes Papers; Bel Geddes, *Magic Motorways,* 6, 8. Bel Geddes's statement of his primary goal and his emphasis on entertainment, with emphasis in the original, appears in "The Proposed Exhibit . . .," 3, 14, file 381 (Correspondence folder), Bel Geddes Papers.

57 *Sales Management,* July 1,1939, 25–26, 60; George F. Pierrot to H. G. McCoy, May 21, 1939, Acc. 56, Box 3, Ford Papers; *New York Post,* clipping, October 26, 1939, *Sunday Mirror* (New York), clipping, April 30, 1939, *Journal American* (New York), clipping, circa. June 31, 1939, file 381 (Publicity folder), Bel Geddes Papers.

Figure 11
Norman Bel Geddes, GM Futurama exhibit, 1929

contributed marginally to the exhibit's success, its stunning popularity clearly derived from more basic elements in its design. By 1939, all of the designers for corporate fair exhibits were seeking that optimal blend of motion, simplicity, spectacularity, and visitor participation that recent observations indicated would be the key to success. Bel Geddes incorporated all of these elements in his design. But the quality that most strikingly set the Futurama apart from competing exhibits lay in its dramatic new techniques of inducing an aura of experiential visitor participation.

These techniques began with the sound system, where the individual speakers, synchronized with the progress of each chair, enabled Bel Geddes and General Motors to tell their story in a conversational tone and avoid the negative visitor reactions to "being talked at through loudspeakers" that surveyors had noted in earlier fairs. As a Bel Geddes lieutenant explained to Richard Grant of GM, it was crucial to perfect the sound system since "the speaker's voice should be very soft with excellent quality and with the sound source apparently close to each individual" to give the effect of "talking individually to each spectator." In many of his descriptions of the ride, Bel Geddes used the word "whispers" to suggest the intimate quality he believed he had achieved in the voice of his mass-produced "personal guide." The New York *World Telegram* confirmed his success by referring to the unseen voice as a "quiet, intimate voice, tensely dramatic, yet direct and almost confidential."[58]

The "easy chairs" carried by conveyor belt were also crucial to the sense of participation. Significantly, in its lessons for future exhibits, the system of moving chairs also solved the problem of maintaining extensive control over the visitor's path, rate of movement, line of sight, and focus of attention. As one of Bel Geddes's staff members later emphasized, "You will remember that these were very comfortable moving chairs that not only permitted, but necessitated, the viewing of the model in the correct sequence and timings."[59] Moreover, the moving chairs did this in synchronization with the verbal guidance of the unseen voice and the controlling qualities of ingenious lighting effects. Moreover, the chairs answered one problem consistently noted at previous fair exhibits, the recurrent tiredness of visitors, by devising a means to hold their attention while affording them "restful comfort (*figure 11*)." And, if all of these devices did not fully create an encompassing "total environment" for the visitor/participant, the climactic emergence into the full-scale city intersection of the future represented Bel Geddes's ultimate theatrical trick to induce his audience "not merely [to] see the events, . . . [but to] *experience* them."[60] With theatrical imagination, he had enlisted the spectator's desire for vicarious participation and given them an opportunity, from a vantage point of comfort and safety, to involve themselves in a time-warp experience more vivid than any

58 "1934 Report on the Fair," 25–26, Acc. 1109, Box 7, Ford Archives; Worthen Paxton to Richard H. Grant, October 10, 1938b file 381 (Correspondence folder), Bel Geddes, "Autobiog.," AE-84, Chapter 77, 1; Press Guide, typescript, 1940, 20, file 381; "This Exhibit . . .,"10, 13, file 384 (Correspondence folder); *New York World Telegram*, July 13, 1939, n.p., clipping, file 381 (Publicity folder), Bel Geddes Papers.

59 Peter Schladermundt, "What is Design" typescript, November 29,1943,14–15, in Bel Geddes, "Autobiog.," AJ-17, Chapters 74–75, Bel Geddes Papers, emphasis mine.

60 "The Proposed Exhibit," 3, file 381 (Correspondence folder), Bel Geddes Papers; Bel Geddes, *Miracle*, 324.

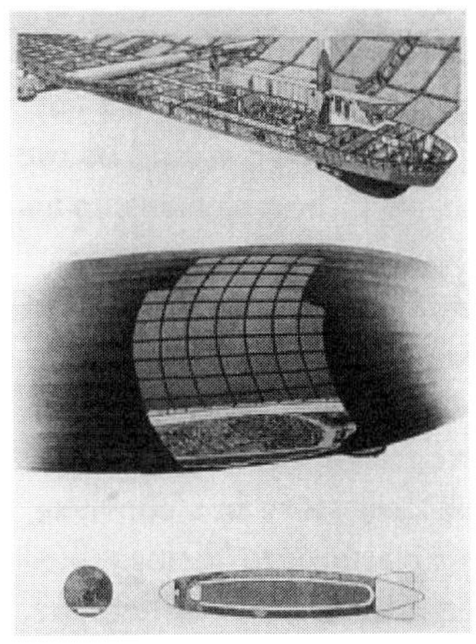

Figure 12
Norman Bel Geddes, Plan for a Zeppelin to carry Futurama exhibit around the United States, 1940

that Edward Bellamy or even H. G. Wells had evoked. In the words of one drama critic, he had combined for his audience "the thrills of Coney Island with the glories of Le Corbusier."[61]

Given such accolades, it is hardly surprising that the demise of the Futurama after the closing of the fair in 1940 was deplored by many observers and, for a time, desperately warded off by Bel Geddes through a series of schemes for preservation or reincarnation. Encouraged by the letters of "hundreds of starry-eyed visitors," including one who lamented that its loss would be comparable to that of a Shakespeare play or a Rembrandt painting, he first proposed turning it into a caravan display, in which 44 trucks would transport it to shifting display sites around the country. On second thought, he conceived a more dramatic device to insure its continuing life and influence. It could be mounted in a giant Zeppelin that would touch down at various of the nation's cities (*figure 12*).[62]

Employing another approach (first in 1940 and later at the beginning of the 1950s), Bel Geddes unsuccessfully implored GM leaders to erect a "General Motors Consumer Building" (actually, in Bel Geddes's phrase, "public relations center") in downtown New York City with the Futurama preserved (or re-created) as a multilevel exhibit. Visitors could tour a version of the Futurama housed in this building by taking an elevator to the top floor and then letting the tow of downward-sloping ramps carry them through the sequential stages of the exhibit.[63] The actual legacy of the Futurama, however, eventually became apparent in the postwar era in the design of amusement park features and corporate industrial exhibits. It was significant that General Motors did not flinch from the implication that it had not had a new idea in 25 years when it recreated a "Futurama" for the 1964–65 World's Fair. To this day, the corporate exhibitors at Epcot have departed little from Bel Geddes's paradigm of the modern public relations exhibit, either in concept or in basic technique.

Even with all of Bel Geddes's enhanced techniques, it was the decisive shift from the concept of "tour our factory" to that of "share our vision" that represented the most significant impact of the Futurama. It is difficult to imagine, for instance, that Bel Geddes's exhibit for General Motors in 1939 would have enjoyed anything like its actual popularity had it transported visitors on an entertaining and educational tour through a model of a General Motors factory. And what of the surprise ending, which not only transported Futurama visitors into a life-sized segment of a world of the future but placed them alongside showroom windows where they could comfortably imagine themselves in the role of consumer? By contrast, a moving-chair exhibit of a model of GM production lines would have hardly gained an equivalent effect if it had suddenly deposited visitors on a

61 "The Proposed Exhibit," typescript [April 7, 1938], 3–4, 14, file 381 (Correspondence folder); *New York Post,* May 11, 1939, clipping, file 381 (Publicity folder), Bel Geddes Papers.

62 *New York News,* October 6, 1940, 80, clipping, file 381 (Publicity folder), Leo Weiselberg to Norman Bel Geddes, October 21, 1939 and Minutes of Meeting, April 26,1940," file 384 (Correspondence folder), "A Presentation of Various Plans for Continuing the Use of the Futurama Following the Close of the World's Fair," April 24, 1940, 18–22, 26–30, file 381, all Bel Geddes Papers.

63 "A Presentation of Various Plans for Continuing the Use of the Futurama," 10–15, "Suggestion for a General Motors Consumer Building at Rockefeller Center," booklet, n.d. (circa. 1949–50),1–3, 18–32, and Alfred P. Sloan, Jr. to Norman Bel Geddes, May 19,1950 (enclosed slip in booklet), Bel Geddes Collection. Ultimately, however, the exhibit was dismembered. One segment resurfaced as the feature of a city planning exhibit in St. Louis in 1941 and the army "borrowed" a large section to use while devising schemes of wartime camouflage. "Futurama Conveyor System," typescript, file 381, Bel Geddes Papers. I have not been able to discover whether any fragments of the original 1939–40 Futurama still exist.

full-scale factory floor, with no evident role for them in play in such an uncomfortably alien, albeit contemporary, world.[64]

Thus the success of Bel Geddes's design lay in concept as well as technique. He had escaped the continuing legacy of the factory visit. Even for Bel Geddes, this escape may have stemmed partly from the circumstances under which he conceived the substance of the exhibit—as the answer to a problem other than that of fair displays. As late as 1935 Bel Geddes himself had proposed a production-oriented, simulated factory-tour display to publicize the contributions of the steel industry to world progress. On a "group of barges tied to a dock at Pittsburgh" this industrial theater would tell "the story of steel from the ore through the mill to the finished product."[65] But the exercise of pondering the solutions to traffic problems oriented Bel Geddes to exploit an idea that had recently been percolating among the creators of industrial exhibits—the idea that, especially for public relations purposes, the future (rather than company history or production processes) might provide better themes for successful image-building exhibits.[66]

By 1939, most of the corporate exhibits had made a substantial break with the production-oriented tradition of trying to display the processes of production. Some, like the 1939 Chrysler exhibit designed by Raymond Loewy, opted for a melange of entertainments—a "Five-Star Show"—while Ford and Du Pont, under the guidance of Walter Dorwin Teague, somewhat awkwardly tried to combine marionettes or musical comedies with stories of products and production or the history of the industry. Ford, with its animated, cartoon-like "Cycle of Production," still tried to impress visitors with the scope and rationality of its processes of production through an entertaining, "educational" review of how cars are made.[67]

In shifting from "the factory" to "the future," Bel Geddes and General Motors managed to introduce many qualities of theatrical entertainment while retaining a prestige-enhancing aura of seriousness. It constituted a major public relations success—not so much for the effectiveness of any of its specific messages (although Studebaker president Paul Hoffman praised Bel Geddes for "blasting open the minds of men as to our highway needs"), but because the great corporation had benevolently offered the public an entrancing "free show" without crossing over the indistinct boundary to pure entertainment. Bel Geddes himself concluded from the immense popularity of the exhibit that he had discovered a new force for change in the world—the educative power of visual dramatization.[68]

On many grounds Bel Geddes's display was evasive. As David Nye points out, the dwarfing and depersonalizing effects of miniaturization on the portrayal of human beings in the model reflected the Futurama's larger failure to make "any attempt to grasp future human relations" in this technological paradise.[69] In fact, Bel Geddes explicitly evaded his own earlier vision of the small town of

64 As GM exhibit designer Allen Orth had earlier reminded company officers, an emphasis on the factory and assembly lines might invite the audience to recall those labor issues that had been "so much in the limelight" as a result of GM's relations with unions and the sit-down strikes in recent years. Allen Orth, "Technical Suggestions Relative to New York World's Fair –1939," July 1,1937, 5, in World's Fair, New York, 1937 file, Kettering Papers.

65 Bel Geddes, "Autobiog.," AJ-14, Chapters 69–70, Bel Geddes Papers.

66 Walter Dorwin Teague to William Hart, January 4,1937, reel 16:21A, Teague Papers; "Chemical Memorandum," Acc 1662, Box 64, Du Pont Papers; "Program for Focal Exhibit of Means of Communication," 2, New York World's Fair, 1939 Papers, Box 57, New York Public Library.

67 On Chrysler, see Vols. 330 and 334, Ross Scrapbooks, Ivy L. Lee Papers, Princeton University and *Knoxville* (Tennessee) *Journal*, October 1,1939, n.p. clipping, file 381 (Publicity folder), Bel Geddes Papers. On Ford and Du Pont, see Marchand, "The Designers Go to the Fair."

68 Paul G. Hoffman to Norman Bel Geddes, July 2, 1940, file 384 (Correspondence folder), Bel Geddes Papers; Bel Geddes, *Magic Motorways*, 4.

69 David E. Nye, "Yesterday's Ritual Tomorrows: The New York World's Fair of 1939," in *Making Exhibitions of Ourselves* (London, 1990); David E. Nye, *Electrifying America: Social Meanings of a New Technology* (Cambridge, Masschusetts, 1990), 368, 371.

the future as dominated by a single multipurpose skyscraper. In the Futurama, the small town on the periphery of the city of the future looked exactly like the traditional idealized portrait, with houses nestled around the single church with lofty steeple.

Speaking of evasions, there were no slums in Bel Geddes's Futurama. All had presumably succumbed to the bulldozers of the highway builders, never to replicate themselves elsewhere. Some admirers noted that he had prettified the future by eliminating such elements as billboards. Even Bel Geddes acknowledged that his highways might create monotony and that "much of the pleasure would be taken from motoring for most people."[70] But no one seems to have perceived the Futurama's greatest evasion of all, the ironic manner in which the fair visitors had been emancipated from the relative tediousness of the old "tour-of-the-factory" display, only to find themselves being carried along on an assembly-line (the moving-chair conveyor belt) while General Motors constructed their vision of the future.[71]

70 "Sound Chair Script," 18, file 381 (Futurama folder), Albert S. Bard to Norman Bel Geddes, November 14, 1939, Bel Geddes to F. S. Chase, October 30,1939, *Bicknell* (Indiana) *News,* October 6, 1939, n.p., clipping, file 381 (Publicity folder), "Notes Taken in Meeting with Mr. Geddes," November 16,1936, file 356, all Bel Geddes Papers.

71 In a similar vein, Jeffrey Meikle notes Walter Dorwin Teague's comment that "people must flow in an exhibit" and observes that by 1939 designers had consciously come to see exhibition buildings as "machines for processing people." It was Bel Geddes who installed the assembly line which most imaginatively and exactingly regulated that flow and undertook that processing. Meikle, *Twentieth Century Limited,* 197.

Harley Earl and the Art and Color Section: The Birth of Styling at General Motors

David Gartman

One day in the early 1930s Harlow Curtice, the new general manager of General Motors' Buick Division, ventured to the third floor of the corporation's headquarters in Detroit, where the Art and Color Section was located. This was the corporate "beauty parlor," as some of Detroit's hard-boiled, no-nonsense automotive men referred to it, where the "pretty-picture boys" dressed up the automobiles that came off the engineers' drawing boards. The section was headed by a California transplant named Harley Earl, a style-conscious man given to wearing white, linen suits and purple shirts. But he was also a huge, powerful man who could curse, drink and womanize with the best of the industry's engineers and production men. And he was determined to wrest the power to design cars away from them.

Curtice eyed the decorations that Earl and his staff had hung on his forthcoming Buicks and did not like what he saw. He quickly got into a heated argument with Earl, who told Curtice that he did not know a "damn thing" about style. After a few more expletives were exchanged, Earl suddenly fell silent and strode toward his office, motioning for Curtice to follow. He picked up the receiver of the phone on his desk, and pushed the button that opened a direct line to the office of General Motors president Alfred Sloan.

"Hello Alfred, how are you?" Earl asked calmly.

"How's Carol, Alfred?"

Curtice listened to the small talk, sensing that the odds in his battle with Earl were slowly shifting.

"And how are the kids, Alfred? All right? That's good."

Now the tone of Earl's voice grew notably harsher.

"Alfred, I'm here in the Buick studio with that son of a bitch Curtice, and he seems to be a little confused. He can't tell who's in charge of Buick and who's in charge of Art and Color. I though maybe you could straighten out his ass for me."

Earl handed the phone to Curtice, to whom Sloan calmly stated: "Let him build anything he wants."[1]

Harley Earl was the creator of the system of modern automobile design that is still practiced throughout the world. By the early 1940s, his renamed Styling Section had almost absolute organizational authority over the look and shape of all the cars produced by the world's largest automaker. During his first years at General Motors,

This material is reprinted with the kind permission of Routledge publishing company from the book, *Auto Opium: A Social History of American Automobile Design*, by David Gartman (1994).

1 This story is pieced together from various sources. See especially Al Fleming, "The Earl of Design," *Automotive News*, (Sept. 16,1983), 232; Barbara Holliday, "Harley Earl, the Original Car Stylist," *Detroit Free Press. Sunday Magazine* (May 25, 1969),13. These sources, however, have cleaned up Earl's language. I have inserted characteristic expletives, relying on the firsthand reports of Earl's associates. See C. Edson Armi, *The Art of American Car Design* (University Park, Pa.: 1988), 32; and "Reminiscences of William L. Mitchell," Automotive Design Center, Henry Ford Museum and Greenfield Village Dearborn, Michigan, 1984), 8.

however he had to struggle mightily against the entrenched power of production-oriented executives to convince them that his vision of automotive style could sell cars. He was a charismatic leader, carrying out a revolution in the industry against the bureaucratic authority of engineers, division heads and sale executives, and depending on the sheer force of his personality to do so. And his unlikely ally in this struggle for styling was Alfred Sloan, whose personal protection and friendship Earl wielded as a weapon in his early battles.

Earl and Sloan were one of the industry's oddest couples. Sloan was the original organization man, a dispassionate champion of corporate bureaucracy and the bottom line. A frail, pale New Yorker who dressed conservatively, Sloan seldom got excited about anything, much less automobiles. By contrast, Harley Earl was a flashy, brash, athletic, perpetually tanned Californian who was easily excited, especially by cars. He absolutely loved them and wanted to transmit his love and excitement through style to the buyers of GM products. The two men could not have been more different. But they needed each other, and they knew it.

In the mid-twenties, Sloan was struggling to break the stranglehold that Ford's Model T had on half of the automotive market. He decided that, instead of confronting Ford directly in a price war, he would cater to the emerging demand for style. So Sloan hired and personally protected Earl to give his mass-produced products the appearance of variety and innovation. Could style, excitement, and change be routinized and rationalized, turned into an predictable cog in Sloan's corporate bureaucracy? This was the question that only a monumental professional and corporate struggle would answer.

General Motors' corporate struggle for style and Earl's professional struggle for stylists were both part of a larger social struggle for style that emerged in the twenties. American society as a whole was struggling to develop a new definition of itself through the visual look of things. The rise of mass production in the previous decade, largely the result of the pioneering efforts of Henry Ford and the automobile industry, undermined the meaning and identity many Americans found in productive activity. Degrading, unskilled, heteronomous work on assembly lines and specialized machines no longer testified to the moral worth and integrity of the individual caught in this collective machinery controlled from above. So after some notable but unsuccessful attempts to resist the degradation of their work, many Americans looked elsewhere for personal meaning and gratification—to a realm of consumer consumption sustained by the higher wages won in labor struggles.

Not just any domestic consumer goods could compensate American workers for the meaning and identity they lost in mass production factories. They wanted commodities with wholeness and unity to compensate for their fragmented and incoherent activities in mass production. They demanded goods offering individuality and variety to provide the distinction that their homogeneous jobs could not. People sought a semblance of the progress and improvement in their personal possessions that they could not achieve in the leveled and segmented occupational hierarchies of Fordist factories. In a word, the working-class recruits into America's consumer army demanded products with "style."[2]

But the structure of Fordism that denied these needs in production also blocked their realization in consumption. The division of labor that rendered workers skilless also prevented products from achieving unity. The standardization of models which eliminated the need for worker discretion also restricted product variety. The high cost of retooling specialized machinery limited the product changes that signaled progress. All of these factors distinguished mass-produced products from the craft-produced goods of the upper classes. The problem that faced mass-producers in the twenties, as production outstripped consumption and competition became fierce, was meeting the escalating demand for stylish goods without undermining the economies of mass production.

The solution to Fordism's dilemma was found by the new profession of industrial design. In the mid-twenties, when saturated markets began to elevate the priority of sales over production, industrial designers or stylists emerged to show mass-producers how to give their products the superficial appearance of individuality, unity, progress, and class without changing the production process of Fordism. The automobile industry was at the forefront of this new wave of industrial design.

Struggle of the Automotive Giants: GM Style versus Ford Utility

The automobile companies that pioneered Fordist mass production were the first to feel its principal contradiction of underconsumption. By the mid-twenties the market for new cars was dangerously soft, but the general weakening of labor that Fordism brought prevented wages from rising enough to bring automobility to lower-income workers. The auto industry faced the dilemma of stimulating the consumption of its product without raising the costs of its production.

During this period there emerged two strategies for overcoming this contradiction, each identified with its corporate champion. The first strategy, pursued by Ford, was an extension of its hitherto successful approach of cost-cutting utility. Ford had risen to dominance in the industry by offering a solid, simple, widely useful vehicle at a low and decreasing price made possible by cost-cutting innovations. When faced with slowing car sales in the mid-twenties, Ford's prescription was more of the same price-cutting medicine. But even the drastic cut of the basic Model T price to $260 in 1924 could not bring back customers. Ford's market share slipped from 50 percent in 1923 to 15 percent in 1927.

Ford's strategy of cost-cutting utility was failing for several reasons. First, finding new production economies to offset lower prices was increasingly difficult and expensive, and workers were

2 On stylish consumption as compensation, see Stuart Ewen, *Captains of Consciousness* (New York, 1976), esp. 77–109; idem, *All Consuming Images: The Politics of Style in Contemporary Culture* (New York, 1988). esp. 57–108.

finding ways to resist them. Second, the demand for low-priced, basic transportation that Ford supplied was increasingly filled by used cars, whose supply exploded as first-time buyers traded in their old cars for new ones. Third and decisively, Americans who traded in their first cars were demanding comfort, convenience and style, all of which were lacking in Ford's car. In their newly constructed domestic refuges from Ford's degraded production process, cars such as the Model T were unwelcome reminders of the ills suffered at work. The ill-fitting assemblage of quickly produced parts reminded people of the hurried, fragmented jobs over which they exercised little control. The rigid standardization of design—consumers could get a Model T in any color they wanted, as long as it was black, Ford had once wryly commented—testified to the standardized, homogeneous work that many Americans performed.

Gradually during this period, possession of such mass-produced vehicles became a social stigma, testifying to an individual's lower-class origins. Popular culture made the Model T the butt of many degrading jokes. One quip asserted that you can go anywhere in a Model T, except in society. Another joke queried: Why is a Model T like an affinity (mistress)? The answer: Because you hate to be seen in public with one. In their domestic refuges, Americans wanted products that obscured their factory lives with wholeness, individuality and style. These attributes were woefully lacking in Henry's humble, homely vehicle. Sensing this, Ford sought in a half-hearted way to stylistically update the Model T, introducing in 1926 a lower, long car available in colors for the first time since 1914. These efforts were too little too late, and Ford was forced to discontinue T production one year later to make way for the more stylish Model A.[3]

The second and ultimately triumphant strategy for stimulating demand to match Fordist production was pursued by General Motors, Ford's second-place competitor in the automotive race. Billy Durant founded the corporation in 1908 as a holding company to monopolize automobile production but, by 1920, his financial manipulations had left General Motors a sprawling, disorganized empire in the control of Pierre Du Pont. Du Pont appointed Alfred Sloan as his executive vice-president. This brilliant young executive turned the loose conglomeration of competing companies into a corporate behemoth that dominated the industry for half a century. Upon assuming the reins of the corporation, Sloan began to devise a strategy to crack Ford's market domination. He ruled out head-on price competition in the low-priced field as "suicidal." GM had tried this in 1915 by introducing a Chevrolet priced just above the Model T. But Ford responded with deep price cuts that GM could not match. Sloan concluded in his policy study of 1921 that: "No conceivable amount of capital short of the United States Treasury could have sustained the losses required to take volume away from him at his own game."[4]

The astute Sloan suggested another strategy—fielding a graded hierarchy of products blanketing all markets. Each of GMs'

3 Jean-Pierre Bardou, Jean-Jacques Chanaron, Patrick Fridenson, and James M Laux, *The Automobile Revolution* (Chapel Hill, N.C. 1982), 93–96: James J. Flink, *The Automobile Age* (Cambridge, Mass ,1988), 229 231; Floyd Clymer, *Henry's Wonderful Model T. 1908–1927* (New York, 1955),128-130. The Model T jokes are from David L. Lewis, *The Public Image of Henry Ford* (Detroit, 1976), 121–125.

4 Alfred P. Sloan, Jr., *My Years with General Motors* (Garden City, NY: Anchor Books, 1972 reprint, originally 1963), 76. See also Ed Cray, *The Chrome Colossus* (New York: McGraw-Hill, 19B0), 137; Bardou et al., *Automobile Revolution*, 93.

car divisions would specialize in one price market, eliminating competition between corporate products. And in each market, GMs' product would be positioned in the upper range, offering a better quality auto for a bit more money than the competition. Behind Sloan's innovation product policy was an awareness of changes in the automotive market. He recognized that, in the 1920s, the mass market for basic transportation at a low cost was being replaced by a "mass-class market," which he defined as "the mass market served by better and better cars . . . with increasing diversity."[5] Rising incomes plus installment buying led consumers to demand higher quality in their auto purchases. Sloan recommended that GM meet the demand for escalating quality with a hierarchy of better cars covering all classes, which would capture consumers' dollars as they moved up the consumption ladder. And consumers would be induced to trade in their old cars by offering them annually a new car in every class that was bigger and better.

In 1921, however, Sloan's innovative product policy was merely a paper strategy with no tactical details. It did not explain how the corporation could offer a variety of constantly improving cars without undermining the standardization and high volume necessary for mass production. The specifics of the policy, especially what constituted "better quality," were thrashed out in an internal struggle that eventually shifted the power structure of Sloan's emerging corporate bureaucracy. The engineering and technical people at GM, led by Charles Kettering, defined "better quality" as improved technical performance and economy. Kettering thought both could be achieved by the innovative air-cooled engine he was developing. And so did some top executives like Du Pont, who pushed successfully for its incorporation in a low-priced Chevrolet to be introduced in 1923 to compete with Ford. Unfortunately, the development of the "copper-cooled" engine ran into technical problems that delayed production and interfered with the strategy to capture a larger share of the market. Sloan's plan boldly stated that the purpose of GM "was to make money, not just to make motor cars."[6] He concluded that the pursuit of this "engineering dream" of a technically superior automobile was interfering with the "commercial-mindedness of our original strategic plan."[7]

Sloan ordered that the air-cooled engine program be sidetracked, and that Chevrolet introduce for 1923 a car new in cosmetics only. The Chevrolet Superior of that year offered nine-year-old technology clothed in a body of the newest style, with a lower roof, higher hood and more rounded lines. Brisk sales of this newly frocked car convinced Sloan that perhaps relatively inexpensive and predictable changes in automotive appearance were more conducive to his "commercial-minded" plan than expensive and risky technological innovations. Sloan wrote that his plan to offer "better quality" cars "was valid if our cars were at least equal in [technical] design to

5 Sloan, *My Years*, 72.

6 Ibid., 70.

7 Ibid., 175.

the best of our competitors in a grade, so that it was not necessary to lead in design or run the risk of untried experiments."[8] Thus, it became the policy of General Motors not to be innovative in engineering.

When Alfred Sloan was appointed president of General Motors in 1923, he began in earnest to implement his strategy of offering "better quality" cars by producing better-looking cars, concentrating on style rather than engineering. In 1925, Chevrolet introduced another restyled version of the same old car, whose major features were, in Sloan's words, a "longer body, increased legroom, a Duco finish, a one-piece windshield with automatic wipers on all closed cars, a dome light in the coach and sedan, a Klaxon horn . . ."[9] This newly clothed Chevy boosted division sales to a new peak and reduced Ford's market share from 54 to 45 percent. Sloan was now sure that the concept of better cars that he had formulated in 1921 could practically mean improved appearance and more accessories. In a letter to Harry Bassett on July 8, 1926, he wrote instructively: "I am sure we all realize...how much appearance has to do with sales; with all cars fairly good mechanically it is a dominating proposition and, in a product such as ours where the individual appeal is so great, it means a tremendous influence on our future prosperity."[10] In that year, the sales of GMs' stylish Chevy nearly doubled, while Model T sales dropped 25 percent.

But Sloan's policy called for not only "better" cars but also "continuous, eternal change" to stimulate automobile turnover. With improvements now defined in terms of appearance, continuous improvements came to mean regular, annual changes in automotive appearance. The annual model change emerged in this period at General Motors as part of the Sloanist style policy. From the beginning of the industry, automakers had traditionally incorporated product changes on an annual basis due to the highly seasonal nature of production. In the early industry, most of the yearly changes were mechanical improvements that enhanced the car's utility. As the use of autos became less seasonal, these innovations were sometimes introduced in the middle of the year, and new models often remained unchanged for several years. But Sloan's policy of offering cars continuously improved in appearance quickly led to a policy of annual style changes that spread throughout the industry.

In July of 1925, the General Sales Committee of General Motors undertook a discussion of "Annual Models Versus Constant Improvement." Some sales executives argued strongly against yearly models, stating that improvements should be quietly introduced whenever available. Arguing for regular, annual models, Sloan replied: "That might be best in connection with some changes but, in the case of a different body it presents serious difficulties."[11] He was already focused on the superficial changes in appearance, designed not to quietly improve performance but to publicly propagandize the impression that GM cars were pioneering automotive progress.

8 Sloan, *My Years*, 72.

9 Ibid., 176.

10 Ibid., 311.

11 Ibid., 190.

Sloan's policy of annual model change, carried the day. It offered consumers the illusion of technological progress to persuade them to buy new cars, while the mechanical realities remained largely unchanged to meet the demands of mass production.

The success of Sloan's product strategy hinged on fielding not just one but a whole hierarchy of "better quality, constantly improving cars" to cover the entire automotive market. He reasoned that the quickest way for GM to increase volume was not to dominate one segment but to increase sales in every market segment, using its unique resource of numerous automaking divisions. To achieve this, Sloan proposed to centrally coordinate the products of the previously independent divisions, making each specialize in one of six price segments. He reasoned that this "teamwork could thus attain increased volume at reduced cost."[12] However, increased volume would reduce costs only if the different divisions standardized and shared components, thus allowing their mass production. Sloan began to implement cross-divisional sharing in 1923 by establishing the corporate-level General Technical Committee. The first fruit of this program was the Pontiac, a new car line introduced in 1926 which demonstrated, in Sloan's words, "that mass production of automobiles could be reconciled with variety in product."[13] The car was planned to fill a gap in the product hierarchy between the low-priced Chevrolet and the middle-priced Oldsmobile. In order to reduce the costs of production and development, the General Technical Committee decided that the new engine developed for Pontiac would be put in a chassis that shared with Chevrolet as many parts as possible, including the body. Although the Chevy body had to be slightly modified, there was so much interchangeability or sharing of parts between the new Pontiac and old Chevy that the cars bore a disturbing resemblance to one another. One GM executive wrote that, when the two cars were placed side by side, "you would have sworn it was the same body."[14]

The new program of corporate interchangeability raised the serious problem of differentiating structurally similar cars. The solution was once again styling. If the different lines were differentiated by appearance, then perhaps consumers would pay more for the same technology in a more attractive dress. In this way, the corporation could give consumers the distinction they desired without violating the standardization of mass production. As Sloan wrote in report to the Finance Committee: "People like different things. . . . It is perfectly possible, from the engineering and manufacturing standpoints, to make two cars at not a great difference in price and weight, but considerably different in appearance and, to some extent, different in technical features, both, in degree, built with the same fundamental tool equipment."[15] As Sloan struggled to put flesh on the bones of his 1921 product plan, it thus became clear to him that the styling of automobiles was the key to the future success of the corporation.

12 Ibid., 73.

13 Ibid.,181.

14 GM executive quoted in Cray, *Chrome Colossus*, 248. See also Richard M. Langworth and Jan P. Norbye, The *Complete History of General Motors*, 1908–1986 (New York: Beekman House, 1986), 93–95.

15 Sloan, *My Years*, 207–208.

1927 and the Triumph of Style

The year 1927 marked the triumph of General Motors' strategy of superficial styling over Ford's strategy of standardized utility. Despite attempts to aesthetically update the Model T. Ford's share of the market had dropped to a disastrous 15 percent by 1927. No longer able to ignore the handwriting on the wall, Henry Ford announced on May 25, 1927 that the company would immediately cease production of the Model T and concentrate on the design and tooling of an entirely new car, the Model A. Because Ford's facilities were so rigidly specialized, the changeover was no easy task. To prepare for the production of the Model A, the company had to gut the factory to the walls and begin anew, which took six frantic months and $18 million. The new car revealed that Ford had yet to learn the lesson of the Model T's decline. The Model A was merely an updated expression of Ford's philosophy of one standardized, unchanging, mass-produced motor car for everyone.[16]

But at least Ford's new standardized car was stylish, showing that he grudgingly was recognizing the style imperative. Like many automotive men of his generation, Henry personally had no use for beauty on a machine, and questioned the masculinity of those who insisted on putting it there. But he was forced by the success of the Chevrolet relative to his homely T to recognize that most car buyers did not share his opinion. So when the Model A went into planning, he relented enough to let his artistically inclined son, Edsel, work with body engineer Joe Galamb to design the body and outward appearance of the car. Edsel, who had been president of Lincoln since 1922, was determined to follow the contemporary trend and bring the custom-made look of luxury to the mass-produced car. The Model A was a scaled-down Lincoln in appearance, and borrowed many of the luxury car's style features including rounded corners, a nickel-plated radiator, sweeping hood lines, and fuller fender lines. In comparison to the Model T, which bore aesthetic testimony to the incivilities of the mass-production factory, Henry's new Model A looked more civilized and acceptable in the world of leisure. One popular songwriter was inspired to declare that "Henry's Made A Lady Out of Lizzie," associating the new car with the gender which supervised the civilized consumption retreat from the barbarous male preserve of production.[17]

But the real styling sensation of 1927 was not Ford's Model A, but General Motors' La Salle, a car from the Cadillac Division, which made its debut in March. This stylish but lower-priced cousin of the Cadillac luxury car was the first mass-produced car to have its appearance completely planned from bumper to bumper by one man. Like Edsel's Model A, Harley Earl's La Salle brought the look of the handcrafted luxury car to the factory-produced vehicle by shamelessly borrowing their superficial style features. Unlike Edsel, who had to fight his art-abhorring father to bring style to Ford, Earl

16 David Hounshell, *From the American System to Mass Production, 1800–1932* (Baltimore: Johns Hopkins University Press, 1984), 278–301; William K. Abernathy, *The Productivity Dilemma* (Baltimore: John Hopkins University Press, 1978), 30–33.

17 David L. Lewis, Mike M. McCarville, and Lorin Sorensen, *Ford 1903 to 1984* (New York: Beekman House, 1983) 75–81; "Reminiscences of Eugene T. Gregorie," Automotive Design Oral History Project, Edsel B. Ford Design History Center, Henry Ford Museum and Greenfield Village, Dearborn, Michigan, 1985, 14, 17, 23–25; Strother MacMinn, "American Automobile Design" in *Automobile and Culture*, ed Gerald Silk (New York: Harry Abrams, 1984), 226; song reproduced in Floyd Clymer, *Treasury of Early American Automobiles, 1877–1925* (New York: McGraw-Hill, 1950), 196.

1927 La Salle convertible coupe, with designer Harley Earl at the wheel and Cadillac head Larry Fisher standing (1927). The first car designed as an integral whole by one man, the La Salle demonstrated definitively that automotive style could be mass-produced. (Courtesy General Motors Corporation)

had the complete support of a corporate president who had already realized that the future of the firm vitally hinged on the appearance of its products.

The La Salle began as another of Sloan's efforts to plug the holes in his automotive hierarchy—this time at the high end, between Buick and Cadillac. The objective was to build a smaller, lighter luxury car that sold for just over $2000, considerably under the $3000 price of the cheapest Cadillac. To hold down costs, the La Salle, unlike the other Cadillacs, was mass-produced on specialized machinery and production lines. Sloan and Cadillac head Larry Fisher knew it could not look like a mass-produced car if they wanted to charge a Cadillac price. As Sloan stated: "We wanted a production automobile that was as beautiful as the custom cars of the period."[18] The task of camouflaging the mass-produced Cadillac was entrusted to the man who was to become the father of American automobile styling, Harley Earl.

The son of a Hollywood coach builder who had migrated to California from Michigan, Earl grew up in the nation's emerging entertainment capital helping his father build vehicles for the spectacular movies and their equally spectacular stars. For example, young Harley designed a custom-built car for Western star Tom Mix which sported a real saddle on the roof and was painted all over

18 Sloan, *My Years*, 313. See also Langworth and Norbye, *History of GM*, 95–99; Joseph Geschelin, "Cadillac Production Keyed to Quality Products at Lower Costs, *Automotive Industries 78* (March 6.1937): 389–403.

with the star's "TM" logotype. Consequently, Earl learned at an early age to think of automobiles as entertainment for the masses, a means of mental transport away from life's troubles, as much as mundane transportation from place to place. Readily admitting his application of the Hollywood entertainment ethos to cars, he stated: "People like something new and exciting in an automobile as well as in a Broadway show—they like visual entertainment and that's what we stylists give them."[19] It was just this sort of obscuring, spectacular style that General Motors needed to divert consumers' gaze away from the mundane mechanicals of the La Salle and its other mass-produced cars.

In 1925, Earl was doing custom body work for a Los Angeles Cadillac dealer, where his spectacular automotive style came to the attention of the new head of the division, the brash and style-conscious Larry Fisher. When the two met at a Hollywood party, Earl bragged: "I can make a car for you, like your Chevrolet, to look like a Cadillac." To this tantalizing taunt Fisher replied: "If you can, you've got yourself a job."[20]

Two facets of Earl's work impressed Fisher. First, unlike other bodybuilders who developed their designs in wood and metal models, Earl used full-scale clay models. This pliable material resulted in designs that were less fragmented and mechanical, and more flowing and organic. Second, unlike many traditional coach builders who concentrated their efforts on the body alone, Earl designed all the visible parts of the car, blending them together into a coherent, integrated form. This was exactly the "unified appearance" of the handcrafted cars that Sloan and Fisher wanted to bring to their production Cadillac. Several major bodybuilding companies had been commissioned by GM to tackle the task, but their designs did not capture the look they were after. So early in 1926, Larry Fisher decided to give Earl a chance to bring his organic, integrated body designs to a mass-production car. Earl was brought to Detroit under a special contract as a consultant on the La Salle. Using the dimensions given to him, Earl developed five full-sized clay models, all unified by a basic theme. These models so impressed top GM executives, including Sloan, that they were immediately accepted and rushed into production.[21]

The sporty little production car with a Cadillac nameplate was an instant and unqualified success upon its debut in March of 1927, evoking unheard of superlatives from journalists. The La Salle was touted as one of the most beautiful cars ever built, and widely compared to the Hispano-Suiza, a luxury sports car from Europe.

The comparison was not gratuitous, for Earl later admitted that "I stole a lot of stuff . . . [from] Hispano."[22] Such design larceny did not bother Sloan or Fisher a bit, for it was just this unified look of luxury that they wanted in their mass-produced Cadillac. For a mere $2500, nearly one-sixth the price of a Hispano-Suiza, the buyer got many of the same custom-car features such as dual side mounts, wire

19 Earl quoted in Stanley Bams, "The Styling Staff," manuscript in the Historic Files of the General Motors Design Staff, General Motors Technical Center, Warren, Michigan 1957, 1.

20 Fisher-Earl conversation quoted in Armi, *American Car Design*, 5–6. See also Holliday, "Harley Earl," 9–10; Stephen Bayley, *Harley Earl and the Dream Machine* (New York: Knopf, 1983) 19–25; Michael Lamm, "Harley Earl's California Years, 1893–1927," *Automobile Quarterly* 20, no. 1 (1982): 34 –44.

21 Holliday, "Harley Earl", 10–1; Sloan, *My Years*, 312–313: Bayley, *Harley Earl*, 43–44.

22 Earl quoted in Holliday, "Harley Earl," 9.

wheels, a folding windshield on open cars, a cross-brace between headlights, and original color combinations. It was not merely the accessories, however, but also the overall proportions of Earl's design that evoked the grace, elegance and speed of the luxury classics. The La Salle was longer and lower than other production cars, with sweeping fenders, elongated windows and a novel molding visually accentuating its horizontal lines. Like the handcrafted luxury classics, Earl's design rounded off all sharp corners, thus replacing the mechanical look of rectilinear lines with the organic appearance of curvilinearity. The whole package, down to the last detail, was blended into one harmonious, unified whole that contrasted sharply with the fragmented, assembled look of most production cars.[23]

The overwhelming success of the La Salle and the final demise of the Model T proved the soundness of Sloan's product policy, with its heavy emphasis on superficial appearance. The events of 1927 also convinced Sloan that he had found the individual to implement his policy. On June 23, 1927, the Executive Committee of General Motors approved Sloan's recommendations to create a new staff department "to study the question of art and color combinations in General Motors products," and to hire Harley Earl as its head.[24] Flushed with the La Salle success, Earl returned to Detroit to inaugurate the Art and Color Section, the first styling department of an American automobile manufacturer.

The Institutionalization of Style: Harley Earl and the Rise of Art and Color

The crucial question facing Sloan and the rest of the industry in the late twenties was whether the one-time styling success of the La Salle could be reproduced on a regular basis within a bureaucracy geared to stable, predictable mass production. Could the aesthetic innovation and variety demanded by Sloanist product policy be reconciled with the bureaucratic uniformity and predictability required by Fordist production? American consumers frustrated in their quest for individuality, empowerment and newness in the mass-production process were demanding consumer products that provided at least sublimated satisfaction of their desires. Ultimately, the question facing not only Detroit but the entire nation was whether consumer dreams could be mass-produced in sufficient volumes to placate restive Americans.

Sloan had reason to believe that Earl could reconcile style and Fordist production, could mass produce consumer spectacles on wheels. After all, he was a native of Hollywood, whose movie industry provided him with a model for the mass production of diverting entertainment. The centralized studios harnessed the creative impulses of actors and directors into a routinized system that produced standardized movies at fantastic profits. They were particularly successful during the 1920s in creating wish-fulfilling spectacles that diverted a nation's attention from widening class

23 Paul C. Wilson, *Chrome Dreams* (Radnor, Pa.:Chilton, 1976),123–124: MacMinn, "American Auto Design," 223; Sloan, *My Years*, 313.

24 Sloan, *My Years*, 313.

inequalities. By 1927 Earl had learned his Hollywood lessons well. What was now required of this son of a Michigan migrant was to take these lessons back to the Midwestern heartland of mass production and translate them into sheet metal.[25]

But when this carrier of the California entertainment ethos arrived in Detroit's auto establishment, he was not welcomed with open arms. The hard-nosed engineers and production men who had built and now controlled the auto industry thought about their product as a utilitarian vehicle of mundane transportation, not an ethereal object of art and entertainment. Before the arrival of Earl and his stylists, the task of designing the bodies of mass-produced cars fell to the body engineers, whose primary goals were strength, durability and efficient production. Ridiculing their disregard for style, one of Earl's pioneering designers, Bill Mitchell, described these engineers as looking like house detectives, "wearing their hats all the time, suspenders and belts, button shoes, with pencils in their pockets and their taste in their mouths."[26] For these men pushing cost-cutting mass production, beauty was a feminine trait that belonged in the parlor, not on machines. They had yet to grasp what Sloan and Earl already knew—that the automobile was increasingly a vital part of the domestic refuge of consumption that compensated for the inhumanities of machine production. Consequently, people were demanding that it be as beautiful as everything else in their parlors, where they sought to temporarily escape their mechanized factory lives. To convince the entrenched automotive engineers of this fact was, however, an uphill battle.

Alfred Sloan knew that Earl's attempts to design beautiful and entertaining cars would challenge the traditional authority of body engineers, but he was reluctant to impose the will of the corporation's central management on its divisions. Sloan was in the midst of constructing a path-breaking divisionalized corporate structure, which centralized general policy decisions in the hands of top corporate executives but left the details of implementation to the operating divisions. Forcing the detail designs on divisions would violate this structure, so he gave Earl's new Art and Color Section a rather ambiguous organizational position. It was made part of the corporation's general staff organization, and merely given the power to advise Fisher Body and the divisions on car appearance. As Sloan recalled: "I said to him, 'Harley, I think you had better work just for me for a while till I see how they take you.' With the support of Mr. Fisher and myself, the new section, I hoped, would be accepted by the car divisions."[27]

By making the Art and Color Section part of the central office staff directly responsible to him, Sloan lent Earl's operations the prestige of his personal support. By denying Art and Color any line authority over divisional executives he avoided challenging the power of divisional executives. This dependency of Earl's work on the personal sponsorship of the president was probably due as much to Sloan's desire to control as to protect the new styling function. In

25 Christy Borth, "Harley J. Earl," *Ward's Auto World 5* (June–July 1969): 33–35; Bayley, Harley Earl, 19–25; *Harley Earl*, as told to Arthur W. Baum, "I Dream Automobiles," *Saturday Evening Post 227* (August 7, 1954): 82

26 The Mitchell quote is a composite from two sources: Jerry Flint, *The Dream Machine: The Golden Age of American Automobiles, 1946–1965* (New York: Quadrangle, 1976). 2; and Bill Mitchell and Karl Wilfert, "Is Romantic Styling Dead? Pro and Con Forum," *Motor Trend* 25 September 1973):113.

27 Sloan, *My Years*, 314.

the 1920s, Sloan was trying to bring unity to Durant's decentralized empire by monitoring the divisional implementation of corporate policy through standardized accounting practices. Such accounting controls were possible because most automotive operations were predictable and quantifiable. But the artistic tasks that Sloan wanted to incorporate into his bureaucracy were inherently uncertain and unquantifiable, and thus impossible to control through bureaucratic rules. How could he harness beauty for the business of building automobiles?

The pioneering sociologist of organization, Max Weber, recognized that the only alternative to bureaucratic control through impersonal rules is personalistic control through ties of kin and loyalty. If subordinates cannot be controlled by detailed instructions, they can often be made to act in the interest of superiors through personal loyalty to them. Sloan cultivated such a personal friendship with Harley Earl, which allowed him to personally influence the highly variant tasks of automobile styling.

The two men were widely different in social background. Alfred Sloan came from a well-to-do New York family and an Ivy League education, both of which trained him in the reserve and cultivated indifference of the upper classes. Earl came from a working-class background and although he attended Stanford University, he never outgrew the earthy language and manners he picked up in his father's carriage-building shops. His speech was reportedly crude and ungrammatical—when he was not shouting expletives, he could usually be caught mispronouncing words, most notoriously, aluminum. Earl was given to temper tantrums and emotional outbursts. Still, he and the reserved Easterner Sloan came to be famous friends. They saw one another socially in Detroit and, each summer, Earl spent a month with Sloan on board his yacht cruising and fishing off the coast of Florida. So when Earl needed some corporate firepower in a battle with an engineer or division head, he could call on his personal friend and patron Alfred. Conversely, Sloan could be sure that in all his activities Earl could be trusted to place the good of the corporation foremost; if for no other reason than his personal loyalty to its head.[28]

Even Sloan's personal patronage did not totally overcome the resistance Earl encountered to his styling efforts for, as one early Art and Color stylist recalled, "the higher-ups . . . didn't always understand these things or were too busy with other things."[29] Some forward-thinking divisional executives like Larry Fisher of Cadillac and Bill Knudsen of Chevrolet eagerly sought the advice of the new Art and Color Section. Others, however, resented a California "pretty boy" telling them how to build automobiles. The conflicts with engineers were particularly vicious. These production-oriented men were very reluctant to alter the mass-production machinery once it had been set up. As Sloan pointed out: "An automobile stylist is an advocate of change to a degree that was at first somewhat startling to

28 Ibid., 19; Bayley, *Harley Earl*, 39; Holliday, "Harley Earl," 7–9; Armi, *American Car Design*, 31–32.

29 "Reminiscences of Frank Q. Hershey," Automotive Design Oral History Project, Edsel B. Ford Design History Center, Henry Ford Museum and Greenfield Village, Dearborn Michigan, 1985, 80–1.

production and engineering executives."[30] In his first years at General Motors, Earl fought the engineers at Fisher Body and the divisions tooth and nail. They were constantly telling him that his designs could not be practically and economically rendered in sheet metal. The conflict with the Fisher brothers of the Fisher body Division were classic confrontations of cultural style as well as business philosophy. Bill Mitchell, an early employee of Art and Color, described their battles in this way: "Now, the Fisher brothers were small, and I can remember when I came, they wore homburgs, and what a contrast to this 6'4" man who had a bronze complexion. He'd wear bronze suits, suede shoes—flamboyant was the word and outspoken, a tough man, and he'd cuss those Fisher brother out. We called them the seven dwarfs. He'd say, 'Goddamn, you don't know what you're talking about.' He didn't have any respect because he was hired by Sloan."[31]

Engineers like the Fisher brothers thought of the stylists as a bunch of worthless "fairies" and "pantywaists," whose interference in design was unjustified. Even when a divisional executive accepted one of Earl's designs, body and production engineers often altered it as they saw fit. Such unauthorized alterations were the cause of Earl's early design disaster, the 1929 "pregnant Buick." Earl designed a body with a slight bulge below the beltline around the entire car. However, Fisher body engineers altered Earl's design to make it conform to standard production procedures, pulling in the side panels at the bottom and adding a full five inches in height. The changes accentuated the bulge in the sides, producing an unpleasant fullness that led some to compare the car to an expectant woman. Earl was furious—"I roared like a Ventura sea lion"—but the car went into production nonetheless and was a sales disaster.[32] This pregnant Buick embarrassment reinforced Earl's conviction to win for his styling section unilateral control over the design of GM cars.

Earl was opposed in winning such control not only by engineers but also by divisional sales managers, who believed that their closeness to the market gave them privileged knowledge of consumer wants. They were often as conservative as engineers—if a model was selling well, they did not want to change it. Divisional salesmen also worried that a central design division controlled by one man could not sufficiently distinguish their cars from those in other GM lines. As GM Sales Director B.G. Koether wrote to Sloan in 1927: "Several people have expressed the fear, that if the art and color end of our business would be dominated by one personality, it might possibly be that in the future all General Motors cars would more or less resemble each other." Sloan wrote back assuring him that Earl was keenly aware of "the importance of having things different," but also speculated that it might be necessary to establish a duplicate styling organization in each division.[33]

Clearly, then, Earl's fledgling Art and Color Section had only a tenuous toehold in the emerging bureaucracy of General Motors.

30 Sloan, *My Years*, 315.

31 "Reminiscences of William L. Mitchell," 2.

32 Earl, "I Dream Automobiles," 19. See also Sloan, *My Years* 317.

33 Sloan, *My Years*, 315–316. See also "Reminiscences of William L. Mitchell," 55.

With little official power and only the unreliable patronage of a few higher-ups, Earl was thrown back on his own personal resources to establish styling as an organizational power. And these, from all accounts, were considerable. Earl was undoubtedly talented, but not as an original designer. Most who worked closely with him agreed that he could not draw at all and rarely sketched his own designs. Nor could he clearly articulate his ideas. Earl stuttered and stammered in his attempts to communicate visual ideas to his designers, and often resorted to expletives and sexual metaphors because he lacked the technical vocabulary of design. Earl's verbal weakness developed into a taboo against design argumentation in his whole organization. At Art and Color it was considered unmanly to talk about design, a norm enforced with the frequent rebuke: "I can see but I can't hear."[34]

Earl's real talent lay in his critical eye for design, which was always focused firmly on the bottom line. Earl was an uncanny commercial critic, with an extraordinary ability to anticipate the sales success of a design. As he once wrote: "The only yardstick for measuring the success of styling is its success in the marketplace. Styling that sells is, in the last analysis, styling that succeeds."[35] Earl kept his finger on the pulse of the American marketplace to pick up trends and fashions. One early stylist reported that he was always bringing in fashionable goods for all sorts and vaguely commanding his employees: "Do something like this."[36] Earl also had a keen understanding of consumer motivation. He knew that consumers wanted to be entertained, wanted to escape the mundane monotony of their daily lives into a dream in which their denied needs could be at least superficially fulfilled. As he once candidly told a conference of GM executives: "The dream of the potential buyer must be discovered and satisfied; and the buyer must be awakened with his dreams turned into cars that he can and will buy."[37] Earl's true talent was this ability to probe the psyches of consumers and turn their repressed desires into successful visual styles.

At the same time, Earl's commercial vision would have been ineffective without the sheer persuasive power of his personality. He used his eye for style to sell not only automobiles but also himself; presenting a powerful, impressive figure wherever he went. Standing 6'4" and weighing 235 pounds, he possessed a perennial sun tan. His physical presence always dominated the scene. As if his sheer stature wasn't enough, he also made himself the center of attention by his flamboyant dress. He loved to wear polychromatic linen suits with brightly colored shirts and ties. He coupled this imposing physical appearance with a tyrannical demeanor that cowered nearly everyone around him. His booming voice filled the largest of rooms with intimidating expletives; and his frequent rages sent all but the bravest of souls scampering for cover. Frank Hershey, one of Earl's earliest employees in the Art and Color Section, recalled: "They were scared of him—physically scared of him 'cause he was 6'6" [sic], and he

34 Armi, *American Car Design*,17, 25–34.

35 Harley Earl, "The Look of Things," booklet based on a film prepared by Earl for General Motors Executive Conference in Lake Placid, New York, October 6, 1952, in the Historic Files of the General Motors Design Staff, Design Library, General Motors Technical Center, Warren, Michigan.

36 Earl quoted in "Reminiscences of Paul W. Gillan," Automotive Design Oral History Project, Edsel B. Ford Design History Center, Henry Ford Museum and Greenfield Village, Dearbom. Michigan 1985, 45. See also "Reminiscences of Richard Teague," in same, 45.

37 Harley Earl, "Setting the Style," in General Motors Corporation, *Opportunities Unlimited—Meeting Tomorrow's Challenge* (transcribed speeches delivered at the General Motors Executive Conference in White Sulphur Springs, West Virginia, September 26–28,1955), in the Historic Files of the General Motors Design Staff, Design Library, General Motors Technical Center, Warren, Michigan, 86.

could look down on you with a fierce look that would just melt even some of the hardest executives."[38]

In other words, Harley Earl had charisma, which was exactly what the pioneers of automobile styling needed. They were revolutionaries, seeking to seize power away from the engineers and production experts who had entrenched themselves in the industry's bureaucracies. As Max Weber recognized, those who would overturn an established order of traditional or legal-rational rule must have extraordinary personal powers. As one Chrysler designer stated of all the early leaders of design: "They weren't exactly professional designers as much as strong, dominant actors. They had strong magnetism and very definite ideas."[39] Charisma is, above all, an act and Earl was a consummate actor. Indeed, GM stylist Frank Hershey stated that his persona was a "calculated image." "Earl had to become very macho to survive, because, is those days, the people in Detroit were pretty crude: big, tough, hard-drinking, hard-talking blacksmiths."[40] Beneath the tough, confident image he cultivated, Earl was often insecure, perhaps, Hershey speculated, because of his rather "ordinary background" and inability to express himself well verbally. In spite of this when the towering, meticulously dressed hulk of a man stepped before an audience of divisional and corporate executives, he seemed to have absolute confidence in himself and his designs.

Harley Earl had insight enough, however, to know that charisma is ephemeral and fleeting. Thus, in his struggle to institutionalize the power of styling within Sloan's impersonal bureaucracy, he also sought to construct networks of personal friendship and loyalty to solidify what Weber called patrimonial rule. Earl created allies through engaging people in interaction rituals of solidarity and ingratiation. He quickly penetrated the automotive social circles of Detroit, cultivating friends at the country clubs and cocktail parties. He fit in well with the physically oriented, working-class culture of engineers and production men, for he too had come up the ranks from the shop floor. Earl was also known to use the resources of his section to do personal favors for influential executives like Larry Fisher, for whose yacht Art and Color craftworkers built a cabin.[41]

In the first few years of his infant Art and Color Section existence, Harley Earl occupied himself not merely with external political struggles, but also with the internal technical organization of the work and workers. Before he could sell his designs to corporate executives, he had to organize a team to produce them. Earl had to find artists, engineers and tradesmen who had the skills to design automobiles which were not only stylish, but also functional and feasible to produce. This combination of skills was in short supply, and no established training programs were creating it. Although Earl did recruit some skilled tradesmen on a tour of Europe, most of the talent to create the initial designs was found in the United States.[42]

Earl turned first to the existing bodybuilding shops, both mass-production and custom, and recruited draftsmen of the caliber

38 "Reminiscences of Frank Q. Hershey," 172. See also Bayley, *Harley Earl*, 12–13; Fleming, "Earl of Design," 225; Armi, *American Car Design*, 19–21, 24–34.

39 Interview with Chuck Gale, Senior Designer, Chrysler Corporation, August 27,1987, Highland Park, Michigan.

40 Reminiscences of Frank Q. Hershey, 92, 90.

41 "Reminiscences of Paul W. Gillan," 40. 49–50; "Reminiscences of George Walker," Automotive Design Oral History Project, Edsel B. Ford Design History Center, Henry Ford Museum and Greenfield Village, Dearborn Michigan 1985, 9–11.

42 Sloan, *My Years*, 314–315.

of Frank Hershey from Murphy Body and Gordon Buehrig from Dietrich Body. Still he feared that the inhibiting traditions of custom coachbuilders might prevent them from delivering the constant newness and difference in style necessary to disguise the standardized sameness of mass-production cars. So Earl also "began to look around at anyone who was interested in design and showed some promise," according to one early Art and Color employee.[43] He hired several trained architects and interior decorators, as well as some ad illustrators. Bill Mitchell, who eventually succeeded Earl as head of GM styling, came to Art and Color from the art department at Collier's advertising agency. Many of these artists and illustrators knew little or nothing about the technical requirements of automobile construction. As Earl stated: "We combed the art schools, and then I had to train the ones we hired from the ground up. They were forever making something look good but you couldn't get into it."[44] For Earl, the main requirement for an auto stylist was neither technical knowledge nor aesthetic training but a love for cars. In Bill Mitchell's metaphor, they had to have "gasoline in their blood," that is, to be excited by autos and able to convey that excitement to others visually.[45] Another requirement, perhaps correlated to this, was that Art and Color recruits be men, and decidedly masculine. Earl was concerned that any hint of femininity would handicap his struggle in the rough-and-tumble, masculine world of the auto industry. By the beginning of 1928 Earl had recruited fifty people for the Art and Color Section, ten of whom were actual designers, of varied backgrounds, but united by their macho love of the automobile.

Harley Earl's next task was to mold this mix of diverse talents into a disciplined, centralized organization to convey a unified vision of automobile style. Centralization of aesthetic decisions was necessitated by several imperatives. First, to facilitate corporate interchangeability or sharing of parts between divisions, all divisional designs had to conform to the basic dimensional packages. Second, corporate executives wanted all GM cars to have a recognizable similarity. This "corporate identity" helped to advertise the corporation and keep those trading up buying GM products. Earl had to balance these imperatives for centralized control with the need for aesthetic diversity in order to differentiate corporate models and justify their different prices. He did so by pioneering an ingenious studio organization.

In the early 1930s, when the cost-cutting exigencies of the Depression forced the divisions to begin to share bodies, Earl created a system of separate studios to disguise these mass-produced similarities. In a central location called the Body Development Studio, he and a handful of his most trusted and talented designers developed three shared body shells, one of which was used by all GM models. Then clay models of these shells were turned over to a series of segregated studios, each carefully locked and shrouded in secrecy, which specialized in one division's automobiles. There, the design-

43 Strother MacMinn quoted in Armi, *American Car Design*, 204.

44 Earl quoted in Holliday, "Harley Earl," 12–13.

45 "Reminiscences of William L. Mitchell." 20. See also Strother MacMinn and Michael Lamm, "A History of American Automobile Design, 1930–1950," in *Detroit Style: Automotive Form*, 1925 1950 (Detroit: Detroit Institute of Arts, 1985), 56.

ers applied to these mass-produced, common bodies the details that made them appear unique and distinct: bumpers, grilles, hoods, fenders, headlights, taillights, trim, and color. As one of Earl's earliest stylists stated: "The idea of isolating the creativity that way was a stroke toward the individuality of each division's design or ideas."[46] At the center of the studio system stood the sole aesthetic authority of Earl, supervising and coordinating all activity.

Such central coordination and control was also necessary to drive Sloan's policy of annual model changes. These annual style innovations had to look fresh and new to give consumers the sense of progress they were searching for in their products. For economic reasons, these changes could not be too drastic. The sale of new cars depended upon relatively high trade-in prices, and drastic changes in style tended to depreciate these. Further, major style changes required new body shells, and to change these frequently, undermined the large volumes necessary to cut production costs.

To ensure annual model change that offered consumers the look of newness while maintaining high production volumes and used-car prices, Earl created in the late twenties and early thirties a three-year styling and once again placed himself at the center. In the first year of the cycle, Earl's Body Development Studio would completely redesign a body shell, allowing the stylists in the divisions that shared the shell to create totally new models. For the next model year, divisional stylists gave these cars what they called a "minor face-lift," changing decorative details such as radiator grilles, taillights and bumpers. In the third year of the cycle, when consumers began to tire of the same old shell, stylists made major changes to disguise it, including new fenders, hood and deck. To hold down annual design and tooling costs, GM staggered the styling cycles of the three shells, so only one was completely redesigned each year. Beneath the dazzling kaleidoscope of sheetmetal, however, the major mechanical components remained unchanged, sometimes for decades, allowing GM to achieve the large volumes demanded by mass production. For example, the "Stovebolt Six" engine that Chevrolet introduced in 1929 remained in production with only minor changes through 1954, over a quarter-century."[47]

Harley Earl amassed the power to control these aesthetic programs by creating a rigidly centralized, personalistic organization of authority, with himself at the center. Because the tasks of the artists, engineers and tradesmen in the Art and Color Section were extremely variant, they could not be controlled initially by impersonal, standardized rules but solely by the personal, direct demands and surveillance of an individual. Earl used the same resources to establish his personal dominance over his inferiors that he used with corporate peers and superiors: charisma, intimidation and favors. His physical stature was such a dominant presence that his employees called him "the shadow." He seemed to be everywhere, examining sketches, directing designs and evaluating personnel. "Mistearl," as

46 "Reminiscences of Strother MacMinn," Automotive Design Oral History Project, Edsel B. Ford Design History Center, Henry Ford Museum and Greenfield Village, Dearborn, Michigan, 1985, 31.

47 Sloan, *My Years*, 318; Cray, Chrome Colossus, 276; Bardou et al., *Automobile Revolution*, 209–211.

he was addressed by all who worked for him, came into the studios and personally examined the designers' sketches. Selecting a few for development, he directly monitored the process every step of the way. Displaying his flair for the dramatic learned from his Hollywood idol, Cecil B. DeMille, Earl often strode into a studio wearing jodhpurs and riding boots, seated himself in a director's chair in front of a full-sized clay model of a car, and began barking orders. Pointing to a line with his toe, he would demand that it be altered. As Bill Mitchell recalled, "he would sit there and everyone would run around like a bunch of monkeys."[48] He brooked absolutely no departure from his personal vision of auto aesthetics. "Either go his way or get the hell out!" was the way Mitchell put it.[49]

Earl enforced his unilateral design decisions through personally dispensing both harsh punishments and endearing favors. He cowered and intimidated his employees by arbitrarily firing anyone he did not like or felt was not working hard enough. Yet there was also an endearing and generous side of Earl that could inspire great loyalty. He did little favors and threw big parties for his employees and their families, playing the role of paternal benefactor. He also engaged in small talk and banter with the designers and tradesmen. As one designer, Gene Garfinkle, recalled: "He'd come in, and we would all huddle up around him—he was like a big Smokey the Bear—and he'd always have something engaging to say."[50]

Earl also controlled his employees by inducing cut-throat competition between them. Most often this competition was informal, such as when Earl told one group of designers that compared to others "what they had wasn't worth a damn."[51] Sometimes the competition became formal contests between different studios for a particular design. In these and other ways, Earl induced a dog-eat-dog, competitive ethos among his designers, insuring that the cooperation and communication necessary to form lateral coalitions to challenge his personal authority were all but impossible to cultivate.

Early on, Earl's dictatorial control over the Art and Color Section did not give him much power to affect the overall aesthetics of General Motors automobiles. His organization merely applied color and trim features to bodies already built by GM's Fisher Body Division. As one historian of the styling staff put it, "someone else built the house; he was merely the 'interior (and exterior) decorator,'—he tried to dress up the designs that came his way."[52] Gradually, however, Earl succeeded in expanding the scope of his responsibilities to include the lines and form as well as the color and trim of the body. And as a result of the pregnant Buick episode, Sloan issued an order in 1930 that no changes be made in designs accepted from the Art and Color Section. Although the divisions were under no obligation to accept Earl's design suggestions, more did so voluntarily as his reputation and sales successes grew. But during the late twenties and early thirties, Art and Color designs

48 Mitchell quoted in Armi, *American Car Design*, 223.

49 Ibid., 224. See also Reminiscences of Strother MacMinn," 26; "Reminiscences of Richard Teague," 42–45; "Reminiscences of Joseph Oros and Betty Thatcher Oros," Automotive Design History Project, Edsel B. Ford Design History Center, Henry Ford Museum and Greenfield Village, Dearborn, Michigan, 1985, 11.

50 Gene Garfinkle quoted in Armi, *American Car Design*, 178.

51 "Reminiscences of Irvin W. Rybicki," Automotive Design Oral History Project, Edsel B. Ford Design History Center. Henry Ford Museum and Greenfield Village, Dearborn, Michigan, 1985, 35. See also Gordon Buehrig interview in Armi, *American Car Design*, 228; Bob Thomas, *Confessions of an Automobile Stylist* (n.p.: R.M. Thomas, 1984), 27.

52 Brams, "The Styling Staff," 27.

General Motors Art and Color Section designer, at work on a full-scale orthographic drawing (1937). These precise renderings were used to define the dimensions of the full-scale clay models constructed at the next stage of the design process. (Courtesy General Motors Corporation)

Art and Color Section sculptors, at work on a full-scale clay model (1933). Harley Earl's innovative use of clay models resulted in designs that were more unified and organic than those modeled in wood or metal. (Courtesy General Motors Corporation)

were still substantially constrained by the predetermined layout of the chassis.[53]

The work of the Art and Color Section typically began when a division seeking its assistance turned over the dimensions or a model of the chassis it was proposing for production. Earl then set his designers to work sketching ideas in small scale on paper. This initial work usually was divided between personnel, with one designer assigned to sketch radiator shells, another grille designs, etc. From these sketches, Earl would select a few for further development; synthesizing the various elements into an overall design. When he was satisfied with the basic themes, he ordered the transformation of the sketches into full-scale orthographic drawings;

53 "The Story of GM Styling," manuscript in the Historic Files of the General Motors Design Staff, Design Library, General Motors Technical Center, Warren, Michigan, 1962,1; Earl, "Setting the Style" 86; "Reminiscences of Frank Q. Hershey," 81.

precise, two-dimensional renderings of the outlines of the car from the front, side, and rear views. Also called surface development drawings, they were made on black paper with colored pencils. Earl learned the importance of these full-scale outline drawings from his coachbuilding days, and spent a great deal of time on them. Once the basic lines were established, designers added color and shading to these drawings to give them a better feel for the form. When Earl was satisfied with the orthographies, they were used to construct wooden templates for the full-scale clay models built next.[54]

These clay models allowed designers to blend the separate dimensional drawings into a unified, organic whole, whose dimensions could be quickly altered. First, tradesmen built a wooden armature or framework, complete with wheels, to the basic dimensions of the design. This armature was turned over to the design team, which applied the clay over it. Although supervised by top designers, most of the sculpting was done by clay modelers, blue-collar tradesmen who were below the drawing designers in organizational rank. They heated up modeling clay until it was soft and pliable, then applied it to the armature using the wooden templates as guides. But sculpting the three-dimensional model required details of form unspecified by the two-dimensional drawings, so Earl and his top designers often worked closely with the modelers. Earl liked to present his design ideas to executives at this clay model stage. The size and fullness of a nine- to twelve-foot sculpture could be quite impressive. Over the years, Earl gradually developed techniques that made the clay models look amazingly like real, operating automobiles: metallic foil to simulate chrome, blacked-out windows, and sheets of colored plastic that looked like lacquer paint when pressed over clay. Once the model was approved for production, Art and Color craftworkers constructed a replica out of wood or metal, from which dies for the sheet-metal presses were produced.[55]

The Maturation of Earl's Styling Organization

Throughout the thirties and forties, Earl's organization consolidated power and gained almost unilateral control over the design of all the products of the world's largest corporation The power of the styling organization gradually came to depend less and less on the personality of its head, and more and more on the regularized rules and regulations of GMs' corporate bureaucracy. In 1937, the name of the section was changed from Art and Color to the Styling Staff at the insistence of Earl, who thought that the former was a "sissy name." On the same day, Alfred Sloan regularized Styling's power by appointing Earl to GMs' all-important Engineering Policy Group, a high-level corporate committee responsible for initiating new product programs. "It will give you more authority when you talk to the presidents of these different divisions," Sloan told Earl of his new position.[56] The real institutionalization of Styling's power, however, came in 1940, when Earl was appointed a vice-president of the

54 Armi, *American Car Design*, 6–7, 27–29; Brams, "The Styling Staff," 51–52.

55 "Reminiscences of Gordon Buehrig," 5–7; "Reminiscences of Strother MacMinn," 51–57: Brams, "The Styling Staff, 52–54

56 Sloan quoted in Holliday, "Harley Earl," 13.

corporation. Each subsequent head of the Styling Staff has held this corporate rank, which ensures him of a place on many of the corporation's most powerful standing committees.

Not only was the power of Styling within the larger corporation increasingly bureaucratized. The exercise of authority within the staff also became more rule-governed and regularized. At the top of the staff bureaucracy was the vice-president, whose authority was guaranteed by his position at the coordinating node of the isolated divisional studios. The fact that all information and communications flowed through this office ensured that subordinates in the studios would be unable to establish the lateral communication and coalitions that could challenge the chief's authority. To enforce his decisions, the Styling Vice-President increasingly relied on rewards and promotions within a routinized career hierarchy; and less on the personal favors and punishments characteristic of the early days.

The aesthetic standards upon which stylists were evaluated were also routinized and standardized throughout the thirties and forties. Earl gradually translated his imprecise sense of style into rules that were objectively taught and enforced. One of the most important of these was the highlight rule, which dictated that a straight, uninterrupted horizontal line extend from the front to the rear of the car just below window height. This "through-line," as it was called, caught the light and increased the apparent length of the car. To ensure that the angle of reflection from this line was right, Earl measured it with a highlight gauge, a protractor device with a leveling bubble. Another important rule governed light reflection from chrome brightwork. Earl discovered that the blinding flash of light reflected from chrome applique could not only disguise gaps, seams and surface flaws in mass-produced bodies but also make shared body panels look distinct. He developed rules to ensure that brightwork reflected light right into spectators' eyes. A final example of Earl's rules was his principle of trickle-down aesthetics. He introduced the newest style features, like tail fins, in the corporation's highest-priced makes to differentiate them from the lower-priced cars and to establish their prestige. In subsequent years, he would gradually transfer some of this prestige to the low-priced makes by simply tacking on the style trinkets of their higher-priced corporate cousins. In order to teach these and other rules of auto aesthetics, Earl established his own training program for stylists in the late thirties.[57]

By the fifties, Earl had been so successful in routinizing his charismatic, personalistic rule that he found he was no longer needed. His bureaucratic system rendered the powerful visionary at the top largely superfluous. The programs of annual model changes and model differentiation did require a styling chief who could invent or inspire new, distinctive designs to be processed through the bureaucracy. But Earl found in the mid-fifties that he could no longer fulfill this narrowed role of aesthetic leadership. He had pushed his auto-as-entertainment aesthetic to its limits, and did not know where

57 Armi, *American Car Design*, 269; Strother MacMinn, "Inside the Prewar Olds Studio," *Special-Interest Autos*, no. 40 (May–July 1977): 41: Walter J. Boyne, *Power Behind the Wheel* (New York: Stewart, Tabori and Chang, 1988),145.

Harley Earl and Alfred Sloan, two pioneers of automobile design at Earl's retirement party (1958). (Courtesy General Motors Corporation)

to go from there. The young stylists, most of whom had received formal training, preferred clean forms over chrome encrustation, and light, subtle lines over Earl's rounded, heavy-looking cars.

This generational revolt brewing inside GM broke out in the fall of 1956, precipitated by Chrysler's introduction of a line of crisp, clean, dart-shaped cars designed by Virgil Exner, one of Earl's protégés. When the young GM designers got a look at them, they scrapped the designs guided by Earl, who was on vacation, and started new ones. When Earl returned, he quietly let the rebel designs go into production. Realizing that he had lost his touch, he withdrew from an active role in design, ceding more influence to his second in command, Bill Mitchell. When Earl retired at the mandatory age of sixty-five on December 1, 1958, he only made official his relinquishment of aesthetic leadership to the younger generation.[58]

But this younger generation of designers at GM and, indeed, the entire automobile industry, merely built upon the system and philosophy of car design pioneered by Harley Earl and Alfred Sloan. The basic principles of superficial disguise and individuation of a mass-produced machine would survive through the sixties. But in the seventies, Americans began to struggle against this brand of ethereal auto design for the sake of mundane environmental responsibility, safety and efficiency.

58 Interview with David R. Holls, Executive Designer, General Motors Corporation, August 14, 1986.

Design at CBS
Dennis P. Doordan

Figure 1
William Golden, CBS Eye, 1951.

The CBS "eye" is an icon of the television age and one of the most successful American logos of the modern era *(Figure 1)*. This simple strong design, centered within the box-like frame of a television screen, is successful because it is instantly recognizable; it conveys quickly and unambiguously the information that one is watching the CBS television network. The flexibility of William Golden's original design for the CBS eye is another factor in the success of this corporate coat-of-arms. Since its introduction in 1951, the eye has appeared in black and white and in color, by itself and as part of a sequence of images, in print ads and in animation *(Figure 2)*. The CBS eye is a powerful example of the ability of designers—graphic artists, industrial designers, and architects—to provide a distinctive visual identity for a corporation.

The eye is not an isolated instance of graphic achievement at CBS; it is, rather, part of a long-established tradition of memorable design produced by talented designers working under the aegis of the Columbia Broadcasting System. The tradition and the history of sensitivity to the role of visual design at CBS comprise the subject of this case study. The graphic designer Paul Rand describes corporate logos and trademarks as symbols, and he notes that:

> Symbols are a duality. They take on meanings from causes—good and bad. And they give meaning to causes—good and bad. The flag is a symbol of a country. The cross is a symbol of a religion. The swastika was a symbol of good luck until its meaning was changed. . . . The trademark is a symbol of a corporation. It is not a sign of quality, it is a sign of *the* quality. . . . A trademark is created by a designer but *made* by a corporation.[1]

How CBS *made* its own distinctive visual identity and what quality it is that CBS wishes to convey through its corporate design efforts, rather than the stylistic pedigrees of individual images and designs, is what is of concern.

As in any case study, there are certain circumstances, personalities, and operations that are specific to the case at hand and that, taken together, constitute the unique history of the subject under consideration. One can also, however, look beyond the specifics of the example under review and ask, what light does this case study shed on the larger issues surrounding design and corporate culture in America? There are at least three questions worth considering in this regard: (1) What is the role of visual design—both two- and

I presented an earlier version of this article in May 1989, in a series devoted to the topic of corporate culture, at the Center for the History of Business, Technology, and Society, of the Hagley Museum and Library in Wilmington, Delaware. I wish to thank Dr. Glenn Porter, director of the Hagley Museum and Library, and Professors Roland Marchand and Mona Domash for their constructive criticisms. I also wish to thank Lou Dorfsman, Adrian Murphy, and Florence Miller Rickard for their suggestions.

1 Paul Rand, *A Designer's Art* (New Haven: Yale University Press, 1985): 24.

Figure 2
Lou Dorfsman, CBS Eye as part of a trade advertisement, *Variety*, May 4,1960.

three-dimensional design—in corporate planning and culture? What tasks have designers been asked to perform? (2) When a conflict arises between corporate policy or goals and the design vision of individual designers, how is this conflict resolved? (3) What are the cultural implications of modern corporate design for American society?

Appreciating the history and tradition of corporate design at CBS necessitates knowing something of the history of the industry.[2] Broadcasting began as a makeshift operation staffed by amateur radio enthusiasts. Corporate design as an integral part of the broadcast industry simply did not exist; indeed, the broadcasting industry as we understand it today did not exist. Instead, individuals or small groups of radio "buffs" broadcast to small, local audiences for a few hours each day or week from crude facilities located in converted garages or from the rooftop of a local highrise. This was the era of the pioneers of radio broadcasting. If the history of technology rather than design was the subject of this article, it would be possible to identify a pattern here—tentative, local beginnings nurtured by inspired inventors and dedicated amateurs—with strong parallels to other experiences, such as the development of the automobile, the airplane, and the camera.

Two men are responsible for managing the transition of broadcasting from the era of pioneers to the era of national broadcasting prominence: David Sarnoff, the father of the National Broadcasting Company (NBC), and William S. Paley, the founder of the Columbia Broadcasting System (CBS). Their backgrounds, interests, and management styles are crucial factors that must be taken into account in any discussion of the growth and direction of the broadcast industry. Backed by the Radio Corporation of America, Westinghouse, and General Electric, Sarnoff built NBC into the larger and richer of the two networks. RCA was the world's largest distributor of radio receivers (it handled receivers manufactured by G.E. and Westinghouse as well as its own product line) and supported NBC in hopes of stimulating the sale of radios. Sarnoff began as a radio man in the era of the pioneers and had a strong personal affinity for the technical side of broadcasting. NBC always enjoyed a superiority in the technical aspects of radio and, later, in television.[3]

William Paley, on the other hand, was a wealthy businessman, not a technician. His earliest involvement with radio was as an advertiser. He sponsored a music program on a small East Coast network, called United Independent Broadcasters (UIB), to promote the sales of the Paley family cigar business.[4] In 1928 Paley purchased UIB and renamed it CBS. In addition to his business interest in the new communication medium of broadcasting, Paley was interested in the visual arts. He traveled frequently to Paris, and under the tutelage of such friends as Averell Harriman and John Hay "Jock" Whitney and his art consultant, Albert Skira, Paley began to assemble an impressive collection of French Impressionist and Postimpressionist paintings. In 1937, he was invited to join the Museum of Modern Art's

2 For a history of the radio broadcast industry, see: Erik Barnouw, *A Tower in Babel*, vol. I, and *The Golden Web*, vol. 2 of A *History of Broadcasting in the United States* (New York: Oxford University Press, 1966 & 1968). Barnouw has also written a good one-volume history of television, entitled *Tube of Plenty. The Evolution of American Television* (New York: Oxford University Press, 1975). Also see: Lawrence Lichty and Malachi C. Topping, *American Broadcasting. A Source Book on the History of Radio and Television* (New York: Hastings House, 1975).

3 For more on Sarnoff and RCA, see: Eugene Lyons, *David Sarnoff. A Biography* (Garden City, NJ: Doubleday, 1979), and Robert Sobel, RCA (New York: St. Martin's Press, 1987).

4 For Paley's own account of his career, see: William S. Paley, *As It Happened* (Garden City, NJ: Doubleday, 1979). Also see: Lewis J. Paper, *Empire. William S. Paley and the Making of CBS* (New York: St. Martin's Press, 1987).

Board of Trustees and, eventually, in 1968, he became chairman of the MoMA board. Paley's discerning attention to design at CBS reflects his own personal passion for the visual arts as well as his professional concern with corporate image.

As head of the Columbia Broadcasting System, William Paley exercised ultimate authority regarding the company's design decisions, but he was not the only management figure intimately involved with forging the design identity of CBS. Another key figure at CBS was Paul Kesten. Kesten came to the network in 1930, from a career in advertising. His position at the network was described by one former employee as "vice-president in charge of the future." Kesten was not an operations manager. Rather, his role was that of a "concepts" man, responsible for a wide range of ideas concerning every aspect of the network. Describing his relationship with Kesten, Paley recalled: "We saw eye to eye from the start on the importance of design and good taste."[5]

A third crucial person in the development of CBS was Frank Stanton. The son of a high school Industrial Arts teacher, Stanton joined the CBS Research Department in 1935, after completing a Ph.D. in Psychology at Ohio State. He rose quickly in the organization and, in 1946, upon Kesten's retirement for health reasons, Stanton was named president of CBS, a position he held until his own retirement in 1973. In his capacity as chief operating officer, Stanton was intimately involved in design decision-making at CBS, even more involved, according to former CBS employees, than Paley himself. It was Stanton, for example, who was responsible for saving the CBS eye. In his account of the design of the new logo for CBS television, William Golden, then creative director at CBS and the designer responsible for developing the original concept of the eye, described presenting the new design to a group of CBS executives who expressed mixed reactions.

> But one man's reaction was immediate and decisive. And that was Frank Stanton, the president of CBS. In fact, a year later, when I timidly suggested we abandon it and do something else (for in this world of "show business," you are under constant temptation to change for the sake of change alone) he reminded me of an old advertising axiom. Just when you're beginning to get bored with what you have done is probably the time it is beginning to be noticed by your audience. So I suspect that the keen eye of Stanton and his sensible decision to stay with it, are more responsible for the success of the "eye" than I am.[6]

Golden's generous acknowledgment of Stanton's role serves to remind us that histories of corporate design efforts that fail to take into account the often active participation of the corporate leadership in design campaigns will remain flawed and incomplete.

There is also a legislative aspect to the history of the broadcast industry that must be considered in order to do justice to the

5 Paley, *As It Happened,* 67.

6 William Golden, "My Eye," *Print* (June 1959) reprinted in C. P. Golden, Kurt Weils, and Robert Strunsky, editors, *The Visual Craft of William Golden* (New York: Braziller, 1962):155.

complexity of the story of design at CBS. The Federal Radio Act of 1927 established the legislative basis of broadcasting. The Radio Act specifically repudiated private ownership of the airwaves and created the Federal Radio Commission to manage the airwaves in the public interest. Private stations had to obtain a license to use prescribed segments of the public airwaves. To maintain their licenses, the networks had to demonstrate responsible management of the public airwaves—they had to be "good citizens"—and, therefore, they had to be conscious of their public image.

From the very beginning of his tenure as head of CBS, Paley recognized the necessity of projecting a positive image to several different constituencies. In addition to the general public and its appointed representatives on regulatory bodies, there were other, equally important constituencies Paley needed to address: the broadcast industry itself and the sponsors of broadcast programming. Both in terms of physical and financial resources, the fledgling CBS network was a distant second to the larger NBC networks.[7] To compensate for the discrepancy in size and wealth between NBC and CBS, Paley decided to project an image of CBS as a young vibrant company on the rise.[8] His professional concern with conveying a certain kind of image dovetailed neatly with his personal interest in modern art and design. In an interview, Paley talked about what he perceived as an affinity between modern design—the kind of design he commissioned for CBS—and the broadcast industry. CBS's self-image was that of a progressive and innovative company in a progressive and growing industry. For Paley, modern architecture and design had a "look" (Paley's own word) expressive of the most progressive aspects of contemporary culture.[9]

This concern with achieving a distinctive corporate look extended to every aspect of the operation. Since its inception, one of the primary tasks of design at CBS has been to project a positive, confident, competent image of the corporation to its diverse constituency composed of federal regulators, commercial sponsors, company employees, others in the broadcasting industry, as well as to the general public. CBS executives have consistently used design to communicate. To the extent that design can structure our perception of a corporation and reinforce the self-image a company wishes—or needs—to project, it is indeed an effective tool for shaping not only the public image but the internal culture of a corporation.

A second important role for designers at CBS has been that of problem-solvers. The production and broadcasting of programs presented the industry with a host of practical problems involving the physical design of studio spaces. Early studios were makeshift facilities housed in old garages or empty theaters. Engineers often draped fabric within these converted spaces to eliminate echo effects or otherwise modify the acoustical properties of the studios. Potted plants and flower arrangements bestowed a genteel atmosphere to these primitive facilities and represented the only conces-

7 Until 1941, NBC actually operated two networks: NBC Red and NBC Blue. The FCC ordered NBC to divest itself of one of its networks. Edward J. Noble, the Lifesaver candy king, bought NBC Blue and renamed it the American Broadcasting Company (ABC).

8 See, for example, Paley, *As It Happened:* 67.

9 Author's interview with William S. Paley, June 14, 1983.

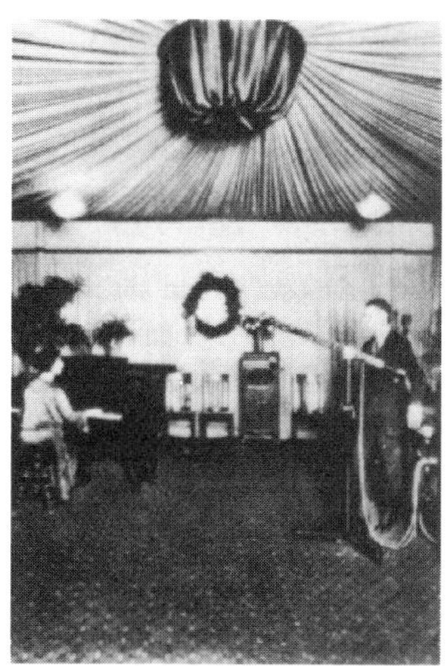

Figure 3
Early Broadcast Studio, Pittsburgh, PA, 1921.

sions to considerations of anything besides technical and acoustical demands *(Figure 3)*.

In addition to working with acoustical engineers, CBS turned to talented architects and industrial designers for assistance in designing more functionally and expressively satisfactory studios. In the mid-1930s, William Paley established a working relationship with the important American modernist William Lescaze. Lescaze was born and educated in Switzerland and came to the United States in the early 1920s. His collaboration, beginning in 1929, with the architect George Howe on the design of the PSFS skyscraper in Philadelphia established Lescaze as one of the foremost practitioners of modern architecture and design in America. His earliest work for CBS, in 1934, involved the conversion of an existing Broadway theater, leased by CBS, into a radio production facility.[10]

Lescaze installed acoustical paneling and engineering control booths within the old theater. The stark character of Lescaze's additions contrasted strongly with the ornate interior of the old theater in a manner that boldly proclaimed the novelty of the new medium of radio *(Figures 4 and 5)*. From the very beginning of his involvement with CBS, Lescaze made no attempt to disguise or camouflage the new forms required by radio facilities. Instead, he identified the essential components of a broadcast studio and sought an appropriate set of forms for the task. He positioned the control booth to provide easy immediate visual contact between the control booth staff and the performers. The STAND BY and ON THE AIR signs are prominently positioned for maximun visibility and the all-important studio clock is isolated for easy reading. The form, location, and graphic design of every detail is carefully considered to ensure that necessary information is conveyed clearly and quickly.

This is a major change from the original and far more primitive studio environments described earlier. Lescaze's early work for CBS also contrasted with the approach adopted by Raymond Hood in his slightly earlier designs for NBC *(Figure 6)*. Hood reasoned that

Figure 4
William Lescaze, Control Booth, Columbia Radio Playhouse, New York, 1934.

10 For a detailed account of Lescaze's involvement with CBS, see: Dennis P. Doordan, "William Lescaze and CBS: A Case Study in Corporate Modernism," *William Lescaze and the Rise of Modern Design in America,* a special issue of *Courier* 19 (Spring 1984). For an account of Lescaze's career, see: Lorraine Lanmon, *William Lescaze, Architect* (Philadelphia: Art Alliance Press, 1987); Christian Hubert and Lindsay S. Shapiro, *William Lescaze* (New York: Rizzoli, 1982).

the broadcast performer lacked the stimulation of traditional concert hall.[11] He tried, therefore, to simulate the effect of an authentic concert hall through the use of theatrical lighting. He attempted to negate the obtrusive presence of the control booth by placing it to the rear of the stage and kept it within the plane of the wall. Hood's studios for NBC were actually mock-theaters. Lescaze's studios, in contrast, were conceived as radio broadcast studios, not dignified parlors (no potted plants here!) or imitation theaters.

In all of his work for CBS, Lescaze functioned as a member of an integrated team of technical experts, acoustical consultants, structural engineers, electricians, and advertising representatives. Lescaze was responsible for the design resolution of a variety of technical, commercial, public relations, and artistic concerns. His solutions reflected the corporate virtues of economy, efficiency, adaptability, and recognizability.

Figure 5
William Lescaze, Signage, Columbia Radio Playhouse, New York, 1934.

Figure 6
Raymond Hood, NBC Broadcast Studio Project, New York, 1928.

Like Paley, Kesten and Stanton were enthusiastic supporters of the new modern style of architecture and design. Given the typically progressive orientation of the corporate leadership at CBS in matters of design, it would seem that the relationship between top management and progressive designers would be a smooth and mutually satisfactory one. Such was not the case, however, as Norman Bel Geddes's experience with CBS demonstrates.[12] In January 1935, CBS commissioned the flamboyant industrial designer to prepare a report detailing the optimal design solutions for radio broadcasting studios in light of current operations and anticipated technological improvements with the understanding that this study of the ideal studio was a prelude to future commissions. Bel Geddes offered two major suggestions regarding the future form of broadcasting facilities.

First, he advocated that future broadcasting facilities be planned as part of larger entertainment centers, complete with dining and dancing rooms, lecture halls, and outdoor gardens. Here Bel Geddes was following the lead of the famous conductor Leopold Stokowski, an early radio enthusiast. In January 1935, Stokowski published an article, entitled "New Vistas in Radio," in the *Atlantic Monthly*.[13] Stokowski described his participation in

11 Raymond Hood, "The National Broadcasting Studios, New York," *Architectural Record* 64 (July 1928).

12 The following account is based upon material preserved in Norman Bel Geddes papers on deposit in the Harry Ransom Humanities Research Center at the University of Texas. I wish to thank Dr. W. H. Crain and the staff of the Ransom Center for their coopention during my research.

13 Leopold Stokowski, "New Vistas in Radio," *The Atlantic Monthly* 155 (January 1935).

recent experiments at the Bell Telephone laboratories involving sound transmission at various frequencies. He then went on to describe his vision of elaborate recreation centers, including performing and visual arts facilities, athletic fields, restaurants, and gardens.[14]

Second, Bel Geddes predicted steady improvements in the quality of sound recordings and recommended that CBS conceive of future studios as "sound laboratories" that would involve the broadcasting of pre-recorded music and programs and the gradual elimination of live audiences. Studios would shrink in size as provisions for audience seating were eliminated, and the engineering facilities would increase in size as more and more of the program was manipulated electronically. Bel Geddes argued that shifting to an increasingly automated studio would generate substantial economies.

Whatever the merits of his proposals were, the Bel Geddes report was quickly and firmly rejected by Paley and Kesten. Indeed, CBS terminated the contract after only a few months. The minutes of meetings, preserved in the Bel Geddes archives, make it painfully clear that, in 1935, the top management of CBS was not prepared to abandon the idea that a live audience was a crucial ingredient of the CBS approach to programming or the network's commitment to broadcasting live, not pre-recorded, programs. Bel Geddes had violated what one of his contemporaries, the industrial designer Raymond Loewy, called the MAYA principle.[15] MAYA is an acronym for MOST ADVANCED YET ACCEPTABLE. The MAYA principle comes into play when a designer's vision—his prophecy if you will—conflicts with company practice. Bel Geddes had proposed something not yet acceptable to his clients.

Corporate design is not a democratic process in which differences can be negotiated and compromises reached. Nor is it a world in which the designer reigns supreme and acts as final arbiter of artistic differences. In corporate culture, designers perform a service role and serve at the discretion of others. Their work, their decisions, and their visions of the future are subject to review and amendment by the leadership of the corporation. As Paul Rand points out, designers *create* possibilities but it is the corporation, not the designer, that *makes* its own identity.

Although Bel Geddes's involvement with CBS was brief, it was not totally without effect. In 1937 CBS began construction on station KNX, the new West Coast headquarters for the network.[16] Designed by William Lescaze, the KNX complex in Hollywood included studio and office space for radio operations; it also included a restaurant and several trendy shops. The extra, non-radio facilities generated some additional revenue for the network, but more important, it represented a step in the direction of the type of recreational complex Bel Geddes had described *(Figures 7 and 8)*.

Lescaze's design solution to the myriad practical problems was flexible, efficient, and uncompromisingly modern. The trade journal *Radio Daily* described the new facility, named Columbia

14 A copy of Stokowski's article is preserved in the CBS project files on deposit in the Bel Geddes archives. For more on Stokowski's involvement with sound recording and broadcasting, see: Daniel Oliver, *Stokowski* (New York: Dodd, Mead & Company, 1982).

15 Raymond Loewy, *Never Leave Well Enough Alone* (New York: Simon and Schuster, 1951): 277–81.

16 For more on the KNX facility, see: "CBS Broadcasting Studio Hollywood, California," *Architectural Forum* 68 (June 1938): 454–64.

Figure 7
William Lescaze, CBS Station KNX, Hollywood, CA, 1936–38, exterior.

Figure 8
William Lescaze, CBS Station KNX, Hollywood, CA, 1936–38, rendering of a broadcast studio.

Square, as: "technically and physically . . . perhaps the most advanced radio home in the world today."[17] Once again, CBS designers had solved operational problems and projected the desired image of a sophisticated and progressive company on the move.

The advent of television after World War II opened a dramatic new chapter in the story of broadcasting. The new form of broadcasting presented the industry with all the challenges attendant upon the introduction of a new technology. But the history of technology and the history of design are two separate tracks within the history of corporate America. The change in broadcast technology altered the technical parameters within which certain functional problems had to be solved, and the cast of designers working for CBS changed with the passage of time. These changes, however, did not generate a corresponding change in the corporate design agenda. Design was still a team effort. Designers were still asked to perform the same tasks—solve practical problems and project a desired image—and designers still had to observe the MAYA principle. The parallels between the design programs of radio and television studio facilities are very strong: the demand for flexible space; the preference for clear, direct expression of the nature of the problem; and the strikingly modern style of the results at CBS are evident in both.

In 1951, CBS began construction of Television City in Los Angeles *(Figure 9)*[18]. Ending more than a decade of collaboration between CBS and William Lescaze, Paley turned to the architectural firm of Pereira and Luckman for the design of this major new facility. In the 1950s and 1960s, William Pereira was one of the stars of contemporary American architecture; his lifestyle as well as his work was profiled in both the popular and the professional press.[19] The selection of Pereira and Luckman conformed to the CBS custom of hiring nationally prominent designers whenever possible.[20] Pereira's partner, Charles Luckman, turned to architecture as a

17 Quote by Paley in *As It Happened:* 116.

18 For additional information on Television City, see: "CBS TV City Starts," *Architectural Forum* (May 1952): 101–10.

19 Pereira, for example, is one of only a handful of American architects to ever be the subject of a *Time* magazine cover story. See: *Time* 82 (September 6,1963).

20 In a related example of the value CBS placed on commissioning work from recognizable designers, CBS, in 1948, once again commissioned Norman Bel Geddes as a production consultant to advise on the ideal format for television studios. Reporting the agreement in its April 7, 1948, issue, *Variety* noted: "Inking of Bel Geddes is regarded in the trade as a result of CBS board chairman William Paley's yen for big names." (Clipping preserved in the Bel Geddes archives.)

Figure 9
Pereira & Luckman, CBS Television City, Hollywood, CA, 1951–52.

second career, after a first, and very successful business career as President of Pepsodent and, later, Lever Brothers. Luckman's earliest contact with William Paley came as a result of advertising, not architecture; he had sponsored a number of CBS radio programs as a way to promote Pepsodent toothpaste and, later, various soap products. After turning to architecture, Luckman approached potential corporate clients as one business man to another, as someone capable of translating business considerations into architectural form, because he was conversant with both the language of architecture and business.[21] One former CBS employee recalled: "We had confidence in our ability to communicate with Mr. Luckman. He spoke our language, and because he also spoke an architect's language, he could translate, supposedly, our desires to Pereira."[22]

This ability to speak two languages is one of the crucial factors in the success of those designers who work within the corporate world. As Paul Rand reminds us, the corporation makes its own identity and it asks designers to translate that identity into workable forms that communicate a sense of the distinctive qualities of the corporation.

In 1946, CBS hired a young graphic designer named Lou Dorfsman.[23] Dorfsman rose through the organization and eventually became vice-president and creative director for advertising and design at CBS. He left his mark on virtually every aspect of the organization, ranging from the design of the letterhead, covers for annual reports to the stockholders, advertising graphics, and office interiors. After the death of William Golden in 1959, Dorfsman more than any other single designer created the visual identity of CBS and maintained the consistently high quality of graphic and industrial design throughout the company. In the 1960s, Dorfsman transformed the seventeenth-century typeface, Didot, into CBS's

21 "The first time I called on a client, I talked to him as one businessman to another, and sold him on the idea of the uniqueness of our firm by saying . . . Pereira will be the architect and I'll be the businessman." Charles Luckman, *Twice in a Lifetime: From Soap to Skyscrapers* (New York: W. W. Norton, 1988): 278.

22 "The William Lescaze Symposium Panel Discussion," *Courier* 19 (Spring 1984): 75.

23 For a comprehensive review of Dorfsman's career, see: Dick Hess and Marion Muller, *Dorfsman & CBS* (New York: American Showcase, 1987).

Figure 10
Lou Dorfsman, Signage, CBS Building, 51 West 52nd St., New York, 1964–65.

contemporary typographic "signature" (known as CBS Didot) used throughout the corporation.

Like Golden, Dorfsman is quick to credit Frank Stanton's role in the design decision-making process at CBS. Although Paley retained ultimate authority regarding design decisions, Dorfsman recalls, Stanton monitored the day-to-day operations and jealously maintained the CBS tradition of distinctive design.[24] Stanton, for example, played an active role in the development of the new CBS headquarters designed by Eero Saarinen at 51 West 52nd Street in New York. Stanton convinced Paley to accept the selection of the dark stone used on the exterior of the building (the source of the building's nickname, Black Rock). It was also at Stanton's instigation that Dorfsman assumed responsibility for the graphics and many of the interiors at Black Rock.[25] Lettering, signage, elevator panels, drop boxes—all those moments and places where one reads and comes into actual contact with a building—were carefully conceived and designed by Dorfsman to ensure the clarity of information and the stylish look that, by the mid-1960s, had become the undeniable marks of CBS design *(Figure 10).*

The move in 1965 to the new corporate headquarters at Black Rock was only part of a major design campaign within the company, a campaign that was increasingly under the direct control of CBS in-house design staff rather than contracted out to free-lance designers. Lou Dorfsman, for example, standardized the letterheads on corporate stationery *(Figures 11 and 12).*[26] No one below the rank of vice-president could have personalized stationery. He replaced the multiple typefaces, paper sizes, and weights then in use with a limited selection. By buying standardized supplies in huge quantities he was able to negotiate with the paper manufactures to substitute the CBS insignia for the paper company's own watermark. Bulk ordering of the new stationery resulted in substantial savings. The result was both elegant and economical. In a company with most

24 Conversation with Lou Dorfsman, May 25, 1989.

25 In his memoirs, Bill Leonard, former president of CBS News, wrote: "Black Rock . . . will be known forever among CBS people as Stanton's building." Bill Leonard, *In the Storm of the Eye. A Lifetime at CBS* (New York: G. P. Putnam's Sons, 1987), 178. For more information on Stanton's role in the development of the 51 West 52nd Street building, see: Paper, *Empire: William S. Paly and the Making of CBS,* 247–248.

26 For more on the design of CBS stationery, see: Hess and Muller, *Dorfsman* & CBS, 35.

Figure 11
Lou Dorfsman, CBS Stationery, 1964–65.

Figure 12
Lou Dorfsman, CBS Stationery, 1964–65.

designers who work within the corporate framework, Dorfsman has always maintained that good design is good business.

Not everyone within CBS accepted standardization of design and procedures as either good design or good business. In his memoir, Paley noted:

> [Stanton] systematized various company procedures, chains of command, even office decor and the way CBS secretaries typed business letters. Some of the "creative" minds at CBS resented what they took to be a loss of their freedom and liberties, but most of what Frank instituted was necessary and gave a special quality to a growing company.[27]

But as CBS grew in size over the years, the standardization of design throughout the organization served another purpose in addition to achieving the economic benefits associated with the bulk ordering of materials. The careful crafting of a corporate look provided a visual anchor, a recognizable constant in a world of explosive growth and incessant change. Design plays a major role in structuring our perception of the world. Through a consistent attitude toward design, a corporation can identify itself—highlight *the* distinctive quality of the organization—both to those within and those without the organization.

The character of the corporate identity visualized by Paley, Stanton, Lescaze, Golden, and Dorfsman is a national one. The Zip codes of CBS facilities change as one moves across the country but not the corporation's basic design presence. Regionalist touches have never had a place in CBS design programs, and here it is worth considering the implications of the design experience at CBS for American culture as a whole.

It was in the years between the world wars that the balance between regional and national cultures in the United States began to tip decidedly in favor of nationally recognizable forms of expression. This shift affected more than a single industry or group of designers; it affected Americans' sense of their national identity. In the very same years that artists, such as Grant Wood and Thomas Hart Benton, were trying to preserve a regionalist flavor in American culture, broadcasting was slowly beginning to subvert regionalism as a significant phenomenon.[28] William Paley and David Sarnoff masterminded the creation of truly national broadcasting networks, and the leaders of the broadcasting industry recognized very early the implications of what they were doing. In a 1924 speech, entitled "Radio and the Farmer," Sarnoff declared that beyond delivering news and entertainment, radio would help as follows:

> To relieve the farmer and his family of the sense of isolation which is, perhaps, the harshest handicap of agricultural life . . . [and] to cope with class and sectional differences and develop greater national unity as between the farmer and other elements of our citizenship.[29]

27 Paley, *As It Happened,* 224.

28 For a discussion of the growth of radio in the 1930s, see: Alice Goldfarb Marquis, "Written on the Wind: The Impact of Radio during the 1930s," *Journal of Contemporary History* 19 (July 1984): 385–415.

29 David Sarnoff, *Looking Ahead. The Papers of David Sarnoff* (New York: McGraw-Hill, 1968): 52.

National networks created the opportunity for Americans from coast to coast to hear the same news and listen to the same entertainment simultaneously. In 1922, there were 30 broadcast stations operating in the United States. After 25 years, there were 1,000 AM stations and 134 FM stations on the air and radio sets were in 93 per cent of American households. Time and distance no longer separated Midwestern farmers and their families from a concert in New York or a football game in California. In only two and one-half decades, radio went from being a curiosity to being a fixture in virtually every American home. Broadcasting was a crucial force in the creation of a truly national culture. Through design, Paley, Kesten, and Stanton projected an image of CBS—and by extension, the entire broadcasting industry—as an expansive and progressive phenomenon unhindered by parochial concerns or regional limits.

Between the early 1930s and the mid-1960s, CBS grew from a fledgling East Coast network into a broadcasting giant. During these same years, the CBS corporate leadership established a tradition of sensitivity to design and skillfully used design to project a dynamic image of the organization. The CBS look emphasized clarity, flexibility, and elegance. The story of design at CBS illustrates several important points of interest to design historians.

First, design serves a crucial purpose within corporate culture. Because design does much to structure our perception of the world around us, it is an effective vehicle for the transmission of a sense of corporate identity to multiple constituencies.

Second, the study of design in the corporation should begin, not with the designer, but with the leadership of the corporation, for it is the corporate leaders who set the design agenda. William S. Paley and his closest associates—Paul Kesten and Frank Stanton—had a clear conception of what they wished to project through design and to whom they wished to project it. Their continued commitment to design is responsible for the impressive accomplishments of CBS design.

Third, having *made* the corporation, Paley and his associates turned to individuals with the special talents required to *create* the visual identity and solve the practical problems posed by design. William Golden, Lou Dorfsman, William Lescaze, and others are recognized by practitioners and historians alike as masters of their respective crafts. In textbooks and trade journals, their work for CBS is consistently singled out as outstanding examples of modern design.[30] Their reputations added an additional lustre to the corporation they served.

Fourth, in exercising their talents these designers had to take into account a whole host of practical, material concerns, things such as budgets, existing technologies, available time, and allotted space. They also had to observe the MAYA principle, to extend but not exceed the limits established by the Most Advanced Yet Acceptable thinking of the moment. The MAYA principle estab-

30 See, for example, Philip B. Meggs, *A History of Graphic Design* (New York: Van Nostrand Reinhold, 1983): 425–27, and Arthur J. Pulos, *The American Design Adventure 1940–1975* (Cambridge, MA: MIT Press, 1988): 274–76.

lishes the boundary between avant-garde and corporate or commercial design.

Fifth, the designers who enjoyed the longest and most prolific relationship with CBS were those who managed to internalize the values of the corporate culture they served. Lescaze was a committed modernist, his new progressive architecture was the perfect expression of the youthful progressive spirit of the young network. Luckman "spoke the businessman's language." Golden and Dorfsman consistently criticized experimental or avant-garde graphic design as art for art's sake and narrowly elitist in its appeal.[31] They accepted the dictum: good design is good business.

The Columbia Broadcasting System can boast of a sustained record of memorable, effective, and functional design accomplishments. Credit for this impressive achievement must be jointly shared by the corporate leadership and the professional designers responsible for creating the image of CBS. Both groups realized that design could be an effective tool for shaping organizational identity as well as solving problems of physical form only when it was treated as an integral part of corporate planning. To appreciate all the ramifications of design in a corporate milieu, future case studies must do more than merely identify designers and describe award-winning or money-making designs.

31 See, for example, William Golden's comments at the Ninth International Design Conference in Aspen, Colorado, June, 1959, reprinted in: C. P. Golden, *The Visual Craft of William Golden,* 57–81.

Promoting Aluminum: Designers and the American Aluminum Industry

Dennis Doordan

Aluminum is one of the ubiquitous metals of the late twentieth century. Designers have used aluminum for everything from aircraft design to cookware; objects as diverse as skyscrapers and lunch sandwiches have been wrapped in aluminum. This pervasive presence of aluminum in the designed environment is not, of course, the result of chance or coincidence. Starting in the late 1940s, the American aluminum industry embarked on a remarkably successful campaign to promote the use of aluminum.

Even a brief review of this campaign, such as this essay offers, can be rewarding for design historians and practitioners. A case study of the design activity sponsored by the American aluminum industry affords historians the opportunity to explicate the complex relationship between design and industry in the modern era. A review of the place and role of design in the American aluminum industry also challenges historians to distinguish between the emerging field of design history and other scholarly disciplines such as the history of technology or business studies.

In order to understand the dynamic role played by industrial designers within the American aluminum industry after World War II, several questions need to be answered:

- What were industrial designers asked to do by the aluminum industry? What was the agenda for design within the industry?
- How were designers integrated into the corporate structure of the industry?
- What was the political and economic situation within the industry that prompted the industrial leadership to engage the services of professional industrial designers?
- How do we assess the impact of the war on design? Is the post-1945 era distinguishable in any significant way from the pre-World War II era?

Aluminum, of course, was a familiar material to designers and consumers alike before the outbreak of World War II. Since aluminum was clearly part of the new "machine esthetic" of the pre-war years in America, it is important to identify the factors that distinguish the post-war history of aluminum. Although the volume of aluminum available to designers was greatly increased after 1945, the post-war story of aluminum is not the result of quantitative factors alone. There was a significant difference in the importance attached to design activities *within* the aluminum industry before and after the war.

Design was a marginal activity within the industry before the war; it was a crucial corporate concern after the war. In order to understand why this is so, it is necessary to know something about the history of the industry and the life cycle of aluminum itself.

The life cycle of aluminum begins with bauxite, which is refined into something referred to within the industry as pig aluminum. Pig aluminum constitutes the basic material from which all end products (often in the form of alloys created to enhance various properties of aluminum) are fabricated. Activities best described as scientific and technological in nature dominate the front end—from bauxite to pig aluminum—of the aluminum cycle. However, activities more properly characterized as design efforts dominate the rear end of the cycle—from pig aluminum to final fabrication.

Before 1940, the American aluminum industry was synonymous with one company, the Aluminum Company of America (Alcoa), founded in 1888. Alcoa was the sole American producer of pig aluminum. Anyone who designed and made anything with aluminum—from architectural elements to cooking utensils—purchased their aluminum from Alcoa. And Alcoa was oriented to the capital-intensive, large-volume front end of the material cycle. The company directed its efforts to basic research and development in the areas of metallurgical science and the production technologies necessary to reduce, refine, smelt, forge, and cast aluminum. It did so because, for most of the first four decades of this century, pig aluminum represented a very substantial share of the value of finished or end-line aluminum products. In 1919, for example, the value of pig aluminum represented fully two-thirds of the value of any finished aluminum product. Industry analysts noted that, as a result, the early stages of the industrial process—from bauxite to pig aluminum—were creating more wealth for the industry than the later stages.[1] In such a situation, it is in the immediate interests of the industry to focus its efforts on scientific and technological research directed to improving the production and handling of pig aluminum.

World War II dramatically changed this. It did so for two reasons. First, the war accelerated one existing trend within the industry. Second, the war ultimately forced a complete reconfiguration of the aluminum industry. Together, these two factors created a postwar climate in which activities we can recognize as design activities (as opposed to strictly technical research and development activities) emerged as important industry considerations.

In the 1920s and 1930s, the value of pig aluminum in relationship to the value of fabricated end products declined. In 1933, it still amounted to more than half the value of any finished aluminum product; but by 1939, pig aluminum's share of product value had fallen to 40 percent. World War II accelerated this decline as more and more new applications and end products were developed. The rear end of the material lifeline—fabrication of finished products—now grew in importance.

1 Nathanael Engle, Homer Gregory and Robert Mosse, *Aluminum: An Industrial Marketing Appraisal* (Chicago: Richard D. Irwin, 1945).

Another factor to note involves the productive capacity of the industry. In order to meet the voracious wartime demand for strong lightweight metals, the United States government subsidized the expansion of the industry's productive capacity. As a result of direct government investment, the production of aluminum increased by more than 600 percent between 1939 and the peak year of 1943. This far outpaced the increase in other critical metals such as steel or copper.[2]

Even before the conclusion of the war, industry executives were concerned with developing new markets to absorb the expanded productive capacity. In an important study of the aluminum industry, published in 1945, industry analysts argued:

> Looking to the future, the transition from war- to peacetime uses of aluminum must take place at the fabricating stage, new products must be discovered, engineered, and produced or there will be fewer jobs at all stages of the aluminum industry.[3]

In 1944, Congress passed the Surplus Property Act; it initiated the process by which the federal government divested itself of the factories built with public money during the war. Alcoa was ready and willing to purchase the new aluminum facilities in order to preserve its monopoly. However, in 1945, the Justice Department initiated an antitrust action designed to break Alcoa's monopoly. The goal of the United States government, repeated by numerous government officials in courtrooms, committee hearings, and legislative chambers, was to promote a free enterprise system based on competition for market share within the industry.[4] The government refused to sell the new productive facilities to Alcoa and, through every possible means, worked to create a competitive industry for aluminum. Alcoa's monopoly was at an end.

Encouraged by the federal government, the R. J. Reynolds Tobacco Company—long a consumer of aluminum for cigarette packaging—and the Kaiser Company—a shipbuilding and heavy construction concern—quickly established independent aluminum companies, acquired aluminum production facilities from the Surplus Property Board, and entered the market as vertically integrated primary producers of aluminum.

The forced reconfiguration of the aluminum industry, together with the recognition on the part of the industrial leadership that the continued vitality of the industry was increasingly dependent upon the rear end or final application stage of the material cycle, ushered in a fundamentally new era in the history of aluminum: the design era.

The Reynolds Metals Company led the way in providing a coherent identity and clearly defined role for design in industrial planning. In 1950, Reynolds created a Styling and Design Department headed by Jim Birnie, a package designer already employed by

2 George David Smith, *From Monopoly to Competition: The Transformation of Alcoa, 1888–1986* (Cambridge: Cambridge University Press, 1988), 223.

3 Engle, et al., *Aluminum*, 189.

4 See, for example, the document published by the U.S. Government Printing Office, *Joint Hearings on the Aluminum Reports of the Surplus Property Administration, October 15, 16, 17, 18, 19, 1945* (Washington, DC: 1945).

Reynolds. In 1955, Alcoa consolidated staff and activities previously scattered throughout the company into a new Market Development Department headed by Fritz Close, formerly of Alcoa's Sales Department. Close immediately hired Sam Fahnestock, an industrial designer previously employed in the design offices of Harold Van Doren, Dan Dailey, and Peter Muller-Munk. Kaiser Aluminum hired Franklin Q. Hershey in 1956 to head up its Industrial Design Department. Hershey was the former chief stylist for Ford.

The size and designation of these design units varied among the three companies. Here we are interested in what they had in common.[5]

- All three design units were clearly distinguished from the more scientific and technologically oriented research and development units within the industry.
- The heads of design units reported to the vice president for sales or to some corporate strategic planning committee, while the heads of R&D reported to the individuals or committees responsible for basic manufacturing processes.
- The personnel in these design units came, for the most part, from a sales background or from design staffs of other corporate and industrial design offices, in contrast to the science and engineering backgrounds of most of the R&D staffs.

What did the aluminum industry ask their in-house design staffs to do? Interestingly, the industry did not ask Birnie, Close, and Hershey to design end products. Designers employed by the aluminum industry seldom competed directly with independent designers or those employed by the industry's customers. Instead, they were expected to work with designers outside the industry, to assist them in understanding the properties and performances of aluminum and aluminum alloys, and to encourage other designers to find new uses for aluminum.

A 1956 Reynolds publication succinctly states the prevailing design wisdom in the industry during the 1950s:

> The fullest exploitation of anything new, whether it is an idea, a technique, or a material, demands understanding and imagination.[6]

To promote understanding and imagination, industry design staffs set out to educate and stimulate designers. At the rear end of the material cycle (i.e., final fabrication), aluminum appears in the form of various alloys, all of which can be produced in a variety of thicknesses, textures, finishes, colors, etc. Aluminum is really an amazingly diverse set of lightweight metals. In order to assist independent designers in identifying and specifying the proper form of aluminum for specific situations, industry designers distributed informative literature and samples, visited design offices to demonstrate new developments, invited outside designers to visit

5 For a profile of designers employed by the aluminum industry, see Hugh B. Johnston, "The Aluminum Industry and Design," *Industrial Design* 3 (August 1956): 50–63.

6 John Peter, *Aluminum in Modern Architecture*, vol. 2 (Louisville, KY: Reynolds Metals Company, 1956),13.

aluminum production facilities, answered questions, and publicized innovative uses for the material.

In 1959, Frank Magee, president of Alcoa, described Alcoa's approach to working with outside designers:

> Our program with industrial designers, begun over the past five years, aims to place Alcoa's knowledge and facilities at the disposal of any designers who can use them. Our own industrial design group was established for the sole purpose of aiding industrial designers in their projects—not in any way to compete with the designer![7]

At Reynolds, Birnie conceived of his design department as an open house where designers were welcome to visit with problems and questions, or just to satisfy their curiosity. According to Birnie:

> Designers are welcome to come in here and stay as long as they like. And they do come, too. And we tell them what tricks we know about designing in aluminum.[8]

How successful were Alcoa, Reynolds, and Kaiser? Extremely successful. Henry Dreyfuss, for example, noted:

> I think most designers would agree that the aluminum people have done a far more effective job of education than other metal suppliers. They have spread the word about the design possibilities of their material, and have succeeded in establishing a connotation of "modernity" which older industries have reason to envy.[9]

Education, then, was an important function performed by the industry's own design staffs. They developed and disseminated a specialized body of information for use by the primary designers of finished products. Industrial design departments served as a crucial link between the industry's research, development, and production divisions and the design community. One of the conclusions to be drawn from this is that this kind of design activity alters the traditional relationship between the designer and the designed object. Birnie, Close, and Hershey designed *information* not *objects*. This is in contrast to the classic (and limiting) model of a designer engaged by an industry to design—or redesign—final products.

The corporate and design leadership of the aluminum industry realized that providing information concerning the physical properties of aluminum was not enough to insure designers would actually employ their product. Alcoa, Kaiser, and Reynolds all worked to stimulate a climate of creative engagement with aluminum on the part of independent designers. Industry publications, distributed free to design offices and schools, were filled not only with technical data but also with articles on design management in large corporations, portfolios of recent distinguished design in aluminum,

7 Frank Magee, "Alcoa and Design," in *Design Forecast 1*, ed. Samuel Fahnestock (Pittsburgh: Alcoa, 1959), 4.

8 Johnston, "The Aluminum Industry and Design:" 53.

9 Henry Dreyfuss, "Product Studies: Aluminum" *Industrial Design* 7 (May 1960): 56.

reports on industrial and design trends, and, significantly, essays on themes such as creativity, innovation, and the phenomenon of change.[10] According to industry publications, the use of aluminum could be justified on the basis of its expressive properties as well as its functional performance criteria. In the hands of creative designers, aluminum could do more than solve technical problems involving strength-to-weight ratios; it could wed art and manufacturing, thus enriching the esthetic dimension of life while serving practical ends.

The widespread application of aluminum at all levels of design activity after World War II was not the product of some vaguely defined but inexorable march of material progress. Historians should avoid accounting for change by advancing the romantic notion of the will-of-the-epoch reified in the form of aluminum foil. Nor can the stylistic analysis of aluminum objects alone reveal the root causes of their pervasive presence, because corporate not esthetic concerns exercised a determining role in the post-war history of aluminum.

The federally mandated reconfiguration of the industry and its expanded productive capacity explains *why* the aluminum industry moved in the direction it did after World War II. But market conditions and production capacity alone cannot explain the *form* design activities assumed within the industry. The design efforts of the aluminum industry were informed by an intellectual and cultural world view as well as a technical one. Design historians must note not only the form and shape of objects but also the constituent elements of the intellectual climate within an industry if we ever hope to portray adequately the complexity of a design culture. The Age of Aluminum did not just happen; it was designed to happen, consciously designed by industrial designers working within the framework of the aluminum industry to provide technical information and to promote a climate conducive to a creative engagement with aluminum.

For Further Reading

Sterling Brubacker, *Trends in the World Aluminum Industry* (Baltimore: Johns Hopkins University Press, 1967).

Charles Carr, *Alcoa, An American Enterprise* (New York: Rinehart, 1952).

Alfred Chandler, Jr., "Technology and the Transformation of Industrial Organization," in *Technology, the Economy, and Society: The American Experience*, ed. Joel Colton and Stuart Bruchey (New York: Columbia University Press, 1987).

E. Raymond Corey, *The Development of Markets for New Materials: A Study of Building Nets End-Product Markets f*or Aluminum, Fibrous *Glass, and the Plastics* (Cambridge: Harvard University Press, 1956).

10 Examples of industry publications include Samuel Fahnestock, ed., *Design Forecast* 1 (Pittsburgh: Alcoa, 1959) and *Design Forecast* 2 (Pittsburgh: Alcoa, 1959). John Peter, *Aluminum in Modern Architecture,* 2 vols. (Louisville, KY: Reynolds Metals Company, 1956). Don Fabun, *The Dynamics of Change* (Englewood Cliffs, NJ: Kaiser Aluminum with Prentice Hall, 1967).

Arthur Gregor, "Aluminum as a Design Material," Industrial Design 7 (May 1960): special issue on aluminum.

Merton J. Peck, Competition in the Aluminum Industry 1945–1958 (Cambridge: Harvard University Press, 1961).

Robert Sheehan, "Look at the Reynolds Boys Now," Fortune 48 (August 1953): 107–13; 170–78.

Section III

Design in the Context of National Experience

Reconsidering the Factory, Art-Labor, and the Schools of Design in Nineteenth-Century Britain

James A. Schmiechen

One of the most widely accepted notions about the relationship between art and labor in nineteenth-century Britain is that the introduction of the machine into industry resulted in the divorce of art from work. Craft disappeared, it is argued, as artisans lost control over production, tools, quality control, wages, and the work environment. Indeed, the disappearance of esthetic activity on the part of the industrial worker is part of the wider notion that the "dark and satanic mills," as the early factories were called, brought on the proletarianization of the working class and the problem of modern alienation. As the artisan fell victim to the division of labor and was replaced by mere machine tenders, designing and making were driven far apart. More and more workers became proletarianized, or, as one historian put it, "very few people designed for machine production."[1] Design itself went from bad to worse and work "was bleaker than ever before in European history."[2] Degenerate design and demise of the artisan were two sides of the same coin.

Contemporary observers, including Friedrich Engels, Thomas Carlyle, and A. W. N. Pugin, wrote about and lamented the separation of art and labor; among them the classic statements on the subject came first from John Ruskin, the century's leading art critic, and then, of course, from William Morris, the socialist and founder of the movement to rescue art-labor from the evils of mechanization. Both held machine society responsible for the atomization of the whole man. As John and Barbara Hammond put it earlier in the present century, "the soul of man was passing into a colder exile."[3]

For a variety of reasons, some ideological and some connected to modern-day historians' distaste for Victorian design, this notion of proletarianization of the art-labor process has followed us into the twentieth century. It is generally held that nineteenth-century mechanization, by directly attacking workers' skills, led to a decline in the demand for skilled labor, including art-labor,[4] and not until the early twentieth century, with the founding of the German Werkbund and the work of Peter Behrens in Germany, do we see a working alliance between industry and art. Although recent design historians have begun to evaluate Victorian design within its own social context and not from within the context of twentieth-century modernism,[5] the notion of the proletarianization

The original version of this text was presented to the Design History Forum of the College Art Association, Boston, February 1986. I thank Ken Carls and Bruce Nelson for their suggestions and comments during the preparation of this draft.

1 John Gloag, *Industrial Art Explained* (London: Allen & Unwin, 1946), 88; or, as it was put, "the factory was the enemy of art."

2 Nikolaus Pevsner, *Pioneers of Modern Design* (Harmondsworth: Penguin, 1964), 45.

3 Barbara Hammond and John Hammond, *The Town Labourer* (London: Longman, 1964), 280. Ruskin's view of industrial production is best stated in his *Stones of Venice*, vol. 2 (London: Smith, Elder & Co., 1859). The best recent critique of Ruskin's thought on this subject is Mark Swenarton, *Artisans and Architects, The Ruskinian Tradition in Architectural Thought* (New York: St. Martin's Press, 1989). See also Kristine O. Garrigan, *Ruskin on Architecture, His Thought and Influence* (Madison: University of Wisconsin Press, 1973).

4 See, for example, Michael Hanagan, "Artisan and Skilled Worker: The Problem of Definition," *International Labor and Working Class History* 12 (November 1977): 29.

5 See, for example, John Heskett, *Industrial Design* (New York: Oxford University Press, 1980).

of art-labor nevertheless still stands tall. One recent reevaluation of design and the machine in the nineteenth century drops it back to the doorstep of an exploitive capitalist system.[6] Most tenacious in their hold onto the proletarian thesis is that school of historians who see William Morris and the "craftsman ideal" as the antithesis to the machine society and bad design. The Morris-led Arts and Crafts movement has, of course, been seen as revolutionary because it was, it is argued, the antithesis of an esthetically bankrupt factory system.[7]

I propose to stand this proletarianization argument on its head; that is, I wish to set forth the notion that early nineteenth-century technology, combined with some important demographic, economic, and cultural changes, induced both a dramatic expansion of art-labor employment and a new interest in art training for working people. All in all, the picture is less one of mass proletarianization than one of improvements in the work status and the job opportunities for workers in industries requiring art-labor. What follows is first a brief description of a dual upheaval in the 1830s and 1840s in Britain that set this expansion in motion—a design revolution of sorts—and then a longer discussion of the impact machinery and its concomitant changes had on the labor force.

The first component in this design revolution of the 1830s and 1840s was a striking economic and demographic change whereby a large portion of the population—namely, the middle and lower-middle classes—became increasingly urbanized and experienced a notable increase in disposable income. They became the first great mass of "consumers" in the modern sense and in so doing exerted enormous pressure on manufacturers to speed up production of cheap household and personal goods. Accompanying this was a second upheaval, a "bourgeois" social and cultural revolution that supported the idea of "design" as a way of communicating certain social ideals.[8] It was precisely at this time that British society embraced the notion that a morally designed physical environment would create a moral individual. This moral component deserves more attention than it has received because it gave an enormous push to mass-produced machine "art" products, everything from teapots to floor coverings. Design (often mistaken for simple ornamentation) sought to convey certain historic truths and moral precepts, hence the values an object conveyed became just as important as its strictly utilitarian purpose. Design had become, by the 1840s, highly didactic in purpose and dedicated to the idea of the union of art and industry—a traffic in symbols whereby ornamentation assumed a social function, or, more precisely, it became an agent of certain "associations" that would serve a social purpose. As the 1849 Select Committee on the Schools of Design put it, the advantage of good design is that it attracts "the people" away "from degrading objects and pursuits."[9]

Central to this design revolution—an age of design mania as it was called—was the machine. It was with a great deal of seriousness

6 Adrian Forty, *Objects of Desire, Design and Society from Wedgewood to IBM* (New York: Pantheon, 1986).

7 The classic statement with regard to Morris's influence on design and architectural theory is Pevsner's *Pioneers of Modern Design.* More recent studies of Morris are Peter Meier, *William Morris: The Marxist Dreamer,* 2 vols. (London: Harvester Press, 1978); Eileen Boris, *Art and Labor: Ruskin, Morris, and the Craftsman Ideal in America* (Philadelphia: Temple University Press, 1986); and Lionel Lambourne, *Utopian Craftsmen: The Arts and Crafts Movement from the Cotswolds to Chicago* (Salt Lake City: Peregrine Smith, 1988).

8 For a further discussion of this, see my article, "The Victorians, Historians, and the Idea of Modernism," *The American Historical Review* 93 (April 1988): 287–316.

9 *PP. Report of the Select Committee on the Schools of Design, 1849,* 434 (IUP *Industrial Revolution, Design,* vol. 3) hereafter cited as *SCSD, 1849.*

and optimism that the early Victorians envisaged the merger of art and technology as a way to uplift society. Contrary to the sentiments of Victorian social critics such as Ruskin, Morris, and Engels, many Victorians believed that machines were both the "friends of labour" because they eliminated "brute . . . and degrading labour" and "brute intellect,"[10] and generators of new art-labor employment. This argument was lucidly set forth by the 1849 Select Committee on Design:

> The value of design in its bearing on the interests of the labouring population is worthy of notice. . . . On the one hand, by the substitution of machine for hand labour, human labour is economized, and the cost of production of simple "products" is diminished, on the other hand, as soon as the public obtains plain manufactures cheap, it seems to desire, almost by a law of nature, to have them decorated and *thus creates an employment for that labour which otherwise would appear for the time superfluous.*[11]

The "otherwise superfluous" labor, of course, is art-labor—that is, labor which required a considerable degree of artistic skill[12] and judgment and which existed because of and alongside of the machine. The machine, in short, was design-intensive. By lowering costs and providing new design technologies, it allowed designer and manufacturer to add artistic "associations" (illustrations from the classical and medieval past, natural and rural images, and other historic or didactic symbolism) to the product—that is, create a new esthetic out of historicist forms—and in doing so create a mass of new art-labor jobs.

The result was dozens of new industries which in Henry Cole's words became "governed by ornamental design," that is, manufacturing in which special knowledge of art is required and which relies on machinery, new materials, or division of labor. Cole's list is staggering (*Table 1*). It suggests that unlike the popular twentieth-century belief that technology was a way of simplifying product designs and bringing about universal design, in reality it made everyday products more varied and ostentatious. Because of the primitive nature of most early machines, artistic skill and esthetic judgment remained an integral part of the work process. Several examples suffice. The production of engraved etchings with photographic negatives became heavily dependent upon highly-trained etchers and engravers, while the new floorcloth industry (made possible because of cheap machine-made canvas) relied on a new class of designers, handblock printers, color mixers, and other art-labor jobs.[13] Further, jobs arose in "architectural decoration" where a variety of machines cut, molded, and polished marble, thereby giving birth to mass merchandising of domestic fireplaces, mantles, door frames, railings, and sculpture for interior use, while at the same time generating a whole new class of sculptors, modelers, and designers.[14]

10 *The Builder* 2 (May 1843):195.

11 *SCSD, 1849,* "Draft Report, Part I, The National Importance of the School," xi, my emphasis. Much the same sentiment had been expressed several years earlier by *The Builder,* which claimed that the machine had resulted in "beautiful products" from "an artistic manufactory" (2 [May 1843]: 195).

12 Here I attach a fairly broad definition to art-labor skill. It is assumed to be labor which demanded both a degree of manual dexterity and a scarce ability which was dependent on acquired artistic knowledge and judgment, all of which centered on some understanding of accepted esthetic principles, both traditional and contemporary. For a helpful discussion of the subject of skill and division of labor, see the "Introduction" in Royden Harrison and Jonathan Zeitlin, eds., *Divisions of Labour, Skilled Workers and Technological Change in Nineteenth Centgry England* (Brighton: Harvester Press, 1985).

13 *The Portfolio* 114 (June 1879): 104–5; for carpet manufacture, see *Architectural Magazine and Journal* (1835): 551–53.

14 George Dodd, *Days at the Factory* (London: C. Knight & Co., 1843). See also *PP. Report of the Select Committee on Arts and Manufacture, 1836,* 619–32 (IUP, *Industrial Revocation, Design,* vol. I); hereafter cited as *SCAM, 2nd Report, 1836.* For carpet manufacture, see Edward Sang, "A Report on the Recent Improvement of Carpet Manufacture," *Scottish Society of Architecture* (1835): 67. Similar results were experienced with regard to the introduction of the wood-planing machine. See *The Builder* 19 (September 1846): 447; and John C. Loudon's *An Encyclopedia of Cottage, Farm, and Villa Architecture* (London: Longman, Brown, Green & Longman, 1842), 1013.

Table 1

Ornamental Design Manufacture ("Cole's List")[15]

Cotton	Silks	Brass and Cast and Hammered Iron Products
Woolen and Worsted	Calicoes and Other Printed Cloth	Gold and Silver Decorative Plate
Silk and Velvet	Velvet and Velveteen	Electro-plated and Ormolu Products
Flax and Hemp Fabrics	Floor Cloths	Jewelry
Muslins (sewed and embroidered)	Wallpaper	Toys and Ornaments
Patterned Woven Carpets	Japanning	Glass Products (blown, molded, pressed, engraved, etc.)
Printed Carpets	Porcelain and Earthenware Painting	Ceramic Potters (hard and soft porcelain, statuary)
Shawls (and other mixed fabrics)	Glass Painting	Porcelain, Stoneware, and Earthenware
Bookbinding and Leather Embossing	Enamelware	
Mousseline de Laine and Cashmere Fabric	Architectural Decoration for Wall and Ceiling	
Table Covers (woolen)	Architectural Decoration in Various Materials	

The expansion of the wallpaper industry is a case in point. Wallpaper imitation of tapestry had been popular for well over a hundred years before wallpaper was mass produced by power-driven machinery in the 1830s. Here the adaptation of steam power to the roller and cylinder printing machines and then the removal (in 1836) of the tax on domestic paper made the 1830s the age of wallpaper. As Charles Dickens remarked, the rich could now throw out their ugly and dirty tapestries, and even those of small means had a chance of "a neat set of walls."[16] Cheap wallpaper meant more designs—as manufacturers found it necessary to issue new designs every six months. As one observer said of wallpaper design in 1836, "the invention of the artist is kept in a constant state of activity for the production of new forms, new combinations, and new arrangements."[17] The number of paper stainers, as these workers were called, increased by 60 percent between 1841 and 1851, and between 1839 and 1847 alone over eighteen hundred new designs were entered on the patent rolls.[18] Because much wallpaper in these early decades was a combination of steam roller and hand-block work, or even, as in some cases, a combination of steam roller and hand-painted work,[19] the traditional hand-block process of wallpaper making entered the factory and existed side by side with machine printing.

The growth and expansion of art-labor in the metal goods trades is remarkably close to that in other art-intensive trades. Here

15 *PP. First Report of the Department of Practical Art, 1852–53,* Vol. 54, Appendix IV, 204 (IUP, *Industrial Revolution, Design,* vol. 4).

16 Charles Dickens, "Household Scenery" *in Household Words* 14 (August 1853): 513.

17 *SCAM, 1836,* 373–82.

18 *PP. Census Returns, 1841, 1851.*

19 For a further discussion of wallpaper production, see Jean Hamilton, *An Introduction to Wallpaper* (London: HMSO, 1983); also *Tbe Builder* 19 (October 1844): 526–27, and *Art Union* (June 1839): 87. I make no attempt in this article to evaluate the worth of the designs. Hamilton claims that although many of the early designs were most bizarre, a look at the pattern books shows primarily simple and attractive cylinder (i.e., machine) prints (Hamilton, 25). The *Journal of Design* (2 [1849–50]: 106), claimed that machine-printed cloth was most probably superior to the traditional block-printed cloth.

too the 1830s and 1840s constituted the take-off stage. Mechanization and the evolution of new technologies such as electroplating (much of this process taking place in and around Birmingham and Sheffield) resulted in an explosion in the mass production of household goods such as iron stoves, tableware, and lighting fixtures. Between 1841 and 1871 the number of persons engaged in these trades increased from twenty-one hundred to thirty-seven hundred, while in 1846 alone over thirty-three thousand new designs were registered. The metal trades relied on a large number of new and traditional art workers: designers, modelers (those who made the design into a wax model), dye-sinkers, engravers, and those who applied ornamentation; to all, as one factory inspector observed, "proficiency in art is of the very highest importance."[20] Indeed, the metal trades worker had the task of translating flat surface design into three-dimensional ornament and had to have an understanding of the changes in the metal when heated and how any particular form would "deliver from the sand."[21]

The early nineteenth-century interaction between machine, worker, and art-labor is perhaps best illustrated in the textile printing industry. Machine "calico" cloth printing by copper plates had existed under a small workshop system in the cotton textile industry since the later eighteenth century, but it was when the power loom caused a dramatic rise in the demand for printed cloth that mechanization in the print works took off. In the 1830s, the successful application of steam power to the engraved metal roller process together with a series of remarkable advances of dyestuff resulted in lowering the cost of printed cloth by about 75 percent, and this ushered in an age of cheap printed cloth, including that lovable old Victorian chintz, as well as thousands of colorful patterned calicoes to dress a fashion-mad (and color-mad) society.[22]

Engels, who argued in 1844 that steam-powered engraved cylinders virtually superseded skilled labor in calico printing, was most probably wrong.[23] For one thing, the traditional blockprinting sector of the trade grew rapidly between 1815 and 1830 as the power loom caused an explosion in cotton cloth production. In reality, the number of workers in the textile print industry increased by 50 percent, for example, between 1841 and 1851,[24] although it is difficult to say if the machine roller factory process involved any more or less art-labor skill than the pre-factory block print "table" process. The factory process appears to be more subdivided, although even under the artisan workshop system the subdivision of work tasks was common (such as the hand application of color by cheaper female labor).

It is not to be denied that the factory and technology fostered considerable disequilibrium in employer-worker relations and, indeed, that the conditions of work for many (including children) in the trade were sub-standard to say the least. Nevertheless, it is fairly

20 J. Howell, factory inspector, in *SCAM 1836*, 103.

21 Kenneth R. Towndrow, *Alfred Stevens* (Liverpool: University Press, 1951), 99.

22 The best accounts of changes in calico printing are Geoffrey Turnbull, *A History of the Calico Printing Industry of Great Britain*, John G. Turnbull, ed. (Altrincham: 1941) and Edward Baines, *History of the Cotton Manufacture in Great Britain* (London: Fisher, Fisher & Jackson, 1835). Also see S. D. Chapman, "Quantity versus Quality in the British Industrial Revolution, The Case of Printed Textiles," *Northern History* 21 (1984):175–92, and M. G. Quimby and Polly Anne Earl, *Technological Innovation and the Decorative Arts* (Charlottesville: University Press of Virginia, 1974). The actual design process in this field has yet to have a good written history. Most helpful is P. C. Floud, "The Origins of English Calico Printing," "The English Contribution to the Early History of Indigo Printing," "The English Contribution to the Development of Copperplate Printing," *Journal of the Society of Dyers and Colourists* 76 (1960): 285–91, 344–49, 425–34. Considerable discussion of this topic can be found in *PP. Report of tbe Select Committee on Copyright of Designs*, 1840 (IUP, *Industrial Revolution, Design*, vol. 2); hereafter cited as *SCCD, 1840*.

23 Friedrich Engels, *Tbe Condition of the Working Class in England*, trans. W. O. Henderson and W. H. Chaloner (Stanford: Stanford University Press, 1968), 219.

24 *PP. Census Returns, 1841, 1851.*

certain that the factory machine print process relied on considerable skill and that overall the number of jobs requiring artistic skill or judgment did not decline. Precisely the opposite appears to have occurred. While it is probable that with the new print factory the proportion of unskilled or semiskilled labor increased, the ratio of apprentices to journeymen seems to have dropped (to the favor of the journeymen) from 3:5 in 1804 to 1:3 by 1875,[25] and the aggregate number of art-labor jobs most probably increased. Although the introduction of the machine and of cheap labor were bitterly attacked by the journeymen (a struggle which stirred up considerable public controversy in the period 1800-1815), by 1830 the journeymen had been transformed from workshop artisans to machine operators in print factories wherein they retained control over the supply of apprentice labor and enjoyed relatively high wages.[26] What the art-labor duties of the machinist were is unclear, but his high wage (the same as a block printer in 1839[27]) suggests that the machinist was a skilled worker.

What is most contrary to the proletarianization thesis is that early mechanized textile printing consisted of several labor-intensive stages all of which required considerable skill in composition of design, drawing, understanding of scale, proportion, and color. First, of course, was the invention of the design, which in some cases took place on the manufacturer's premises, but was just as often done outside the factory itself. Inglis and Wakefield, the Glasgow printworks, for example, hired two in-house designers in their London office, other in-house designers at the Glasgow factory, and six out-of-house designers in the city of Glasgow.[28] Overall, for Britain, the number of pattern designers doubled between 1841 and 1851, and in Manchester in just one year (1840) five hundred designers turned out over a half-million textile designs.[29]

The machine itself invited more design, because it allowed for an increased draftsmanship not possible under the old system, while new dye stuff, including chrome yellow and dark green (heretofore unavailable), allowed the designer to avoid masking color misregistrations and to undertake greater use of shading and gradation of color; and, as in the case of the discovery of Turkey Red dye, opened the door to design possibilities (particularly for the export market) which had not previously existed.[30] Next, the design had to be made to suit the cloth. Pattern-drawing consisted of making out or copying the pattern to paper by the *drawer* or sketch maker to the required scale. A worker then assumed the task of the *putter on* who transferred the pattern to the roller. Next, engraver engraved the roller itself, a process which often meant making alterations in the design before or after the printing took place. Finally, the *color mixer* selected the colors appropriate to the design and would, if necessary, adjust the color during printing. This was a skilled task, as indicated by the fact that color mixers' wages were

25 Turnbull, *Calico Printing*, 211, 223; and Robert Glen, *Urban Workers in the Early Industrial Revolution* (London: Croom Helm, 1984), 86. The ratio of child to adult male labor in block print workshops was 1:1.

26 Glen, *Urban Workers*, 84–91. Machine printers' wages varied greatly from printwork to printwork, but were in the range of 25s to 42s per week in the 1810s and 40s to 50s in the 1860s (Turnbull, *Calico Printing*, 215–17). Calico printers were among the best organized workers in the textile industry. See Sidney Webb and Beatrice Webb, *The History of Trade Unionism* (London: Longman, 1911).

27 Turnbull, *Calico Printing*, 212.

28 *SCSD, 1845*,1025–55.

29 *PP. Census Returns, Occupations, 1841, 1851;* and *SCCD, 1840*, 4567, 4596, 4600.

30 In his history, Baines states that calico printing was an art that combined the knowledge of "taste, chemistry, and mathematics" *(Cotton Manufacture*, 253). For an excellent discussion of this process, see Forty, *Objects of Desire*, chapter 3, "Design and Mechanization."

higher in 1849 than those of the traditional block printers. Furthermore, the *block printer* found that because mass-produced factory printed cloth was very often a combination of machine and block printing, the block printing process became more design intensive, and therefore the block printer worked alongside the machine in the factory.[31]

Developments in factory weaving followed somewhat the same pattern. It was necessary for a larger number of workers to understand the entire design-execution process while at the same time they were acquiring more narrowly defined skills. Designing and other art-labor tasks in woven, as opposed to printed, textile design underwent significant change as a result of the introduction of the seam-powered jacquard loom, which in the 1840s made the traditional hand-drawn (or "harness") domestic and small workshop process nearly obsolete. Mechanization meant that not only could a patterned shawl, for example, be woven in one day as compared to the hand-loom shawl which took two weeks to weave, but equally important the mechanized jacquard, because it allowed for new design possibilities, was design and preparation intensive. The demand for art-labor at all three stages of weaving, design, transfer, and application, increased. In the design stage, for example, the jacquard allowed for greater variety and versatility in design and permitted "finer definition" and greater imitation possibilities.[32]

As with printed cloth, a multitude of new patterns were designed each year as manufacturers used design to exploit new markets at home and abroad—not the least of which was the shawl trade that profited from a shawl fashion boom from about 1800 to 1870. After the initial pattern was designed, either by an in-house designer or contracted from the outside, the pattern had to be redrawn by the *drawer* onto lined paper, which was called "point paper." This, in effect, was both a mathematical and artistic process which demanded that the design be converted to the proper scale to fit the cloth. Next, another worker took this point-paper design and used it to make the punched cards (often many hundreds) which were hooked up to the jacquard loom.

The jacquard was, in a sense, a sort of primitive computer. In France, this would have been done by the designer himself because it took considerable skill and understanding of the pattern. In Britain, however, the process was given to someone of lesser stature, thus providing the British a decided financial advantage, but creating yet another class of worker trained in particular artistic and mathematical skills while still having an understanding of the overall design. The last crucial task was to transfer the design to the actual loom—setting the *loom* by way of the punched cards. As was claimed in 1836, the person who sets the loom needs to be "imbued with the principles of design; he should have certain taste, and know what forms will have the best effect upon the tissue."[33] The result of

31 For color mixer wages, see Turnbull, *Calico Printing,* 212; for an account of block printing in the factory, see *SCCD, 1840,* 4581–97, and *SCSD, 1849,* 1055; also Turnbull, *Calico Printing,* 58, 93, 107, 212.

32 *Designs for British Dress and Furnishings Fabrics, Eighteenth Century to the Present* (London: Victoria and Albert Museum, 1986), 36; see also, *SCAM, vol. 5,1835,* 813–15, and Maureen Lochrie, "The Paisley Shawl Industry," (Ph.D. diss., University of Strathclyde, Glasgow, 1987).

33 *SCAM, vol.* 5, *1835,*1512.

all this was that manufacturing centers specializing in patterned woolens built up a large design labor force. Such was the case of Paisley where one family in sixty was engaged in shawl design.

It is, therefore, difficult to argue, as the proletarian thesis does, that with mechanization the range of skills narrowed and the degree or level of skill declined. What did happen is that within a process of highly uneven industrial-capitalist development, skill was redefined and the relationship between skill acquisition and the status of the worker changed; in short, over the course of the several decades after about 1830, mechanization was accompanied by a near revolution in how the art-labor force was formed and trained. This change was the heart of what we now regard as the Victorian design crisis. The gradual, uneven, and incomplete manner in which technology transformed industry created an awkward void in skill acquisition—a void that caused panic on the part of the Victorians who were convinced their system of art training for industry was grossly deficient and had led to bad design. Henry Cole, that ever-busy Victorian organizer of education, art, and industry, claimed to have studied all fifty-six thousand new designs between 1839 and 1848 and found them wanting.[34] A busy Victorian indeed. Our knowledge of art-labor training and the transmission of skill is rudimentary, but I would like to suggest what may have happened.

For many of these new or reconstituted industries engaged in "art-manufacture," a traditional patrimonial apprenticeship system had existed whereby the worker exercised not only a considerable amount of skill (including artistic skill) but also acted as part of a craft group or union, and exerted considerable control over production and working conditions. Wages and the number of new entries into the trade were, historically, upheld by the craft group (or even guaranteed by statute). The skill or craft aspect was passed from family member to family member (usually from father to son), although in some trades (such as lace manufacture) the old hand-production system served as a disincentive to design and art-labor.

Many of these elements of the old system were still in place in the early Victorian decades, as work shifted from workshop to factory,[35] although in some trades the cement of the old system, apprenticeship, was under attack and drying out. Because, as we have seen, the machine and its frequent companion, the subdivision of labor, open required either a different level or range of creative invention and esthetic judgment (i.e., skill), and because of the small scale of most of these new enterprises, the old apprenticeship system reappeared in the factory only in a weakened state. Although some manufacturers, as entrepreneurs, began their careers by physically running the production process on their own,[36] most did not seek to control skill acquisition and therefore did little to train their employees. As one designer observed, art-labor workers "have scarcely any opportunity in life to make themselves generally acquainted with the various proportions of

34 Cole termed them "abortions and only fit for the fire." *SCSD, 1849*, xxxviii, 2032.

35 For a reference to the absence of design in domestic lacemaking, see *SCAM, 2nd Report, 1836*, 144–203. I am indebted to the late John Ward for allowing me to read his "Textile Trade Unionism in Nineteenth-Century Scotland" (unpublished paper, 1987). See also Turnbull, *Calico Printing*, 93, 223. Certainly "masters" and "journeymen" alike in the traditional (prefactory) manufacturing process relied on guide books for some of their design and construction needs, but it appears that the new mass-production factory mode of production did not generate a new literature. The call for guide books and "principles" for designers and art-laborers is frequently heard in the early nineteenth century (see, for example, *Architectural Magazine and Journal* 2 [1835]: 42). Curiously, the age saw a remarkable proliferation of cheap artistic reproductions which, in a sense, gave a mass of workers access to self-education in the arts. In recent years the study of apprenticeship has been important to labor historians because it raises the question of who controlled the workplace—employer or employee. Richard Price, "The Labour Process and Labour History," *Social History* 8 (1983) has argued that control of the workplace was central to the conflict between classes. For further discussion of Price's argument and the arguments of others on the subject, see William Knox, "Apprenticeship and Deskilling in Britain, 1850–1914," *International Review of Social History* 31 (1986).

36 The firm of Turnbull and Stockdale in Bury, for example, began in 1881 with William Turnbull working his own printing machine. Turnbull, *Calico Printing*, 219.

the human form, with animals, architecture, and especially botany, and the principle of combining colours so as to form pleasing effects."[37]

Simply "watching" the process, as in the case of much art-labor skill acquisition in the past, was no longer enough. The result was that the worker-apprentice had to go elsewhere—as both manufacturer and worker complained of the paucity of training opportunities. In Lancashire, in print manufacturing, for example, apprenticeship still existed but there was no art training for pattern drawers or designers. In porcelain-ware manufacture a shortage of artists meant that production slowed down, and in the metal trades where modelers had little or no access to educational opportunity art-labor training hardly existed. For example, the center of this trade, Sheffield, in 1836 had only four modelers. Across the industrial midlands and in Scotland much the same tale of woe was told by the workers themselves.[38]

This deficiency was an important development in art-labor history. Although apprenticeship lingered on as a way of controlling the labor supply and maintaining wages, and now and then we find a case whereby an employer set up his own in-house training system, generally speaking workers managed on their own. Significantly, it appears that rather than become victims of change as the proletarian thesis suggests, *workers themselves took much of the initiative* in what became a reorganization of art-labor training. In city after city in the 1830s and 1840s art-labor workers sought their own instruction outside the factory: setting up Mechanics Institutes which offered classes in drawing, mathematics, and so on; hiring their own drawing masters; and attending fee-paying lectures at local art societies. Workers in art manufacture, one observer found in 1836, were more interested in art education than were their employers and were not only picking up lectures and drawing classes wherever they could but were asking for the establishment of free public museums and free instruction in the applied arts.[39]

One result of this flurry of activity was the establishment in 1837 of the government Schools of Design (there were twenty-one by 1849). These schools have not fared well with historians and must stand as one of the most neglected chapters in the history of both Victorian reform and Victorian design. Usually viewed in much the same negative light as Henry Cole viewed the early schools, they remain one of the whipping boys for bad design in the nineteenth century. When addressing the schools, most historians simply repeat Cole's argument that the schools failed to pay attention to practical design and were, in effect, "enfeebled and hardly functioning."[40]

There are a number of reasons for this negative view, the most important perhaps is that Cole, the greatest art politician of the century, purposely exaggerated the negative features of the schools, particularly the early ones, in order to gain public support and funding for his

37 *SCAM, vol.* 5,1835,129–43,141–43, 216, 838, 1528–32, 1681–94. The factory inspectors likewise pointed to the need of design education. See *SCAM, vol. 5, 1835,* 71–140.

38 James Crabb, "Education of the People," *Leigh Hunt's London Journal* 28 (November 1835): 424.

39 *SCAM, 2nd Report,* 1836, 72–105. When the new Museum of Manufacture was opened in London in 1853, it attracted over eight hundred visitors a day, many of whom were workers, probably using the museum as an educational opportunity. But by no means was the urban middle class unaware of the need for new means of art education. A Society for the Promotion of Practical Design was in operation by 1830, offering classes to the public; and a remarkable number of new magazines, such as the *Art Union* and John C. Loudon's *Architectural Magazine and Journal,* were dedicated to the improvement of public taste and art-labor skill. By mid-century many of the industrial towns (such as Preston) boasted of public access to art collections—something unheard of several decades earlier (see, for example, the comments of *The Builder* 18 [January 1851]: 49).

40 Elizabeth Bonython, *King Cole, A Picture Portrait of Sir Henry Cole, 1808–1882* (London: Victoria and Albert Museum, 1981), 7; other criticisms of the schools are found in N. Pevsner, "The Cole Circle," chapter 16 in his *Some Architectural Writers of the Nineteenth Century* (Oxford: Clarendon Press, 1972); and Fiona MacCarthy, *A History of British Design, 1830–1970* (London: Allen & Unwin, 1979),17, who regards the schools "an out-and-out fiasco." The standard history of the subject is Quentin Bell, *The Schools of Design* (London: Routledge and Paul, 1963); although a valuable work, Bell's book approaches the history of the Schools of Design as one of "scandal, confusion, and disaster," 1. The most recent discussion of design education in early Victorian Britain is Adrian Rifkin, "Success Disavowed: The Schools of Design in Mid-Nineteenth-Century Britain. (An Allegory)", *The Journal of Design History* l, no. 2 (1988); Rifkin sees the schools as allegory for the confusion and contradictions within Victorian design—an "ideal *non sequitur,*" 91.

proposed reforms of the schools.[41] But the nearly constant attack on the schools was partly a result of the dilemma in which British industry had found itself as the pioneer in industrialization. The primitive nature of machinery and technological innovation (and the concomitant division of labor) required the workers to wear two hats: that of a specialist who could perform well and even invent a particular aspect of the process, and that of the generalist who understood the entire design and art-labor process. As a result the organizers of the schools, from the outset, could not decide whether to emphasize general art education or specialist skill training, and hence the schools became a center of controversy and considerable criticism. If Cole's motives were honorable, his views (and those of many twentieth-century historians) have kept us from looking at the schools in a more serious light.

Evaluated in terms of the art-labor training system of the time, these Schools of Design look entirely different. Between 1837 and 1848, over fifteen thousand men and women attended them. In this period and the decade following, the schools went some distance in revolutionizing factory art-labor apprenticeship and training. Some workers were now selected on provable skill *prior to employment* and not on the patrimony basis of many of the old craft unions. For others, the Schools of Design became a way to move up in one's position to the point even of avoiding formal in-house apprenticeship. Whatever the case, some employers began to use school attendance as a prerequisite to employment or formal apprenticeship. By 1850 a notable proportion of Britain's art-laborers were using the schools to replace some or all of the traditional apprenticeship system, that is, to acquire nonapprenticed skill [42]

For example, an 1849 survey of forty-six "art-intensive" firms (ranging from carpet manufacture and glass manufacture to cloth printing and so on) found that 28 percent of the workers had attended or were attending a School of Design. Further, a survey of the students at the Glasgow School found that 47 percent were already employed in some sort of art-manufacture.[43] Although the early Manchester School appears to have been less than a success, others proved to be fairly prodigious. The Glasgow School seems to have done what critics and historians say the schools did not do: use the classroom to bring about practical design solutions for industry.[44] The Sheffield School was only a few years old when it was claimed that every firm engaged in the traditional Sheffield trades "had an apprentice, or a young man, or workman" in the School of Design.[45]

If the experience of the designer Alfred Stevens is typical, it may be said that it was common for designers in industry to take on assistants from the local school. Stevens, working for the Sheffield firm of Hoole, not only took on students from the school, but spent considerable time at the school studying and discussing design with the students.[46]

In the potteries, two Schools of Design, one at Stoke-on-Trent and one at Hanley, were established and in the first years trained

41 Cole stacked the parliamentary commission set up to investigate the schools, he manipulated the witnesses, and he directed the tone of the reports. For example, he grossly exaggerated the importance of French design competition and used his own students to attack the Schools of Design. See *SCSD, l849,* 1124–77. For a discussion of this, see Lochrie, *Paisley Shawl Industry.*

42 Students attended the Schools of Design for different time periods, at different times of the day (but generally at night), and at different times of life. For evidence of the schools in the workforce, see *SCSD, 1849,* app. 5, 441. For a discussion of the nature of nonapprenticed skill and the problem of identifying how workers moved from the less skilled to the skilled grades, see Charles More, *Skill and the English Working Class, 1870–1914* (New York: St. Martin's Press, 1980), 230–35.

43 The first of these surveys is found in *SCSD, 1849,* app. 5. The Glasgow survey is from *PP. Schools of Design, Reports and Papers Relating to Head and Branch Schools,* 1850 (IUP, *Industrial Revolution, Design,* vol. 4); hereafter cited as *Reports and Papers,* 1850, 179. Charles Dickens found, in his visit to a wallpaper factory at about this same time, that the in-house designer had been trained at a School of Design. *Household Words* 14 (August 1853): 513.

44 *SCSD, 1849,* 1011–55.

45 *SCSD,* 1849,1197.

46 Stevens even had students from the school serving him without pay. Towndrow, *Alfred Stevens,* 98–100.

hundreds of workers for the pottery industry. Mintons, for example, took four of its seven designers from the schools in addition to forty-two of three hundred fifteen of its total workforce. It was from the Nottingham School that designers produced the first original British lace designs, and in Belfast the school encouraged the birth of a new branch of art-manufacture in the linen industry.[47]

To say about machine production in the nineteenth century, as Pevsner has,[48] that the shape and appearance of all products were left to the uneducated manufacturer, is to exaggerate the importance of the manufacturer and the machine and, at the same time, miss the fact that working men and women directed significant change in the face of technology. Such a view, as well, hides the fact that the first efforts to bring about the union of art and industry were in the period after about 1830, not in the decades surrounding 1920 as our "modernist" orthodoxy has so long held. Most important, these preliminary findings suggest that we reconsider some of our long-standing notions with regard to art-labor in the age of the factory. Was the only art-labor that took place that found in the Morris-inspired cottage workshops? The picture, as we have seen, appears to have been otherwise.

Mechanization, as Raphael Samuel reminds us, "was a process rather than an event," a process "neither linear nor smooth but, on the contrary, discontinuous and subject to a whole complex of competing claims, pulling in opposite directions."[49] Overall, the flow of industrial art-labor activity in the nineteenth century was in reality *toward* and not away from the factory—first because the machine caused certain trades to become more art-labor intensive, and second because the traditional method of skill acquisition and transfer proved inadequate and was therefore augmented by a new system of art training under the public domain. It cannot be denied that technological change threw some art-laborers into proletarian status and made the artisanal workshop obsolete for the acquisition of skill; but, overall, proletarianization appears to be a less significant feature of the history of design during this seminal period in British design history than was the expansion of art-labor opportunities. Whereas under the preindustrial system, worker independence was symbolized by possession of personal tools and passage through a patrimonial and group-controlled apprenticeship, now much of that had been replaced by external education. If, indeed, proletarianization is "increased dependence upon the dictates of capitalist relations," it is possible that for those workers connected to art-labor industries, the machine generated not proletarianization but rather considerable new art-labor opportunities and new skill acquisition opportunities, both of which may have led some workers down the road of deproletarianization. Perhaps we need to squelch the din of the critic Ruskin and his tribe, refocus our perspective on the workplace and the Schools of Design, and listen to the workers themselves.

47 These schools are considered in *Reports and Papers, 1850,* 78–85.

48 Pevsner, *Pioneers of Modern Design,* 45.

49 Raphael Samuel, "The Workshop of the World: Steam Power and Hand Technology in Mid-Victorian Britain," *History Workshop,* no. 3 (Spring 1977):10.

Evolutionary Affinity in Arthur Mackmurdo's Botanical Design

Larry D. Lutchmansingh

If nineteenth-century religion and science may be said to have frequently verged on open warfare, art and science in that period existed in a condition of mutual indifference or distrust. Few other artists or designers of the latter part of the century, therefore, could make the remarkable claim of Arthur Heygate Mackmurdo (1851–1942), who said that he was "an artist with a scientific training" and that the two disciplines constituted the absorbing allegiances of his life. Indeed, Mackmurdo himself supposed, with an uncharacteristic immodesty, that not since the day of Sir Christopher Wren (1632–1723) had a European artist commanded both fields of endeavor in quite the way he did.[1] And although at the height of his career as an architect and designer he stood among the first rank of the Arts and Crafts Movement and came to be hailed as an important precursor of art nouveau, Mackmurdo soon abandoned that work for social criticism and reform, driven by his scientific interests. In retrospect, despite his reputation as a designer, Mackmurdo insisted that he attached more importance to his work as a social theorist and reformer than as artist and designer. Although time has reversed that particular judgment, Mackmurdo's assessment indicates an enriching, complex, and yet uneasy conjunction of forces in his activity as artist, designer, and social thinker.

The particular development of Victorian science to which Mackmurdo adhered was evolutionary theory, particularly its Spencerian version. In his "Autobiographical Notes," Mackmurdo records that he had studied "Social Statics and Social Dynamics" and "the positiv [sic] sciences . . . from Mathematics to Ethics, and from Astronomy to Sociology," under Herbert Spencer, a friend of the family.[2] These studies must have occurred sometime in the 1870s. Apparently at Spencer's insistence, Mackmurdo furthered his studies by attending the lectures of Thomas Huxley and William Tyndall in 1876–78.[3] To the influence of these men Mackmurdo curiously added that of Auguste Comte and accordingly avowed himself a "staunch Positivist." Around 1883 he even lectured at Newton Hall in Fetter Lane, the London center of Positivism, on one occasion with the Positivist leader, Frederic Harrison, in the chair, and on another, with Spencer and George Eliot in the audience.[4]

During these same years, Mackmurdo pursued a parallel career in art and design. This career began with an unsuccessful apprenticeship, at age 18, to the architect T. Chatfield Clarke, and then, more successfully, to James Brooks (1825–1901), a designer of

1 Arthur H. Mackmurdo, "Autobiographical Notes" (Walthamstow, London: William Morris Gallery, 1936), unpaginated typescript.

2 Mackmurdo, "Autobiographical Notes." "Social Statics and Social Dynamics" was the title of a chapter of Spencer's *Social Statics* (London: John Chapman, 1851). The term, *social statics* had also appeared in Comte's *Cours de Philosophie Positive* of 1830–42 (translated into English by Harriet Martineau in 1854), whence it was taken by John Stuart Mill and used in *Principles of Political Economy* of 1848. See Sidney Eisen, "Herbert Spencer and the Spectre of Comte," *Journal of British Studies* 7, no. 1 (November, 1967): 51.

3 Mackmurdo, "Autobiographical Notes."

4 Mackmurdo, "Autobiographical Notes."

churches in the Gothic Revival style. Study with Ruskin at Oxford was followed by traveling with him in 1874 to Italy; establishing contact with such leaders of the Arts and Crafts Movement as Ford Madox Brown (1821–93), Richard Norman Shaw (1831–1912), Philip Webb (1831–1915), and William Morris (1834–96); and setting up an architectural practice in London in 1875.

But all the while Mackmurdo burned with, in his own words, an "overmastering discontent with things as they were." Especially in the sphere of art and design, his criticism was frequently articulated with references to such common and ill-digested concepts of popularized evolutionism as the "law of nature," the "organism" of society and "organic evolution," the "fierce struggle" of competitive commerce, and the need for "social synthesis."[5] It seems that not even such revered figures as Thomas Carlyle, Robert Browning, John Ruskin, and William Morris availed Mackmurdo in his disillusionment. Instead, he saw light in two disparate principles: traditional craftsmanship, perceived to be increasingly threatened by industrial manufacture and the operations of the free market, and the urgent need for a new, scientific basis of historical understanding and social reconstruction. These two interests guided Mackmurdo's artistic career and were drawn together, briefly and symbolically, in some of his decorative designs of the 1880s.

Figure I
Arthur Heygate Mackmurdo, cover, *Wren's City Churches*, 1883.

A major achievement of Mackmurdo's decorative work, and the one regarded as his most innovative and influential upon subsequent art nouveau pieces, was a series of botanically derived designs he created during the early and mid 1880s, for fabric, wallpaper, furniture, and a book cover. Nikolaus Pevsner evocatively defined this element of the designs in his influential 1936 study, *Pioneers of Modern Design*: "If the long, sensitive curve, reminiscent of the lily's stem, an insect's feeler, the filament of a blossom, or occasionally a slender flame, the curve undulating, lowing, and interplaying with others, sprouting from corners and covering asymmetrically all available surfaces, can be regarded as the leitmotif of art nouveau, then the first work of art nouveau which can be traced is Arthur H. Mackmurdo's cover of his book on *Wren's City Churches* published in 1883"[6] (*Figure 1*).

In tracing "so amazing a design" to such disparate sources as the pre-Raphaelite artists Burne-Jones and Rossetti, the Gothic Revival, and preceeding these, William Blake, so that "the most original compositions of the early and late nineteenth century are firmly linked," Pevsner only partially accounts for its innovative qualities, such as its radical planarity and compressed, rhythmic unity.[7] In his *Sources of Art Nouveau* (1956), Stephen Tschudi Madsen similarly relates the art nouveau and modernist aspects of Mackmurdo's designs to the overgeneralized concept of a nineteenth-century "cult of plant and line."[8] But this association, too, overlooks some of the distinctiveness of the designs, in part because

5 Mackmurdo, "Autobiographical Notes."
6 Nikolaus Pevsner, *Pioneers of Modern Design: From William Morris to Walter Gropius* (Harmondsworth: Penguin, 1978), 90.
7 Pevsner, *Pioneers of Modern Design*, 90.
8 Stephen Tschudi Madsen, *Sources of Art Noveau* (New York: Da Capo Press, 1980), 152, 154.

Figure 2
William Morris, *Acanthus Hanging*, c. 1880. London, Victoria and Albert Museum.

Figure 3
George Lemmen, cover, *L'Art Moderne*, 1894.

of Madsen's dichotomization of two naturalist tendencies that, in fact, are inseparably linked in Mackmurdo's designs, namely the rhythmic use of flower and stem and the constructive evocation of fitness, logic, and structure.[9]

Although Mackmurdo's botanical motifs of the early 1880s take their place in a long and well-established tradition that goes back at least to designers such as Owen Jones (1809–74) and Christopher Dresser (1834–1904) and looks forward to art nouveau, some of their explicit features set them distinctly apart. This distinction becomes clear through comparison of Mackmurdo's cover of *Wren's City Churches* with, two related designs by other artists. The small embroidered *Acanthus* hanging (*Figure* 2), designed by William Morris and executed by Morris and Company approximately three years earlier; observes a strict symmetry about the central vertical axis, a more intricate interweaving of two different vegetal patterns, and a deeper spatial effect, notably aided by the contrasting tones of the brown-gold vegetation and the blue background. The lateral distribution of the ornate pattern gives neither a directed focus nor the suggestion of a single source of growth. On the other hand, Mackmurdo achieves a more direct and concentrated expression of organic vitality by use of asymmetrical organization on a single plane, a greater economy of imagery, and a dramatic juxtaposition of alternate black and white bands that sprout from a source near the lower center of the composition in a swinging, rhythmic motion and terminate in three unequal blooms and flame-like tendrils. The vitality of this remarkable pattern is carried over into the waving banner and even within it, to the irregularly composed letters that spell the book's title. The most distinctive feature of this work is the way everything seems to be responding to an equally dynamic, external force. In contrast to this dynamism, only the elongated figures of the peacocks at the vertical margins and the letters and numbers giving details of authorship and publication provide any suggestion of stability.

Comparison with an example that is clearly art nouveau, George Lemmen's magazine cover for *L'Art Moderne* of 1894 (*Figure* 3), further distinguishes Mackmurdo's design—in this instance, from the style that his book cover is supposed to have anticipated. Lemmen's design, though suggestive of a certain vitality, verges on visual confusion. Its flow of linear energies is restless, its juxtaposition of transparent and opaque planes is unclear, and its imagistic elements are difficult to distinguish from its calligraphic, which spell *Art/Moderne/Bruxelles*.

The repeat pattern of Mackmurdo's *Single Flower* cretonne, from about 1882 (*Figure* 4), anticipates several features of his book cover design. The economical design appears in a single plane, though this piece employs color, and elongated leaves and single

9 Madsen, *Sources of Art Noveau*, 171. The citation from Mackmurdo is found in his review of Lewis F. Day's *Nature in Ornament* in *Century Guild Hobby Horse* 7 (1892), 64.

Figure 4
Arthur Heygate Mackmurdo, *Single Flower,* cretonne, c. 1882. Walthamstow, William Morris Gallery (F80).

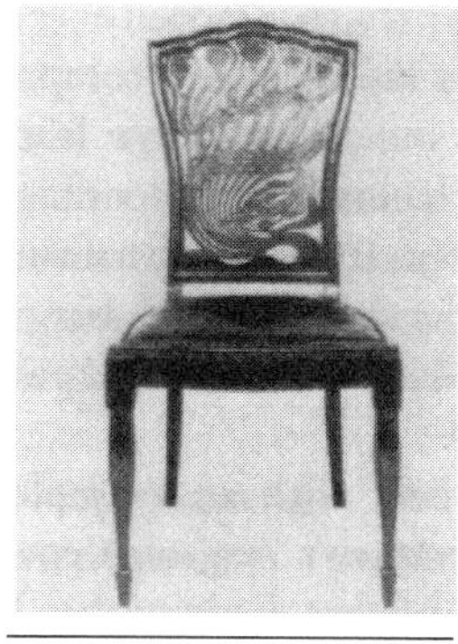

Figure 6
Arthur Heygate Mackmurdo, *Dining-chair,* c. 1882. Walthamstow, William Morris Gallery (G36).

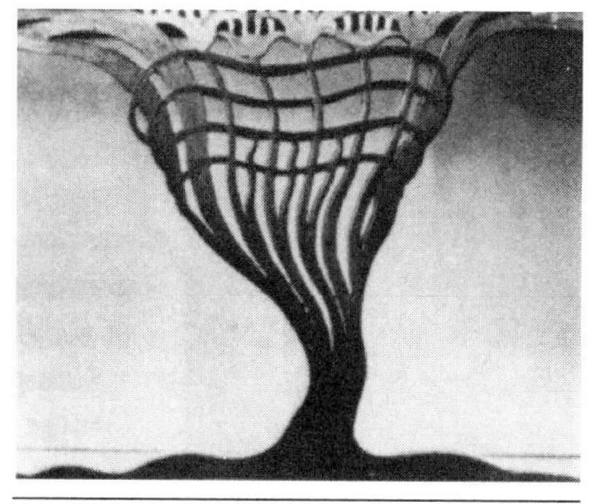

Figure 7
Arthur Heygate Mackmurdo, *Cabinet shelf-bracket,* mahogany, c. 1886. Walthamstow, William Morris Gallery (G9).

flowers waft in different directions, again as if in response to the external force of wind or water. Incidentally, the initials C.G. straddling the small leaved stem near the root of the cluster denote the Century Guild, a craft organization founded by Mackmurdo and a few associates in 1882. *Cromer Bird* (*Figure 5*), another cretonne, from about 1884, even more forcefully suggests marine vegetation being swayed by water, with long leaves undulating in the opposite direction of the many-petalled lilies above and the birds in pairs and threes flying to the right. In a background plane, on a reduced scale and in lighter tones, a more regular arrangement of leaved stems curves around lotuses.

Figure 5
Arthur Heygate Mackmurdo, *Cromer Bird,* cretonne, c. 1884. Walthamstow, William Morris Gallery (F84).

Closer yet to art nouveau is the fretwork back of a dining chair from about 1882 (*Figure 6*). The dimensions, spacing, and arrangement of meandering and interlaced flat bands, evoke, with remarkable effect, the vitality of a marine plant swaying to the gentle push and pull of water, from the single sinuous trunk at the bottom to the spreading and criss-crossing stems, the buds curving downward and left, and the row of florets at the top. A more subdued version of this type of design is used in three fretted shelf brackets for a cabinet, from about 1886 (*Figure 7*).

As suggested above, the force and originality of Mackmurdo's designs are the result of two inseparable elements: a distinctive use of botanical imagery and the function of that imagery as the symbolic embodiment of a constructive and ordering force in the processes of nature. By subordinating the data of nature to certain rules of abstraction and the requirements of decorative design, Mackmurdo was observing his own dictate to the designer not to "literally depict the model," which is but to make oneself a slave of mere chance, but rather to strive for "a more profound knowledge of nature."[10] This rejection of "realistic rendering" was not the function of traditional artistic idealism.[11] Instead, Mackmurdo was resorting

10 Mackmurdo, review of Day's *Nature in Ornament,* 66.

11 For idealism, see Joshua Reynolds, Discourse III, in *Discourses on Art* (New York: Collier Books, 1966), 43–52, and Erwin Panofsky, *Idea: A Concept in Art Theory,* translated by J. S. Peake (Columbia: University of South Carolina Press, 1968), especially chapter 4, "The Renaissance," and chapter 6, "Classicism."

to an interpretive device commonly used in evolutionary reflections of his day to infer an abstract principle underlying concrete images of nature. In the last paragraph of *On the Origins of Species*, with which Mackmurdo was probably familiar, Darwin makes such an inference. After surveying the complex and interdependent organic life of "an entangled bank, clothed with many plants of many kinds, with birds singing on the bushes," and abundant other creatures, Darwin infers the operation of "laws acting around us."[12] Earlier, in 1857, Spencer had posited an underlying law in nature that regulates the development of organisms from a state of homogeneity to one of heterogeneity.[13] Mackmurdo likewise inferred "a cosmic unity behind the phenomenal appearances, one law harmonizing seeming opposites; a single process under which everything animate and inanimate is being kneaded to an all-embracing perfection."[14] He characterized an object in nature as "that which it will be when its development is complete" and offered the following example: The "purple clematis that climbs about my porch interests my imagination as an artist only so far as it has qualities and *tendencies*."[15] Thus, the embodiment of law in nature is a means of approach to the symbolic function of the botanical designs that Mackmurdo provided. On the artist's part, "the trained imagination" or "imaginative reason," the faculty in him that discerns the natural law, is itself regulated by a corresponding mental law, so that his design captures "that unity of character, that rectitude and entirety of form, which the mind anticipates as the net result of the *tendencies* of the greatest number in a sort."[16]

In practical terms, the design would distill "that ordering of parts which the imagination discerns throughout nature, . . . that inevitable sequence which informs a living whole and gives such integrity to design," in addition to the two other essential qualities of nature—rhythm and arbitrariness.[17] Criticizing the attempt of his fellow-artist, Lewis Foreman Day, to "demonstrate the natural development of ornament from nature, [and] to show its constant relation to natural form" as being impossible on the too narrow terms offered by him, Mackmurdo proposed instead the following organizing first principles: (1) Because the formative imagination plays an independent role in art, transcription of nature should not be the primary aim. (2) The same "law" that governs all of life governs the operations of imagination and "is made vocal by the instrument of art" when art observes "a strict conformity with all organic structure, a determined uniformity of plan, a certain inevitableness in the sequence of parts and . . . a severe simplicity of economy of means, directed toward one end, an end predetermined from the first inception in the artist's imagination." (3) A design is "a work of nature as a plant may be said to be a work of nature," both giving evidence of the "same prime influence," the one in human nature (as manifested in art), the other in external nature. (4)

12 Charles Darwin, *The Works of Charles Darwin*, P. H. Barrett and R. B. Freeman, eds. (London: W. Pickering, 1988), 347.

13 Herbert Spencer,"Progress: Its Laws and Its Cause," in *Essays Scientific, Political, and Speculative*, 1 (New York: D. Appleton & Company, 1910), 9–10.

14 Mackmurdo, *The Human Hive: Its Life and Law* (London: Watts & Co., 1926), 276.

15 Mackmurdo, *The Human Hive*, 66.

16 Mackmurdo, *The Human Hive*, 66.

17 Mackmurdo, *The Human Hive*, 67.

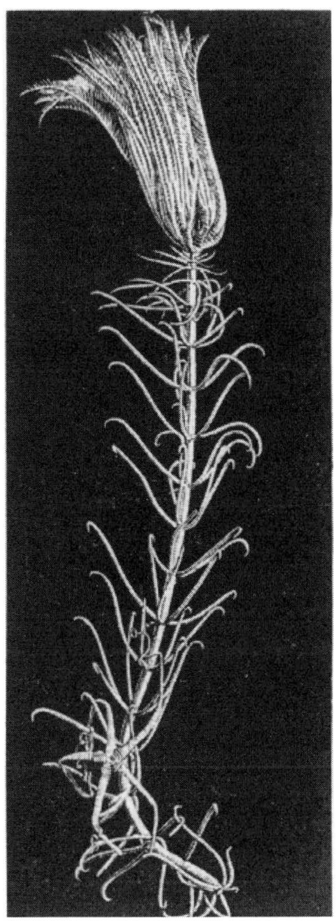

Figure 8
Pentacrinus asteria, figure 70, C. Wyville Thomspon, *The Depths of the Sea* (New York & London, Macmillan and Co., 1873), figure 30.

The artist must be schooled both in the history of art and in "all living forms," which will enable him to match his technical means to his grasp of the developmental principle in nature.[18]

Mackmurdo made much of this seemingly schematic appropriation of evolutionary theory between the mid 1870s and early 1880s, when scientific literature was giving particular attention to plant life, including that of the seas. Darwin's *The Movement and Habits of Climbing Plants* appeared in 1865, his *The Different Forms of Flowers on Plants of the Same Species* in 1877, and his *The Power of Movement in Plants,* which according to one critic, influenced Mackmurdo's designs, appeared in 1880.[19] This kind of writing sometimes had a poetical ring, as in the following passage by Spencer, which seems to offer an appropriate gloss on Mackmurdo's botanical-designs: "Streams of water produce in opposing objects the same general effects as do streams of air. Submerged weeds growing in the middle of a brook, undulate from end to end. Branches brought down by the last flood, and left entangled at the bottom where the current is rapid, are thrown into a state of up and down movement that is slow or quick in proportion as they are large or small. . . ."[20]

The principles of organic evolution that Spencer derived from observations of natural phenomena are directly applicable to Mackmurdo's botanical designs: (1) Because matter is perceived in terms of forces of attraction and repulsion, all things exhibit the aspect of resistance to both dilation and compression. (2) Considering the law of attraction and repulsion of bodies, movement is determined by traction and resistance and, thus, rarely follows a straight axis. (3) Exact regularity is rare, for the dynamic of action and reaction never brings about a return to a previous state.[21] These terms are congruent with Mackmurdo's design guidelines and the qualities of his own designs, especially their dynamic rhythms, their suggestion of the reciprocal action of internal and external forces, and the consequent aspects of irregularity, arbitrariness, and economy of form. These principles can also be seen in the illustrations that accompanied the two reports of marine expeditions by Sir C. Wyville Thomson on H.M.S. "Porcupine" and H.M.S. "Lightning" from 1868 to 1870 and H.M.S. "Challenger" in 1873, upon which Huxley lectured in 1875[22] (*Figures 8 and 9*).

Mackmurdo's two fundamental propositions, that nature is regulated by a law of progressive development (which he held in common with Spencer), and that a work of art is similar to a plant by also being a work of nature (which was entirely original) gave his theory of design a moral and civilizing impulse. These propositions mark the break in his thought from the historicism and retrospection that prevailed in his day and its reorientation along the line from the present to the future. They also make more intelligible Mackmurdo's defection from Ruskinian medievalism and Morris's

18 Mackmurdo, review of Day's *Nature in Ornament,* 66–67.

19 Malcolm Haslam, "A Pioneer of Art Nouveau: Arthur Heygate Mackmurdo," *Country Life* 157, no. I (February 27,1975): 127.

20 Herbert Spencer, *First Principles,* 4th ed. (New York: A. L. Burt, 1904), 228–29.

21 Spencer, *First Principles,* 208–09, 215, 233.

22 See Thomas Henry Huxley, "On Some of the Results of the Expedition of H.M.S. 'Challenger,'" in *Discourses Biological and Geological: Essays* (New York: D. Appleton & Company, 1897).

utopian communism, on the one hand, and his sympathy with the modernist esthetic of artists such as James McNeill Whistler, on the other. The principles of organic form and purified design that informed his botanical designs and his ideal of social transformation through art prefigure modernism in a wider yet more specific sense than is indicated by a straightforward comparison of those designs with art nouveau. But what remained, on the whole, distinctive about Mackmurdo's role as an early modernist was his conviction that science could play a part in the formation of a style that was serviceable to modern needs.

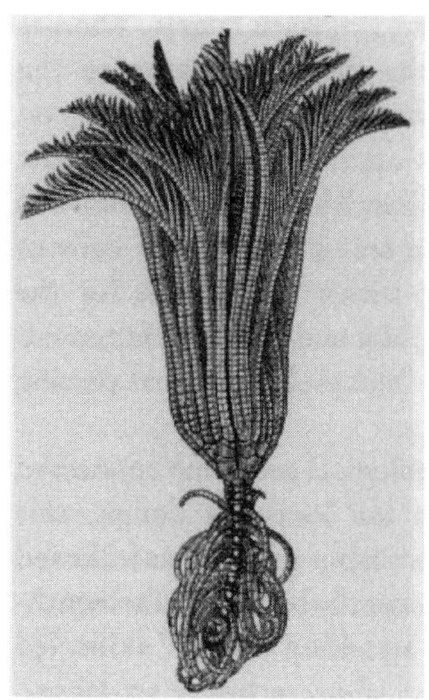

Figure 9
Pentacrinus Maclearanus, figure 31, from C. Wyville Thomson, *The Voyage of the "Challenger:" The Atlantic* (New York, Harper & Bros., 1878), fig. 31.

The Design Prototype as Artistic Boundary: The Debate on History and Industry in Central European Applied Arts Museums, 1860–1900

Mitchell Schwarzer

The twentieth-century association of modernity with utility validated a modernist design genealogy characterized by increasingly simple, mechanized forms. The thesis of historical development leading toward industrialization, which important historians of modern design like Nikolaus Pevsner, Siegfried Giedion, and even Reyner Banham argued, was based on the opposition of progressive and regressive ontological realities: simple and complex, mechanized and hand-crafted, ascetic and historicist, avant garde and mainstream. Furthermore, the representation of modern design in terms of progress, and its unceasing flow of inventions, also pointed to the attainment of a heroic age, generally the period between 1918 and 1939, by which all other eras of modern design could be measured.[1]

More than any other movement, the Bauhaus was identified as that absolute laboratory of modern design. As such, historical representation of the characteristics of Bauhaus design became a point of reference for situating progressive trends in both preceding and succeeding periods. Because historical representation gestured to specific and exclusive genealogies, it became incumbent upon historians to ignore or condemn "unprogressive" historical moments and praise "progressive" eras. In histories mentioning German design, for example, this historiographic approach resulted in the linkage of Bauhaus design to disparate historical movements such as the Biedermeier age between 1815 and 1848, solely on the basis of a perceived preference in each for simple forms and an absence of historical ornament.[2] This representation of the culminating achievements of Bauhaus philosophy similarly amalgamated movements with sharply contrasting philosophies: the utilitarian (but anti-machine) ideas of the Arts and Crafts Movement in nineteenth-century England and the advocacy for mechanization within the union of artists and industrialists known as the Deutscher Werkbund in Germany after 1907. What both of these movements held in common was their opposition to the rigid historicist and academic attitudes of the second half of the nineteenth century; we are told in each case that new design models emerged because historical artistic models were rejected.[3]

1 The overall argument, for example, of Siegfried Giedion's *Mechanization Takes Command, A Contribution to an Anonymous History* (New York: Norton, 1969), posited as the conflation of historical destiny and productive attainment, is that the heroic age was depicted as the absolute character of design modernity.

2 See Edward Lucie Smith, *History of Industrial Design* (New York: Van Nostrand, 1983), 50.

3 The historical work primarily responsible for establishing this most lasting genealogy has been Nikolaus Pevsner's *Pioneers of the Modern Movement* (London: Faber & Faber, 1936).

At the very least, the linear and monolithic qualities of these historical representations obscure an infinitely more complex set of significative relationships behind the emergence of industrial design in modern society. They also betray tendencies to disguise historiographic prejudices and suppositions for the appearance of monolithic historical reality and to obliterate societal difference in favor of universality. The efforts of paradigmatic historians of modern design to collapse disparate historical occurrences into an integrated and consistent schema have been increasingly challenged in recent years. Clive Dilnot describes these interpretative efforts as more indicative of the particular historiographic point of view "dominant at the time the history was written" than of any omnipresent reality.[4] Consequently, contemporary historians have begun to construct new representations of design movements not on the basis of comparisons with a limited set of progressive qualities, but through complex descriptions of a large set of historical moments previously considered unprogressive.[5]

Any historical re-evaluation of modern design in terms of heterogeneity mandates an investigation of those historical moments repressed by canonical modernist historiography. This approach should not seek, however, to replace one historical genealogy with another and supplant utilitarian modernism with a historically or artistically reinvigorated postmodernism. Rather, it must reject the totalizing claims and linear paths that are emblematic of most historical approaches since the eighteenth century. This re-evaluation, therefore, encourages a representation of history that exhibits how dissenting, marginal, and fragmentary design movements are of value in and of themselves. More importantly, it recognizes that these movements are also deeply implicated in the discursive structures of canonical modernism itself and, hence, are of fundamental value in understanding contemporary structures of design knowledge.

For example, take the topic of this essay: the definition of modern mechanization, with its objectives to express movement and progress, can be related to earlier (and seemingly antithetical) efforts to define modern historicism. In other words, the objectivization of both modern mechanization and historical identity emerged from similar motivations to set boundaries to artistic expression through the use of prototypes. What has been often neglected by histories of modern design is that the shift to a mechanistic philosophy by German thinkers after 1900 was ignited by a profound series of earlier inquiries into the historical nature of the applied arts (Kunstgewerbe). Many of these studies, by such divergent thinkers as Rudolf Eitelberger and Julius Lessing, occurred between 1860 and 1900 at the newly founded museums of the applied arts (Kunstgewerbemuseen) throughout Austria and Germany.[6] In analyzing the interdependence of social and artistic issues in the museum promotion of historical models, a principal issue of this essay is the museum's advocacy of modeling as an

4 Clive Dilnot, "The State of Design History. Part 1: Mapping the Field," *Design Issues I (Spring* 1984), 6.

5 The investigation of the congruences of twentieth-century modernism with nineteenth-century historicism has been a deep concern of recent architectural and design history. See, for instance, Gillian Naylor, *The Bauhaus Reassessed, Sources and Design Theory* (NewYork: E.P. Dutton, 1985), 2.

6 For a comprehensive history of the *Kunstgewerbemuseen* movement, see Barbara Mundt's *Die deutschen Kunstgewerbemuseen im 19. Jahrhundert* (München: Prestel, 1974). As Mundt relates, before the 1860s, the words *Kunst* (art) and *Gewerbe* (product) were infrequently combined. The concept of *Kunstgewerbe* attained its greatest currency between the 1860s and 1890s. Throughout its period of usage, however, *Kunstgewerbe* contained within itself competing voices. Its history, therefore, is indicative of the indeterminacy regarding issues of art and utility in applied arts design during the modern era. After 1900, and the association of Kunstgewerbe with historicism, the use of the concept fell into gradual disuse (13–15).

instrument for situating socioartistic boundaries for applied arts production in industrial culture.

Applied arts museums were one expression of a much larger series of attempts during the nineteenth century to hold artistic culture together amid the centrifugal forces of industrialization. Like many reactive constituents of their age, museum directors were greatly fearful of the new divisive forces of individualism, specialization, and utilitarianism. They energetically combated the decentering of artistic ideals by industrial irrationality, and sought to bring about a regulating climate for the mass production and consumption of applied arts products. To a great extent, this notion of a rational climate meant the restoration of the traditional artistic values of aristocratic culture. The museum program sought, to put it simply, to tame both the machine and industrial society through artistic exemplars.

What complicated the museum attempt to develop a conclusive set of deductive prototypes for the industrial applied arts was the fact that its constituency often had opposing social goals and differing esthetic sensibilities. Unlike the English Arts and Crafts movement, applied arts museums never rejected industry and took great efforts to create an educational environment for industrialists and art dealers, as well as artists, historians, and the general public. Undoubtedly, it was extraordinarily difficult to create a regulating pattern language for the disparate segments of this population. For example, the museum objective, which embraced the Enlightenment ideal of a uniform and progressive artistic rule, ignored the extent of class and ethnic differences in nineteenth-century Austria and Germany. Historical modeling also disregarded the fresh energies and forms of industry, as Julius Lessing (director of the Berlin Museum of the Applied Arts after 1873) pointed out in the 1890s.

Lessing's insights contested the habitual acceptance of historic artistic culture by theorists of the applied arts museum movement. In the 1860s and 1870s, Rudolf Eitelberger had only superficially accepted the machine and industrialization, and had actually tried to convince industrialists to mass-produce artifacts in accordance with fine arts models. Now, in contrast to Eitelberger, Lessing forcefully recommended that applied artists take their forms from industrial processes and not from history. Nevertheless, shared affinities were present in both Eitelberger's preoccupation with historical modeling and Lessing's advocacy for industrial processes at the turn of the century. In spite of distinct aspirations, ideas of modeling—the inferential use of literal or analogical prototypes—were proposed in both cases to combat perceptions of degeneracy in modern society. Lessing's double movement, rejecting historical identification and accepting technological determinacy, foreshadowed an important strand of twentieth-century modernism, and, in particular, the Werkbund's theory of industrial types, or *Typisierung*.

The initial elaboration of historical modeling

The origins of the applied arts ideal of historical modeling occurred in the period between 1730 to 1850. During this extraordinary time, a series of major technological inventions ranging from the steam engine to the railroad transfigured economic and social relations in Europe. By 1850, the inexpensive, easily reproducible products of machine industry had displaced hand crafts throughout Austria and Germany. Old hand vocations, characteristic of the applied arts in furniture, glassware, linens, and metalwork, vanished.[7] Machine-produced goods gained dominance in the urban marketplace and shaped the tastes of the rapidly growing urban consumer class. This destruction of the hand crafts and folk culture was later described by the art critic Albrecht Kurzwelly as a consequence of an increasing incompatibility of urban and rural life: "The growth of transportation through the railroad and the spread of industry throughout the land accelerated the decline of [rural life]. City-oriented tastes favored inexpensive, poorly made, and ultimately phony machine products which displaced the hereditary logic of rural ways."[8] Kurzwelly's comments implied that rural life should be considered by reformers as the primary model for any intended renewal of the hand crafts. As we will see, such was not to be the case until the end of the nineteenth century.[9]

From the late eighteenth century to the beginnings of the applied arts museum movement in the 1860s, reformers looked to the fine artist, and not to the folk artist, as the agent of revitalization. These reformers, consisting largely of government bureaucrats, hoped to hold artistic culture together under the guiding hands of those artists unstained by the commodifying and degenerate practices of industrial production. Machine industry was defiling the esthetic singularity of hand craft products. Arbitrariness, especially as exercised by poorly trained handicraftsmen or machine designers, was replacing the centralizing precepts of artistic tradition. Reformers, who deplored this profanation of the applied arts, argued for protection from disjunctive industrial culture. Not surprisingly, defensive barriers emerged in the guise of the artistic academies, and the orderly integration of the applied arts under the sign of the fine arts.

Academicization of the applied arts in Central Europe was ironic because the detachment of the applied arts from high culture owed as much to the evolution of court society and the concept "fine arts" as to industrialization. Well before large-scale mechanization, the rise of a humanist notion of the "individual artist" instituted a chasm between the fine and applied arts. The growth of art academies and general reinforcement of classical artistic training at the expense of hand craft guilds furthered this separation.[10] But, rather than viewing the academicization of the applied arts as potentially leading to the cleavage of its creativity from the productive energies of everyday life, the principles of the artistic academy

7 The industrial specialization of the period after 1850 encompassed textiles, fashions, and luxury articles. By the end of the 1850s, certain trades, such as furniture, were greatly commercialized. Hans Bobek & Elisabeth Lichtenberger, *Wien, Bauliche Gestalt und Entwicklung seit der Mitte des 19. Jahrhunderts* (Graz: Hermann Böhlaus, 1966), 40.

8 Albrecht Kurzwelly, "Lage und Zukunft der Volkskunst," in Richard Graul, ed. *Die Krisis im Kunstgewerbe: Studien über die Wege und Ziele der modernen Richtung* (Stuttgart: J. G. Cotta, 1855), 91.

9 Consideration of the peasantry as the ultimate source and foundation for national culture is closely connected to the development of ethnology in Germany after the 1850s. Wilhelm Riehl's science of *Volkskunde* contributed to great interest in the daily life of Germanic peasants. See his *Naturgeschihte des Volkes* (Stuttgart: J. G. Cotta, 1855). Still, despite the medievalist movement of the 1840s and the growth of Germanic ethnology during the second half of the century, expansive interest among theorists of the applied arts in rural life and the Germanic peasantry emerged only amid the new *Volkskunst* movements in the 1890s.

10 In Prussia, on the French model, an Akademie der Künste was founded in 1696, and included courses in architecture, geometry, and perspective. In 1786, the Academy was directed to pursue the cultivation of all aspects of the arts and crafts, and finally in 1799 a separate architectural section was established as the Bauakademie. Hermann Muthesius, "Geschichtliche Entwicklung des Kunstunterrichts im XVIII. Jahrhundert," *Hohe Warte* 2,1905–1906, 458. In Austria, in 1773 the diverse Viennese schools of art were united into one institution, the K. K. Akademie der vereinigten bildenen Künste. The new school included sections of painting, sculpture, architecture, copper engraving, and metalworking. Yet, although a manufacturer's school had been founded in Vienna in 1758, its absorption into the Academy in 1787 did little to shift the focus of the academic institution's attention to practical affairs of industrial commerce and production. "Kunstgewerblicher Unterricht in Oesterreich im Vorigen Jahrhundert," *Blätter für Kunstgewerbe* 6, 1877, 23.

were initially regarded as a salvation. During the closing decades of the eighteenth century, associations of crafts artists *(Gewerbevereine)* were formed in Germany and Austria to awaken the public's sense of the artistry of the applied arts.[11]

By the 1820s, the regeneration of the applied arts envisaged strict guarantees for artistic purity. For many, the deleterious effects of industry could only be reversed through the structuring of everyday applied arts production by universal artistic prototype and the subordination of the applied artist to the fine artist. Applied arts reformers looked to the fine artist as tastemaker and tried to centralize applied arts production according to a small series of fine arts models. This attempt to turn industrial production into the sublimated expression of a small set of historical prototypes was characterized as the modeling movement *(Musterbewegung* or *Vorbilderbewegung).* The architect Karl Friedrich Schinkel's model drawings of furniture, silverware, and numerous other applied arts products in 1830s Prussia are perhaps the most famous example of how a state artist acted as the primary designer for an entire range of subservient producers in the applied arts. Alongside Schinkel in Berlin, Peter Wilhelm Beuth provided tremendous impetus for the Vorbilderbewegung in the applied arts.[12] Beuth, actively engaged throughout his life in modernizing Prussian industry, also subordinated applied artists to a much smaller circle of fine artists. He recommended that the latter develop ideal prototypes—taken from historical sources—for all applied arts products, from which copies would then be made.[13] In Prussia, this role of the artist as tastemaker represents one of the earliest attempts by an entire nation to rationalize applied arts production according to unified esthetic principles at the expense of specialization and fragmentation.[14]

The stringent ideology of the modeling movement was in large part the impetus for the establishment of museums of applied arts in Central Europe during the last third of the century. Insofar as artistic selection and modification from historical sources became integral for an applied arts renewal, the permanent showcasing of important artistic types or models to the public assumed increasingly greater relevance.[15] Additional inspiration for founding public applied arts museums came from recent developments toward artistic centralization in France and England. In Paris, the applied arts curriculum of the Conservatoire des arts et métiers (1799) stimulated the founding of technical schools throughout Central Europe.

In fact, the public museum of applied arts objects was pioneered in London. Because of early industrialization, the English reform movement was the first to struggle against the injurious effects of mass production on the hand crafts. Propelled by an 1835 report on the state of the arts in England, an informal group of English reformers (including Henry Cole, A.W.N. Pugin, and Owen Jones) developed the idea of a practical alliance between the applied artist and the manufacturer.[16] As a consequence of these efforts and

11 The first union of artists and friends was established in 1792 in Nürnberg. J.F. Ahrens, "Die Reform des Kunstgewerbes in ihrem geschichtlichen Entwicklungsgange," in *Deutsche Zeitund Streit-Fragen,* ed. Franz von Hoftzendorff (Hamburg: J.F. Richter, 1886), 22–23. During the early nineteenth century, state commissions were established in the various German lands to develop drawing schools for *Kunstgewerbe* on the model of the fine arts. Hans Waentig, *Wirtschaft und Kunst* (Jena: Gustav Fischer,1909),107.

12 See especially Beuth's *Vorbilder für Fabrikanten und Handwerker* (Berlin: Beuth, 1826).

13 Barbara Mundt, "Theorien zum Kunstgewerbe des Historismus in Deutschland," in *Beiträge zur Theorie der Künste run 19. Jahrhundert, I,* eds. Helmut Koopmann and J. Adolf Schmoll (Frankfurt am Main: Vittorio Klostermann, 1971) 318–21.

14 Gert Selle, *Design-Geschichte in Deutschland: Produkultur als Entwurf und Erfahrung* (Köln: Dumont, 1987), 43 .

15 Perhaps the most important early private collection of applied arts products in Central Europe was that of Alexander Freiherr von Minutoli. Started in the 1830s, this collection, housed in the Liegnitzer Palace, numbered around 19,000 objects by 1865, and shortly afterward formed the basis for several German applied arts museums. Mundt, *Die deutschen Kunstgewerbemuseen im 19. Jahrhundert,* 31. Another early important collection of applied arts objects was that of the Stuttgarter Institut zur Gewerbeförderung.

16 For accounts of the English reform movement in the 1830s and 1840s, see Clive Bell, *Art In England* (Harmondsworth: Penguin, 1938); Bernard Denvir, *The Early Nineteenth Century: Art, Design, and Society from1789 to 1852* (London: Longman Group, 1984); and Lyndel Saunders King, *The Industrialization of Taste: Victorian England and the Art Union of London* (Ann Arbor. UMI, 1982).

the financial profits generated by the Great World Exhibition in London in 1851, the first public applied arts museum in Europe, the South Kensington Museum, opened in 1852.

To those interested in the applied arts in the German-speaking lands, French and English actions were decisive.[17] The 1851 Exhibition and its successors in Paris (1855, 1867) and London (1862) made possible for the first time a direct comparison of the applied arts in different nations. What Central Europeans found was demoralizing. Time and time again, art critics lamented the impoverished state of the applied arts in Austria and Germany.[18] To them, the English museum's promotion of elevated models represented an archetype for improving and regulating artistic taste and production. It is no wonder, therefore, that Austrians began preparations in the 1850s for the founding of a Viennese version of the South Kensington Museum.[19] Rudolf Eitelberger's renewed pronouncements about continuing English ingenuity at the 1862 London Exhibition further stimulated interest; and, finally, the Österreichische Museum für Kunst und Industrie was opened to the public in 1864.[20]

Support was also building at the same time for public applied arts museums in Germany. Catalyzed by Hermann Schwabe's 1866 book, *Die Förderung der Kunst-Industrie in England und der Stand dieser Frage in Deutschland (The Advancement of Art Industry in England and the State of this Question in Germany)*, an extensive study of English industrial arts, and the tremendous public interest for the 1867 Paris Exposition, the Deutsches Museum für Kunst und Gewerbe opened in Berlin in 1868.[21] In subsequent years, numerous museums of the applied arts were founded in large cities throughout the German and Austrian empires.

The museum offered the possibility for rationally examining historical laws of progress in the applied arts, and presenting a compelling exhibition of deductive laws for the construction of a

17 Rudolf Eitelberger remarked positively on the South Kensington Museum's encouragement of the practical needs of art education and production for the public at large. Rudolf Eitelberger v. Edelberg, "Die Gründung des Österreichischen Museums" [1864], in *Gesammelte Kunsthistorische Schriften,* II (Wien: Wilhelm Braumüller, 1879), 85.

18 After each international exhibition it was common for art critics in Central Europe to write long comparative reports highlighting national achievements in the applied arts. For example, see Friedrich Pecht, *Kunst und Kunstindustrie auf der Weltausstellung von 1867* (Leipzig: F.A. Brockhaus, 1867); *Kunst und Kunstindustrie auf der Wiener Weltausstellung* (Stuttgart: J.G. Cotta, 1873); *Kunst and Kunstindustrie auf der Weltausstellung von 1878* (Stuttgart: J.G. Cotta, 1878).

19 Eitelberger and his successors at the future Austrian Museum were indebted to Joseph Daniel Böhm, whose collection of applied art objects was the focus of activities among those involved with antiquities in Vienna after 1830. During the 1850s, Count Leo Thun's reorganization of the state educational system of Austria along empiricist lines similar to those of England also contributed to the strongly reformist climate. Around 1859, the *Niederösterreichische Gewerbe-Verein and the Handels-und Gewerbekammer* began to discuss in earnest the founding of an Austrian Museum for the arts and crafts. Elisabeth Springer, *Geschichte und Kulturleben der Wiener Ringstrasse* (Wiesbaden: Franz Steiner, 1979), 12, 260.

20 Jacob Falke, "Das Kunstgewerbe," in Wien, 1848–1888, ed. Gemeinderathe der Stadt Wien (Wien: Commissions-Verlag von Carl Konegan, 1888), 257–59.

21 On its founding and collections, see C. Grunow, *Das deutsche Gewerbe-Museum zu Berlin (Berlin,* 1868).

vital arts culture in the industrial marketplace.[22] Its program encouraged factory owners and dealers to produce and sell applied arts goods that simulated the historical models displayed in museum collections. These new collections exhibited a wide range of applied arts materials: precious metals, crystal and glass, ivory, enamels, porcelain, church relics, furniture, and tapestry. By no means, however, were museums limited to assembling collections of prototypes *(Mustersammlungen)*. Given their pervasive mission, museums backed a variety of activities aimed at increasing their influence among industrialists and the general public. A series of schools for the applied arts were created to train artists in the techniques of simulating historical models.[23] Furthermore, museums and their directors became principal patrons of a new series of journals on the applied arts, forums for a great deal of subsequent debate on the philosophical direction of the modeling movement.[24] The breadth of these museum activities, which also included lecture series and exhibitions, opened up dialogue among participants in the increasingly public debate on the applied arts. As we will see, however, the pluralist format for debate built into the museum offerings contained the seeds of destruction for its program of historical modeling.

Historical modeling at the applied art museums

True to his conviction in artistic traditions, Rudolf Eitelberger, director of Vienna's Museum of Art and Industry, revolted against the extent to which mass production had damaged the state of the applied arts. In his 1876 essay "Kunstgewerbliche Zeitfragen" ("Contemporary Issues in the Applied Arts"), he was quick to point out the replacement of the artistic hand by the unartistic machine. He charged that modern industrialists would rather copy imperfect old works and foreign designs than encourage independent thought and creation.[25] By cheaply reproducing the high-quality hand-made products of the traditional crafts, machines were forcing the age-old home industries (Hausindustrie) to isolated rural regions.[26] For Eitelberger, such a decline in the quality of local crafts led to artistic degeneracy, leaving the population no choice but to buy inferior local goods or superior foreign crafts.

The ruin of handwork by the debased techniques of modern industry, which so disturbed Eitelberger, could only be countered by a movement to revitalize unsullied artistic traditions (die Techniken der Alten).[27] To this end, Eitelberger and other historically minded theorists of the modeling movement were indebted to Gottfried Semper's theories on the integrative evolution of the applied arts and his proposal for a museum which would visually demonstrate these historical relationships.[28] The German architect and theorist Semper, who lived in London during the 1851 exhibition, directed his observations and recommendations to German readers in his 1851 essay "Wissenschaft, Industrie und Kunst: Vorschläge zur Anregung nationalen Kunstgefühls" ("Science, Industry and Art:

22 For a discussion of events in the development of an industrial philosophy at the Smithsonian Institution, see Arthur P. Molella, "The Museum that Might have Been: The Smithsonian's National Museum of Engineering and Industry," *Technology and Culture 32* (April 1992), 237–63.

23 The School of the Austrian Museum, as the Museum itself, was first housed in an armory. The new Museum building by Heinrich Ferstel was opened in 1871. A separate School building was completed adjacent to the Museum in 1877. Falke, "Das Kunstgewerbe," 260.

24 Among the more prominent of these early applied arts journals were *Kunstgewerbeblatt*, Leipzig (1884); *Mittelungen des k.k. Österreichischen Museums für Kunst and Industrie*, Wien (1865); *Kunst und Gewerbe*, Berlin (1867).

25 Eitelberger, "Kunstgewerbeliche Zeitragen," in Gesammelte *Kunsthistorische Schriften*, II, 274.

26 A few years earlier, Julius Lessing favorably observed the extant hand trades of the Slavic lands of the lower Danube and Russia where peasants still decorated their homes in a true style. *Das Kunstgewerbe auf der Wiener Weltaustellung 1873* (Berlin: Ernst Wasmuth, 1874), 28.

27 Eitelberger, "Kunstgewerbeliche Zeitfragen," 277.

28 For a collection of Semper's writings on these themes, see Gottfried Semper *The Four Elements of Architecture, and Other Writings*, trans. Harry Francis Mallgrave & Wolfgang Herrmann (Cambridge: Cambridge University, 1989).

Suggestions for the Revitalization of the National Spirit in Art"). Like others of the time, Semper had a profound desire to approach modern design problems with an understanding gleaned from historical models. Advancing beyond Schinkel's vision of a universal artistic language, however, Semper viewed the applied arts as part of a continuous web of human technological creation reaching back to the earliest days of mankind.

Semper's 1852 essay "Plan eines idealen Museums" (Plan for an Ideal Museum"), emphasized the importance of the techniques of production in reuniting pieces of artistic culture torn apart by the disruptions of industrial life."[29] Believing that collections of art had historically stimulated artistic development by setting forth values that shape national character, Semper advocated an awareness of extant, but frequently obscured, tectonic and technological traditions in the arts. He believed in taking into account both the common origins of different objects and their dissimilar historical development: "A perfect and comprehensive collection must represent the complete history of culture."[30] First, a comparison of the original motives *(Urmotive)* and related origins of all applied arts products demonstrates the unity of practical and esthetic aspects in artistic development. Second, their arrangement reproduces historical forces of creation and dispersion, energies active up to the present moment and of great importance to all involved in modern artistic creation.

The collections at the Austrian Museum are a telling display of some of Semper's ideas. By bracketing the arts with technology, Semper motivated Eitelberger and the incipient applied arts museum movement to consider any artistic renewal of the applied arts in concert with industrial concerns.[31] Eitelberger's call for links between the applied arts and industry epitomized the widespread realization during the second half of the century that Central Europeans must confront the new social and material forces of their age. This plea, then, must be understood as part of a larger turn to notions of a realistic economic and industrial policy *(Realpolitik)*, argued by such German writers as Ludwig August Rochau.[32]

Above all, however, Eitelberger hoped to reintegrate industrial production of the applied arts under the tutelage of the fine arts. Hence, his demand for a "real" connection between industry and the applied arts depended upon the primacy of the artistic-historical tradition. He felt that most contemporary industrialists and commercial dealers had too narrow an education and a very one-sided mercantilist viewpoint.[33] Especially important for Eitelberger was the demand that all levels of society—consumers, art dealers, industrialists—become familiar with the great historical exemplars of the applied arts tradition. In the ethic of the modeling movement, Eitelberger saw the museum as a forum for raising consciousness and argued that the improvement of the small crafts *(Kleingewerbe)* would be brought about only "through the visual inspection, use, and study of outstanding or instructive works."[34]

29 Gottfried Semper, "Plan eines idealen Museums" [1852], in Wissenschaft, *Industrie & Kunst*, ed. Hans M. Wingler (Mainz & Berlin: Florian Kupferberg, 1966), 72.

30 Semper, "Plan eines idealen Museums," 76.

31 Eitelberger, "Kunstgewerbeliche Zeitfragen," 312.

32 See his *Gründsätze der Realpolitik angewendet auf die staatlichen Zustände Deutschlands* (Stuttgart: K Göpel, 1853). Harold James, *A German Identity, 1770–1990* (London: Weidenfeld & Nicolson, 1989), 62.

33 Eitelberger, "Kunstgewerbeliche Zeitfragen," 296.

34 Eitelberger, "Die Gründung des Österreichischen Museums" in *Gesammelte Kunsthistorische Schriften*, II, 111.

Under Eitelberger, the Austrian Museum adopted a pedagogical course between that of empirically oriented England and classically traditional France.[35] Thus, despite inspiration from English Arts and Crafts theorists on the utilitarian aspects of design, the ideals of the applied arts movement promoted a strong allegiance to French artistic notions of composition and convenience. Adopting imitative practices similar to the Greek Revival and Beaux-Arts traditions in architecture, Eitelberger framed historical boundaries for applied arts production as a literal counterpart to those boundaries operative for artistic forms in preindustrial aristocratic Europe. Borrowing from what was considered by Semper to be the most advanced era of decorative arts production, the Austrian Museum structured its collections around vessels, implements, and other objects imbued with the visual signs of the classical artistic language. Unlike Semper, however, Eitelberger's desire to classicize and estheticize industrial production focused strongly on softening the contrast between the fine artist and applied artist and turning lowly machine products into works of high art. It all too often ignored Semper's notion that the forms of the applied arts were deeply inspired by the practical forces of industry in any historical period.

Eitelberger's critique was nevertheless influential in Austria and Germany, and led to a framing of applied arts production by the morphological systems of historical epochs.[36] The strength of the modeling movement in applied arts museums between the 1860s and 1880s led to a preoccupation with formal, visual qualities, stressing the need to translate the works of classicism into modern artistic languages through imitation and modeling from pattern books.[37] Adopting this viewpoint, Jacob Falke, the second director of the Viennese museum, blamed the nineteenth century's deterioration of taste on the applied artists' infatuation with the new and fashionable. In *Geschichte des modernen Geschmacks (A History of modern taste)*, Falke cast the museum's purpose as establishing a set of rational principles of taste gleaned from a comparison of the most splendid historical models.[38] Neither of the Viennese museum directors were alone in exposing the importance of historically minded restoration for Kunstgewerbe. As head of the Hamburgisches Museum für Kunst und Gewerbe in the north German city-state, Justus Brinckmann also advocated historical models and listed goals which would promote an understanding of the historical development of art industry, and improve upon the formation of taste; provide authentic prototypes for the crafts; resuscitate lost or neglected technical methods; and, finally, provide examples of modern art industry.[39]

The privileging of industrial processes

In the 1890s, Julius Lessing's vision for industrial and technological processes as a creative boundary for the applied arts was one of the clearest arguments for a wholesale break with historical modeling.

35 Stephan Muthesius, Das *englische Vorbild: eine Studie zu den deutschen Reformbewegungen in Architektur, Wohnbau, & Kunstgeschichte im späten 19 Jahrhundert* (München: Prestel, 1974), 53.

36 As Elisabeth Springer observes, Eitelberger's approach was embodied by a desire to determine the artistic principles for the present which are in harmnony with those of the past. Overall, he sought to institute objective criteria in place of free discovery. *Geschichte und Kulturleben der Wiener Ringstrasse*, 269.

37 Muthesius, *Das englische Vorbild*, 283–84.

38 Jacob Falke, *Geschichte des modernen Geschmacks*, (Leipzig: T.O. Weigel, 1866), 349.

39 As described by John Heskett in *German Design 1870–1918 (N.Y.:* Taplinger, 1986), 21.

Lessing's turn to industrial workings emerged, however, from his earlier belief in the restorative power of models. Thus, well before he broke with the philosophy of the historical modeling movement, he advocated the value of the past for the future, and insisted that it was the duty of his contemporaries to reintroduce the lost traditions of the arts.[40] This restoration of former artistic mores owed its urgency to Lessing's perception in the 1870s, during his directorship of the Berlin Museum of the Applied Arts, that integral historic contributions were cut short by events early in the century. He blamed ruptures in artistic continuity on the French Revolution, the Napoleonic Wars, and the radical climate of the nineteenth century. The first task of artistic renewal would be a reconnection with the models of the late eighteenth century. It was thus clear for Lessing that "in order to master the tasks at hand, all lost areas of historical technic must be enlivened."[41]

In his texts of the 1890s, written when he was no longer director of the Berlin Museum, Lessing aggressively substituted a belief in modern technology *(moderne Technik)* for his former faith in historical models. His exchange of history for industry, and model for process, were crucial for later developments in modern design. Influenced more than Eitelberger by the materialist aspects of Gottfried Semper's writings, Lessing stipulated that the artistic rediscovery of past states of handwork *(Handwerk)* would not be complete without deliberate consideration of new materials and technic. If one had to single out the reason for Lessing's reversal, it would be the growing perception among art theorists and critics that the aims of the historical modeling movement were failing.

By the 1880s, as the German art critic Heinrich Waentig later observed, it was becoming clear that the concerted attempts by the museum movement to invigorate the artistic quotient of the applied arts through historical modeling were not succeeding. Industrialists copied historical forms without sufficient regard for quality, and they reaped immense profits from these mass wares.

> So it was that the last and highest goal (of the applied arts movement), the artistic ennoblement of applied arts production, was not achieved. Quicker than one realized, the modern mass industrial technologies fashioned new forms for themselves. Thus, the Renaissance which arose from the 'machine's graces' must be labeled as a crass caricature of its noble predecessor.[42]

In the 1890s, Lessing came to the conclusion that historicism had caused the applied arts to become stale and inexpressive of new needs and desires. He charged that historical imitation had failed to yield adequate forms for the modern age and was in fact leading to a sharp antihistoricist reaction:

> As long as the fundamental conditions of the time remain the same, the (copied) form finally stiffens into unrecognizability and appears to the later generation only as a conceptless flourish. This later generation is then quickly ready to throw to its death the entire cultural period with which this form is associated.[43]

40 Julius Lessing, *Das Kunstgewerbe auf der Wiener Weltausstellung 1873* (Berlin: Ernst Wasmuth, 1874),10.

41 Lessing, *Das Kunstgewerbe auf der Wiener Weltausstellung 1873,* 12.

42 Waentig, *Wirtschaft und Kunst,* 270.

43 Julius Lessing, "Aus Alten Kultur," *Dekorative Kunst* 1898, 2, 33.

Lessing also sharply contrasted a historicist view of creativity, satisfied with imitating the results of earlier centuries to the point of stupor, with the emerging creative attitude of the moderns: "They explain forcefully that tradition is not useful anymore, and that the new age in which we live must have its own independent expression. This must emerge out of the depths of modern thought, out of the fresh sunlight consideration of nature."[44] Modern, for the Berliner Lessing, meant the fresh discovery of new forms by the rapidly growing industrial sector. It also meant a more thorough abandonment of historical heritage than was possible in traditionally conscious Austria.

Inasmuch as Lessing denied history in the name of industrial logic, his writings represent a breach with the historicism prevalent in texts on the applied arts during the nineteenth century, and the start of theorizing on the applied arts as purely constructive.[45]

For Lessing, it had become obvious that technology and science had separated the modern age from all prior historical eras. As far as the applied arts, the new industrial methods were so complex and efficient that it was no longer possible to clothe them in historical forms.[46] He admonished, "What is now demanded with a scream is the rejection of the forms of art that have predominated until now."[47] In a remarkable reversal Lessing now accused historical modeling of degeneracy.

In thus calling for the creation of new forms to embrace a shifting societal mood, Lessing required that forms must respond to—and not ignore—the concrete manifestations of industrial society. His understanding of the problem of the practical arts in the late nineteenth century revolved around this point: "Because of the modern factory industry, we stand before a fully changed system of productive activity, but we have not yet determined to reconfigure our knowledge of forms to these circumstances."[48] Lessing did not directly refer to the standardization of industrial products according to technological or functional prototypes. Nonetheless, his calls for the development of new forms to correspond to new technologies anticipated the theory of industrial types by Hermann Muthesius and other members of the Deutscher Werkbund.

It seems undeniable that Lessing's construction of limits based on industrial methods and materials was a transfigured—if less literal—expression of his earlier endorsement of historic models. Whereas Lessing now deplored direct imitation, he retained faith in the importance of drawing boundaries for the artistic imagination and industrial productive system. Continuity between historical modeling and industrial theories of twentieth-century design turns on the ideal of boundaries and their significance in recentering unrestrained artistic production. The dissimilarity between Lessing and Eitelberger was in the actual make-up of boundaries, and not in a belief in their necessity.

In the 1890s, Lessing's critique had repercussions within the applied arts museum world, and brought up serious questions on

44 Julius Lessing, *Das Moderne in der Kunst* (Berlin: Leonhard Simion, 1898), 3–4.

45 For similar developments in architecture, see Hermann Muthesius's early article, "Ist die Architektur eine Kunst oder ein Gewerbe?" *Zentralblatt der Bauverwaltung 13.* 1893.

46 Lessing *Die Moderne in der Kunst*, 18.

47 Lessing, *Die Moderne in der Kunst*, 5.

48 Julius Lessing "Neue Wege," *Kunstgewerbeblatt*, Neue Folge 6. 1895, 2.

the hierarchical character of this recentering of the applied arts. Bruno Bucher, the third director of the Austrian Museum of Art and Industry, felt compelled to address contradictions which had surfaced in regard to the applied arts museum's dual role for industry and history. Although the historical collection had customarily been viewed as the basis for artistic regeneration, Bucher attacked this orientation as potentially numbing for creativity amid the world of industrial products.[49] Like Lessing, Bucher was convinced that contemporary concerns were overshadowed by scholarly aspirations. Rather than stimulating living artistic projects, museums strove for historical breadth. He urged reorienting the goals of the applied arts museum from their hitherto emphasis on comprehensiveness and quantity to one of operative intentions toward contemporary artists and industrialists. Less ambitious historically, the pedagogic worth of the collection would engage in lively debate with the various art industries.[50] These suggestions emerged from Bucher's understanding of the depths to which industrial life differed from earlier historical eras. As industrial products have created an entirely new world, it would be wrong to design and decorate according to the conditions of an earlier age.[51] For one thing, commented Bucher, the wholesale import of the antique forms of Rome during the Renaissance cut off the natural development of art in northern Europe. The renewed historicism of the nineteenth century presumably had led now to a similar predicament.

It would be a mistake, however, to conclude that empirical observation of industrial life and nature had really replaced historic modeling as a paradigm for creativity within the applied arts museum movement. Historicist attitudes remained strong within the official museum program, while it was outside this program that antihistoricist attitudes were strongest.[52] Indeed, Bucher did not follow Lessing's radical utilitarianism. In a compromise position, not all that different from Eitelberger's earlier stance, Bucher argued in 1897 that artistic progress resulted from both the study of historical models and contemporary technologies—the development when necessary of traditions which are at hand.[53] Although aware of discrepancies between art history and industrial art, Bucher advocated a balance between the museum's scientific and scholarly aims and its practical calling for contemporary artistic activity. After all, he stated, "our museums are neither archaeological institutes nor solely stores for idea-seeking designers."[54]

Like Bucher, Wilhelm Bode, director of the Kaiser Friedrich Museum in Berlin in 1890, argued for a compromise position among the interests of contemporary art, industry, and historical tradition. In his 1896 article "Aufgaben der Kunstgewerbemuseen" ("Tasks of the Applied Art Museum"), the conservative leanings of this compromise position are apparent and led Bode to conclude, like Eitelberger, that applied arts museums should stress their existing collections: "The goals of the founding of applied arts museums

49 Bruno Bucher, "Die Sammlungen im Kunstgewerbemuseen und ihre Aufgabe," *Kunstgewerbeblatt* Neue Folge 3.1887, 151–52.

50 Bucher, "Die Sammlungen im Kunstgewerbemuseen und ihre Aufgabe," 152.

51 Bruno Bucher, "Styl im Zimmer," *Blätter für Kunstegewerbe* IX.1880, 4.

52 Arthur von Scala's brief tenure as the director of the Museum for Art and Industry in Vienna in 1897–98 is evidence of the strong opposition to new ideas within applied arts museum culture. See Adolf Loos's defense of Scala's English functionalism in his essay "Der Fall Scala" [1898], in *Die Potemkinsche Stadt*, ed. Adolf Opel (Wien: Georg Prachner, 1983).

53 Bucher, "Styl im Zimmer," 2.

54 Bruno Bucher, *Die Aufgaben der Kunstgewerblichen Museen* (Wien: Verlag des K.K. Oesterr. Museums, 1897), 9.

were almost exclusively didactic, technological—the reawakening and elevation of the applied arts through the gathering together of valuable models in all directions."[55] Yet, a year later, Bode felt obliged to acknowledge that his views were not universally shared. Many applied artists—especially those of the growing nationalist movements in England and Germany—were opposed to the intensive study of old art. From their perspective, wrote Bode, the copying of old forms and methods of decorating does not correspond to the needs of modern life.[56]

The social politics of artistic boundaries

The museum debate was part of a larger social controversy on the role that history and technology should play in shaping artistic production within industrial society. Through the course of its forty years, the debate unleashed sharp disagreement on the relevance of historic recuperation for contemporary industrial creativity as well as veiled agreement on the need for some sort of boundary for the applied arts. Without doubt, in modern times industrial production had detached the applied arts from their associations with historical artistic practices. If we look again at the underlying assumptions of the Central European museum program to restore those historical associations, however, we see two mutually contradictory dimensions. On the one hand, museums ingeniously extended their socioartistic mission to industrialists and the battlefield of machine production. On the other, they retained an allegiance to a set of literal models drawn from a centered vision of unified aristocratic culture, emphatically refusing to acknowledge the fragmentary social networks of industrial society.

First, the museum program sought a central position in debates on the applied arts, and aspired to influence artistic events as well as social ones. The Central European museums presented a vision of the applied arts more in tune with industrial culture than the antimachine attitudes of English theorists like John Ruskin and William Morris. Through a persistent desire to understand the applied arts in their productive associations, the modeling movement foreshadowed twentieth-century attempts at a cultural praxis that results from the merger of artistic and industrial modes of comprehension. The 1890s challenge by Lessing to the domination of industrial innovation by historic artistic models established, moreover, a discursive milieu of special consequence for the Deutscher Werkbund. The Werkbund retained the applied arts allegiance to the need for artistic and productive boundaries, and, yet, crafted new boundaries more along the abstract analogical framework of process recommended by Lessing than the literal modeling notions of the museum movement. Because of this constancy, the Werkbund debate of 1914 inverted the nineteenth-century conflict between Eitelberger and Lessing on the importance of liberating industrial forces from historical artistic traditions. Artists like Henry

55 Wilhelm Bode, "Aufgaben der Kunstgewerbemuseen," Pan 2.1896, 122.

56 Wilhelm Bode, "Kuenstler im Kunsthandwerk," Pan 3.1897, 41.

Van de Velde argued for the value of a free artistic imagination independent from the restrictions imposed by industrial utility.

In the second case, museums stuck to a unified and fine arts-centered world view. Despite the fact that functionalist and popularizing opinions were multiplying rapidly after 1900, association between historical modeling and creativity remained central to the museum agenda. This meant that the new social demands on the museum, represented most powerfully by Lessing's industrial realism but also by the new Volkskunst movement, were not met. Within the Werkbund, the radical utilitarians Friedrich Naumann and Hermann Muthesius revolted against the same sterile formalism that Lessing had seen as the outcome of the applied arts attempt to contain the applied arts by traditional artistic models. In a different vein, as part of the growing nationalist movement in the 1890s, Volk-oriented writers of the Heimat (homeland) movement vehemently criticized the aristocratic and frequently foreign models of the modeling movement as soulless formulas extraneous to the German spirit.[57]

The assumptions behind the historical collections had isolated the museum from the emerging industrial and nationalistic mentalities among those writing about the applied arts. Drawing the wrath of both Industrie and Heimat, the importance of applied arts museums in applied arts discourse diminished markedly in the twentieth century.[58]

The rise and fall of the Central European applied arts museum revolves around the history of its conceptualization of boundaries for artistic degeneracy. As we have seen, degeneracy exemplified the threat to the applied arts posed by undisciplined and disorganized industries, and established a rhetorical case for the museum's sharply constricted range of historical prototypes. Despite appeals to industry, the ideology of the modeling movement resisted expression of the enormously varied significatory languages indigenous to industrial modes of production and living. Although museum directors introduced new audiences to their activities, the largely aristocratic orientation of their collections refused recognition of the populist background characteristic of much of the new urban population. What mattered to theorists from Beuth to Eitelberger and eventually Bode was the imposition of a monologic vision of aristocratic artistic culture upon the disparate social contexts of industrial applied arts culture.

In Lessing's case, resistance to the historical modeling movement was directed against these hegemonic models for applied arts knowledge. Nonetheless, while Lessing rejected the imposition of historical models on industrial society, he did not attack the idea of artistic boundaries. Lessing was no more drawn to the multifarious social qualities of industrial bourgeois culture than was Eitelberger. Looking to create boundaries for applied arts production around a limited set of new technological developments, he eschewed the

57 Exemplifying of the critique emerging from the nationalistic right in the 1890s is Julius Langbehn's *Rembrandt als Erzieher* [1890] (Weimar: Alexander Duncker, 1922).

58 See Mundt, *Die deutschen Kunstgewerbemuseen*, 20.

diffuse and ostensibly arbitrary historical languages of industrial society. Whereas earlier Eitelberger had associated degeneracy with estrangement from artistic traditions, Lessing now identified it with the harmful effects of historical traditions on the modern age's will to industrial form. In both cases, different ideas of degeneracy were posed as the negative impetuses for equally different visions of authentic and restorative models.[59]

What these observations lead to is an awareness that scopic debates on boundaries for the applied arts were, and remain, a crucial issue for design theorists and historians. Their particularities articulate the epistemological ambivalence of modern society, while their similarities reflect the centralizing nature of nineteenth-century attempts to eradicate this ambivalence. As a consequence of these comments, historians of design might well reconsider the relevance of a lineal design genealogy for the modern era. It may be fruitful to explore more fully the numerous concurrent and conflicting narrative fictions which have competed during the last 200 years to designate an authoritative center of design knowledge.

59 Degeneracy dominated discourse as well in the *Heimat* movement. Yet, somewhat differently, *völkisch* theorists revolted against the scholarly and empirical orientation of museum collections and its acceptance of industrial culture at large. *Volkskunst* models for the applied arts were derived from a metaphysical assessment of the qualities of the medieval German peasant culture. See Robert Mielke, *Volkskunst* (Magdeburg Walter Niemann, 1896).

Early Modern Design in Hong Kong

Matthew Turner

What distinguishes the history of design from the history of art or architecture is surely the narrowness of its geopolitical compass. The design literature is almost exclusively concerned with the First World, that is to say, with the industrial and commercial development of the Organization for Economic Cooperation and Development (OECD) region.

Whereas we may turn to historical studies of Chinese art or architecture, for example, and draw on a wealth of Chinese and foreign scholarship, a corresponding history of Chinese design is yet to be seen. There is no history of design in India or in a hundred other places that lie outside the triad of Western Europe, North America, and Japan. The effect is as though no significant design had ever taken place in the rest of the world, except in the remote sense of the vernacular, or in oases of Western influence.[1]

The extent to which this imbalance in historical resources gives rise to a certain chauvinism, enjoyed by contemporary designers within the triad, and to the difficulties faced by designers elsewhere is a question that ought to concern practitioners of design history. For it may be asked whether the discipline has become a form of neoimperialism?

Most historians of design, particularly those writing from a Marxist viewpoint, would be affronted by such a question. Pretending that the discipline's horizons are expanding or that it will follow the history of science and reach the Sinic world before long is unacceptable. Clive Dilnot argues that the teleological character of design history, its mission to pave the *via regia* of Western modernism, has had its day;[2] Adrian Forty points out that factory production and standardization evolved contemporaneously, but independently, from mechanization;[3] John Heskett suggests somewhat radically that the study of design need not be predicated on modern sources of energy to the extent that third-century India may fall within the purview of the discipline;[4] and Simon Jervis claims that the greater number of significant designers lived and worked before the period conventionally studied by design historians.[5] Why, then, does there seem to be no evidence that the First World's monopoly on the history of design is about to be shaken.

The simplest explanations include that (1) nobody has yet looked for the history of design outside the modern, industrialized, capitalist nations, or (2) evidence is not readily available, and (3) by Western definitions, there can be no real history of design outside the First World. The first explanation is perhaps the most congenial

1 Objections may be made that aspects of design outside the OECD have been described, for example, by developmental economists or railway enthusiasts, but through conversations with designers across Asia, one learns that such accounts are not believed to comprise a history of design.

2 Clive Dilnot, "The State of Design History," *Design Issues* Vol. I, No. 1 (Spring 1984): 4–23.

3 Adrian Forty, *Objects of Desire* (New York: Pantheon, 1986), chapter 1.

4 Hazel Conway, ed., *Design History—A Student Guide,* 1986/87 article by John Heskett.

5 Simon Jervis, *Penguin Dictionary of Design and Designers* (London: Penguin, 1984), Introductory Essay.

to those who come to design history by way of art history. After all, is not the history of design a relatively new field, which has yet to establish itself even in many OECD nations, such as Yugoslavia? Perhaps the late Sir Nikolaus Pevsner should be regarded as a latter-day Vasari, and John Heskett, *et alia,* as figures such as Giordano Bruno ("There are only as many true rules as there are true artists"), or Zuccari ("Man forms within himself various designs . . . therefore his design is accidental")? Germany today, tomorrow the world?

However, only the third explanation seems plausible. Appeals to the novelty of the subject or to the dearth of subject matter are not well-founded. After all, more than half a century has passed since Pevsner's *Pioneers* was published in the West and design, as well as design education, was established in many non-Western countries. Given the twentieth-century internationalization of communications and the global expansion of industrial forms of production, the complete absence of any but a Western history of design for three-quarters of the world cannot be explained away by a lack of interest or evidence.

The proposition that, by Western definitions, there cannot be a history of *design,* properly speaking, outside the tradition of the First World has the merit of frankness and, moreover, offers greater explanatory power. In this form, the proposition does not deny that from ancient to modern times there was not a vast daily output of goods and images manufactured for domestic or export purposes, around the globe; it merely asserts that the planning and shaping of such goods and images should not be confused with modern, Western, industrial notions of design—for if everything is design, then design has no meaning.

Entering into a review of definitions of design may not be necessary because the laconic and generalized definitions that have been made do not in themselves preclude application to almost any form of visualization or productive activity. But who, then, advances such a proposition? Indeed, nobody has seriously proposed that the history of design is the exclusive inheritance of the First World, yet neither has anybody seriously contested the terms of the inheritance or suggested it to be a modern forgery. Rather, in line with the old saw that history is written by the victors, the history of design seems to be written by the economically powerful. Japan, for example, was not equipped with a history of design (or with a workable system of management) until her emergence as an economic superpower made such a history inevitable. Until the late 1960s, Japan was assumed to have copied her way onto the industrial ladder; after that point, she was revealed to have possessed a long and complex history of innovation in design.[6]

The example of Japan suggests that the teleological current in design history runs deeper than merely the justification of whatever style currently happens to be in fashion or the provision of a

6 The transition point seems to be the *Exhibition of Modern Design in Japan* (Kyoto: National Museum of Modern Art, 1969); the catalog begins: "In the field of modern design, Japan's history is brief."

hagiography of great names. The lineage it provides for modern industrial power may be on an altogether larger scale. Points of friction are instructive; for example, the interpretation of Russian design during the revolutionary period, the discussion of German design in the context of National Socialism or in the German Democratic Republic, and the accounts of design in developing countries. Talking about design in the context of Communism, Fascism, or poverty is never easy. Is this because the history of design is a discourse embedded in the ideological formations of the postwar, liberal, capitalist world?

For some time, now, Occam's razor has been hovering over this tenuous thread of reasoning and, having entered into Discourse's hall of mirrors, only an investigation on the scale of a Foucault or a Said[7] would be sufficient. Such an investigation must demonstrate that the history of design has developed into a useful buttress of values central to the First World and, to such an extent, that its retrospective application elsewhere is problematic. Of course, what these central values might be is a question open to much speculation. Supposing that the history of design embodies a number of key beliefs about First World development seems reasonable. These beliefs are in economic growth and technological development, in progress through free competition and consumer choice, in aspirations toward the comforts and sophistications of affluence, in the importance of individuality, creativity, and innovation fused with the benefits of standardization and mass production. If a demonstration that design is less a description of a process and more a representation of an ideology (conveniently depoliticized and positive, filling the vacuum left behind by science, which has lost so much of its innocence since the 1950s) could be made, a fruitless search for essences might be avoided. After all, an essence being distilled from practices as varied as engineering, design, and fashion design has never seemed likely.

Would such an investigation yield any positive result? Yes, for it would open a perspective on an immense, unexplored storehouse of knowledge about the developing world in the modern era. While enlarging the understanding of world design, valuable material for other disciplines would be provided and a much needed boost would be given to the growing confidence of designers working outside the First World.

The following discourse represents a fragmentary contribution to this ambitious program, focusing on early twentieth-century design in Hong Kong. Other methodologies and perspectives will need to be forged because Hong Kong is in many ways atypical of the developing world. Hong Kong is one of the newly industrialized countries (NICs) of Asia, which, although outside the triad, share many of its values. South Korea and Taiwan[8] had a long colonial history of manufacturing under Japanese colonialization, and Singapore and Hong Kong were industrialized during the period of

7 See Edward Said, *Orientalism* (New York: Pantheon, 1978).

8 See J.L. Lau, ed. *Models of Development: A Comparative Study of Economic Growth in South Korea and Taiwan* (San Francisco: ICS Press 1986).

British colonial rule.[9] In addition, all four "little dragons" are well-known for their unique postwar rates of growth and for the volume and variety of goods exported from their factories.

If the Asian NICs lack of indigenous histories of design seem surprising, remember that the "inheritance" of design history is administered by the First World. Delaying recognition of competing economic power centers as long as possible may be in the interest of the triad, whether by trade protectionism or intellectual protectionism. The intellectual property laws in Hong Kong, for example, protect foreign firms far more than local firms.[10] Uniquely, the trademarks and copyrights of all other countries are enforced within the Territory to attract foreign firms seeking a place to manufacture their goods. That such laws discourage local innovation (it is impossible for a company to check the registers in every country) has not been considered a disadvantage by those who frame the law. The colonial view never considered it likely that Chinese design would make a significant contribution to exports. The corresponding instruments of trade protectionism toward the NICs need no elaboration.

These issues, however, concern postwar Hong Kong design. The concern here is rather to investigate earlier developments, that began some time before the British landed at Possession Point in 1841. China's foreign trade had been concentrated in its coastal cities for many centuries, particularly in the Pearl River delta. This region had been a center for foreign trade since the Han dynasty (202 BC–220 AD) and for export manufacturing since the Sung dynasty (960–1279 AD), when vast quantities of mass-produced ceramics were made in the provincial kilns of Guangdong. When Emperor Qianlong closed all trading ports with the exception of Guangzhou in 1757, the Pearl River delta became the focus of China's commerce and export industry.

The development of industry in China's Pearl River delta[11]

The economic strategy of this region was characterized by first, a labor-intensive system of serial or mass production; second, a strong export orientation; and third, a process of adaptive design. As the successive waves of foreign merchants brought with them new products, the early industries of the Pearl River delta became the crucible for export designs that adapted the world's goods to Chinese materials and manufacture. From the tenth to the nineteenth century, Chinese export ceramics were designed in a vast range of adaptive styles, from rough Southeast Asian *kendi* to refined Japanese *imari* wares and Dutch coffee pots. Decorations ran from Arabic to Latin and English, interlaced with Chinese motifs and symbols. The epitome of mimicry was reached when fanciful Western *chinoiserie* designs were self-consciously copied by Chinese artists for European markets.

Design for manufacturing industries around the Pearl River delta, therefore, adopted a strategy unlike that developed by the

9 The *Report on the Industrial Development of the Colonial Empire* (Colonial Office 1934) was intended to further "Mass production by highly mechanized industrial techniques, a Western device which the east has not found difficult to copy [leading to] progressive social development which will raise the standard of life and the demand for comfort, recreation, and even luxury on the part of Oriental populations" in Singapore and Hong Kong.

10 Michael Pendleton "Discouraging Local Innovation and Design Expertise in Hong Kong's Colonial Intellectual Property Law," in Hong Kong University's Conference *Design and Development in South and Southeast Asia*, December, 1988.

11 The following account is a variation of my catalog essay published originally as "A History of Export Design in Hong Kong (1900–1960)" in *Made in Hong Kong: A History of Export Design 1900–1960* (Hong Kong: Hong Kong Museum of History with the Urban Council 1988).

textile manufacturers of Ahmedabad, where predominantly Indic designs were produced in varying quality to suit different markets. As industrialization gathered speed in Europe, the Chinese strategy of design adaptation, labor intensive production, and export orientation also ran counter to the strategies of manufacturers and traders in the West, preoccupied as they were with an integrated expansion of mechanization and empire.

From the perspective of a commercial and military power such as Britain at the turn of the nineteenth century, that all other systems of manufacturing should give way before the great partnership of machine production and expanded foreign markets must have seemed inevitable. Indeed, this situation became the fate of proto-industrialization outside the West. Traditional systems of trade and manufacture gave place to a colonial economy that depended on supplying raw materials to the West and importing machine made goods. The East-West flow in the world's circulation of goods was soon reversed.

But the trading and manufacturing centers of the Pearl River delta, together with Japan, were an exception to the rule. This exception is more surprising because Japan enjoyed a favorable situation in relation to the expansion of empires in the nineteenth century, whereas a good part of the Pearl River delta came under effective foreign control. Indeed, the survival of design adaptation, labor intensive production, and export orientation into modern times became, as with imperial *laissez-faire* capitalism, an economic anachronism. Yet this combination later led to industrial "hypergrowth" in the modern Asian economies of Hong Kong, Singapore, Taiwan, and South Korea.

Hong Kong was the direct descendant of a unique system of design and manufacturing that had established itself over the centuries along the commercial thoroughfares of the Pearl River delta. The evidence for this may be found in the remarkable continuities of design, during more than a century, in product types and styles, manufacturing and printing companies, and families of artist-designers, that can stretch back to the earliest years of Hong Kong.

If, a century later, Hong Kong artificial flowers were made of plastic and new products, such as radios and flashlights, had joined the list, the continuities rather than the new developments were more remarkable.

To those who assume Hong Kong's industrialization was a postwar phenomenon, its long history of manufacturing is equally surprising. In 1846, the second governor, Sir John Davis, noted: A large number of Chinese are employed in their respective shops in the exercise of industrial trades and manufactures, and there are scarcely any wants of the inhabitants which do not meet with a ready supply within the town.[12]

By 1846, one-third of all Chinese properties were registered as factories. With a Chinese population of 20,338 by 1848, some 700 industrial enterprises must have been founded within the first

12 In 1956, for example, the combined value of Hong Kong "Imperial Preference" export products to British Africa, Malaya, India, and Pakistan and the rest of the British Commonwealth amounted to more than HK$ 264,000,000 (excluding Great Britain) while exports to the United States totaled a mere HK$ 20,457,311.

decade of Hong Kong's history. Records from 1853 suggest that more than 500 of these were ship chandlers, boat builders, and rope manufacturers, however, other arts and crafts also flourished. The 1865 census lists 44 silversmiths, 14 painters and photographers, 17 rattan furniture makers, 10 watch and clock makers, and 5 portrait artists.

During the late nineteenth century, local industry expanded and diversified to include feather-dressing, match factories, soap, cement, coal, briquette and rattan works, sugar refineries, and spinning mills. In 1906, Sir Matthew Nathan promoted the first exhibition of industrial arts to provide visual evidence of what could be made in Hong Kong. A forerunner of the annual industrial products exhibitions, organized by the Chinese Manufacturers' Association founded in 1934, Nathan's Arts and Crafts show was, in the memory of Horace Kadoorie: A revelation of the artistic temperament of Chinese craftsmen in our midst. Above all, it showed the way in which local artisans sought to express their feelings for beauty in the works of their hands.[13]

Early modern Hong Kong graphic design

Hong Kong design, particularly graphic design, also strongly developed during these years by synthesizing the widest variety of Chinese traditions and foreign influences. Chinese asymmetrical and diagonal composition, learned from the wood block prints in artists' manuals, for example, the *Mustard Seed Garden* (the blank areas were ideal spaces for commercial trademarks) provided a sound design basis. New, brighter colors were added, derived, in part, from the bold primaries of Guangdong New Year prints and, in part, from the more subtle, but equally colorful bird and flower painting of the Lingnan school. Drawing on the heritage of export porcelain decoration and the infinitely detailed techniques of Pearl River "China Trade" oil painting, early Hong Kong posters, labels, and packaging assumed a distinctly modern Chinese appearance. Foreign motifs, such as the wistful girls and flowers—especially roses—typical of late Victorian imagery, and European styles from art nouveau to art deco, both of which were of Oriental inspiration were easily adapted. Another source for commercializing tradition was derived from the mass-produced travel prints, calendars, and posters of late *Meiji* and *Taisho* Japan, in which national motifs were adapted to the sale of such modern articles as cosmetics, dry goods, and wine.

To follow the history of the Kwan family is to trace a complete history of Hong Kong graphic design. In 1845, the China Trade artist Kwan Chuk Lam, known to the West as Lamqua, settled in Hong Kong. He was the only known pupil of the English painter G. Chinnery and had exhibited paintings at the Royal Academy in the style of his master. His "Handsome Face Painter" shop followed a system of serial production and a division of labor. His descendants, a family that currently numbers more than one hundred, followed this commercial principle, moving into the related fields of

13 Turner, "A History of Export Design," 9.

photography, lithography, poster design, and advertising. Kwan Wai Nung (b. 1880) learned Western painting from his family and Chinese painting from Gui Koo Chuen. Kwan was employed as a printer, producing the first five-color lithographic works in China. In 1911, Kwan became art director of the *South China Morning Post,* which he left in 1915 to found the Asiatic Lithographic Printing Press, Ltd. Art and business were wholly compatible to Kwan.

The status of designers

Many designers enjoyed considerable status as directors of companies, and not printing companies only. Fan Chai, a Shanghainese-trained designer of enamelware patterns, vacuum flask casings, and exhibition plans for the Chinese Manufacturers' Association, became a director of I-Feng Enamelling Co., (H.K.) Ltd. and Freezinhot Bottle Co., (H.K.) Ltd., the famous vacuum flask manufacturer. Cheng Ho, who trained in France and Germany and established his own design and manufacturing studio in Kowloon Tong after World War I was also a director of Union Metal Works, Ltd., where the American "Boss" cooker was redesigned for the Asian market. A number of companies set up their own studios. The Wing On Department Store studio, under the direction of Chan Chut Man from 1928, designed displays, advertisements, and stationery. Kwong Sang Hong, Ltd., the cosmetics company, founded in 1905, maintained departments specializing in the design and manufacture of their distinctive glass bottles and a lithographic printing department for pamphlets, labels, and advertising posters. In the early years Kwong Sang Hong, Ltd.'s posters were drawn by Kwan Wai Nung and printed by his Asiatic Lithographic Printing Press, Ltd.; later versions were printed by China Can Co., (H.K.) Ltd., a Shanghai firm that established a printed can and tin toy factory in Hong Kong in 1934. The art department of China Can Co., (H.K.) Ltd. was staffed by five Shanghai-trained designers who produced posters and packaging for major Hong Kong industries, such as Garden Co., Ltd. (bakers and confectionery), and Amoy Industries, (International) Ltd. (canned foods and preserves).

Hong Kong's prewar industrialization

The arrival of Shanghainese firms was a gradual process that quickened during the late 1930s as Japan bombarded Shanghai, but the influence of these firms was not decisive for Hong Kong's industrialization. Government *Blue Books* for 1927 record 1,523 manufacturing industries, whereas the Chinese Chamber of Commerce *Directory,* including more traditional industries, lists approximately 3,000 companies during the same year. A century after the founding of the colony, business directories such as the *Hong Kong and Macao Business Classified Directory* (1940), record 7,500 factories and workshops. The figures for domestic exports (excluding re-exports) for 1937 vary between the Government's estimate of HK$ 400,000 and the Brilliance Cultural Undertakings Company's figures, of HK$ 800,000, published in their A *Century of Commerce.* But for the year 1939, both sources agree on HK$ 600,000. Postwar inflation raised the value of all manufactured products and textiles six- or sevenfold. The possibility exists that Hong Kong did not recover its average prewar real value of exports until two decades later, that is, at the beginning of Hong Kong's phenomenal hypergrowth. In other words, Hong Kong's "Industrial Revolution" began much earlier than is conventionally supposed.

A comparison between Hong Kong's pre- and postwar domestic exports discloses much the same continuities noted above. The adaptive designs for products most associated with Hong Kong's modern industrial success story can be frequently traced to an earlier time.

Of these companies, many of which still exist, the great majority were set up as branch factories of firms originating in Guangzhou, the Shanghai companies arriving during the 1930s. Two new postwar products, the 1952 alarm clock of Chiap Hua Manufactory Co., Ltd. (founded in 1947) and the 1957 Halina brand cameras by W. Haking Industries were both products of the two Cantonese companies. A great boost to Hong Kong industry came with the postwar establishment of Shanghainese spinning and weaving factories which made use of the abundant cheap labor of newly arriving refugees.

However, the greatest diversification of Hong Kong products came with plastics, first introduced by China Plastics Co. (later, Wah Sun Hong) in 1947. The ease with which designers could adapt the form and pattern of plastic goods, the high degree of hand finishing combined with mechanization, and the opening of world export markets in the postwar boom years made these materials ideal for an economy based on design adaptation, labor intensive production, and export orientation. Plastics became the China Trade ceramics of the twentieth century, and design became an everyday expression.

Concepts of design

Although the term *design* and its Chinese equivalent first appeared in the context of registered design trademarks and advertising company productions (more than one dozen advertising houses existed in Hong Kong by 1941), design was more fully developed in furniture, interior, product, engineering, and exhibition work. Trade literature from the 1930s highlights design as a selling point in steel furniture, architectural services, dressmaking stands, printing machines, and in the industrial products exhibitions of the Chinese Manufacturers' Association. An advertisement from the Association's second exhibition catalog of 1939 uses *design* as a term associated with marketing, scientific production, artistic pattern, and new style—a comprehensive definition of modern design, wholly translated into Chinese long before reaching many other countries.

Early modern Hong Kong industrial design

Hong Kong industrial design during the first half of the twentieth century developed much the same adaptive and synthetic strategies as that of graphic design. The silversmithing of Wang Hing Jeweller and the furniture of You On Co., during the early 1900s, show the same articulation of Chinese, Japanese, and Western imagery, material, and technique. Wang Hing Jeweller's silver matchbox in the form of a dancing bear is part miniature of a contemporary Japanese wine bottle design (in detailed chasing as well as modeling) and part Western dancing bear with collar and chain. Equally, the Italianate dolphins supporting the cardholder of the same date are Sinicized by transforming themselves into Chinese dragons. In the same way, the enameled products or glass lamps of the 1930s not only combine Eastern and Western forms, but also include motifs and details drawn from their markets in Asia, the Middle East, and Africa.

Until recently, few Western designers worked for such markets, but following the Ottawa Agreement of 1932, products manufactured in the British Crown Colony of Hong Kong could be exported to other colonies (and later to Commonwealth countries) without import duties. Hong Kong designers, as with designers anywhere else, had to work according to the demands and, more important, the limitations of their market.[14] One of the founders of Star Industrial Co., Ltd., a large plastics company, explained that the use of bright red, blue, and yellow in their domestic plasticware was dictated by customers in Asia, the Middle East, and Africa who would not accept tasteful brown and cream; and the company had the failures to prove it. Much the same story was told by the son of the founder of Sunbeam Manufacturing Co., which produced flashlights in Hong Kong, beginning in 1930. Although Sunbeam formed an engineering and design department after World War II and experimented with modern styles, customers in Africa and Asia rejected the slightest changes in pattern, regarding them as inferior imitations. Thus, the earliest products built a reputation for Hong Kong design that effectively prevented any improvements. At the same time, Sunbeam's exports of aluminum ware to Europe now demand regular re-design.

The quality of such Empire Made products was surprisingly good. For example, the "505" and "555" cotton singlets, manufactured by Chuen Sun Knitting Factory, Ltd., used expensive yarn imported from Switzerland, a three-stage fulling process, and hand cutting to ensure maximum durability and fit. Production of these items was scaled down after more than 40 years, because of competition from cheap American T-shirts. However, as Chuen Sun Knitting Factory, Ltd. began fashion production (Marco Polo brand), the American film star Bo Derek appeared in a publicity poster wearing a "555" singlet and little else. By then, the decline in traditional quality and manufacturing made the rush of American orders for this item difficult to meet. That the very symbol of modern

14 Turner, "A History of Export Design," 9.

Western glamour should wear a garment first produced in Hong Kong during the 1930s is a delightful irony of design history.

The decline of early modern Hong Kong design

With the decline of the British Empire, the stamp Empire Made became less significant, and the 1950s saw an attempt by the Chinese Manufacturers' Association to expand into new Asian markets. Trade missions were dispatched to Japan, Thailand, Malaya, Australia, Singapore, the Philippines, Korea, and Indonesia. By 1956, Asian countries were importing products Made-in-Hong Kong at a value level equal to that of the rest of the Commonwealth. But wider political changes were taking place in the world that would transform Hong Kong design.

Although Hong Kong's domestic exports to China had been declining since the turn of the century, China had always been a major trading partner. With the Korean War, the United States effectively sealed off Hong Kong's trade with the new Peoples' Republic. Simultaneously, the Hong Kong government began to acknowledge the fact that Hong Kong was a major industrial society, as well as a trading port.

U.S. foreign policy aimed at stimulating industrial and commercial development that was linked to its own economy—particularly in Japan, South Korea, Taiwan, and Vietnam. Hong Kong suddenly became favored by American importers. This relationship was in part facilitated by the Hong Kong government's new Federation of Hong Kong Industries, established in 1960; membership was open to all. Three significant changes followed: First, American trading companies appeared, armed with detailed specifications of designs to be manufactured at low cost by Hong Kong firms. Second, the federation assisted six American specialist designers to set up in Hong Kong in 1961. Soon, they were dominating the local design scene. Third, Chinese traditional crafts, no longer available to America or Europe, began to be produced, with suitable modifications, to fill the vacuum.

These changes were not fundamental departures from the manufacturing strategies of the Pearl River delta, namely design adaptation, labor intensive production, and export orientation, but the quality of indigenous Hong Kong Chinese design rapidly declined. Increasingly, the design of export goods was carried out either in America or by Americans in Hong Kong. Local designers could not compete. For one reason, although many of the prewar generation of designers had received a solid art education in Guangzhou or Shanghai the younger generation had had no similar opportunity. Even though the well-known portrait painter Chan Hoi Ying's Hong Kong Academy of Fine Arts included a Design Department since 1955, and the Hong Kong Technical College, sponsored by the Chinese Manufacturer's Association, opened a Commercial Art and Design Department in 1960, they alone could not sustain the broad program needed to modernize the esthetic traditions once current in China's art schools. The subtle coloration, asymmetry, complex adaptations, sensitivity to the demands of non-Western markets, and achievement of an indigenous yet modern Chinese design were gradually lost to a younger generation that had no opportunity to assimilate its own tradition. Innovative companies, such as Tai Ping Carpets, Ltd., founded in 1959, which reworked traditional Tianjin carpets for semi-industrial export manufacture, employed British and American designers, even in the production of Chinese patterns. Their chief designer still recalls her early difficulties in drawing dragons. The design of embroidery, fashion garments and accessories, wood carving, and other crafts came to be dominated by foreign buyers. In the design and packaging of modern plastic and electronic consumer goods, Western concepts of design went unquestioned.

The Western view of Hong Kong design

In part, the prestige of Western design in the Hong Kong of the 1960s was derived from the West's prevailing belief that the modern style of design was one universal visual language, which had originated in the West and which, as with the English language, should be learned by everybody else as a key to industrial and commercial progress. That China lacked any useful design principles of its own was a belief that rested on almost two centuries of critical opinion in the West.

In 1793, at the height of the Western fashion for *chinoiserie,* the failure of the British Macartney Mission to interest the Qing Court in Manchester carpets, Sheffield plates, Birmingham "toys," and Wedgwood pottery was ascribed by manufacturers to the failure of the Chinese to appreciate the high quality of British products, as well as to unfair Chinese trading practices. Emperor Qianlong replied to the English throne: "We possess all things, . . . have no use for your country's manufactures." By the mid-nineteenth century, British writers on world art, such as Fergusson and Owen Jones, were convinced that China was wholly devoid of either architectural design or ornament. In Owen Jones's encyclopedic *Grammar of Ornament (1856)* we may detect the economic threat of a competing export power coloring his esthetic judgment: In their ornament, with which the world is so familiar through the numerous manufactured articles of every kind which have been imported into this country . . . the Chinese are totally unimaginative, and all their works are accordingly wanting in the highest grace of art.[15] In nineteenth-century commercial guides of Hong Kong, locally manufactured products are often described as "fantastic in design," "odd," "coarse," "peculiar," or "inferior."

Hong Kong workers were capable of producing acceptable designs if, however, "copies are made of designs furnished from abroad." Thus, in 1904, the firm of Art and Crafts was established in Hong Kong by London furniture designers "due to the inability of Chinese people to grasp the fundamentals of European design."

15 Turner, "A History of Export Design," 15.

These views echoed through the postwar era and came to be widely accepted in Hong Kong. Speaking at the founding ceremony of the Hong Kong Technical College in 1955, the president of the Chinese Manufacturer's Association, Hui Ngok, had to remind his audience that: "We are sometimes criticised [sic] for producing low quality goods with old fashioned designs; however, our markets are in areas where the purchasing power is limited and where designs have a background in tradition."[16]

By this date, Hong Kong products had established a reputation for quality in much of the world. Indeed, by 1955, Hong Kong manufacturers were complaining that Japan was exporting goods with fake Empire Made labels, and that Britain was substituting Made-in-United Kingdom labels on Hong Kong gloves and textiles, even while imposing voluntary restrictions on Hong Kong's textiles exports.

Some manufacturers believed that the Chinese tradition had much to offer modern design. Horace Kadoorie had argued in a business symposium of 1957 for: "an amalgamation of Chinese art and Western productiveness in the development of goods for export . . . such as the plastics industry where at times designers are borrowing forms from the East."[17]

Yet, by the 1960s, the designs and the designers of the early modern period of Hong Kong had begun to disappear as American markets and styles came to predominate. A few designers, such as Cheung Yat Man, son of the 1930s calendar artist Cheung Yat Luen, abandoned all attempts to modernize Chinese forms and imagery and became a successful designer in the Western manner. Through his designs of the 1950s and 1960s, Chinese motifs gradually disappeared and were replaced by American advertising imagery.

As manufacturing and printing in Hong Kong increasingly came to depend on foreign buyer-supplied design, with specifications that left little room for creative adaptation, the tradition of adaptive design turned to mere copying, leaving many young designers with a sense of creative inferiority.

At present, there are no signs that Hong Kong designers really believe in the existence of an earlier, Hong Kong Chinese design. True, a few have used nostalgic motifs (mostly for packaging), but these relate rather to the Western *chinoiserie* of *Shanghai Surprise* and *The Last Emperor.* No challenge to the authority of First World design, supported as it is by a plethora of design history from the West and Japan seems possible. Colonial/commercial education has further sealed local sources of originality, as Chinese culture, arts, and calligraphy (itself a plausible basic design course) have been progressively weeded out of curricula as irrelevant to the pursuit of excellence in design.

Perhaps this is the fate of design in Hong Kong, which largely survives on translating the samples and specifications brought by foreign firms. When designs are successfully originated in Hong Kong, they are almost always marketed abroad under

16 Turner, "A History of Export Design," 15.

17 Turner, "A History of Export Design," 15.

foreign brand names. Few realize that certain products retailed as Braun, Melitta, Philips, Habitat, Pifco, Mothercare, and so on, were wholly designed and manufactured in Hong Kong; nor, is there any indication that anybody wishes this to be known. But, for the most part, local industry, employment, and 22 percent of Hong Kong's gross national product must rely on supplying the First World with whatever the market demands.

Yet, the recovery of Hong Kong's early history of design, a history that was not so much presumed lost as simply not believed to exist, hints at the vaster resources beneath industrial giants such as China, India, and other independent nations. There would be a great waste if this material were simply to disappear because design historians in the First World continue to write as if design were the exclusive inheritance of their own culture.

Chinese Modern Design: A Retrospective

Shou Zhi Wang

Introduction

Postmodernism is currently a hot topic in Chinese architectural and design circles. The Beijing International Exhibition Center, a sizable complex for foreign exhibitions, is the first large project in this style.[1] Chinese architects and designers discuss the esthetic details of postmodern work, and imported publications on the subject, such as *Architecture Today* by Charles Jencks, are widely read by young practitioners and students. In addition, articles on the subject have had widespread coverage in art and architectural magazines in China.[2] In a conference to study and review design projects for resort hotels held in the city of Zhongshang in Guangdong province in the summer of 1988, 60 percent of the projects presented by delegates from all corners of China were Chinese versions of the postmodern style.[3] Whether on the subject of graphic design, product design, interior design, or art, people are talking widely of a new age in Chinese design: a postmodern age. There is a feeling among Chinese architects and designers that is understandable: China cannot afford to miss out on design as an aspect of international competition, and it is necessary to catch up with everything new. For most Chinese intellectuals, postmodernism is a brand new movement, though it has already had 20 years of history in the Western world.

Without a good knowledge of what has happened and is happening in design, it is impossible to understand the Chinese efforts to modernize. Postmodernism, as a counter-current to the international modern movement, is still a showcase event for the Chinese, and it is premature to refer to it as a school or movement. The most crucial questions for a study of Chinese design, in my opinion, involve the Chinese modern movement: is it a real movement or just an immature foreign imitation? When did it begin to penetrate architecture and design in China? What does modern Chinese design look like? To begin to answer these questions is one of the prime motivations of this paper, to try to outline the contours of modern design in China.

The Four Modernizations of Prime Minister Deng Xiou-ping, and the ambitious attempt to upgrade China's economy, have received widespread attention around the world. On the surface, all of the Four Modernizations—agriculture, industry, science, and defense—have little to do with the development of Chinese design. However, as a part of economic activity, design has to be brought to

1 *China Pictorial*, December 1988.

2 See the following journals for the years 1986–88: *Mei Shu* (Fine Art), *Jian Zhu Xue Bao* (Architectural Journal) and *Zhong Guo Mei Shu Bao* (China's Art News).

3 Cited from an unpublished report by Zhujiang Enterprises Ltd. the official sponsor of the conference.

the forefront of China's reform of its economy and the restructuring of its bureaucracy. Despite the attitudes of officialdom, in the past decade the demand for new design has accelerated to a previously unbelievable extent. New apartments, new service buildings, new hotels and office buildings, and other public facilities are mushrooming all over the country. Hundreds of thousands of new products are being poured onto the market. Foreign competition is fierce, with more and more products, from cars to cosmetics, being imported. There is a Holiday Inn in Guangzhou and a Sheraton in Beijing, Kentucky Fried Chicken faces Mao's portrait in Tien An Mien Square, and the showcases of Sony are a magnet for thousands of pedestrians in Nanjing Road, Shanghai. Without the development of design, all battles to compete with foreign products will be lost. The demand is so strong and urgent that Chinese architects and designers are unable to expand the time they spend in designing and planning. Too often, the easiest way for design agencies to complete commissions from clients and make quick money is to copy foreign models.

A good example is the construction of the city of Shenzhen, the first Special Economic Zone (SEZ) in China. Before 1979, the city was a small village, just a bus stop between the mainland and Hong Kong. There were barbed wire fences everywhere and no one could go there without a special security permit. The whole population of the area was less than 20 thousand in 1977. In 1979, however, the government decided to turn this small village into a large experimental area of Chinese socialist capitalism, which was a priority of its new economic reform blueprint. Shenzhen virtually changed overnight: hundreds of skyscrapers sprouted and covered the Shenzhen River valley; the population ballooned to nearly half-a-million; the gas station signs of Texaco, Shell, and Chevron are everywhere.[4] The buildings erected in Shenzhen in this period of hectic contruction can be roughly grouped into four categories:

- Functional apartments and office buildings resembling Ernst May's low-cost apartments in Bruchfeldstrasse, Frankfurt (1926–28).
- 1950s–1960s International Style "glass boxes" such as the Seagram Building in New York. The Shenzhen International Trade Center and other commercial business complexes totally resemble either Gio Ponti's Pirelli Building in Milan (1961) or Mies van der Rohe's and Walter Gropius's glass and steel giants in Manhattan.
- Quasi-Chinese national postmodern, which means International Style with a Chinese pavilion top or glazed tile roof and frieze. The Shenzhen City Library is an example.
- International postmodern. Some hotels and business buildings are in this category.[5]

To build Shenzhen into a modern city in a very short time, architects and other professionals were called from throughout

4 *Shenzhen Annual Report 1987* (Shenzhen: Shenzhen City Government, 1988).

5 *Shenzhen—The Special Economic Zone: A General Review of SEZ* (Shenzhen: Shenzhen City Government, 1987).

China to design something wholly beyond their previous experience. Shenzhen epitomizes the present condition of Chinese design because the whole of China is rushing into economic development. There is no time to digest the new style, not even time to digest China's own rich traditions, before architects and designers start work on a new project. The slogan of the Shenzhen project is "Time is Money." Time is indeed valuable, and market demand is high. Government and foreign investment in the city is now so abundant that it is unnecessary to worry about the style of the projects. By 1986, the total investment in the Shenzhen SEZ by the central government was 6 billion Chinese Yuan, or 1.7 billion U.S. dollars.[6] Copying and imitating foreign design, especially the style and design of Hong Kong, which is less than 20 miles from Shenzhen, is the most convenient way to design a new project.

A dozen similar new cities have arisen over the past few years in the Pearl River Delta, and thousands of new construction projects have also appeared in all parts of China, even in Tibet, as a result of this construction fever. Designers are flooded with commissions that pour in from their clients—government agencies, joint-venture enterprises, and private entrepreneurs. They do not have time to focus their over-heated minds on style or esthetic aspects. However, in these special circumstances a style has emerged, the hurried imitation of foreign style. From huge gymnasiums to cassette recorders, from jeans to TV commercials, from sneakers to billboards, everywhere imitation is the main characteristic of modern Chinese design. In most cases it is impossible for a foreigner to distinguish Chinese-made products from those of other countries.

Charles Jencks's view on the plurality of modern style is relevant here. Speaking about its use in modern architecture, he commented: "Those who use it are either unaware of the plurality of live architectural traditions, or else they hope to coalesce this plurality into some integrated movement. For instance, when one hears a historian say, 'The Modern Movement,' one knows what to expect next: some all-embracing theory, one or two lines of architectural development, something called 'the true style of our century,' and a single melodrama loaded with heroes and villains who perform their expected roles according to the historian's loaded script."[7] Modern design is not just a style, or a single and coherent movement. It is rather a phenomenon happening or appearing in the modern age. Modern design is the logical expression of the machine age in architecture and products. It is like the skin over the mechanical monster. It is the symbol of a highly productive, competitive society—a span of time Marxists refer to as "The Capitalist Period."

Viewed from a pluralist standpoint, Chinese modern design or Chinese modernity has several main points:

- China did not have a really modern design movement until 1979, although there were some fragmented attempts from the late nineteenth century through the first half of the

6 *Annual Report of Construction of SEZ in Shenzhen* (Shenzhen: Basic Construction Committee of the Shenzhen City Government, 1986).

7 Charles Jencks, *Modern Movements in Architecture* (Garden City, NY: Doubleday, 1973) 11.

twentieth century to use design to modernize the Chinese economy. China simply missed a chance to be modernized.

- The reasons why China missed this chance lie in the following facts: China's traditional hostile attitude to all non-Chinese cultures, an attitude formed in the late Ming and Qing dynasties; foreign aggression and expansion in China since the 1840s, the worst being the Japanese occupation from 1931 (Manchuria) through 1945 (these wars and occupations totally destroyed any possibility of modernizing the Chinese economy); the mismanagement and malfunctioning of the national economy under the Communist government from 1949 to the late 1970s; and the Soviet Union's influence over the Chinese economy, culture, and education after 1949, as well as the isolation of China from the rest of the world after it broke off relations with the Russians in the 1960s.
- China's modernity is now being shaped by several pressures: the high economic rate of development now required by the leadership in Beijing as well as at the local level; a strong desire among the Chinese people for a better standard of living; and China's open policy, which attracts more and more foreign competition, investment, and imported products, as well as new ideas, new culture, and new problems.
- Chinese designers' and architects' knowledge of Western modern movements in design and architecture is not comprehensive; it is fragmented, full of misunderstandings and exaggerations. This is because China is still mostly closed off in terms of intellectual, personal, and cultural exchange. The reason for this half-open state originates from a typical Marxist ideological concept: the fear of being "spiritually polluted and contaminated" by Western civilization and life-style, which could shake the ideological stability of the puritan-style Chinese communist beliefs.
- The special nature of Chinese bureaucracy is another factor shaping Chinese modernity. Design education is especially affected by this bureaucratic virus.
- The development of Chinese modern design is, or will be, in terms of the following model: imitating foreign modern design (and postmodern, or whatever is new), especially in the design of expensive consumer products, such as stereos and televisions, and also in big architectural projects; maintaining the production of daily necessities and cheap apartment buildings with basic functions, generally with a mechanical and engineering appearance. If economic development proceeds smoothly, if three-digit inflation such as that of late 1988 is controlled, if a society based more on the rule of law is assured, and if a rational long-term economic policy is established to guide national economic develop-

ment, then China may possibly evolve its own design style and modernity.

China's Early Efforts to Modernize

China was not transformed from an agrarian society into a predominantly industrial one until relatively recently. According to Albert Feuerwerker, the transformation was incomplete by the time of World War I.[8] Indeed, if we consider the percentage of industrial output in Gross National Product as the key figure to judge a nation's level of industrialization, China was still an agrarian society even by the end of World War II.

China was forced militarily to open its doors to the rest of the world in the 1840s. The foreign consulates, concepts of extraterritoriality, concession areas, foreign expatriates, and Treaty Ports, as well as foreign ideas and culture, were all forced upon the Chinese after the Opium Wars of the 1840s, when the country was not yet ready for them.[9] China was struggling to establish a republic when most of the Western nations were already thinking in terms of their experience of the new technology and esthetics which matched the way of life of the new age. Throughout the remainder of the nineteenth century and into the first decade of the twentieth, China suffered deeply from setbacks in wars with major foreign powers: two Opium Wars with the British, a confrontation with the French and several with the Japanese and Russians, and so on. There were also several civil wars which wrought terrible damage on the Chinese economy and social stability, such as the Taiping Rebellion in 1860 and the Boxer Rebellion in 1900.[10] After these conflicts, more coastal cities were forced to be opened as Treaty Ports to foreign trade; the Chinese Customs and Excise Service was established under British supervision; and some industries, the official armaments factories and civilian small manufacturers, were established along the east coast area and the Yantzu River region.

From the setbacks of these wars, some smart Chinese scholars and government officials realized the importance of the "New Learning" (i.e., Western culture and technology) and the urgent need to reform the Chinese political structure, a movement resembling the Enlightenment in France or the Meiji reform movement in Japan. A program was introduced but is known as the Bai Ri Wei Xing, or One Hundred Days Reform, from its brief duration before it was suppressed by the conservative political establishment headed by the Empress Dowager Ci Xi. Some of the leaders of the reform were executed, and one, Kang You-wei, fled to Japan. Emperor Guang Xu, who supported the reforms, was placed in custody in the Forbidden City. Every new issue and experiment raised in the reform was abandoned.[11]

Why has it been so difficult for China to accept something new or foreign? This is probably one of the most perplexing questions facing Sinologists. One important fact is China's traditional

8 Albert Feuerwerker, *China's Early Industrialization: Sheng Hsuan-huai and Mandarin Enterprise* (Cambridge: Harvard University Press, 1958) 1.

9 Bai Shou-yi, *A History of China* (Beijing: Foreign Language Press, 1983). See chapter 14.

10 Shou-yi, *A History of China.*

11 Shou-yi, *A History of China.*

physical and psychological isolation from the rest of the world for a thousand years. Siberia, the Gobi Desert, the Himalayan mountain chain, and the Pacific Ocean form a physical barrier for China to the rest of the world. Chinese culture has developed in a vacuum of inadequate contact and interaction with other civilizations. There were some cultural and religious interchanges in the Han and Tang dynasties, which brought about a magnificent cultural and art boom in China. But this kind of interchange dwindled after the Song dynasty, and total isolation from the world was complete again by the time of the Qing dynasty.[12] China retreated into the security of the "Central Kingdom," stayed in its gilded cage of a brilliant past, and avoided contact with any foreign culture.

Unfortunately, the modern age was opening at the same time China was becoming increasingly negative toward world affairs, knowing less about the world while becoming more suspicious. Over the last 200 years, the suspicion became distilled into hatred and fear of everything foreign. Several emperors of the Qing dynasty repeatedly refused to communicate with Westerners and Japanese.[13] The Chinese people had all kinds of nicknames for foreigners; "foreign devils" is simply one of the many terms indicating China's heritage of antagonism toward outsiders.

The wars in the second half of the nineteenth century between China and other world powers resulted in a large Western trade expansion in the Chinese market. However, although Britain had turned India into a huge imperial possession, China was another story—it was so different from the West, and its traditional culture was too strong to be changed. Moreover, the potential of its huge market attracted too much attention from the opponents of British trade. Therefore, in handling China the British and the other foreign powers used a different model: China was superficially independent, but half-colonial in fact. The means devised by the British to achieve effective control over trade included the Treaty Port for international trade, concession areas for foreign residents, and the concept of "extraterritoriality" for legitimating the protection of foreign subjects. All these efforts created a strange situation, with two Chinas existing at the same time. There was an urban China, mainly in the Treaty Port cities, such as Shanghai and Wuhan, where trade and industry developed quickly under foreign economic domination, and where foreign-trained intellectuals were playing a more important role in business, trade, the stock exchange, management, modern education, and cultural activities. There was also a rural and agrarian China which remained intact from a thousand years ago: self-sufficient but backward. This situation remained relatively unchanged until recent times.[14]

The history of China in the twentieth century has been one of political turmoil and endless wars. Two decades of struggle to overthrow the Qing dynasty resulted in a fragile republic headed by Dr. Sun Yat-sen in 1911. Dr. Sun resigned from his Presidency several

12 Shou-yi, *A History of China*. See chapter 8 on the Song dynasty.

13 Shou-yi, *A History of China*. See chapter 13.

14 Hu Sheng, *Chinese Revolutionary History* (Beijing: Chinese Youth Publishing House, 1979). See the preface and chapters I and 2.

months after his inauguration, and the new President, Yuan Shi-kai, crowned himself Emperor in 1916. He was overthrown after ruling for two months and died six months later. Dr. Sun was re-selected President but died in 1925, his health broken by a hopeless effort to solve the political and military power struggle between his government and war lords in northern China. He was succeeded by Chiang Kai-shek.

The Chinese Communist Party was formed in 1921 and became an increasingly important political force. For a short time in the early 1920s there was a honeymoon between the Communists and the ruling Nationalist Party, or Kuomintang (KMT). However, a deteriorating relationship finally broke down in 1927, and fighting between the Communists and KMT continued for several decades.

At the same time, Japanese expansion in China created another tension: northeastern China (Manchuria) was occupied in 1931, Beijing and parts of north China were occupied in 1937, and Shanghai and Wuhan were lost in 1938. Therefore, long before war broke out in Europe and the Pacific, China had been at war for several years.[15] The losses in every sense were enormous. More than 10 million people died, and the economy was destroyed—except for the heavy industrial base in Manchuria, which served Japanese military requirements. After World War II, huge areas of China were in ruins.

With the war's end in 1945, most Chinese were relieved and believed peace could be established. But the civil war between the Communists and the KMT broke out again in 1946, despite American attempts to mediate.[16] As a result of the civil war, the KMT fled to Taiwan, the smallest province and the largest island of China, and the Communists took power with the founding of the People's Republic of China in 1949. In short, for a century after the 1840s, there was no peace in China, not even a ten-year interval. The conditions for the development of a national industry and economy simply did not exist.

Germany, France, Britain, America, and other Western nations also suffered from the nightmare of war in the first half of the twentieth century, but war did not have such a sustained and destructive effect on them. Cultural life still flourished in those countries. There was still the architectural and design work of Walter Gropius, Mies van der Rohe, Frank Lloyd Wright, Le Corbusier, Theo Van Doesburg, and Alvar Aalto. Why hasn't China had one person who could be listed with the masters of modern design? The main difference is that until the 1950s China had no modern industry, which by that time had been developing for almost two centuries in the Western nations. Moreover, Western nations had a breathing space between the two world wars that China lacked. Shanghai and a few other Chinese cities enjoyed a short economic boom during and after World War I, in which some industries developed, but this was cut short by the Japanese occupation of 1938. In the whole period of unrest from the mid-nineteenth century until the 1950s, China had no possibility of developing a national industrial base or

15 Hu Sheng, *Chinese Revolutionary History.* See chapter 11.

16 Barbara W. Tuchman, *Stilwell and the American Experience in China, 1911–45* (New York: Macmillan 1971). See the last several chapters.

of embarking on major construction projects. It is, therefore, understandable that Chinese modern design, whether architecture or product design, did not emerge in this period.

The first effort to establish modern industry in China began with the modernization of the armaments industry. As Feuerwerker points out, the desire to acquire Western military technology was one of the themes of the decade of the "Tung-chih Restoration," the first decade following the final treaty settlement of 1860.[17] Zeng Guo-fan (1811–1872), commander of the Hunan military district and chief architect of the victory over the Taiping Rebellion, first became interested in Western methods in his desire to improve China's defenses. As early as 1855, Zeng established small arsenals in Jiansi province. In 1861, he opened an arsenal and shipyard at Anqung in Anhui province. Zeng's principal industrial project was the Jiangnan Arsenal at Shanghai in 1865, established by himself and Li Hong-zhang (1823–1901), then acting governor at Nanjing. The enterprise eventually produced several small armored naval vessels, as well as rifles, cannon, gunpowder, and cartridges.[18]

To train the qualified personnel necessary to run these enterprises, a new teaching institution was set up in Beijing in 1861. The courses offered included astronomy, mathematics, chemistry, physics, biology, minerology, metallurgy, mechanics, anatomy, physiology, political economy, and international law. Several hundred Chinese students were also sent to America and other Western countries to master the secrets of Western technology in order to underpin the efforts at "self-strengthening" that Zeng and Li had initiated.[19] In Chinese history textbooks, these efforts to modernize are known as the Yang Wu Yun Dong or Foreign Affairs movement.

In addition to the defense industry, other areas of manufacturing were started: cotton spinning and weaving, silk reeling, fabric dyeing, pottery and glass, soap and candles, matches, leather goods, cement, paper making, flour milling and rice husking, tobacco and cigarettes, oilpressing, and sundry food products. In addition, beginnings were made on establishing the necessary infrastructure: steamships, telegraph lines, coal and gold mines, railroads, and electricity production.

There was virtually no design activity in a specific sense in any of these early industries. The machinery and equipment were purchased from foreign countries and set up under the supervision of foreign engineers. The products were then manufactured according to the prototypes of foreign designs: from cigarettes to steamships, from soap to rifles. The only indigenous design from this period was in the field of graphics, mainly the packaging of cigarettes, soap, and matches. Pottery was still a traditional Chinese craft, which had very little to do with machine mass production.

As mentioned earlier, there was one chief exception to this general pattern. Through the 1920s until occupied in 1938, Shanghai, then the largest city in China, enjoyed a brief period of development

17 See Feuerwerker, *China's Early Industrialization;* Kung Chun, *An Outline History of the Development of Modern Industry in China* (Shanghai 1935); and Ssu-Yu Teng and John K. Fairbank, *China's Response to the West: A Documentary Survey, 1839–1923* (Cambridge: Harvard University Press, 1954) 61–131.

18 Feuerwerker, *China's Early Industrialization,* 1.

19 See Feuerwerker, *China's Early Industrialization,* 2; History Books Editing Committee, *The Foreign Affairs Movement [Yang Wu Yun Dong]* (Shanghai: Shanghai People's Publishing House 1974) chapter 3.

which made it the country's most important industrial center. Design also developed as an aspect of this boom, although it lagged behind economic development. Shanghai had functioned as a commercial city since the mid-nineteenth century, when it became one of the first Treaty Ports. It was China's principal point of contact with the world. In a five-year period (1927–31), 43 percent of China's foreign trade passed through Shanghai. Subsequently, with the loss of Manchuria and the elimination of its ports from the trade returns, Shanghai became even more important in relative terms: the share of total foreign trade it handled rose to 54 percent in 1933–34.

There were also much greater advances in modern manufacturing industry in Shanghai than in any other city of China. The fairly adequate data on individual factories and industries may be taken as evidence of the city's relative standing. For example, of 133 cotton spinning and weaving mills in China proper in 1933, Shanghai had 61, with 55 percent of the total spindles and 57 percent of the looms. Shanghai was already a manufacturing center as well as a commercial city when the foreigners first entered it. In the account of the march of British troops to take the city in 1842, there is a reference to buildings they believed to be distilleries.[20] Lindsay, in his account of the visit of the ship *Lord Amherst* in 1832, refers to the spinning and weaving of cotton carried on by every family in the many small villages dotting the area around Shanghai.[21]

When China finally began to accept and adopt the industrial system of the West, Shanghai was most advantageously located for the new manufacturing industries. In addition to the Jiangnan arsenal and dockyard mentioned earlier, two small silk filatures opened in 1862 and 1866. They closed within a short time, but a more permanent filature, using Italian experts and machinery, began operation in 1880. Agitation for the construction of a modern cotton spinning and weaving mill was begun in 1881, and after some delay the mill finally opened in 1890. Other industries followed, but cotton spinning and weaving, replacing the old handicraft textile industry, became dominant among the modern industries in Shanghai.

In 1895, the Treaty of Shimonoseki, which concluded the war between China and Japan, gave the Japanese and, through the operation of the most-favored nation clause, all foreigners the right to establish manufacturing industries in China. Numerous factories were subsequently set up by Japanese, Germans, British, and Americans, and as a result, Shanghai experienced its first boom. A second boom came during and after World War I, when increasing demand for manufactured goods as well as difficulties in importing from Europe led to a great expansion of productive capacity. The involvement of European nations in the war, therefore, gave China, and especially Shanghai, an opportunity to develop its national economy without much foreign interference.

Design came into demand in Shanghai as the economic boom attracted more domestic and foreign investment. Shanghai, as

20 See H. Lang, *Shanghai Considered Socially*, 2nd edition (Shanghai, 1875).

21 See H. H. Lindsay and Charles Gutzlaff, *Report of Proceeding on a Voyage to the Northern Ports of China in the Ship Lord Amherst: Extracted from Papers by Order of the House of Commons Relating to the Trade with China* (London 1833); Bai Shou-yi, *A History of China*.

well as Guangzhou, Tientjin, Wuhan, Nanjing, and other Treaty Ports, had foreign concession areas for the French, British, German, Japanese, etc. Modern design was first introduced in these foreign domains. In Shanghai, the luxury Jiangjing Hotel had the most up-to-date art deco interior, and most of the business buildings along the Huangpu River had an obvious Neo-Classical style, but these buildings were mainly designed by foreigners in design and architectural offices based in Europe.

However, low-cost apartment dwellings were a geniune Chinese design, although the designers adopted the example of the Western town house to develop these dwellings in the Shanghai downtown area. They were called *Nong Tang Gong Yu,* or apartments in lanes, and first appeared as early as the end of the nineteenth century. The *Nong Tang Gong Yu* totally changed traditional Chinese concepts of dwellings for big families, which were based on a vertical and symmetrical layout; these were replaced with a row-house style, although some traditional elements such as a walled courtyard were retained. This was probably one of the earliest attempts to bring a Western design concept to China to improve living conditions in an urban area. With Shanghai continually developing and needing more labor, the demand for housing rapidly increased. The *Nong Tang Gong Yu* were highly successful in filling the demands of a growing Chinese middle class in the city.[22] Many of these houses are still in use.

Manufacturing continued to expand in range. In the mid-1930s, a small factory in Shanghai produced the first Chinese bicycles on the prototype of the British Raleigh model of 1903. The first Chinese sewing machine was also made at that time, based on the American Singer. Fountain pen manufacturers also used an American model. As a result, design was a very limited activity in this early stage of development.

The real development in design was in the area of graphics, where advertising billboards, commercial posters, and packaging for all kinds of Chinese commodities provided numerous opportunities. Several young people embarked on careers as graphic designers and by the mid-1930s had their own design offices in Shanghai—the first design agencies in China. Ding Hao, former chairman of the Department of Design at the Shanghai School of Light Industry; Xu Bai-yi, now head of the Shanghai Advertising Company; and Cai Zhen-hua, retired art editor of the Shanghai Publishing House, are three men who pioneered early commercial graphic design in Shanghai. In interviews, Ding and Xu recounted that clients in the 1930s were numerous, coming from all corners of China and even from Japan. A Japanese clientele developed, Ding said, because graphic work in Shanghai was better than work in Japan at that time. The design careers of these young people began in local printing houses where they worked as apprentices. Some of these printing houses were owned by foreign publishers, and in that

22 See *A History of Cbinese Urban Development* (Beijing: China's Architectural Publishing House, 1985) chapter 19.

way the designers learned advanced techniques of printing and graphic design before establishing their own agencies.

The main design projects were for wrapping paper, comic cards for cigarette packs, and cardboard box packaging for a variety of miscellaneous products, such as matches, soap, candy, needles, and thread. Illustrations for these projects were based on Chinese traditional linear brushwork, but the subject matter was mainly "modern Shanghai beauties" in 1930s Western fashions and with short hair. The layout, the typography, and even the logotypes were also becoming more Western looking, with some obvious influences of art nouveau, art deco, and even De Stijl. The Chinese sans serif—*Hei Ti* (black style)—was created on the basis of Western sans serif developments of the time.[23] Publishing was also a good market for designers' talents. Woodcuts were widely used for book covers and illustrations and these show very strong evidence of German Expressionist influences. This probably stemmed from Lu Xun, a left-wing writer, who was a very powerful advocate of German Expressionism as a model for Chinese graphic design in Shanghai during the 1930s.[24]

In this period, Shanghai was known as "the Paris of the Orient," but design in what can in retrospect be called a golden age for the city still needs considerable further research. However, its fame and brilliance were wiped out by the Japanese occupation of 1938.

Modern Design in China

Formation of a centrally controlled and centrally planned market in mainland China.

The foundation of the People's Republic of China in 1949 marked a new communist, socialist stage in Chinese history. Immediately after the Chinese Communist Party took power, a large-scale reform and remodeling of the national economy was carried out. Its main elements were:

- Removal of all foreign businesses and interests in China. The foreign companies and other enterprises were taken over and confiscated by the Chinese government. All foreign business and trade were controlled by the government. All relations between private Chinese enterprises with foreign partners were eliminated.
- Confiscation of all Chinese private monopoly enterprises (known in Communist political terms as "bureaucratic capital"), which were nationalized and controlled by government departments of either industry or trade.
- Elimination of "guilds" in rural areas—small syndicates of trade in rural China, which had controlled most business in rural markets before 1949—by having private property socialized. The aim was for the government to control the rural market.
- Building up a network of national department stores and

23 Author's interviews with Ding Hao in Shanghai (May 1984) and Xu Bai-yi at the Shanghai Advertising Company (March 1983).

24 See *Lu Xun and the Chinese Woodcut Movement* (Shanghai: Shanghai Fine Arts Publishing House, 1964); *A History of Chinese Publications* (Beijing: Shangwu Press, 1983).

national cooperative supply centers. This network finally became the only business and trade organization in all of China.

- Financial and monetary affairs controlled by the central government. The currency, commodities, and other products were all under the strict control of the government.[25]

Having taken all these steps, the Chinese Communists turned the Chinese market into a highly controlled, highly planned supply and distributing economy based on rationing. This effort temporarily eased the chaos in the market but merely postponed economic crisis.

From a free market to a centrally controlled one, China has followed four main phases of evolution: 1949–56, transition period; 1956–58, formation of a centralized Chinese market; 1958–79, a cumbersome and poor national market; 1979–present, period of economic reform.

1949–56, transition period

During this period, the Chinese market had two parallel lines of development: co-existence of public and private business. Because control of national economic power had yet to be consolidated, the government was unable to carry out immediately its plans for socialization and nationalization. Five main forms of business organization existed at that time: nationalized business, cooperative businesses based on a contract between the government and a private group under the control of the former, large monopoly private companies formed before 1949 and left untouched for the time being (most located in eastern, coastal China in ports such as Shanghai, then the largest business center in China), small private businesses (e.g., small workshops, factories, shops, restaurants), and private salespeople and shopkeepers.[26]

Within the six-year period, the Chinese Communist Party transformed this five-fold division on the basis of the Soviet Union market model. The purpose of this transformation was to establish a pure socialist market that would have very little private ownership, be highly controlled by the central government, and be based on planning and a ration-supply system. The method of transformation was four-fold: a great expansion of nationalized or socialized business enterprises, a limited and careful expansion of small cooperative businesses, gradual government purchase of all large monopoly private firms, and elimination of small private businesses. This latter was achieved by using the businesses for the time being but preventing their further development, and eventually transforming them into either a cooperative or a nationalized form. This effort to have the whole Chinese market nationalized and centrally controlled was partly finished by the end of 1955. This prepared the stage for the next step: the complete elimination of all private businesses.

25 Shijun Ma, ed., *Chinese Marketing* (Guilan: People's Daily News Press, 1986). See chapter 1. For a general view of China's economy see Liu Suinian and Wu Quangan *China 's Socialist Economy: An Outline History, 1949–84* (Beijing: Beijing Review Press 1987).

26 Shijun Ma, *Chinese Marketing*. See chapters 1 and 2. See also *China's Economy* (Beijing: China's Foreign Language Press 1984) chapter 1.

1956–58, formation of a centralized Chinese market

A government-initiated movement of redemption or buy-out of all private business throughout the country was carried out in 1956. It was called *gong si he ying,* literally translated as "operating both public and private." All private businesses—factories, trading companies, shops, restaurants, small workshops—were forcibly redeemed by the government. The method of compensating private owners was *ding xi* or fixed interest. According to the official explanation, *ding xi* was "an annual rate of interest paid by the state to the national bourgeoisie on the money value of their assets for a given period of time, after the 1956 conversion of capitalist industry and commerce into joint state-private enterprises." By the end of 1956, almost all former private enterprises and businesses became publicly owned, except for a limited number of small businesses, although the latter were tightly controlled by market control departments that functioned across the nation.

Chinese productivity at that time was poor. A self-sufficient rural economy was still thriving across the vast rural area of China. The *gong se hi ying* movement brought very little improvement to the Chinese people. It created a highly controlled and nationalized economy and market, which temporarily relieved problems in the chaotic domestic market. However, it also began to eliminate a dynamic and competitive market and put a heavy financial burden on the government because it had to subsidize the supply of commodities used in everyday life.

1958–79, a cumbersome and poor national market

After 1956, a few private shopkeepers still existed. However, in 1958, Mao Tse-tung announced the concept of a state monopoly of the market. This was part of a utopian effort to upgrade the national economy to the standard of the technologically advanced nations within an impossibly short time period. According to Mao's idea, even one person in business as a shopkeeper was a capitalist, and could pose a threat to the communist, socialist economy. It was, therefore, ordered that all such businesses be closed down and forcibly annexed by nationalized or cooperative organizations. With this move, a single mainland Chinese market was finally formed: a cumbersome production-and-supply structure based on two forms of trading organization:

- The nationalized trading organization (e.g., nationalized department stores, nationalized Xing Hua bookstores as the only bookstore chain in the whole of China, the Chinese People's Bank as the only bank in the country, etc.).
- Nationalized Gong Xiao He Zuo She—a supply and marketing cooperative responsible for supplying productive tools and daily commodities (e.g., fertilizer, agricultural machinery, etc.) to farmers in all of China. This market was proudly proclaimed by the government as a "socialist

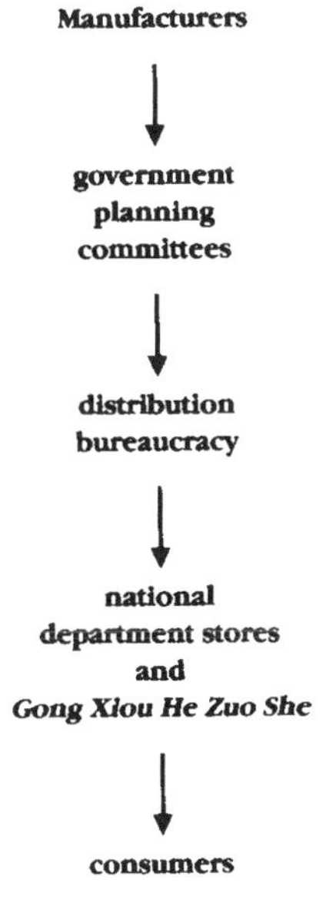

Figure 1
Model of the Market

united market." In it, commodities were distributed by a system of rationing. There was no competition and only one trade channel, that of distribution through the inefficient bureaucracy of the central government. There was also very poor feedback to producers *(Figure 1)*. Like other communist countries, China's economy developed in isolation. The result, at first, was to make the Chinese economy dependent on Soviet aid. After relations with the Soviet Union broke down in the mid-1960s, and after a series of disastrous economic policies and political upheavals, China's economy was on the edge of bankruptcy by the early 1970s. The annual income per person in the mid-1970s was less than 200 U.S. dollars.[27] There were constant shortages of almost all kinds of commodities, from food to clothing, and most commodities were only available with ration coupons. These coupons became a way of life for all mainlanders throughout the 1960s and 1970s. Because demand for commodities in the market was always higher than supply, product, packaging, and advertising design were unnecessary. The major concern of manufacturers as well as consumers was quantity—the more the better. Quality and design were less important. A poor, underdeveloped consumer market was, therefore, the basic reason for the lack of design and design education in China from 1949 until the late 1970s.

1979–present, period of economic reform

The disastrous Cultural Revolution (1966–76) finally ended with the death of Mao in 1976, followed by the trial and imprisonment of the "Gang of Four." Soon after, China again started an economic reform effort to transform its backward economy into an advanced one. Although it is impossible here to discuss all details of the reform, some of the main issues which have influenced the market and design are:

- Permitting limited private ownership and encouraging small-scale private businesses, such as light manufacturing and service-sector enterprises.
- Splitting the power of management in all enterprises between the communist leadership and management leadership. More operating control is given to the latter; the professional leaders of businesses and the executive power of communist organizations in enterprises has been correspondingly diminished.
- Introducing in 1988 bankruptcy law for nationalized and cooperative enterprises.
- Disbanding People's Communes in rural areas and giving land back to individual peasants, who may use their "own" land for 50 or more years, dependent on the contract signed

27 See the Annual Summary of the Domestic Situation published by the *People's Daily*, Beijing, December 31, 1979.

with the government. The land belongs to the state, but peasants have all rights of use, except the right to buy and sell.

- Partly relaxing the former fixed prices of commodities. The price of basic necessities, such as rice and cooking oil, are still fixed and heavily subsidized by the central government. The goal is for a more dynamic consumer market that will bring the Chinese domestic market into a balance between supply and demand. A flexible price system can encourage competition between nationalized and private enterprises, resulting in a richer market both in quantity and quality. Changing the old and stagnant rationed market into a modern one is the aim of the effort.
- Partly opening Chinese markets to foreign trade, foreign investment, and joint-venture projects with foreign partners. A dozen port cities have been chosen as Special Economic Zones (SEZ) to attract foreign investment and trade on liberal terms with preferential treatment. (Recall the example of the city of Shenzhen mentioned earlier in my introduction.)
- Importing many high-technology, industrial products, transportation vehicles, machines, and so on, in order to boost the Chinese Four Modernizations. This requires encouraging Chinese exports to provide the necessary foreign currency.
- Reducing the defense budget and retiring one million men from the army. The funds saved have been invested in economic development.
- Creating a more liberal political atmosphere with fewer political initiatives from the center. The authorities understand that a stable and peaceful political atmosphere is important to develop the national economy.[28]

The consequences of these economic reforms in China in the last decade have been remarkable. Productivity is higher and the annual income per person is more than 300 U.S. dollars. The coastal area of China (especially the Pearl River delta), site of the SEZs, is richer than most other parts of China. Foreign investment is increasing, and imported foreign products such as VCRs, cameras, cars, stereos, and cosmetics are giving the Chinese people their first experience of consuming modern commodities and of modern design. The ability of Chinese people to purchase these goods has increased largely because their income is getting higher. The Chinese market is changing from a rationing distribution system into a new one in which consumers can be more discerning about quality, design, and even the brand of products. Competition among businesses is becoming more intense and acute.[29] All these changes have attracted much attention in the world, but there still remain numerous problems in the reform process. Many contradictions remain untouched,

28 See Dixin Yu, *Transformation of China's Economy: China's Search for Economic Growth* (Beijing: New World Press, 1982) 1–27; Shijun Ma, ed., *Chinese Marketing,* chapter 2.

29 Lu Dong, "China's Economy, a Healthy Stride Forward," *Beijing Review* (January 12, 1987).

some of them having persisted for a long time. The most notable contradictions and problems of present-day China are:

- The contradiction between the political structure and the changing economic structure. The Communist Party is always placed above the three branches of government, so China is still a country governed by a group of Communist political leaders rather than by the rule of law. The policy of the nation can be changed at will by one of several top political leaders rather than as a result of legal processes by legislative bodies.
- As the key part of Chinese socialism, public ownership is still adhered to by the central government of China as well as the Communist Party. The whole reform of the economic structure is for varied kinds of market elements (private, foreign, cooperative and nationalized) existing on the basis of a "public ownership" model fixed by the government. With this "public ownership" or centralized national economy, a huge bureaucracy of low efficiency came into being. There is a two-track price system: a public one based on government subsidy, and a private one dependent on market competition. The goods subsidized by the government are generally lower in price but of limited availability controlled by a group of bureaucrats. Obtaining "public products" from the hands of bureaucrats and selling them on the open market is very profitable. Consequently, corruption and bribery are widely prevalent now. There is no way to stop this corruption in China except by random checks and political education of officials.
- The country as well as markets are governed by political leaders, not by law. Because market regulations can be arbitrarily subjected to radical change, the market lacks a key element of healthy development: a good legal system. Red tape, low efficiency, and sudden changes of economic policy and market regulations are reflections of this political situation in China.
- Because public ownership is still at the core of policy, ownership of real estate is still illegal, the stock exchange is limited, and the foreign currency market is closed. Whenever citizens earn some money, there is no way for them to invest it to make more. Spending it on commodities, which they may or may not need, is the only outlet for this earned money, these new savings. Furthermore, the open-price sector of the two-track price system has brought to China that endemic problem of a free market: inflation. And amid double-digit inflation in recent years, spending of savings on commodities, whether needed or not, has increased even more—in order to maintain the value of one's "savings." This rush to purchase was particularly

acute in 1987–88 and brought on a nationwide panic. In addition, government employees in China, on low, fixed salaries, have been especially hurt by inflation. The psychological effect of all these troubles has been to throw serious doubt on the reform program.

- The government maintains an artificially high exchange rate of the Chinese currency to foreign currencies, but in fact the value is much lower than this official exchange rate. This creates a lively black market for currency in big cities in China.
- Confusion in foreign trade results from its being controlled mainly by foreign trade departments at either central government or provincial level. After 1980, some independent rights for foreign trade were given to some local nationalized companies or local governments. The channels of imports and exports are also overlapping. Most authorized foreign trade agencies are government bureaus that have no experience of such trade, but have political and policy-making power. This creates uncertainty and hesitation among foreign companies considering business with China.
- In the case of the "open policy," the government often tends to mix materialist issues with ideological ones. It takes from the West technology, science, management, and "good culture." But there are no criteria to distinguish between "good" and "bad." The only standard is the subjective judgment of the officials involved. This creates another kind of confusion and chaos.[30]

Graphic Design

Graphic design in China is called *Zhuang Huang,* or decoration. After early development in the 1930s, it separated into two main categories by the 1950s: *Zhuang Huang* continued to mean decoration or graphic design, but a specialized sector came to be recognized as *Shu Ji Zhuan Huang,* or publication design. Publication design was given high priority in China because publications were considered to be important means of propaganda. All private publishers were banned in the early 1950s, and the government set up its own publishing houses. Each province had its own People's Publishing House, which was authorized to produce important government publications, such as Mao's works. In addition, a range of specialist publishing houses were established. Books on science, technology, art, music, literature, architecture are published by presses directly responsible to the relevant ministry at national level. For example, the Architecture Publishing House is under the Ministry of Construction; the People's Fine Art Publishing House, the People's Music Publishing House, and the People's Literature Publishing House are all under the direction of the Ministry of Culture. In all these presses, graphic designers are in charge of

30 Several articles criticizing "capitalist spiritual pollution" appeared in the *People's Daily* and other leading Chinese newspapers in October 1983. See also "Opposing Ideological Pollution," *Beijing Review* (October 31, 1983) and "Clearing Cultural Contamination" *Beijing Review* (November 7, 1983).

designing books. Their work includes cover design, illustration, lettering, layout, typography, and logotypes. In publication design, Chinese designers have had some significant achievements in the past four decades, winning major prizes in international publications exhibitions. This is a reflection of the fact that in China publications have been subsidized by the government and the publishing houses have had adequate budgets. Without financial problems to influence their work, designers were able to do a better job.[31]

In commercial graphic design it was another story. Commercial graphics were considered a symbol of "Western lifestyle" and accused of "encouraging unnecessary purchasing and waste of national resources." Throughout the whole period from the 1950s to the 1970s, they were deliberately ignored by the government. However, in the late 1950s and early 1960s, in Shanghai, Beijing, Guangzhou, Xi'an, Wuhan, and several other cities, advertising agencies were formed under the Gong Shang Guang Li Ju, or Industrial and Commercial Supervisory Bureau. The term "advertising" in Chinese is *Guang Gao,* which means "announcing to the public." It has no commercial connotations at all. These agencies became the places where the government commissioned political billboards and posters, and portraits of Mao and other political leaders.

Managers and designers of these agencies interviewed by the author in recent years include Chen Liang of the Shanghai Advertising Company, Ren Ji-wu of the Beijing Advertising Company, and Zhang Xiou-ping of the Guangzhou Advertising Company. In the 1950s and 1960s, 70 percent of their work was political posters and billboards, and during the Cultural Revolution (1966–76), 100 percent of their work was political.[32] Political posters were designed on a common model: the great leader waved his arm to guide the people to move forward; the foreground and background were oceans of red flags; the people were surging ahead to eliminate all enemies such as the KMT, Americans, and Russians. In fact, there was very little scope for design in the agencies, since the poster had been prepared by artists in the official publishing houses before being sent to the advertising companies. The job of the latter was to copy these designs onto large billboards.

Commercial advertising in China at this time was very limited. All news media were mouthpieces of communist propaganda, and it was impossible for them to carry "corrupt advertising." Political billboards on the street were considered a means of educating the people; commercial versions were a means of seducing them. There was, therefore, no adequate medium for advertising. In addition, because of the shortage of most commodities and the existence of a demand economy, there was little need for most enterprises to advertise.

In some special cases, commercials had a limited development and were permitted by the government. For example, in the mid-1970s, there were dozens of commercial billboards for the

31 Author's interview with Ren Yi, well-known book designer and illustrator and provost of the Shanghai Fine Art College (Spring 1984).

32 Author's interview with Chen Liang, an editor of *Advertising* magazine and a designer at the Shanghai Advertising Company (October 1983).

Guangzhou Export Fair. But these were always overshadowed by huge political billboards with red flags and political slogans.[33] The only place where commercial advertising had no problems was on the walls of buildings alongside railroad tracks. Roughly hand-painted, these advertisements were mainly for Chinese traditional medicine, tooth brushes and paste, fountain pens, flashlights and batteries, etc. The cost of these commercial posters was very low: an advertisement measuring 16′ × 6′ cost less than 20 U.S. dollars (100 Chinese Yuan) in the early 1960s. Most posters were blue and white or black. The designs were very simple, usually with a big logotype, the name of the manufacturer, and a simple illustration. However, this form of advertising was also banned during the Cultural Revolution. Since 1976, it has reappeared with its characteristics generally unchanged. The Shanghai Advertising Company has had many of these advertisements commissioned by clients in recent years.[34]

There were also many limitations on the development of packaging design in the last three decades. The Chinese word for packaging is *Bao Zhuang,* which means "wrap and pack." Wrapping was a very common means of packaging for sale in China and most of the nations of the Far East. Indeed it is still very popular in China and Japan. Wrapping expresses a special symbolic value of openness and truth. Over the past thousand years, Chinese commodities such as ceramics, tea, and silk fabrics were wrapped with paper and straw, string or rope, or set in large wooden chests for delivery and sale. Even in the 1970s, this method of wrap and pack was the main method of packaging, with even machinery and heavy tools set in wooden chests. All kinds of wine, soft drinks, soy sauce, and cooking ingredients were kept in reusable bulk glass containers. Many commodities had no selling packaging at all: they were simply shipped to the shops and displayed on the shelves. Buyers frequently had to provide their own containers, bags, or bottles, to transport such commodities home. Small items, such as tea and candy, would be wrapped in a piece of paper for the purchaser to take away. In such a situation, packaging design too was undeveloped.

However, for export commodities, packaging was necessary and important. Without good packaging to satisfy international standards and foreign buyers' requirements, it was impossible to export. To service this need, several packaging agencies were formed in the 1960s under the control of central and provincial departments of trade. The Guangdong Provincial Packaging Company under the Guangdong Provincial Foreign Trade Corporation was one of these. It is responsible for packaging design for many export goods, including hardware items, stationery, cosmetics, crafts, textiles and clothing, ceramics, electronic products, radios, flashlights, and batteries. In the 1960s and 1970s, designs focused on label decoration. Most packages were paperboard or corrugated paper boxes supplied to the company in different sizes. All products were set in these boxes, with paper strip, straw, and

33 See the photos showing the street and city look of China during the Cultural Revolution in *China Pictorial*, 1967–72.

34 "The Ads Along the Railroad," *China Advertising*, vol. 12 (1985).

foam plastic used for packing. Labels carrying the names of products, the manufacturer, and information about quality and quantity were finally attached to the boxes. In this sense, design was still limited to a decorative function.[35] The logos were often so picturesque and complicated as to conceal the identity of product or manufacturer. Corporate identity design was unheard of in China until the mid-1970s.

Product Design

Product design was less developed than all other forms of design until the 1970s. Poor productivity, innumerable people, and endless political chaos brought a common factor to life in China: a shortage of everything. From food to cloth, from hardware items to lumber, even salt and rice were in constant short supply. Rationing coupons, first introduced around 1958, were a symbol of Chinese daily life for the next two decades. (Coupons for rice, cereals, cooking oil, and meat were reissued in late 1988 in several big cities in China.) In this situation, quantity was the constant number one concern for all. Design was less important, and many manufacturers used the same design for two or three decades without any change. Thermos bottles, which are a major item in Chinese homes because most houses and apartments do not have hot water, remained unchanged from the 1930s until the 1980s. Desk lamps, telephones, fountain pens, electric fans, and bicycles were other products whose design never changed.

The Chinese motor vehicle industry was first established in the late 1950s. The need for a motorized road transport vehicle was desperate. With aid from the Soviet Union, China set up its first factory in Changchun, Jiling province in Manchuria in 1957. The first product was a 1.5 ton Jiefang truck, based on the prototype of the Soviet Union GAZ truck produced at the Maxim Gorky plant. For the Chinese it was a dream truck. Earlier China had featured the GAZ truck, which at that time was imported, on the one-cent bill issued in 1953. Until the mid-1970s, the Changchun plant was the only truck manufacturer in China, producing for the whole country, with an output of around 200,000 units per year from four assembly lines. Domestic demand alone was higher than this figure, and in addition China had to ship some of the trucks as part of foreign aid to Third World nations and to its allies, such as Albania, Vietnam, and North Korea. This demand forced production higher, and design or styling was unnecessary under such circumstances. The Jiefang truck was in production from 1957 to 1984 without any change of design, and broke the Ford Model T record (1907–25) for continuous production.

There was no competition in the Chinese domestic market because the government had a very strict import policy for autos. The only exceptions were some GAZ-69 jeeps from Russia and Rumania, limited production cars such as the Babeda (Victory) from Russia and Poland, Tatra trucks from Czechoslovakia, and buses

35 Author's interviews with Hu Yao-wu and Su Sen-tao of the Guangdong Packaging Company, Guangzhou (November 1986). See also the magazine *Packaging and Design*, nos. 1–3 (1983) edited by the Guangdong Packaging Company.

from Hungary and Czechoslovakia. A Chinese tractor, the Dong Fang Hong produced by the Luoyang Tractor Facory in Luoyang, Henan province, and bicycles such as the Yong Jou (Phoenix) produced by the Shanghai bicycle factory had similar design histories as the Jiefang truck: no change for years.[36]

In most Chinese manufacturing, engineers were generally responsible for everything, from mechanical function to appearance. Sometimes artists would be called in to decorate and beautify products. Such artists who work in factories in this way are still known as *Mei Gong* or "art workers".

China began to make its own cars in 1958 with a model called the Dong Feng (East Wind); it was not produced on a production line but was made individually in a workshop in Beijing. Mao took a five-minute ride in it. Several instructors from the Central Academy of Arts and Craft's were asked to decorate the car, which took on the appearance of an art deco fantasy. The two rear lights were in the shape of traditional Chinese lanterns, the hood ornament was a dancing golden dragon. Yet, although reminiscent of some of the products in London's 1851 Crystal Palace exhibition, it was the precursor of modern Chinese automobile design.[37]

In 1962, China produced its first limousine, the Hong Qi (Red Flag), at the First Auto Factory in Changchun. It was heavily derived from the Russian Seagull limousine, a standard car for senior officials and distinguished foreign guests. It had a V-8 engine and a typically diplomatic look: black color, heavy and wide, bulletproof glass windows. At this time, the rift with the Soviet Union was becoming ever wider, and the production of the Hong Qi was an indication of the desire of Chinese leaders to be free of dependence on Soviet Union vehicles, feeling they lost face by using them to go to work or to meet foreign diplomats. The total production of the limousine was very small, varying from 20 to 50 per year, depending on the level of government orders. All American presidents visiting China have used the Hong Qi, which was the official vehicle for top visitors. Production was halted in 1984, because Chinese leaders were no longer satisfied with its quality.[38]

The first Chinese factory devoted to car production was set up in Shanghai in the early 1960s. Its initial product was named after the city, the Shanghai. It was shabby looking, with a four-cylinder engine, four doors and an auto-shift option; but most important, it was an original Chinese design, by engineers from the factory—and with no artists involved. It had the distinct appearance of an art nouveau-type Russian Volga car. The front bumper was chromed and heavy, as were the radiator grill and other exposed parts. The most popular color was light apple green.

In the early 1970s, a new model appeared, which eliminated most of the art nouveau detail, giving a simpler look. The form was boxier. Even the contour of the lights was changed from round to square. However, because no designers were involved in the project,

36 "Industrial Design and China's Modernism." *Design* magazine, vol. 1 (1988), published by the Industrial Design Research Center Guangzhon Academy of Fine Art, Beijing.

37 *China Pictorial*, November 1958.

38 Author's interview with engineers of the Limousine Section, First Automobile Factory Changchun (Spring 1985).

the car was rather like an assembly of jigsaw puzzle pieces, with each piece derived from some part of foreign cars. The Shanghai had a very bad maintenance and repair record, and production ended in the early 1980s. At present, the Shanghai car factory is a joint-venture manufacturer with Volkswagen. It produces a small VW Shanghai-Santana and assembles some Audis.[39]

China now produces many kinds of trucks, jeeps, and military vehicles. These include the Jiefang truck from the First Auto Factory; the Dongfeng (Great Leap Forward) truck from the Second Automobile Factory in Shiyan, Hubei province, now the largest automobile manufacturer in China; the Hunghe (Yellow River) truck, based on the Czech Skoda heavy-load truck, by the Jinan Auto Factory in Shandong province; and the Hongyian truck by Chongqing Auto in Szechuan province. Of these plants, the first two mentioned produce engines which are supplied to the other plants.

The main Chinese jeep producer is the Beijing Jeep Factory, which began by making the famous Beijing jeep. This solid-looking four-wheel drive vehicle had its debut in the mid-1960s and was used by Mao to parade his Red Guards during the Cultural Revolution. A large quantity was shipped to Vietnam during the war there as aid from China. The Beijing was designed on the model of the Russian GAZ-69 but with a different front end. A modified version is still the main jeep for the Chinese army.[40]

Development of Chinese Design Since 1979

The Chinese market has changed rapidly since 1979, when the Chinese government introduced its ambitious plan of economic reform and "open policy" in foreign affairs. Reform partly changed the old market situation of "demand is higher than supply," and a new consumer market is appearing. As a result, demand from consumers for better-designed, high-quality commodities is growing. This is the background to recent developments in Chinese design and design education. Because many problems in the economic reform program remain unresolved, as discussed earlier, the development of Chinese design is uneven and unbalanced. Of all design activities, advertising design and interior design have had a comparatively faster development. Product design, or industrial design, lags far behind.

Advertising

Until 1979 there were very few advertising agencies, and all were in big cities. Shanghai, a city with a population of 11 million, had two agencies, the Shanghai Advertising Company and the Shanghai Decoration Company. There was just one in Beijing at that time, the Beijing Advertising Art Company, responsible for making all the political billboards in downtown Beijing, including the portraits of Mao that hung in the Tien An Mien Square area. Such work was the

39 Product catalog of VW-Shanghai Auto Company 1988.

40 Author's interviews with engineers of the Second Automobile Factory, Shiyan and the Beijing Jeep Factory [Jinnan Auto Manufacture] (Spring 1985).

common pattern for all similar agencies. Commercial advertising was very limited.[41]

After 1979, as business competition became more intense in China, advertising as a means of market promotion came to be considered a key competitive element. The demand for advertising services is therefore increasing and thousands of agencies have mushroomed almost everywhere in China. By 1984 there were almost 200 advertising agencies in Shanghai and a similar number in Beijing. Since there were no proper laws regulating commercial advertising in China, anybody could register a new agency for a relatively low fee. Advertising was considered an easy and profitable thing to do, which is why there was such fast expansion. It came not only through agencies; even some government organizations, such as the national railway and airline, set up their own agencies in an attempt to make greater profits. One of the largest agencies in the SEZ city of Shenzen is the Advertising Company of the Railroad Bureau of Shenzen.[42]

Many problems remain, however, in building a real advertising business in China:

- The Chinese market is still immature and in the unstable process of transformation. Business competition is still not acute enough for high cost, high quality advertising.
- There is a lack of regulation and laws to control Chinese advertising.
- News media are still considered to be a means of ideological propaganda and are strictly controlled by the Department of Propaganda of the Communist Party. Commercial advertising gets very limited space or time on TV, on radio, or in newspapers. About 30 minutes of advertising are permitted on the national TV network each day. One page of advertisements is the maximum in all newspapers, which are usually four-page dailies, with the *People's Daily* and the *Guangzhou Daily News* having eight pages. News media have their own advertising sections or companies which have a monopoly on creating advertisements for these media. The quality of work is so bad that it actually discourages viewers from watching them.
- Billboards are limited in number and are under the control of either urban planning or environmental development agencies. For example, there was a total of 80 billboards in Xi'an in 1984. Before 1979, all 80 were assigned to one agency, the Xi'an Advertising Company. By 1984, there were almost 20 advertising agencies in the city, but due to urban construction the number of billboards was reduced to 70. The agencies soon realized that billboard advertising was not very profitable. There were similar occurrences in other cities.
- Most "designers" in advertising agencies have no design qualifications or training. Some have an ability to paint and

41 Author's interviews with managers of the Shanghai and Beijing advertising companies (1985 and 1986).

42 Author's interview with two managers of the Shenzhen Railroad Advertising Company (October 1985).

draw but little understanding of real commercial design. So the average quality level is very poor, sometimes even ugly, with negative consumer reaction.

- Foreign advertising is controlled by a few government-authorized agencies, such as the Guangdong Advertising Company of the Foreign Trade Bureau of Guangdong province. There is very limited flexibility for foreign advertisements to compete with their Chinese opponents in a situation of unequal competition.[43]
- There are no direct mail advertisements in China. Both industry and consumers think it a waste.

In this situation, the rapid expansion of Chinese advertising agencies has slowed down, and many existing agencies are seeking to expand into other more profitable areas of work, such as interior design for tourist projects.

Graphic design

After 1979 the field of graphic design saw remarkable developments in the art of "wrap and pack," particularly in relation to the expansion of exports, where the pressures for effective competition were severe. In addition, commodity damage in shipping and transportation in the home market was resulting in very heavy losses due to inadequate packaging. Losses in 1983 went into billions of Yuan.[44] To address both the above problems, the central government established a National Committee for Packaging Technology in 1982.[45] It has several independent subcommittees, including one for design, located in Suzhou, Jiansu province. Several government-sponsored packaging magazines have been issued, and foreign package technology and design exhibitions have been held in China. The government also spends substantial amounts of foreign currency to import technology, machinery, and factories. As a result of this strong government support, China is rapidly catching up in the field of packaging engineering and technology. Design is the weakest point in this development. Design is seen as software, while technology and engineering are viewed as hardware in the eyes of most Chinese officials, who think design is just "beautification and decoration" and therefore logically of less importance.

Many ministries of the central government are also developing packaging for their own commodities and products. In recent years, the Ministry of Health and Medicine has held a series of training classes for its designers of medical packaging, and at the same time has also organized exhibitions of packaging from Western countries. Similar activities have been carried out by other ministries, such as those for the Chemical Industry, Light Industry, and Textiles. In this sense, packaging, engineering, and technology have gained the most support from the government. However,

43 Liu Jian-jun, "Advertising Comes into Its Own," *Beijing Review* (June 1, 1987): 18–20.

44 "Poor Packaging Brought Damage to the National Economy," *Package Design*, vol. 2 (1983).

45 *Package Design*, vol. 3 (1984).

packaging design has fared less well because the main concern of government officials is still better "wrapping and packing." Market competition is still too new to be accepted by most officials.

Packaging design depends mainly upon manufacturing, and since there is very limited private manufacturing in China, packaging design naturally receives very little demand from private business. Foreign rnanufacturers, such as Coca-Cola and Pepsi, generally import existing packaging design and therefore do not need Chinese designers. Because Chinese packaging design is a government-oriented activity, it exists in a very different context from advertising design.

Product design

Of all the forms of design, industrial design or product design is the most ignored. The reason for this neglect can be found in the still-underdeveloped consumer-product manufacturing sector. Although the Chinese market has changed considerably since 1979, it is still basically in a condition where demand exceeds supply, and the shortage of many consumer products is obvious. According to official government statistics, in 1983 China produced 10.8 million sewing machines, 34.6 million wrist watches, 6.8 million TV sets, 27.58 million bicycles, and 14.88 million meters of fabric. In 1986 China produced 9.86 million sewing machines, 32.35 million bicycles, and 3.8 billion pieces of tableware.

China has attracted more and more attention from the world since its ambitious reforms began in 1979. Its GNP has maintained an annual increase of 10 percent, and people's income has also rapidly increased. But the figures are dwarfed by the stark fact of China's one billion population. Eighty percent of Chinese are farmers who live in the countryside. In this fundamental sense, China is still an agrarian country, although the proportion of industry in GNP is growing higher. China's main export items are minerals or agricultural products. To feed one billion mouths is a tough task by any standard, and the issue of quantity is the first priority for most Chinese people.

In terms of the quantity of modern manufacturing, China holds world records for producing the most bicycles, watches, clocks, clothes, and so on, all the products necessary to maintain its one billion people. The figures are amazingly high, but what they conceal is that the design of these products is still very old and conservative. Most products are still based on foreign prototypes from several decades ago. In most Western countries, one-speed, heavy-looking Raleigh bicycles are kept in museums, but in China they are still being used by millions and are hot items in department stores.

However, a recent phenomenon has attracted the attention of government officials and designers. Millions of products without any styling or design are pouring off Chinese production lines. With income levels increasing and more people having their basic needs satisfied, the poorly designed, old-fashioned products are filling warehouses and cannot be sold. What is just beginning to happen in China is that more people are seeking better-quality and better-looking products; this is indeed a new tendency in the domestic market. According to a news report in May 1987, one million old-fashioned bicycles with little-known brand names, 10 million wrist watches, and 2.6 million sewing machines could not be sold and were sitting in storage. It was the first time in China that goods were not sold out. It indicates that productivity is increasing, which brings more products into the market; but it also shows that the sensitivity of Chinese people toward design and quality is growing.

There is also another new trend in China's economic boom. More and more foreign companies are coming to China in varying forms of business cooperation, such as investment in Chinese manufacturing, setting up foreign companies in China, or joint-venture enterprises. The Special Economic Zones have been extended in number and have been the main location for establishing hundreds of overseas companies. By the end of 1986, China had attracted 20.6 billion U.S. dollars in foreign investment, imported 14,000 new items of high technology, and had 7,800 joint-venture projects established.[46] The latter include such well-known names as Volkswagen, GMA Jeep, Peugeot, Canon, Yamaha, Hitachi, Coca-Cola, Pepsi-Cola, Kodak, and Kentucky Fried Chicken. All have been established since 1980 and all are profitable. The product design of these manufacturers is just the same as their models in overseas markets. It is non-Chinese design but gives the Chinese people a chance to feel and experience what good design is in comparison with their old and conservative products.

Many Chinese factories have imported foreign assembly lines, machines, technology, and management. Since the factories use foreign technology, the easiest way of manufacturing products in the shortest time is to rely upon foreign prototypes. Design imitation in such factories is therefore very popular. In most cases, factories just change the logos of foreign products or make minor adjustments to details of design in order to avoid violating copyright regulations. However, there is still a clear resemblance to foreign products. An example is Guangzhou's Wanbao Refrigerator Manufactory, one of the largest plants producing refrigerators, freezers, air conditioners, and other cooling appliances. Over recent years it has imported several assembly lines from Japan and Singapore. The design of the Wanbao refrigerator looks exactly like its Japanese prototype; even the color of the body is the same, a pale olive green, which is not popular in Western countries.[47]

The examples we have noted illustrate the two tendencies current in Chinese modern product design. One is keeping old designs and not changing them. Most products in this category are either well-known brands, such as the Shanghai and Tianjin bicycles, or products still in shortage in the market, such as trucks and

46 Gao Shang-quan "Progress in Economic Reform 1977–86," *Beijing Review* (July 6, 1987): 23–24.

47 Product catalog of the Wanbao Corporation, Guangzhou,1987.

automobiles. (The government still strictly controls imports of foreign automobiles to protect and encourage the domestic auto industry.) The second tendency is to copy and imitate foreign design. Since China is still a nonsignatory of most copyright treaties, it is difficult for foreign manufacturers, whose product design has been copied by Chinese competitors, to use lawsuits to protect their own copyrights.

An interesting example of Chinese violation of international copyright is Walt Disney's cartoon characters. As part of Disney's global strategy of promotion and marketing, in 1986 China's national TV network was offered several hundred hours of classical Disney cartoon movies. When shown in 1987, they attracted millions of Chinese children as well as their parents. Mickey, Donald, Goofy, and Pluto became favorite characters among the Chinese people, and more and more Chinese manufacturers started to decorate their products, such as T-shirts and shoes, with images of these characters. Disney canceled the remainder of the screenings while awaiting the decision of a Chinese court on a lawsuit charging Chinese manufacturers with copyright violations.

Why is it that China has such a strange situation in design? The first reason is the country's special political and economic background. In the past three decades, the Chinese national economy stagnated, and any tendency toward a consumer market or any materialist tendency was labeled "corrupt" and "capitalist." The concept of "consuming" at that time meant merely filling the stomach and securing basic shelter and clothing. The government discouraged any interest and desire among the Chinese people for a new, luxurious, or comfortable life. What is plain and old-fashioned looking is still considered by some Chinese, especially the old generation, as a symbol of virtue. Indeed, three decades of an austere, poor, and simple way of life have formed an esthetic standard in China that favors a conservative and plain style. The longer this economic situation lasted, the more this old, simple style became accepted as part of the Chinese national character.

Chinese traditional philosophy also hampers people from seeking what is better looking. The essence of Confucian philosophy is nonindividualism in a fixed social order. It requires people to be obedient and polite, always using others' viewpoints to adjust one's own behavior. On the surface, Taoism is the complete opposite, telling people to pretend to be unselfish in order to manipulate others for their own self-interest—in short, to be hypocritical. This traditional philosophical heritage was exaggerated and used by Mao in arguing for people who were "unselfish and devoted to communism." Mao's efforts resulted in an official version of traditional philosophy with a communist label. A comfortable life, luxurious surroundings, and self-enjoyment were all considered to be non-Chinese, whether communist Chinese or traditional Chinese. Under this new puritanism, the moral atmosphere of which invaded political, philosophical, and social life, it was very easy to ban all foreign culture, including modern design. In the post-Mao era, although many young Chinese do not like old and never-changing products, there is still a large number of Chinese who are willing to suffer the inconvenience of old products rather than tolerate those dazzling foreign devils.

Since design has been so much ignored, there are very few product designers in China. Whenever China opens its doors to the world and enters the international market, all Chinese manufacturers face the problem of a lack of designers. In recent years, some Chinese manufacturers have even gone bankrupt because of poor quality and design of products. But it is impossible to train large numbers of designers in a short time, and certainly China does not have enough good design schools. Therefore, for most manufacturers the key to survival is to imitate foreign designs that have proven successful in international markets.[48]

After nine years in preparation, China's Industrial Design Council was finally approved by the central government and established in Beijing on October 14, 1987. At its opening, Qiang Xue-sen, a graduate of California Institute of Technology in the 1940s and now head of China's nuclear and space project and a four-star general in the Ministry of Defense, gave a constructive speech. He emphasized the need for concern about the problem of poor design in Chinese products and expressed hope for rapid development with cooperation among engineers, artists, and designers. This event was a very important indication of progress in product design in China and shows the government's awareness and positive attitude to design affairs.[49]

The Design Council is a very special organization because China's complicated bureaucratic structure restricts overall design cooperation. The Ministry of Light Industry is reluctant to develop design for electronic products, such as TV sets, stereos, and VCRs, because all these items are considered the responsibility of the Ministry of Electronic Industry; the Ministry of Textiles is in charge of textile design and manufacturing, but not of clothes manufacture, which comes under the Ministry of Light Industry. In his opening speech, Qiang Xue-sen expressed his concern at this overlapping bureaucracy and its influence on design.

The structure of China's Design Council gives an interesting insight into the complexity of this bureaucratic tangle. It has 10 special societies which are focal points for major design specialties: electronic product design, graphic and decoration design, ceramic design, furniture design, glassware design, display and exhibition design, medical equipment design, construction material design, paper cutting and paper wrapping art, and the society of higher education in design. There are also numerous provincial and city branches of the Council in Shanghai, Liaoning, Jilin, Shanxi, Zhejiang, Guangdong, Jiansu, Sichuan, Nanjing, Chansha, Chongqing,

48 "Industrial Design and Chinese Modernization," *Design,* vol. 1 (1988): 18–20.

49 Wu You-hui, "China's Industrial Design Council," *Design,* vol.1, Beijing (1988): 44–45.

Qingdao, Shijiazhuang, Shansi, Yantai, Wuxi, Xi'an, and Xiangtan.[50] In addition to meetings on matters of professional interest, the Council promotes interchanges and contacts between design schools, institutes, and manufacturers. Books on design and design history and theory are published by arrangements between the Council and various publishing houses. The total number of members of the Council was 6,500 in 1988. The board of the Council consists of 77 members with an executive committee of 23 members.[51]

The foundation of China's Design Council as the organizer of design activities in the country is a great step forward. Of course, the Council is a very loose organization and has limited power in policy making on design for the nation. It is a symbol of progress rather than a practical step forward in design. However, the foundation of the Council also indicates the level of government support for design that is developing in China. Its establishment was approved at the highest level of the Chinese government. This can be seen as part of a growing awareness by government leaders of the importance of good standards of design in market competition, in both domestic and international markets. This awareness is evident in China's Seventh Five-Year Plan, which focuses on "gradually increasing the proportion of manufactured products in all export items" and the need to "improve the quality of commodities and strengthen their capability in competition."[52] There is still a need for much more development and change if design is to play a full part in China's modernization, but important steps have been taken and the potential is evident.

50 You-hui, "China's Industrial Design Council."

51 You-hui, "China's Industrial Design Council."

52 "Seventh Five-Year Plan, Major Economic Index," *Beijing Review* (April 7, 1986): 27–34.

Present at the Beginning

Svetlana Sylvestrova

> *"It was hard to work—we had no experience; we had to do everything for the first time. . . . "*
> *"It was an easy job—there were no set ways, we had to figure everything out for ourselves, it was the first time. . . ."*

This juxtaposition of contrary opinions probably reflects the most truthful estimation of that postwar time. Speaking today about the Architectural-Artistic Bureau (AAB) within the Ministry of Transport Machine Building in the Soviet Union, its former associates do not even notice how easily they have reconciled these two concepts: hard and easy. It was a time of untrodden and therefore difficult roads to industrial design, of active and therefore joyful labor of enthusiasts. AAB set up the methodological basis for modern industrial design and offered an example for organizing designers' work. And its activity provided the impetus for a new stage in the development of Soviet industrial design. Researchers are still faced with the task of filling in the gaps in the study of Soviet postwar experience in industrial design, especially of the practical scientific experience of the AAB. This article will only paraphrase the recollections of a few AAB specialists who began their work there 40 years ago.

The Minister's brief

In 1945 the Soviet Union was returning to peacetime labor. Plants were being reconstructed to manufacture new products, closed factories were being restored and opened. Particular difficulties existed in the transportation field: The rails were in bad condition, the rolling stock had been destroyed, and there was a shortage of urban transportation as well. Decisive measures had to be taken to restore the nation's complex transportation system in a short time; not simply to restore it, but to raise it to a new technical and qualitative level.

The Minister of Transport Machine Building in those years was Vyacheslav Mikhaylovich Malyshev, a highly qualified professional and an activist. He was called the country's "number one engineer." Malyshev was directly responsible for the supervision of many urgent tasks. He picked bold, talented people for the job. He assigned the chief task of designing an all-metal passenger coach to the Kalinin Railway Coach Construction Plant.

Before World War II, railway coaches were made of wood, and inside were dark and small, with little windows and hard seats. Because the technical basis was to be different, the coach compart-

This article was originally published in Russian in *Teckhnicheskaya Estetika* 6 (1985). The editors wish to thank Lauren Leighton for his help with the translation of this manuscript.

Figure I
Soviet prewar third-class passenger coach.

ment also had to be different. The technical brief signed by the Minister formulated the task concisely: maximum comfort and minimum material expenditure. The Engineering Design Bureau at the plant understood the seriousness of the proposed work and invited Yuri Soloviev, then a young Moscow specialist, to help the department in its work.

The railway coach design: from intuition to methodological principles

Yu. Soloviev invited two architects, Yuri Solomonovich Somov and Georgy Georgievich Lebedev, and an electrotechnical engineer, Igor Aleksandrovich Kulakov, to work together on the project. Intuition told the project director that professionals should be spoken to in their own language. The shortcomings of the old coach interior were obvious: It was ugly and uncomfortable. But these were mere words. To negotiate with clients, this team had to acquire experience, that is, conduct experiments and gather analytical data.

So they made an analysis. The upper and lower berths were completely flat. It was uncomfortable to sit or lie on them, and they were heavy. The mechanism for raising the upper berth to a sleeping position was useless: The berth hung along the wall, and in order to raise it, the passenger on the lower berth had to be disturbed. There was no storage for bed linen and no dining table. The lighting was dim. Ventilation was nonexistant.

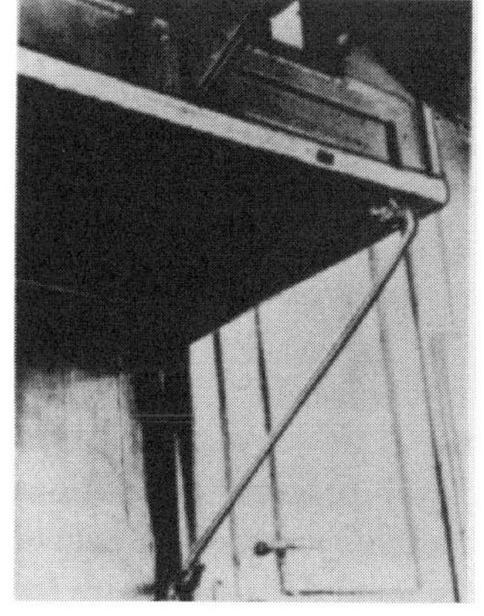

Figure 2
Soviet prewar third-class passenger coach interior.

As Yu. Somov recalls today, "The ideas poured out of us as if from a horn of plenty." The team rejected half of the ideas without bothering to develop them (they were too fantastic), but worthy ideas were put to strenuous test. To avoid errors, they consulted specialists.

The idea of lightening the weight of the wooden shelf, replacing it with a new lacquered panel, was checked and approved by production engineers in the aircraft industry. The designers also consulted these specialists about using "pure aviation" technology

Figure 3
An all-metal passenger coach. Designers: Yu. Soloviev and Yu. Somov, with the participation of G. G. Lebedev and I. A. Kulakov, 1946.

Figure 4
An all-metal passenger coach. Designers: Yu. Soloviev and Yu. Somov, with the participation of G. G. Lebedev and I. A. Kulakov, 1946.

Figure 5
An all-metal passenger coach. Designers: Yu. Soloviev and Yu. Somov, with the participation of G. G. Lebedev and I. A. Kulakov, 1946.

and materials, that is, light aluminum alloys with mat anodized finishing, for the lock and handle. These ideas were justified by experience itself. And even today, 40 years later, many Soviet trains have coaches that contain berths and the mechanisms to raise them designed by Yu. Soloviev, step ladders designed by Yu. Somov, and stop alarms and ashtrays designed by G. Lebedev. With slight modifications, this coach compartment has been retained even in the modern model now being made for us in the German Democratic Republic.

In less than two months a mock-up of the coach was completed and presented to the ministry. However, the difficulties involved should not be concealed. Not everyone could see and evaluate the advantages of a rationally designed object. And the designers in those years were dealing with such problems for the first time. The designers were called *craftsmen* in those days, as the term *designer* for this kind of professional was not in use in 1945.

Concurrent with the artistic mock-up of the compartment, a new version of the coach interior was presented by the plant engineers. The two were presented side by side at the meeting of the technical committee, and the comparison was fatal for the plant version. The interior of the compartment presented by the artists seemed spacious and airy as a result of the light from the windows, the light color finishing—natural colors of wood and aluminum—and the spotlight illumination. The compartment furnishings were in harmony with the idea of an all metal railway coach.

The plant designers, who offered only superficial cosmetic changes in the interior, had weighty rebuttals ready: The projected coaches were intended for mass transportation; they had to be traditional and cheap, and the design of such coaches could do without the "aviation motifs" for their decoration. However, the Minister's order put an end to hot discussions. The artists' project was approved as standard and put into production. This work decided the fate of the first specialized organization: In early 1946, the Architectural-Artistic Bureau was set up within the Ministry of Transport Machine Building. Yu. Soloviev was appointed director.

Ship designs: the activity field widens

The bureau director quickly drew some practical conclusions from the lessons of the first project. If industry needed the help of artists, then they needed specific professional skills and means for efficient interaction with industry. They needed workshops for making models, testing rigs, and also some help from economists.

To set up an experimental model workshop, it was necessary to find first-rate cabinet makers, and Yu. Soloviev found just one such enthusiast, Aleksandr Iosifovich Sabov, who was nominated as head of the workshop. He understood that the objective was to make new furniture prototypes that would be principally innovative, both in design and quality. He gathered highly qualified professionals to work in the new experimental workshop, which

Figure 6
A new convertible furniture set for children: wardrobe bed and desk. Designers: Yu. Soloviev and S. Logginova, 1947.

was subordinate to the AAB. The workshop needed modern machine tools and orders for high-quality work so that these highly trained workers would not lose their skills. Both were achieved. But now the work was different. The ideology for this young creative team was clearly defined from the very beginning. Unique and expensive goods were not wanted, but rather, mass-produced items, that is, items needed by everybody. And these items needed to be attractive, durable, rational, and in good taste. For the 1950s, such a trend in design was innovative. And AAB personnel worked out the principles—compactness, variability, economy, and technological rationality—while designing domestic furniture.

These ideas were skillfully used in ship designs. Maya Yurevna Kaplinskaya, a former staff member of AAB, recollects: "From the moment I first came to work for AAB in 1947, I was plunged into the special atmosphere of team work that reigned there. At that time, AAB was developing the architectural and artistic part of a project for a river passenger ship. I remember how surprised I was to be invited to take part in discussing a sanitary unit design. I had come with an electrical engineer's diploma, and I couldn't understand how I could be of any use in solving questions of sanitation and hygiene. But I was wrong. For the little group at

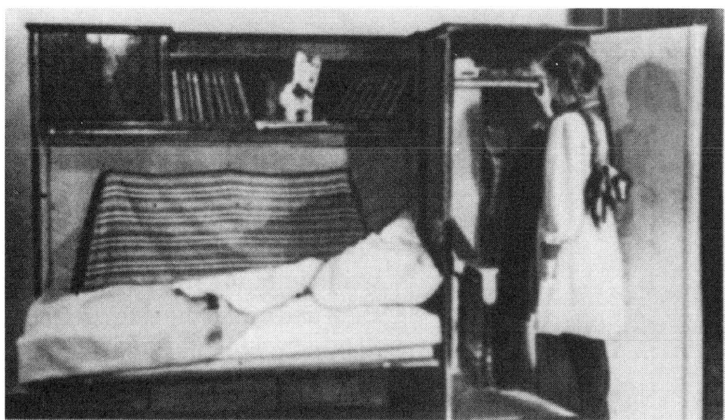

Figure 7
A new convertible furniture set for children: wardrobe, bed, and desk. Designers: Yu. Soloviev and S. Logginova, 1947.

Figure 8
A new convertible furniture set for children: wardrobe, bed, and desk. Designers: Yu. Soloviev and S. Logginova, 1947.

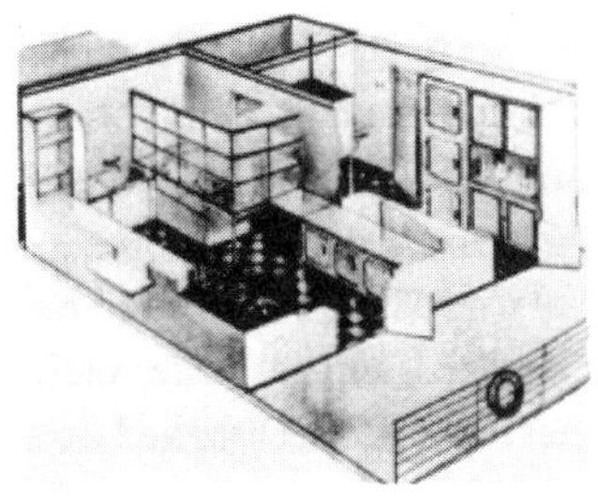

Figure 9
The galley unit of a river ship. Designer: O. G. Lebedieva, 1949.

AAB it was customary to think together, inasmuch as everything they did was designed for the first time, everything was novelty."

Today we are accustomed to such expressions as *ergonomic analysis*, *space zoning*, *work posture*, and *human factors*. But at that time, these words had not been born yet, although the methods themselves were in the process of being born. M. Kaplinskaya was astounded by the test of a wash basin mock-up: The force of the water from the faucet and the direction of the water being splashed were measured. But then she began designing lighting fixtures for the ship's cabins, and she already knew what was expected of her: She had to provide for maximum comfort and coziness through the lighting. This was the first time that a new type of lighting—luminescent lamps—was proposed for use on ships.

Artists were asked to introduce nothing less than an "artistic order" in the ship's interior. But they undertook to change the very basis—the interior layout. They studied errors in the deck arrangements, and identified inconveniences of exits and entrances, excessive steepness of the ladders, and difficulties of getting around. For example, lack of coordination in the layout of the galleys and restaurants obliged the waiters to walk almost 40 kilometers a day. The designers therefore proposed to break up an old tradition in the shipbuilding industry by placing the galley in the stern and arranging the cafeteria in two stories on a single vertical. Naturally, this and some other proposals brought about changes in the ship exterior, as well.

New design projects are seldom accepted fully. That was the case here, too. The clients from the shipbuilding plant in Kiev were sufficiently upset to insert the following in the protocol: ". . . the exterior of the ship was designed by architects who are nonprofessionals in shipbuilding; as a result, the ship looks very strange and unusual." However, experience has shown that this "unusualness, " which was a good design solution, was dictated by a concern for people, their comfort, and their health. The new principle of the arrangement of the galleys and restaurants was accepted and implemented in this ship and subsequently became a commonplace standard in shipbuilding. The first postwar river passenger ship, built in Kiev, became the pioneer of comfortable river ships.

The architect Georgy Nikolayevich Botcharov recollects: "Our work on what was for that time the largest river ship, the diesel electric ship Lenin, went forward with vast scope. This ship was designed at the Red Sormovo factory in Gorky, the most venerable ship design bureau in Russia, and to compete with such experienced shipbuilders as these was not easy." Nevertheless, the predesign proposal worked out by Yu. Soloviev contained ideas that had the effect of a bomb going off. Instead of a three-deck ship 100 meters long, it was proposed to design a five-deck ship 120 meters long, something unheard of in the world of shipbuilding practice. Two things helped support Yu. Soloviev's defense of this project: first, his experience in battles like this and, second, the goodwill of Professor Vyacheslav Mikhaylovich Kerichev, Red Sormovo's chief designer and a man of great erudition who never lost his taste for innovation.

A large ship required hard work. In addition to working out the general arrangements (the decks), cabin and salon interiors of all classes, and even the design for the crew's uniforms (this work is now called complex design), the designers solved ideological problems as well. They had to prove that their efforts to guarantee equal comfort in all cabins was correct; they had to justify the selection of "strange and unusual" finishing materials such as polymers, glass, and aluminum instead of bronze, velvet, and velours; they had to explain the advantages of built-in convertible furniture in the cabins instead of the bulky and heavy sofas and armchairs that looked as

Figure 10
The exterior of the five-deck diesel electric ship built by the Red Sormovo factory in Gorky. Designers: Yu. Soloviev, G. Botcharov, 1951.

if they were brought from palaces. Not incidentally, this was the first time that anyone had proposed to establish "intersector unification," that is, to use for the sleeping berths those suspended wooden shelves that had been designed for railway coaches and were already in production. Their use significantly reduced the cost of building the ship.

Figure 11
The cabin interior of the nuclear-powered icebreaker Lenin. Designer: S. Logginova, 1957.

An essential job was performed for the ships by the craftsmen of the experimental workshops. The wood used for ships had to meet specific requirements: Wooden finishes had to withstand contrasts of temperature, humidity, moisture, and so forth. The designers concerned themselves with these aspects. They constantly trained their craftsmen at the experimental workshops to look for and evaluate the advantages of new technological processes for woodworking. They therefore developed a new process of finishing by combining polishing with the application of a nitrovarnish

Thus, they ensured the required properties and the quality of wood and essentially reduced material and time expenditures. The furniture and equipment looked spectacular. But just before the acceptance of the ship by the responsible commission, somebody saw the brilliant polish on both sides of the shower doors and decided to take them off, because he did not trust "those artists' gadgets." The inventor of this new finish technology, an engineer named Ingber at the AAB experimental workshop, insisted on testing this new finishing process. The shower cabins were filled with hot steam three times and then exposed to cold drafts. The varnished surfaces of the doors remained smooth and brilliant on both sides.

Figure 12
The interior of the passenger cabin of a river ship with a convertible sleeping berth. Designer: O. G. Lebedieva, 1949.

Design and development of the river ships significantly enriched the designers' experience. At first intuitively, then with increasing confidence, they accumulated an arsenal of professional skills and methods and worked out a strategy for cooperation with engineers and design engineers. Having the design drawings approved twice—by the engineering design bureau at Red Sormovo and by AAB—became standard practice at that time. At Red Sormovo they quickly adopted the practice of not releasing the working drafts for production without the written authorization of the chief engineering designer and the chief architect.

There were certainly designs of AAB that ended up on the shelf. Those are now called initiative designs: They were developed parallel with the current orders of the clients, and the inventors themselves did not understand where they found the time for this work. An example of this "postponed" work was a complete reconstruction of the captain's bridge. Yu. Soloviev proposed to move it from its long-established position in the center of a motor ship to the bow and to supply it with a system of TV cameras for improving the field of view. (20 years later this solution became standard practice.)

Another example was a project for a long-distance passenger train with separate compartments and salons organized as reading rooms, sports and music halls, and so forth. These had appropriate equipment, down to a public telephone that connected a passenger with any town in the country while the train was standing in a station. "Pure fantasy," said some when they rejected the projects; "Too soon for something like this," said others.

But these projects were not empty fantasies; they raised the morale of the designers, broadened the scope of their work, and gave them new work skills. These projects added spice to designers' work when they undertook solutions to vital industrial tasks.

A city trolleybus—a full-cycle design project

In 1949, a city trolleybus was designed for the Uritsky factory. This project deserves attention because it was carried out most reliably in terms of organization, methodology, and creativity. In this case, the designers' proposal outstripped the work of the factory design engineers who had developed only the basic plan for the chassis and had not yet worked on the body. The designers undertook this work on their own, from scratch, which meant that time was not wasted reworking a draft. A detailed analysis of the existing prototype helped expose its shortcomings, above all those from the passengers' point of view. The analysis completed, the designers began a new elaboration of the project.

Figure 13
A city trolleybus (original design).

Figure 14
A new comfortable city trolleybus. Designer: Yu. Soloviev, with the assistance of T. A. Shepeleva, 1949.

The new trolleybus had an entirely different appearance. It had a larger glazed surface; it was wider with higher windows encased by thin framing. Passengers no longer had to bend down to see streets, store signs, and house numbers. By changing the doorways and the door construction to open wider and by lowering the height of the steps, the designers made entering and exiting easier. In addition, a special platform was provided near the doors where the passengers could prepare to exit. Everything was designed anew, even the shape of the seats, the lighting, and the interior of the driver's cab. Thus, 35 years ago, the design project was developed according to methods now considered elementary, almost classic, practice: drawing up a brief (with the client), analyzing the project, sketching, preparing full-scale mock-ups, producing design documentation, and making a tested prototype.

Without mutual understanding with the factory specialists, achieving success would have been impossible. But this working method is, as they used to say at the AAB, "the most happy"; the

Figure 15
A speed boat. Designer: Yu. Soloviev, 1958.

chief design engineer of the factory and the team fully shared the designers' striving to make a comfortable, attractive trolleybus. And this model is still in use.

After the design of the trolleybus, designers developed more and more interesting products for industry, including electric-train coaches, a street car, excursion launches, and sets of furniture and interior designs for a nuclear-powered icebreaker. These projects were designed by graduates of Moscow's Stroganov School, the Moscow Architectural Institute, and the Moscow Aviation Institute. These young people established a new profession in the Soviet Union: industrial design.

A quote from Yu. Soloviev, former chief architect at AAB, summarizes the overall experience: "My work in AAB was excellent training for me. I learned a lot from my colleagues, because each of them had a specific talent that enriched us all, the members of a friendly creative team. I learned a lot from the craftsmen of our experimental workshops, not only a knowledge of the secrets of producing superior wooden structures, but also high respect for the profession. I'll never forget how a master cabinetworker once replied to my question, 'Why do you want to work for us, even though you are making more where you are?' by saying 'Because you require high-quality work, and I'm afraid of losing my skills at my present job.' The accumulated experience and methods that were developed at that time by a small team at AAB were later developed on a broad scale in the practice of Soviet industrial design."

The Irish Design Reform Movement of the 1960s

John Turpin

It is sometimes mistakenly believed that contemporary design awareness came to Ireland with the celebrated report, *Design in Ireland*, prepared by a group of Scandinavian designers in 1962. However, Ireland has a long historical design background that includes the eighteenth-century School of Ornament of the Dublin Society, the nineteenth-century Schools of Design, and the traditional urban and rural crafts as well. In 1853, 1865, and 1907, large international exhibitions of art and industry comparable to those abroad were held in Dublin, and these gave Irish manufacturers some idea of foreign design. However, these exhibitions tended to be dominated by luxury products, which only highlighted the inadequacies of Irish production. Irish linen, silk poplin, lace, and the cast iron of Richard Turner were the most distinguished local products.[1]

There were also trade exhibitions of art and industry that did not attempt to compete with international quality products, that is, those in Dublin in the 1880s and at Cork in 1852 and 1902. Twentieth-century design was marked by the exhibitions of the Irish Arts and Crafts Society between 1895 and 1925. Because of the arts and crafts and even fine art orientation of the exhibitors, however, these were not spring-boards for modern design. In this respect, the Irish arts and crafts exhibitions resembled those of England's Arts and Crafts Exhibition Society, rather than the Deutscher Werkbund of Germany. The emphasis was on items such as enamels and stained glass to the exclusion of functional mass-produced products. Harry Clarke's book illustrations and trade designs of the 1920s were the most notable graphic design work of that period in Ireland.[2] It is interesting to note that when Ireland's most famous industry, Guinness Stout, began advertising between the wars, it turned to English graphic designers, as Dublin did not have high quality advertising agencies that could provide an integrated advertising program of words and images to promote a product.

Since the nineteenth century when Ireland was part of the United Kingdom, the Irish Free State (which became a self-governing dominion of the British Commonwealth in 1922) pursued an economic policy of free trade. However, with the advent of a new Fianna Fáil government in 1932, with its strongly nationalist, separatist, and self-reliant ideology, a policy of protective tariffs was inaugurated to shelter nascent Irish industries, such as clothing, footwear, and car assembly. These substituted for direct imports, primarily from Britain. The issue of industrial design had to be

I am indebted to Mr. Paul Hogan of Córas Tráchtála (the Irish Export Board), Dublin, and Mr. John Heskett of Ravensbourne College of Art and Design, England, for advice in connection with the preparation of this paper, but I take full responsibility for it.

1 On these exhibitions see John Turpin "The Irish Arts and Industries Exhibition Movement 1834–1864," *Dublin Historical Record* XXXV, 1 (December 1981): 12–13; John Turpin "Dublin Exhibitions of Art and Industries, 1865–1885," *Dublin Historical Record* XXXV, 2 (March 1982): 42–51; John Turpin "Ireland's Progress: The Dublin Exhibition of 1907," *Eire –Ireland* XVII: 1 (Spring 1982): 31–38.

2 See Nicola Gordon-Bowe, *The Graphic Work of Harry Clarke* (Dublin: The Dolmen Press 1983), which details the design background of the early twentieth century in Ireland. On Irish crafts see David Shaw-Smith, *Ireland's Traditional Crafts* (London: Thames and Hudson, 1984).

addressed, and on October 22, 1937, Sean Lemass, Minister for Industry and Commerce, set up a departmental committee "to advise on matters affecting the design and decoration of articles" manufactured in the Irish Free State.[3] Although the committee met 42 times, little seems to have resulted, and it ceased to exist in 1939 when war broke out; its final recommendation was for an exhibition of design in industry, but nothing came of this until 1954, under new aegis. Nevertheless, as in Britain, there was a great deal of useful innovation during World War II, spearheaded by Seán Lemass's Ministry of Supplies. To take only one example, James J. Drumm's "Traction Battery" train was an Irish innovation.[4] (Locomotive and carriage building had been an important feature of late nineteenth-century Irish heavy industry at Dundalk and Inchicore, Dublin.)

New post-World War II initiatives must be seen against this rather stagnant background. Thomas Bodkin, director of the Barber Institute, Birmingham, and former director of the National Gallery of Ireland, was commissioned to write a report on the arts in Ireland. Taking up its initiative of ten years before, the Department of Industry and Commerce insisted that this report include consideration of industrial design. Bodkin's remarks in this area inaugurated the post-World War II story of Irish design consciousness. Bodkin stated in his report of 1949: "There never has been a sustained alliance between the arts and industry in Ireland; and little has been done in the last fifty years to promote such a desirable aim, beyond the efforts made for over thirty years by the Arts and Crafts Society."[5] He admitted that the Irish Countrywomen's Association, through the energy of Dr. Muriel Gahan, had done much to encourage handicrafts and to facilitate their sale through country markets in Dublin. Bodkin pointed to Sweden as an example for Ireland and also showed what Britain's Council of Industrial Design had done since 1944, particularly its propaganda for design reform by Gordon Russell and Robin Darwin. By contrast, Bodkin saw a picture of poor industrial design in Ireland. "No civilized nation has neglected art to the extent that we have done during the past fifty years, with consequent injury to our national industries."[6]

During the 1950s, while Britain and Europe were rebuilding their industries, the Republic of Ireland's economic situation with a declining population was stagnant. Although the Republic may not have been *au courant* with modern design in the 1950s, it was at least little affected by the ugliness of modern industrialization. The built environment of Dublin largely consisted of quality Georgian and Victorian terraces. The elegance of Dublin's Grafton Street, its shop fronts, and traditional lettering had not yet been lost in modernization. E. A. Maguire, owner of Brown Thomas, the most fashionable shop in Dublin, promoted the best of textile design, whereas Richard Alan was a leader in fashion design.

3 Thomas Bodkin, *Report on the Arts in Ireland* (Dublin: The Stationery Office, 30 (September, 1949, 42.)

4 Locomotive and carriage building had been an important feature of late nineteenth century Irish heavy industry at Dundalk and Inchicore, Dublin. The coming of the railways marked the advent of the Industrial Revolution in most parts of Ireland outside the Belfast hinterland.

5 Bodkin, *Report on the Arts in Ireland,* 36.

6 Bodkin, *Report on the Arts in Ireland,* 40.

As a consequence of the Bodkin Report, the Irish Arts Council was set up in 1951, with the promotion of industrial design as one of its aims. The council sought to generate design awareness by holding two important exhibitions in the mid-1950s. The first was the International Design Exhibition 1954, produced by the Design Research Unit of Ireland, with Misha Black, the prominent British design theorist, as consultant. The three introductory essays to the catalog, from which the following quotations are taken, are an interesting summary of Irish design theory. Patrick J. Little, director of the Irish Arts Council, wrote that the exhibition's aim was "to impress upon our people the vital importance of attractive craftsmanship in our industrial products, first because it helps to raise the standards of good taste and artistic judgment at home . . . and again because without it our exports cannot compete in world markets."[7] He cited the Example of Olivetti in Italy, a recent exhibition of Art in Industry at Burlington House, London, the reorganization of British art schools, and especially the Royal College of Art, London. Even so, he hailed the leading role of Denmark, Sweden, Italy, and the United States in the field of design.

E. A. Maguire, member of the Arts Council and Ireland's leading fashion retailer, pointed to John Ruskin and Eric Gill in support of the esthetic value of design and stated, "To achieve good design, the manufacture and his workmen must be educated in principles of good design. Taste can be acquired, and the purpose of this exhibition is to help in this matter."[8] He dismissed academic art but hailed abstract art as the stimulus for design, all high-minded, mandarin, modernist sentiments.

The third essay came from Herbert Read, who cited Sweden, Finland, and Denmark as examples to be followed. "Ireland has a great tradition—Dublin is its witness. But that tradition has been lost . . . but there is no reason why it cannot be recovered."[9] The clear message was that Irish design should model itself on Scandinavia.

The exhibition contained a selection of good international modern design, including furniture, carpets and rugs, fabrics and wallpapers, light fittings, ceramics, glass, domestic equipment, commercial and industrial equipment, and packages and containers. Among the designers exhibited were Jacques Guillon, Ronald Inglis, Kenneth Lamble, Ronald Grierson, Margaret Leichner, Marianne Straub, Milner Gray, Graham Sutherland (who designed a tea service), Brandt Friberg, P. Nenni, S. Palmqvist, N. Landberg, and E. Hald. Products came from Heals and Sanderson of London, Rima and Arteluce of Italy, Royal Copenhagen Porcelain, Wedgewood, Olivetti, and others. The exhibition gave a very good idea of what might be attempted at home, particularly in furniture and fabrics. A follow-up exhibition of contemporary Italian industrial art, as well as two exhibits on contemporary architecture, were also added.

Another major Arts Council design exhibition was devoted to Irish products. It was called simply *Irish Design Exhibition 1956* and

7 *International Design Exhibition 1954,* presented by the Irish Art Council and produced by the Design Research Unit of Ireland, 3.

8 *International Design Exhibition 1954,* 6.

9 *International Design Exhibition 1954,* 8.

was also produced by the Design Research Unit of Ireland, with Misha Black as consultant and Thurloe Connolly as designer. Åke Huldt, director of the Swedish Council of Industrial Design, was invited to select the exhibits. P. J. Little commented about Huldt that "although searchingly critical, he was most encouraging. He emphasized the importance of freshness of imagination, grace, simplicity, and practical utility of articles in ordinary use, rather than stressing luxury articles. Whilst good tradition was not condemned, unimaginative imitation was not approved. Our textiles, especially our tweeds, received the commendation as leading in their kind for Europe."[10] E. A. Maguire's catalog essay was an example of standard modern design theory. The designer was to "subordinate his design to his machine, to the resources and requirements of his employer and to the desires of the consuming public."[11]

The exhibition showed Irish products: furniture, carpets and rugs, ceramics and glass, domestic equipment, fabrics and wall papers, leather goods, agricultural equipment, packages, containers and prints, and a series of three case studies demonstrating how a team of designers could redesign a corporate image. Among the participating designers were Barney Herron, Thurloe Connolly, Grattan Freyer, Kenneth Lamble, Louis Le Brocquy (painter and tapestry designer), Peter Wildbur (graphic designer), Raymond McGrath (government architect and carpet designer), Colm O Lochlainn (printer of fine books), Patrick Scott (painter, architect, and tapestry designer), Guus Melai (Dutch graphic designer), and Jock Kinnan. Among the firms showing were Andrew Thompson (furniture); Dun Emer Guild (fabrics), which provided an interesting link with the original Irish arts and crafts movement; Arklow and Carrigaline pottery; Waterford Glass; Newbridge Cutlery; Avoca Handweavers; Gaeltarra Eireann (knitwear); Pierce and Co. (engineering); Tullamore Dew (whiskey); and Irish Ropes (carpets). It was a sampling of the leading designers of the 1950s and of those Irish firms that were interested in design. This 1956 exhibition traveled from Dublin to Waterford, Cork, Limerick, Galway, and Sligo, and, thus, for the first time, there was an attempt to reach a countrywide audience and to spread the gospel of good design.

Undoubtedly the Irish Arts Council, under its chairman P. J. Little, did a lot of useful work to promote design and awarded premiums (that is, prizes) for design.[12] These initiatives eventually led to the design grants offered by Córas Tráchtála (CTT), the Irish Export Board, in the 1960s. Most important of all, the Arts Council introduced the Design Research Unit of Ireland, which had an office in Dublin headed by Thurloe Connolly. As mentioned above, this unit produced the design exhibitions sponsored by the council. The Design Research Unit led, in turn, to the formation of Signa Consultants, which was founded by Michael Scott and Louis Le Brocquy and which influenced graphic and packaging design standards.

The National College of Art in Dublin was the principal insti-

10 *Irish Design Exhibition 1956*, presented by the Irish Arts Council and produced by the Design Research Unit of Ireland, 4.

11 *Irish Design Exhibition 1956*, 5.

12 This concept of premiums went back to Rev. Dr. Samuel Madden of the Dublin Society who was the first person in Ireland to offer premiums for drawings of ornament in the 1740s.

tution where design was taught. In the early twentieth century, there had been a flowering of crafts, such as enameling and metalwork, stained glass, lace and embroidery, and illustration and illumination at the College.[13] However, the impetus had died away, and by the 1940s the crafts, apart from embroidery, had disappeared from the school. During the 1950s, partially as a result of Thomas Bodkin's strictures, there was a strong move to restore them; stained glass, metalwork, pottery, weaving, and lithography were introduced, but the school had to function in the adverse conditions of lack of money and accommodation. Staff were mostly local, working in the arts and crafts tradition, and there was no bridge to industry.

Figure 1
Guus Melai, *Symbol for the first "Tostal" silk screen print festival* (1954).

The School of Design at the college had been headed since 1939 by Bernardus Romein, from Rotterdam, a man with a respectable reputation in Holland in the 1930s. He was an artist-designer who believed in superb hand lettering in the pre-World War II tradition. However, he gave no instruction in typography or reprographic techniques. Nevertheless, this form of commercial art was the nearest the National College of Art got to the industrial world. Roman hand lettering, posters and showcards, plant drawing, and black-and-white work comprised the syllabus that aimed at advertising and illustration. Romein's students were not welcomed by the commercial advertising agencies, and the unfavorable public reception of an exhibition of his students' work at the school in 1953 was a grievous disappointment to him. Furthermore, by temperament Romein was difficult to deal with and he made no effort to link up with industry in Ireland or with the design profession.

Apart from the Design Research Unit and Signa Consultants, the major impetus to innovation in Irish design in the 1950s came from an influx of post-World War II-trained Dutch graphic designers, a generation younger than Romein. Aer Lingus, Ireland's airline, which was the main success story of modern Ireland, sought designers in Holland who had done design work for KLM and could promote an airline image. Guus Melai who came in 1951, as the first of these, and others, such as Jan de Fouw, followed; an interesting attraction for these Dutchmen was that in comparison to the desperate housing situation in post-World War II Holland, one could get a house and garden easily in Dublin. The training of the Dutch graphic designers was based on Bauhaus principles, which they introduced into Ireland. Their work at Sun Advertising had an immediate public impact, as it was seen in Irish publications, bill boards, shops, and offices; it crystallized the advent of modern design in Ireland. Irish fashion, primarily through Sybil Connolly, was in advance of Irish graphic design; she was trained in London, and was also acquiring an international reputation, notably in the United States in the 1940s and 1950s. Connolly demonstrated the possibilities of using traditional Irish materials such as linen and tweed in an *haute couture* context.

13 See Jeanne Sheehy, *The Rediscovery of Ireland's Past: the Celtic Revival, 1830–1930* (London: Thames and Hudson, 1980). For an account of the College in the early twentieth century see John Turpin, "The Dublin Metropolitan School of Art, 1900–1923," *The Dublin Historical Record* XXXVII, 2 (March 1984): 59–78; XXXVIII, 2 (March 1985), 42–52; XXXVIII, 3 June 1985): 86–102.

Figure 2
Guus Melai, *Brochure for Aer Lingus* (1953).

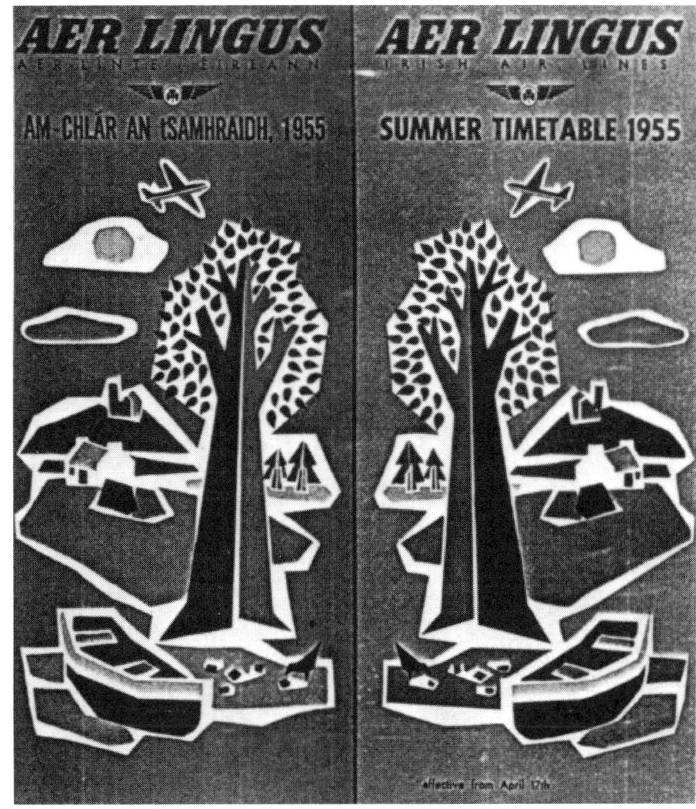

The design profession was itself beginning to develop in the late 1950s. The Irish Packaging Institute was established in 1958, and in 1960 the Institute of Creative Advertising and Design was founded. Both were forerunners of the Society of Designers in Ireland, founded in 1972. By 1960, there was already significant design awareness and a modern outlook in certain circles in Ireland; because of this, a more wide ranging initiative developed in the 1960s.

The main government agency that pushed for improvements in design for industry was Córas Tráchtála which was set up in 1952. It had taken over responsibility for design promotion from the Arts Council, through its new responsibilities as outlined in the Export Promotion Act of 1959, and confirmed in 1960 by Sean Lemass, Taoiseach (Prime Minister), in the Dáil (Parliament). This led immediately to the establishment in 1961 of a Design Section within CTT. William H. Walsh, manager of CTT and a former businessman, was thus in a strong position, having the confidence of the Taoiseach (Prime Minister) to recommend policy changes.

In this advantageous position, Walsh became the central catalyst of the design reform movement of the 1960s. Walsh knew the value of design in marketing through his personal experience in private enterprise. He had a particular interest in contemporary design in Denmark, a country parallel in some respects to Ireland as it was small and largely agricultural. Walsh was instrumental in having a panel of distinguished Scandinavian designers visit Ireland

Figure 3
Piet Sluis, *Poster, Exhibition of the Institute of Creative Advertising*, silk screen print, (1964).

to advise on what had to be done or, rather, to put international weight behind what Walsh believed should be done. (In the 1950s, the Scandinavians were acknowledged as design leaders in Europe.)

With Ireland's entry into the Common Market, Irish products had to compete with foreign ones in a free-trade environment. This, too, was a spur to better design.

A group of Scandinavian designers: Kaj Franck (Finland), Erik Herlow, Gunnar B. Petersen, Erik Sorensen (Denmark), and Åke Huldt (Sweden) visited Ireland at Easter 1961 and made a well-focused, if brief, study of textile printing and design; linen; woolen and woven cloths; poplin; Donegal tweeds; hand knitwear; hand-made, machine-made, and sisal carpets; souvenirs; graphics; packaging; and stamps (to which they devoted exhaustive analysis). Huldt was important in that he already knew Irish design, having selected the items for inclusion in the Irish Design Exhibition in 1956.

Their report *Design in Ireland* (February 1962), a manifesto for modernism in design, was the most controversial one on the visual arts ever written in Ireland. The authors severely criticized the level of Irish design and stated: "Lasting results, however, cannot be hoped for unless the vital matter of design education is tackled with energy and foresight. We think it is impossible for Ireland to make progress in Design without a radical change in existing educational institutions."[14] They recommended that young Irish crafts people go to Scandinavia on study trips. They reserved their strongest condemnations for Irish art schools and particularly for the National College of Art which, "as it is presently constituted cannot be a starting point for the education of people in the different crafts or indeed for the education of painters, sculptors, or designers."[15] One of their particular theories was that design education was to be linked closely to architectural education; they envisaged a new Irish Institute of Visual Art including architecture to spearhead reform in design education.

The main value of the report was not in the evidence it collected or its recommendations, but in its exposure of Irish design to the shock of international comment. The report came like a bombshell into the provincial and complacent atmosphere of Irish art and design education. The reaction of the editors and correspondents of *The Irish Times*, the leading Irish newspaper, was generally favorable.[16] It led to questions in the Dáil when Dr. Noel Browne, a radical member of Parliament, and former Minister of Health, attacked Dr. Patrick Hillery (Minister for Education), for inaction, inasmuch as the college came directly under Hillery's responsibility.[17] The late Dr. T. O'Raifeartaigh (Secretary of the Department of Education), criticized the Scandinavian report as inadequate because its authors had spent merely two hours in the National College of Art during a holiday period. Another public reaction articulated by Desmond Fennell was that godless Scandinavia was telling nationalist and Catholic Ireland what to do (a recrudescence of Viking and Celtic

14 *Design in Ireland,* Report of the Scandinavian Group in Ireland, April 1961, (Córas Tráchtála, [February] 1962), 40.

15 *Design in Ireland,* 45.

16 *The Irish Times,* Saturday, 3 February, 1962 carried a front page photograph and editorial on the Report: "We have a very long way to go before we can claim that our Industrial Design reaches the same standards of Germany or France not to mention those of Denmark and Finland." One Irish designer Cormac Mehigan of Youghal Carpets felt the Seaninagians were unrealistic (*The Irish Times,* 13 February, 1962); a correspondent, Mac An Ceannaide, argued that Irish industries were too small to afford designers (*The Irish Times,* 15 February 1962); Brigid Ganly, a prominent artist, said that if Irish industrial designers did not go abroad they were "set to the hard work of adopting foreign ready made patterns for a public untrained in the appreciation of design of quality." (*The Irish Times,* 17 February, 1962); another correspondent, John Tate, praised the Dublin advertising agencies but said that Irish manufacturers preferred "the poorest type of fussy Victorian period designs" (*The Irish Times,* 24 February, 1962).

17 Dáil Debates, 193, (22 February ,1962).

conflict). Fennell had lived for a while in Scandinavia before he turned against its "materialism."

In retrospect, it can be seen that the educational requirements of design reform were not well presented by CTT. Had pressure been applied in cabinet by the Department of Industry and Commerce and had the Department of Education been involved with the formulation of new policy, the latter might not have been so defensive and resistant to design reform; thus it might not have delayed the necessary reforming legislation of the National College of Art until 1971. In fact, there was a clear dichotomy between the go-ahead capitalist modernism of the Department of Industry and Commerce favoring design, and the traditional cautious conservatism of the Department of Education, which was not convinced by the case for thorough reform in design education.

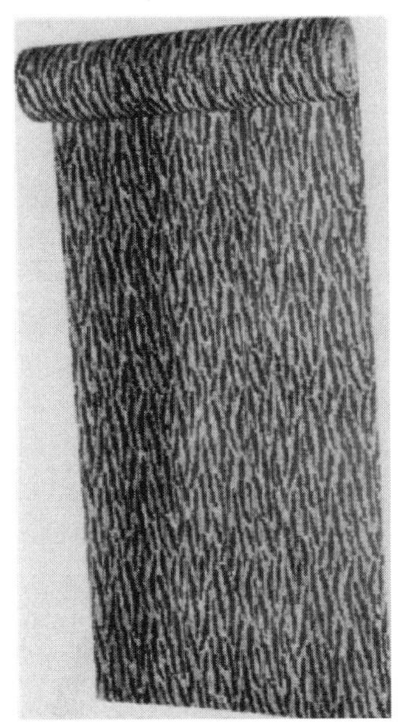

Figure 4
Margaret Leischner, *Carpet*, woven sisal, (early 1960s).

At the NCA, Bernardus Romein retired as professor of design in 1959. Dr. Patrick Hillery, the Minister of Education, on the advice of his department, put in two temporary stop-gap acting professors of design in the early 1960s; the first was Karl Koehler, an American graphic designer, and then, Giles Talbot Kelly, an English graphic designer who had a successful design practice, Group Three, in Dublin. However, Kelly was never given any clear authority by the department and was not able to initiate change. Eventually, Lucie Charles was promoted internally to be acting professor of design in 1964. She had studied painting at the NCA and in Paris before becoming an inspector of art in the department from which she transferred to the NCA. Stopgap measures did not satisfy Dr. Noel Browne, who pressed in Parliament for a full commission of inquiry into the college and its design teaching.

On the publication of the Scandinavian report, Lemass as Taoiseach delegated government responsibility for dealing with its design recommendations to CTT. This signalled the design section of CTT to make new plans to implement design reform.[18]

A method of promoting design consciousness among industrialists and the public was by means of exhibitions. As a direct consequence of the Scandinavians' visit to Ireland in 1961, CTT commissioned Gunnar Petersen, professor of graphic design at the Royal Danish Academy, to go to Japan and assemble an exhibition. He was instructed to select objects that demonstrated how a country could maintain its traditional individualism within a modern industrial idiom. This exhibition, Tradition in Modern Japanese Production, opened in the Danish Arts and Crafts Exhibition Center in Copenhagen in 1962 and in the Municipal Gallery in 1963. It showed traditional lacquerwork and modern plastic versions, tea services for Japanese National Railways, handtools, textiles, and basketwork. CTT maintained this momentum by sponsoring two exhibitions in the new exhibitions gallery of Trinity College, Dublin; one on chairs and a second on Irish textiles, selected from Irish mills by Jack Lenor Larsen, the prominent American textile designer. At the Royal Dublin

18 See *Report on the Council of Design*, an internal Civil Service Memorandum, The Department of Industry and Commerce Ms. 7.05 (413), Library of Córas Tráchtála Dublin.

Figure 5
Bertel Gardberg, *Tea Set*, stoneware, Kilkenny Design Workshops, (1968/69).

Society, CTT mounted an exhibition of product design from nine countries in the European Economic Community (EEC).

With respect to Irish industry itself, CTT identified three problems: first, the low level of design consciousness in the country, particularly among manufacturers; second, the absence of skilled personnel in design management; and third, the need to develop a modern education for designers. By 1967 (following the Export Promotion Act of that year) CTT's strategy was to divide Irish industry into sections: engineering, textiles, fashion, and so forth and to draw up an annual program of advice for each section. They also held seminars for management, kept a register of designers, and held exhibitions. The main policy initiative was to import foreign design expertise and to give grants to manufacturers so that professional designers would be employed. This was a successful short-term program, and approximately 200 designers worked with exporters during the 1960s. The advent of these professionals contributed to a general raising of design awareness in business and manufacturing circles.

Figure 6
Bertel Gardberg, *Chandelier*, wrought iron, Kilkenny Design Workshops, (1969).

The Irish furniture industry was a particular success in the 1960s. Herbert Berry, a leading British furniture designer, was brought over by CTT as was Andrew Milne, to energize the Irish furniture industry (for example, at Navan). Good modern furniture was produced for the first time. In the textile industry, CTT brought

DEAD WITH TEA AND DEAD WITHOUT IT

IS MINIC
DO BRIS
BÉAL
DUINE
SRÓN
MANY A TIME A MAN'S MOUTH BROKE HIS NOSE

THE FAR OFF HILLS ARE GREEN

FILLEANN AN FEALL AR AN BFEALLAIRE
TREACHERY RECOILS ON THE TRAITOR
MADE IN THE REPUBLIC OF IRELAND

Figure 7
Oisin Kelly, *Glass cloths*, printed textiles, Kilkenny Design Workshop, (1967).

in designers from France (such as André Courrèges) and from the United States to work with Irish weavers and to promote lighter weights and more fashionable colors; sometimes these high-fashion ideas were too far in advance of Irish companies. One of the most prominent companies' designers was Doreen. Another trend setter was Irish Ropes, which employed Margaret Leichner (from Britain) and Louis Le Brocquy, the artist, to design carpets in sisal and other materials. Although the Scandinavians had praised the outlook of Irish architects, there was in fact no cross fertilization between Irish architecture and product design, not even in furniture; in this respect Ireland followed the British, not the Continental Bauhaus-inspired model.

In the field of training, CTT effected a major breakthrough. Walsh had been impressed by the Plus Craft Workshops at Frederikstad in Norway (set up by the Norwegian entrepreneur Per Tannum). He resolved to set up something similar in Ireland. This led to the establishment of Kilkenny Design Workshops (KDW) in 1963, although the work areas themselves did not open until 1965. The workshops took over the old stables beside Kilkenny Castle, formerly the home of the Dukes of Ormonde. At first, they were staffed by designers from Britain, Denmark, Sweden, and Germany; the earliest ones were for silversmithing, candlemaking and poplin weaving (all traditional eighteenth-century Dublin crafts). Afterward, came ceramics and textiles (both woven and printed); only later did Kilkenny Design Workshops become involved with furniture, graphics, fashion, and packaging. Some visiting crafts-people, such as Edna Martin, a major textile designer from Stockholm, came to demonstrate their skills. Initially, Kilkenny was seen as a center for innovation and experiment, rather than of direct service to manufacturers as clients. In 1966, it established its own management independent of CTT, with W. H. Walsh as its executive chairman. Walsh, having become so involved with design reform, transferred from CTT to take this job.

On the positive side, the encouragement of the workshops led to a vast improvement of craft output, and many of the foreign craftspeople settled permanently in Ireland of their own accord. However, this tended to obscure (in the 1960s at least) the other aim of improving high technology-based industrial design. Nevertheless, during the 1970s design for noncraft-based industries gradually became the main function of the Kilkenny Design Workshops.[19]

The prime mover in design thinking during the 1960s was, as previously noted, W. H. Walsh. However, he worked closely with Paul Hogan of the CTT Design Section. It was largely due to Hogan that the Design Advisory Committee was set up in 1969 under CTT, with representatives of the Ministries, business, and the design profession. This led, among other things, to the CTT scholarship scheme, which enabled talented young Irish designers to work

19 For a brief account of Kilkenny Design Workshops and a photographic survey of their products, see Nicholas Marchant and Jeremy Addis, *Kilkenny Design, Twenty One Years of Design in Ireland* (Kilkenny and London: KDW and Lund Humphries 1984). See also *Export* (House Magazine of CTT) I, 1 (1967); III, 2 (1969); IV, 3 (1970); VI, 3 (1972). See also "Twenty Years of Kilkenny Design," *Business and Finance*, supplement (Dublin 19 May, 1963, and 23 August, 1979).

abroad. In particular, the committee was responsible for the Industrial Design Seminar at Killarney in November 1970. Kilkenny Design Workshops opened a retail shop at Kilkenny and made a big breakthrough with a highly commercially successful shop in Dublin in 1976, stocking Irish-designed products. It was the nearest Ireland came to a Design Center. An Irish Design Center, on the lines of the London Design Center, Haymarket, as discussed in CTT, was to be an exemplary showcase for foreign rather than indigenous design.

Irish society was changing in the early 1960s; the advent of Irish television with its chat shows and advertising introduced the public to foreign life-styles, foreign products, and a view of Ireland itself as interpreted by the media. This modernized Irish opinion by introducing an interest in the world of art and design. Simultaneously, the Republic of Ireland began to industrialize and urbanize in a large way. Free secondary education, greater literacy, leisure, travel, a shift to a more secular and less religious-oriented society, all contributed to a more questioning and better-informed public. The articulate modernist cultural lobby, which might safely have been ignored in the 1940s as a minority "alien" import, had to be reckoned with by government in the 1960s in view of membership of the EEC and of voter reaction at home. The Irish Design Reform Movement was merely an aspect of a larger cultural change. This concern for design reform in the 1960s had an analogy in 1830s Britain, when it was realized that Britain was far behind its continental competitors in terms of design education for a commercial world.

Pressure was coming from those who wanted education to be related to Irish industrial development, and to have commercial relevance in view of the Common Market free-trade conditions. There was also a general desire to modernize Irish art educational institutions, which had not changed significantly since before World War I. In addition, the development of economic activity in Ireland led to a general increase in affluence and disposable income. This made the production and marketing of high-quality goods more viable; there was a growing market for well-designed products.

Apart from the establishment of the Kilkenny Design Workshops, another important result of the Scandinavian report was the establishment of the (First) Council of Design by Dr. Patrick Hillery in September 1963. It included Sybil Connolly and Sir Robin Darwin and was to advise on the training of industrial designers in state establishments, design policy in general, and on fostering links between industry and the School of Design of the National College of Art.

The council, which held nine meetings and 46 subcommittee meetings and visited Irish art schools, as well as those at Cologne and Ulm, published its report in 1967. It embodied the conventional modern attitudes to design of the 1960s. The main intellectual thrust of the report was toward industrial design. It recommended that a Faculty of Industrial Design be set up in close association with faculties of architecture and technology and fine arts.[20] It called for a

20 *Report of the Council of Design,* 1967, Chairman Dr. Michäel French O'Carroll, 67; see also page 24: "The School of Design is inadequate;" the report noted the introduction of the Crafts since World War II but concluded that "nothing more can be done to develop an adequate modern School of Design until the needs of staff, equipment, finance and above all accommodation have been met."

National Design Council to promote design for industry, with a reformed National College of Art under its control. (A minority report favored a strictly technological theory of architecture and worked to avoid "contamination" by fine art.)[21] The report tabled a reformed structure for the new College, but Sir Robin Darwin criticized the suggested industrial design faculty as a craft department, lacking the specific category of industrial design (engineering), which he regarded as central to the practice of design. Darwin was attempting to bring the experience of the Royal College of Art to Dublin.

Simultaneously, the Commission on Higher Education made a comprehensive review of third-level education in Ireland, including the National College of Art, and reported in 1967. It recommended a renewed college with a new building. This report complemented that of the Council of Design.[22]

Despite these two major government reports, a policy statement or schedule for restructuring the National College of Art or providing it with new buildings was not made by the Minister for Education; it is known, however, that his art inspectors, Gerald Bruen and Micheál O Nualláin, pressed for special attention to be given to the college, particularly in view of the need for design reform.

A spirited controversy developed in the correspondence columns of *The Irish Times* in January and February 1968, calling for reform, once again with special reference to design.[23] There was a general feeling that art and design education had lost out in the generous disbursal of state funds for education during the 1960s. Donough O'Malley, the Minister for Education, was called upon by Fergus O'Farrell, a former student of the NCA and then practicing as a craftsman, to do something about the situation. Terence de Vere White, the Dublin journalist and man of letters, put the view succinctly: "The College should be removed from the Department of Education and set up on the model of the Royal College of Art, London. Dublin could learn from Belfast as well as from London."[24] O'Malley admitted these shortcomings and committed himself publicly to reform at the NCA on January 26, 1968.

The analogy of the School of Art, Belfast was salutary.[25] Although in a roughly similar position to Dublin in 1914, it sustained its design teaching, largely because of the importance of industry in Belfast and the British political connection and funding. It had long-standing specialization in ceramics, silver, jewelry, and graphic design since the nineteenth century. Belfast had just received a new school building, which was the envy of Dublin and showed the Republic what could be done. There was also the example of the new design courses approved by the National Council for Diplomas in Art and Design in the United Kingdom which applied in Belfast. Clearly, the Republic was lagging behind these new developments, which "Modernizers" saw as worthy of imitation.

The pressure for reform at the National College of Art came originally from the design lobby outside the school. The students'

21 *Report of the Council of Design*, 29; Sir R. Darwin's dissenting view was on pages 36–37.

22 *Report of the Commission on Higher Education 1960–67* (Dublin: The Stationery Office, 1967), Part II, Report Vol. I, 499; the Report included a comprehensive analysis of the National College of Art.

23 In particular *The Irish Times*, 10 January, 1968: 11, carried a letter by "A Lover of Art " which assessed the results of the original Scandinavian Report. "The setting up of the Council of Design and its subsequent Report was the result of Dr. Hillery's rude awakening to the realities of the situation." The letter was an extensive critique of the lack of informed policy on visual education at the Department of Education over the years.

24 Tenence de Vere White in the Irish Edition of *The Sunday Express* (London: 14 January, 1968).

25 See James Warwick to the editor of *The Irish Times*, 20 April, 1968: 19.

Figure 8
Kor Classen, *Record Jacket*, "Understanding our vocation/Women in the Church," Mercier Press, (1969).

Representative Council within the school began to agitate for change in late 1967, and by 1968 student revolution was in progress.[26] A major landmark was the Arts Council Symposium of April 18 at Trinity College Dublin, when Sir Robin Darwin said that, in Ireland, art schools were very much behind the times. "The vast number of plaster casts in art schools in Dublin and Cork should be taken out and smashed. They are symbolic of the Victorian era in which they were introduced and in such an atmosphere there can be no development in art and design." He called for a "Faculty of Industrial Design, engineering, science and mathematics" in the new University of Dublin. (The idea of new university arrangements in Dublin was aired by politicians at that time.) "Ireland by giving the world finer artistic designs on its produce could increase its industrial exports as does Scandinavia today. . . . If I lived in this blessed but benighted country, I would set up a society for the prevention of cruelty to art schools."[27] Some students took Sir Robin at his word and smashed the antique cast collection in May 1969, during the subsequent student revolution at the NCA that lasted from 1969 to 1971.

Parallel to the agitation at the National College of Art, Córas Tráchtála's Design Advisory Committee organized a three-day seminar at Killarney, on industrial design education, March 26–28, 1970.[28] There were 130 delegates, including businessmen, designers, civil servants, and some students. The chief recommendation of Paul Hogan's introductory paper was that a two-year postgraduate course in industrial design be set up in University College Dublin

26 An interesting document, if written from an exclusively student viewpoint, is P. Gillen, *The National College of Art, a Case History of Education under Neo-Colonialism*, duplicated typescript (Dublin: May, 1971), Archives of the National College of Art and Design, Dublin. For an overview of the 1960s in Irish art education, see Joan Fowler "Art Colleges in Southern Ireland, Against the Odds," *Circa* 24, Belfast (September–October 1985): 3–11.

27 Quoted in *The Irish Times*, 19 April, 1968, and *Cork Examiner*, 19 April, 1968.

28 *Industrial Design Education Seminar*, sponsored by the Department of Education and Córas Tráchtála, Killarney (26–28 November 1970), typescript volume of papers Library of Córas Tráchtála, Dublin.

and that the art college should *not* be the basis of this development. Kilkenny Design Workshops were also to concentrate on postgraduate work. Hogan noted that the concept of design as applied art still lingered on in Ireland despite its rejection elsewhere. The reporting committee felt that this was the single most important obstacle to be overcome in establishing modern design education. Discussions with industry had disclosed massive discontent with the prevailing situation of the availability of designers and training facilities. Industry had no clear idea of what was wanted in design. The most intellectually trenchant paper at the conference was that of Misha Black, the well-known British industrial designer. He disagreed with the current student call for generalists, putting his faith instead in the virtues of excellence and specialization; he emphasized industrial design particularly and the need to transcend craft-based thinking. This Killarney seminar was important, as it focused attention on the type of industrial design course that had to be devised for Ireland.

Surveying the 1960s, the Department of Industry and Commerce stated, "The only progress in relation to Industrial Design since the Scandinavian Report is due directly to the work of CTT and its subsidiary KDW." The Department's view was that industrial design was "a matter of business at least as much as art. An industrial designer must be creative and inventive, but he is essentially a member, permanent or temporary, of the management of an industrial concern. . . . The job is to solve problems, finding a creative and preferably elegant solution where a new product is required. A good design is honest. . . ."[29]

When, eventually, as a result of the student agitation and the recommendation of the two government reports, a bill to restructure the National College of Art as the National College of Art and Design (NCAD) was introduced into the Dáil in 1971. The debate on design was not forgotten. J. Keating (Labour) said, "One does not have to travel far from Ireland to see that there is a higher level of design awareness in most of the countries we are so anxious to join [in the EEC]. We will need to produce beautiful goods efficiently and at the right price if we are to be in a competitive position. . . .We are notably deficient in the area of design. . . ."[30] Barry Desmond (Labour) said: "Our Government publications, our stamp designs, many of them downright bad and ugly . . . reflect little credit on Ireland at present. We can hope that in future, our Irish industrial products which have suffered so much on domestic markets and in the export market—from the absence of a tradition of industrial design in the country and the failure of the Government to develop and nurture a more dynamic and fruitful atmosphere of industrial design."[31] The bill, as passed in December 1971, however, spoke only in general about "arts, crafts, and design."

Also in 1971 was the establishment of the Crafts Council of Ireland at the Royal Dublin Society headquarters, which was in line

29 See note 18.

30 Dáil Debates, opening of the 2nd reading, 225, (29 June, 1971):142.

31 Dáil Debates, 225:158.

with the traditions of the Society, which in 1756 had established a School of Ornament that was taken over by the Board of Trade in 1849. James Warwick, principal of the Belfast School of Art, was the first chairman of the Crafts Council; P. Hogan was the first secretary, and he sought to demarcate the differences between crafts and industrial design, an area of confusion which stemmed from the Scandinavian report. There was a considerable growth of handcrafts in the 1970s fostered by Kilkenny Design Workshops and facilitated by the Royal Dublin Society. In the 1980s, the Industrial Development Authority began to help craftsmen to set up their own businesses. Indeed, many independent craftspeople set up particularly in the south and west of Ireland.

As the primary purpose of this article is to discuss the design developments of the 1960s, only the landmarks of the 1970s will be mentioned. So far as design education was concerned, the NCAD Act of 1971 opened the way for the introduction of a new college Department of Industrial Design, which paralleled the new product design push at Kilkenny. James Warwick, with a lifetime of experience in art education, was consultant director of the National College of Art and Design in 1973–74 and introduced a reformed faculty structure with faculties of design, fine art, pre-diploma, and history of art and complementary studies. The establishment of a Department of Industrial Design in 1976 was led by David Sherlock, an industrial designer from Nottingham Polytechnic in England, and Michal Ozmin, a Polish designer and postgraduate of the University of Manchester's Institute of Science and Technology. The new industrial design course, formed in response to a decade of agitation, was run in tandem with the newly established National Institute of Higher Education, Limerick, where high technology (but no artistic) facilities were available. Graphic design was modernized and a new course in fashion design was introduced at the NCAD. A course in the history of design was inaugurated at the college by this author to relate to these new diploma courses, subsequently mutated into degrees.

The second crucial development in design education was the establishment in 1972 of a state award-giving body, The National Council for Educational Awards (NCEA), which later set up a Design Studies Board in 1976. A proliferation of courses in crafts and graphic design in the Regional Technical Colleges around Ireland were submitted to the NCEA for validation; these new craft and design courses, often supported by EEC funds, showed that education in crafts was being diffused countrywide.

The establishment of the Society of Designers in Ireland in 1972 finally gave recognition to the profession of Irish designers. It became a focus for discussion about design in general and was seen as part of the international profession of designers by the holding of the 10th International Congress and the General Assembly of the International Council of Societies of Industrial Design (ICSID) in Dublin in 1977.

The design reform movement began in the 1950s in the wake of Thomas Bodkin's report. It was fueled by the promotional exhibitions of the Arts Council and by the growth of the Irish design profession, particularly of graphic design, where the influence of immigrant Dutch designers was strongest. This momentum led to the Scandinavian *Report* of 1962, which precipitated the crisis of the 1960s. Its fruitful results included the establishment of Kilkenny Design Workshops. While noting the role of institutions, tribute should also be paid to the influence of W. H. Walsh of Córas Tráchtála, who more than anyone, formulated and activated what needed to be done in Irish Design for industry in the 1960s.

The industrialization of Ireland and its entry into the Common Market were crucial factors that forced the pace of design in Irish industry and education. Ultimately, however, in terms of Irish social history, the design reform movement must be seen in the context of the modernization of Irish society during the 1960s, when international concepts, including art and design, became more generally appreciated, particularly through the media.

Sources

All of the essays in this volume appeared originally in the journal *Design Issues.*

Volume 1, number 2 (Fall 1984): Paul Shaw, "Tradition and Innovation: The Design Work of William Addison Dwiggins," pp. 26–41.

Volume 2, number 1 (Spring 1985): Bradford R. Collins, "The Poster as Art; Jules Chéret and the Struggle for the Equality of the Arts in Late Nineteenth-Century France," pp. 41–50.

Volume 2, number 2 (Fall 1985): Enric Satué, "Super Veloz: A Typographic System for the Small Printer," pp. 9–17.

Volume 3, number 1 (Spring 1986): John Turpin, "The Irish Design Reform Movement of the 1960s," pp. 4–21; Svetlana Sylvestrova, "That Was the Beginning," pp. 54–63;

Volume 3, number 2 (Fall 1986): David Brett, "Drawing and the Ideology of Industrialization," pp. 59–72.

Volume 6, number 1 (Fall 1989): Matthew Turner, "Early Modern Design in Hong Kong," pp. 79–91; Shou Zhi Wang, "Chinese Modern Design: A Retrospective," pp. 49–78.

Volume 6, number 2 (Spring 1990): Dennis P. Doordan, "Design at CBS," pp. 4–17; Larry D. Lutchmansingh, "Evolutionary Affinity in Arthur Mackmurdo's Botanical Design," pp. 51–57; James A. Schmeichen, "Reconsidering the Factory, Art-Labor, and the Schools of Design in Nineteenth-Century Britain," pp. 58–69.

Volume 7, number 2 (Spring 1991): György Haiman, "Imre Kner and the Revival of Hungarian Printing," pp. 43–53.

Volume 8, number 1 (Fall 1991): Roland Marchand, "The Designers go to the Fair, I: Walter Dorwin Teague and the Professionalization of Corporate Industrial Exhibits, 1933–1940," pp. 4–17.

Volume 8, number 2 (Spring 1992): Roland Marchand, "The Designers go to the Fair, II: Norman Bel Geddes, the General Motors 'Futurma,' and the Visit-to-the-Factory Transformed," pp. 23–40.

Volume 9, number 1 (Fall 1992): Mitchell Schwarzer, "The Design Prototype as Artistic Boundary: The Debate on History and Industry in Central European Applied Arts Museums, 1860–1900," pp. 30–44.

Volume 9, number 2 (Spring 1993): Dennis P. Doordan, "Promoting

Aluminum: Designers and the American Aluminum Industry," pp. 44–50.

Volume 10, number 2 (Summer 1994): David Gartman, "Harley Earl and the Art and Color Section: The Birth of Styling at General Motors," pp. 3–26; Ellen Mazur Thomson, "Alms for Oblivion: The History of Women in Early American Graphic Design," pp. 27–48.

About the Contributors

David Brett teaches the History of Design at the University of Ulster in Belfast, Northern Ireland. He has written extensively on architecture and decoration.

Bradford R. Collins is an art historian, art critic, and poet. He teaches in the Art Department at the Unitversity of South Carolina.

Dennis P. Doordan is an editor of *Design Issues* and an Associate Professor in the School of Architecture at the University of Notre Dame. He is the author of *Building Modern Italy: Italian Architecture 1914–1936.*

David Gartman teaches sociology at the University of South Alabama. He is the author of *Auto Slavery: The Labor Process in the American Automobile Industry* and *Auto Opium: A Social History of American Automobile Design.*

György Haiman is a typographer and graphic designer and a member of the Kner family of bookbinders and printers. He teaches graphic design at the Hungarian Academy of Craft and Design in Budapest.

Larry D. Lutchmansingh is an Associate Professor of Art History at Bowdoin College. He has published articles on the Pre-Raphaelites and on the Arts and Crafts movement.

Roland Marchand is a Professor in the Department of History at the University of California, Davis. He is the author of *Advertising the American Dream: Making Way for Modernity, 1920–1940.*

Enric Satué is a free-lance graphic designer in Barcelona, Spain. His design activity includes magazine and book design, and corporate identity programs.

James A. Schmeichen is a Professor in the Department of History at Central Michigan University. He has been a visiting professor at the University of Strathclyde in Glasgow and a former Fulbright Fellow to Great Britain.

Mitchell Schwarzer is an architectural historian and has published articles on the historiography of art, German architectural theory, and the philosophy of historic preservation. He teaches at the California College of Arts and Crafts in San Francisco.

Paul Shaw is a free-lance designer specializing in lettering and calligraphy. He is the author of *Black Letter Primer* and has published articles on typography, calligraphy, and rubber stamps in various publications.

Svetlana Sylvestrova is Deputy Editor of the Russian design magazine *Technicheskaya Estetika.*

Ellen Mazur Thomson is a librarian, printmaker, and author of *American Graphic Design: A Guide to the Literature.*

Matthew Turner teaches Design History in Edinburgh, Scotland. Previously, he was a Senior Lecturer in Design History at the Swire School of Design at the Hong Kong Polytechnic. In 1988, he curated a major exhibition on the history of Hong Kong design for the Hong Kong Museum of History.

John Turpin is Professor of Art History at the National College of Art and Design in Dublin, Ireland. He has written extensively on Irish artists, the history of Irish art and design education, and 19th-century art and industry exhibitions in Ireland.

Shou Zhi Wang teaches in the College of Design at the Art Center of Pasadena. Prior to joining the faculty in Pasadena, he was a Professor of Design in the Department of Design at the Guang Hu Institute of Arts.